THE STANDARD EDITION OF THE COMPLETE PSYCHOLOGICAL WORKS OF SIGMUND FREUD

VOLUME V

THE STANDARD EDITION OF THE
COMPLETE PSYCHOLOGICAL WORKS OF

Sigmund Freud

VOLUME V
(1900–1901)

THE INTERPRETATION
OF DREAMS

(Second Part)

and

ON DREAMS

TRANSLATED FROM THE GERMAN
UNDER THE GENERAL EDITORSHIP OF
James Strachey

IN COLLABORATION WITH
Anna Freud

ASSISTED BY
Alix Strachey and Alan Tyson

V

VINTAGE
THE HOGARTH PRESS
AND THE INSTITUTE OF PSYCHO-ANALYSIS

Published by Vintage 2001

7 9 10 8

Translation and editorial matter
© The Institute of Psycho-Analysis 1953

'The Interpretation of Dreams' is included
by arrangement with George Allen and Unwin Ltd,
London

First published in Great Britain in 1953 by
The Hogarth Press
Reprinted with corrections 1958

Vintage
Random House, 20 Vauxhall Bridge Road,
London SW1V 2SA

Addresses for companies within The Random House Group Limited
can be found at: www.randomhouse.co.uk/offices.htm

The Random House Group Limited Reg. No. 954009
www.randomhouse.co.uk/vintage/classics

A CIP catalogue record for this book
is available from the British Library

ISBN 9780099426561

The Random House Group Limited supports The Forest Stewardship
Council (FSC), the leading international forest certification organisation.
All our titles that are printed on Greenpeace approved FSC certified paper carry
the FSC logo. Our paper procurement policy can be found at:
www.rbooks.co.uk/environment

Printed and bound in Great Britain by
CPI Antony Rowe, Chippenham, Wiltshire

CONTENTS

VOLUME FIVE

THE INTERPRETATION OF DREAMS (1900)

ON DREAMS (1901)

CHAPTER VI *(continued)*

(D)

CONSIDERATIONS OF REPRESENTABILITY

WE have been occupied so far with investigating the means by which dreams represent the relations between the dream-thoughts. In the course of this investigation, however, we have more than once touched upon the further topic of the general nature of the modifications which the material of the dream-thoughts undergoes for the purpose of the formation of a dream. We have learnt that that material, stripped to a large extent of its relations, is submitted to a process of compression, while at the same time displacements of intensity between its elements necessarily bring about a psychical transvaluation of the material. The displacements we have hitherto considered turned out to consist in the replacing of some one particular idea by another in some way closely associated with it, and they were used to facilitate condensation in so far as, by their means, instead of *two* elements, a single common element intermediate between them found its way into the dream. We have not yet referred to any other sort of displacement. Analyses show us, however, that another sort exists and that it reveals itself in a change in the *verbal expression* of the thoughts concerned. In both cases there is a displacement along a chain of associations; but a process of such a kind can occur in various psychical spheres, and the outcome of the displacement may in one case be that one element is replaced by another, while the outcome in another case may be that a single element has its *verbal form* replaced by another.

This second species of displacement which occurs in dream-formation is not only of great theoretical interest but is also specially well calculated to explain the appearance of fantastic absurdity in which dreams are disguised. The direction taken by the displacement usually results in a colourless and abstract expression in the dream-thought being exchanged for a pictorial and concrete one. The advantage, and accordingly the purpose, of such a change jumps to the eyes. A thing that is pictorial is, from the point of view of a dream, a thing that is *capable of being represented*: it can be introduced into a situation in which abstract expressions offer the same kind of difficulties to representation in dreams as a political leading article in a newspaper would offer to an illustrator. But not only representability, but the interests of condensation and the censorship as well, can be the gainers from this exchange. A dream-thought is unusable so long as it is expressed in an abstract form; but when once it has been transformed into pictorial language, contrasts and identifications of the kind which the dream-work requires, and which it creates if they are not already present, can be established more easily than before between the new form of expression and the remainder of the material underlying the dream. This is so because in every language concrete terms, in consequence of the history of their development, are richer in associations than conceptual ones. We may suppose that a good part of the intermediate work done during the formation of a dream, which seeks to reduce the dispersed dream-thoughts to the most succinct and unified expression possible, proceeds along the line of finding appropriate verbal transformations for the individual thoughts. Any one thought, whose form of expression may happen to be fixed for other reasons, will operate in a determinant and selective manner on the possible forms of expression allotted to the other thoughts, and it may do so, perhaps, from the very start—as is the case in writing a poem. If a poem is to be written in rhymes, the second line of a couplet is limited by two conditions: it must express an appropriate meaning, and the expression of that meaning must rhyme with the first line. No doubt the best poem will be one in which we fail to notice the intention of finding a rhyme, and in which the two thoughts have, by mutual influence, chosen from the very start a verbal expression which will allow a rhyme to emerge with only slight subsequent adjustment.

In a few instances a change of expression of this kind assists dream-condensation even more directly, by finding a form of words which owing to its ambiguity is able to give expression to more than one of the dream-thoughts. In this way the whole domain of verbal wit is put at the disposal of the dream-work. There is no need to be astonished at the part played by words in dream-formation. Words, since they are the nodal points of numerous ideas, may be regarded as predestined to ambiguity;

and the neuroses (e.g. in framing obsessions and phobias), no less than dreams, make unashamed use of the advantages thus offered by words for purposes of condensation and disguise.[1] It is easy to show that dream-distortion too profits from displacement of expression. If one ambiguous word is used instead of two unambiguous ones the result is misleading; and if our everyday, sober method of expression is replaced by a pictorial one, our understanding is brought to a halt, particularly since a dream never tells us whether its elements are to be interpreted literally or in a figurative sense or whether they are to be connected with the material of the dream-thoughts directly or through the intermediary of some interpolated phraseology.[2] In interpreting any dream-element it is in general doubtful

(a) whether it is to be taken in a positive or negative sense (as an antithetic relation),

(b) whether it is to be interpreted historically (as a recollection),

(c) whether it is to be interpreted symbolically, or

(d) whether its interpretation is to depend on its wording. Yet, in spite of all this ambiguity, it is fair to say that the productions of the dream-work, which, it must be remembered, *are not made with the intention of being understood*, present no greater difficulties to their translators than do the ancient hieroglyphic scripts to those who seek to read them.

I have already given several examples of representations in dreams which are only held together by the ambiguity of their wording. (For instance, 'She opened her mouth properly' in the dream of Irma's injection [p. 111] and 'I could not go after all' in the dream which I last quoted [p. 336 f.].) I will now record a dream in which a considerable part was played by the turning of abstract thought into pictures. The distinction between dream-interpretation of this kind and interpretation by means of symbolism can still be drawn quite sharply. In the case of symbolic dream-interpretation the key to the symbolization is

---

[1] [*Footnote added* 1909:] See my volume on jokes (1905c) [especially the later part of Chapter VI] and the use of 'verbal bridges' in the solution of neurotic symptoms. [See, e.g., the synthesis of Dora's first dream at the end of Section II of Freud, 1905e (where the term 'switch-words' is also used), and the solution of the 'Rat Man's' rat-obsession in Section I(G) of Freud, 1909d.]

[2] [The remainder of this paragraph was added as a footnote in 1909 and included in the text in 1914.]

arbitrarily chosen by the interpreter; whereas in our cases of verbal disguise the keys are generally known and laid down by firmly established linguistic usage. If one has the right idea at one's disposal at the right moment, one can solve dreams of this kind wholly or in part even independently of information from the dreamer.

A lady of my acquaintance had the following dream: *She was at the Opera. A Wagner opera was being performed, and had lasted till a quarter to eight in the morning. There were tables set out in the stalls, at which people were eating and drinking. Her cousin, who had just got back from his honeymoon, was sitting at one of the tables with his young wife, and an aristocrat was sitting beside them. Her cousin's wife, so it appeared, had brought him back with her from the honeymoon, quite openly, just as one might bring back a hat. In the middle of the stalls there was a high tower, which had a platform on top of it surrounded by an iron railing. High up at the top was the conductor, who had the features of Hans Richter. He kept running round the railing, and was perspiring violently; and from that position he was conducting the orchestra, which was grouped about the base of the tower. She herself was sitting in a box with a woman friend* (whom I knew). *Her younger sister wanted to hand her up a large lump of coal from the stalls, on the ground that she had not known it would be so long, and must be simply freezing by now. (As though the boxes required to be heated during the long performance.)*

Even though the dream was well focused on a single situation, yet in other respects it was sufficiently senseless: the tower in the middle of the stalls, for instance, with the conductor directing the orchestra from the top of it! And above all the coal that her sister handed up to her! I deliberately refrained from asking for an analysis of the dream. But since I had some knowledge of the dreamer's personal relations, I was able to interpret certain pieces of it independently of her. I knew she had had a great deal of sympathy for a musician whose career had been prematurely cut short by insanity. So I decided to take the tower in the stalls metaphorically. It then emerged that the man whom she had wanted to see in Hans Richter's place *towered high above* the other members of the orchestra. The tower might be described as a composite picture formed by apposition. The lower part of its structure represented the man's greatness; the railing at the top, behind which he was running round like a prisoner or an animal in a cage—this was an allusion to the unhappy man's name[1]—represented his ultimate fate. The two ideas might have been brought together in the word 'Narrenturm'.[2]

Having thus discovered the mode of representation adopted by the dream, we might attempt to use the same key for solving its second apparent absurdity—the coal handed up to the dreamer by her sister. 'Coal' must mean 'secret love':

> Kein *Feuer*, keine *Kohle*
> kann brennen so heiss
> als wie *heimliche Liebe*,
> von der niemand nichts weiss.[3]

She herself and her woman friend had been left unmarried [German '*sitzen geblieben*', literally 'left sitting']. Her younger sister, who still had prospects of marriage, handed her up the coal 'because she had not known *it would be so long*'. The dream did not specify *what* would be so long. If it were a story, we should say 'the performance'; but since it is a dream, we may take the phrase as an independent entity, decide that it was used ambiguously and add the words 'before she got married.' Our interpretation of 'secret love' is further supported by the mention of the dreamer's cousin sitting with his wife in the stalls, and by the *open* love-affair attributed to the latter. The dream was dominated by the antithesis between secret and open love and between the dreamer's own fire and the coldness of the young wife. In both cases, moreover, there was someone 'highly-placed'—a term applying equally to the aristocrat and to the musician on whom such high hopes had been pinned.[4]

The foregoing discussion has led us at last to the discovery of a third factor[5] whose share in the transformation of the dream-

---

[1] [*Footnote added* 1925:] Hugo Wolf.
[2] [Literally 'Fools' Tower'—an old term for an insane asylum.]
[3] [No *fire*, no *coal*
So hotly glows
As *secret love*
Of which no one knows.
German *Volkslied*.]
[4] [The element of absurdity in this dream is commented upon on p. 435.]
[5] [The two previous ones being condensation and displacement.]

thoughts into the dream-content is not to be underrated: namely, *considerations of representability in the peculiar psychical material of which dreams make use*—for the most part, that is, representability in visual images. Of the various subsidiary thoughts attached to the essential dream-thoughts, those will be preferred which admit of visual representation; and the dream-work does not shrink from the effort of recasting unadaptable thoughts into a new verbal form—even into a less usual one—provided that that process facilitates representation and so relieves the psychological pressure caused by constricted thinking. This pouring of the content of a thought into another mould may at the same time serve the purposes of the activity of condensation and may create connections, which might not otherwise have been present, with some other thought; while this second thought itself may already have had its original form of expression changed, with a view to meeting the first one half-way.

Herbert Silberer (1909)[1] has pointed out a good way of directly observing the transformation of thoughts into pictures in the process of forming dreams and so of studying this one factor of the dream-work in isolation. If, when he was in a fatigued and sleepy condition, he set himself some intellectual task, he found that it often happened that the thought escaped him and that in its place a picture appeared, which he was then able to recognize as a substitute for the thought. Silberer describes these substitutes by the not very appropriate term of 'auto-symbolic'. I will here quote a few examples from Silberer's paper [ibid., 519–22], and I shall have occasion, on account of certain characteristics of the phenomena concerned, to return to them later. [See p. 503 ff.]

'*Example* 1.—I thought of having to revise an uneven passage in an essay.

'*Symbol.*—I saw myself planing a piece of wood.'

'*Example* 5.—I endeavoured to bring home to myself the aim of certain metaphysical studies which I was proposing to make. Their aim, I reflected, was to work one's way through to ever higher forms of consciousness and layers of existence, in one's search for the bases of existence.

[1] [This paragraph and the subsequent quotation from Silberer were added in 1914.]

'*Symbol.*—I was pushing a long knife under a cake, as though to lift out a slice.

'*Interpretation.*—My motion with the knife meant the "working my way through" which was in question. . . . Here is the explanation of the symbolism. It is from time to time my business at meals to cut up a cake and distribute the helpings. I perform the task with a long, flexible knife—which demands some care. In particular, to lift out the slices cleanly after they have been cut offers certain difficulties; the knife must be pushed carefully *under* the slice (corresponding to the slow "working my way through" to reach the "bases"). But there is yet more symbolism in the picture. For the cake in the symbol was a "Dobos" cake—a cake with a number of "layers" through which, in cutting it, the knife has to penetrate (the "layers" of consciousness and thought).'

'*Example* 9.—I had lost the thread in a train of thought. I tried to find it again, but had to admit that the starting-point had completely escaped me.

'*Symbol.*—Part of a compositor's forme, with the last lines of type fallen away.'

In view of the part played by jokes, quotations, songs and proverbs in the mental life of educated people, it would fully agree with our expectations if disguises of such kinds were used with extreme frequency for representing dream-thoughts. What, for instance, is the meaning in a dream of a number of carts, each filled with a different sort of vegetable? They stand for a wishful contrast to '*Kraut und Rüben*' [literally, 'cabbages and turnips'], that is to say to 'higgledy-piggledy', and accordingly signify 'disorder'. I am surprised that this dream has only been reported to me once.[1] A dream-symbolism of universal validity has only emerged in the case of a few subjects, on the basis of generally familiar allusions and verbal substitutes. Moreover a good part of this symbolism is shared by dreams with psychoneuroses, legends and popular customs.[2]

Indeed, when we look into the matter more closely, we must recognize the fact that the dream-work is doing nothing

---

[1] [*Footnote added* 1925:] I have in fact never met with this image again; so I have lost confidence in the correctness of the interpretation.

[2] [The subject of dream-symbolism is treated at length in the next section.]

original in making substitutions of this kind. In order to gain its ends—in this case the possibility of a representation hampered by censorship—it merely follows the paths which it finds already laid down in the unconscious; and it gives preference to those transformations of the repressed material which can also become conscious in the form of jokes or allusions and of which the phantasies of neurotic patients are so full. At this point we suddenly reach an understanding of Scherner's dream-interpretations, whose essential correctness I have defended elsewhere [pp. 83 ff. and 227]. The imagination's pre-occupation with the subject's own body is by no means peculiar to dreams or characteristic only of them. My analyses have shown me that it is habitually present in the unconscious thoughts of neurotics, and that it is derived from sexual curiosity, which, in growing youths or girls, is directed to the genitals of the other sex, and to those of their own as well. Nor, as Scherner [1861] and Volkelt [1875] have rightly insisted, is a house the only circle of ideas employed for symbolizing the body; and this is equally true of dreams and of the unconscious phantasies of neurosis. It is true that I know patients who have retained an architectural symbolism for the body and the genitals. (Sexual interest ranges far beyond the sphere of the external genitalia.) For these patients pillars and columns represent the legs (as they do in the *Song of Solomon*), every gateway stands for one of the bodily orifices (a 'hole'), every water-pipe is a reminder of the urinary apparatus, and so on. But the circle of ideas centring round plant-life or the kitchen may just as readily be chosen to conceal sexual images.[1] In the former case the way has been well prepared by linguistic usage, itself the precipitate of imaginative similes reaching back to remote antiquity: e.g. the Lord's vineyard, the seed, and the maiden's garden in the *Song of Solomon*. The ugliest as well as the most intimate details of sexual life may be thought and dreamt of in seemingly innocent allusions to activities in the kitchen; and the symptoms of hysteria could never be interpreted if we forgot that sexual symbolism can find its best hiding-place behind what is commonplace and inconspicuous. There is a valid sexual meaning behind the neurotic child's intolerance of blood or raw meat, or his nausea at the sight of eggs or macaroni, and behind the

[1] [*Footnote added* 1914:] Abundant evidence of this is to be found in the three supplementary volumes to Fuchs (1909–12).

enormous exaggeration in neurotics of the natural human dread of snakes. Wherever neuroses make use of such disguises they are following paths along which all humanity passed in the earliest periods of civilization—paths of whose continued existence to-day, under the thinnest of veils, evidence is to be found in linguistic usages, superstitions and customs.

I will now append the 'flowery' dream dreamt by one of my women patients which I have already [p. 315] promised to record. I have indicated in small capitals those elements in it that are to be given a sexual interpretation. The dreamer quite lost her liking for this pretty dream after it had been interpreted.

(*a*) INTRODUCTORY DREAM: *She went into the kitchen, where her two maidservants were, and found fault with them for not having got her 'bite of food' ready. At the same time she saw quite a quantity of crockery standing upside down to drain, common crockery piled up in heaps.* Later addition: *The two maidservants went to fetch some water and had to step into a kind of river which came right up to the house into the yard.*[1]

(*b*) MAIN DREAM[2]: *She was descending from a height*[3] *over some strangely constructed palisades or fences, which were put together into large panels, and consisted of small squares of wattling.*[4] *It was not intended for climbing over; she had trouble in finding a place to put her feet in and felt glad that her dress had not been caught anywhere, so that she had stayed respectable as she went along.*[5] *She was holding a* BIG BRANCH *in her hand*[6]; *actually it was like a tree, covered over with* RED BLOSSOMS, *branching and spreading out.*[7] *There was an idea of their being cherry-*BLOSSOMS; *but they also looked like double* CAMELLIAS, *though of course those do not grow on trees. As she went down, first she*

[1] For the interpretation of this introductory dream, which is to be interpreted as a causal dependent clause, see p. 315. [Cf. also pp. 319 and 325.]

[2] Describing the course of her life.

[3] Her high descent: a wishful antithesis to the introductory dream.

[4] A composite picture uniting two localities: what were known as the 'attics' of her family home, where she used to play with her brother, the object of her later phantasies, and a farm belonging to a bad uncle who used to tease her.

[5] A wishful antithesis to a real recollection of her uncle's farm, where she used to throw off her clothes in her sleep.

[6] Just as the angel carries a sprig of lilies in pictures of the Annunciation.

[7] For the explanation of this composite image see p. 319: innocence, menstruation, *La dame aux camélias.*

had ONE, *then suddenly* TWO, *and later again* ONE.[1] *When she got down, the lower* BLOSSOMS *were already a good deal* FADED. *Then she saw, after she had got down, a manservant who—she felt inclined to say—was combing a similar tree, that is to say he was using a* PIECE OF WOOD *to drag out some* THICK TUFTS OF HAIR *that were hanging down from it like moss. Some other workmen had cut down similar* BRANCHES *from a* GARDEN *and thrown them into the* ROAD, *where they* LAY ABOUT, *so that* A LOT OF PEOPLE TOOK SOME. *But she asked whether that was all right—whether she might* TAKE ONE TOO.[2] *A young* MAN (someone she knew, a stranger) *was standing in the garden; she went up to him to ask how* BRANCHES *of that kind could be* TRANSPLANTED INTO HER OWN GARDEN.[3] *He embraced her; whereupon she struggled and asked him what he was thinking of and whether he thought people could embrace her like that. He said there was no harm in that: it was allowed.[4] He then said he was willing to go into the* OTHER GARDEN *with her, to show her how the planting was done, and added something she could not quite understand: 'Anyhow, I need three* YARDS (later she gave it as: *three square yards*) *or three fathoms of ground.' It was as though he were asking her for something in return for his willingness, as though he intended* TO COMPENSATE HIMSELF IN HER GARDEN, *or as though he wanted to* CHEAT *some law or other, to get some advantage from it without causing her harm. Whether he really showed her something, she had no idea.*

This dream, which I have brought forward on account of its symbolic elements, may be described as a 'biographical' one. Dreams of this kind occur frequently during psycho-analysis, but perhaps only rarely outside it.[5]

[1] Referring to the multiplicity of the people involved in her phantasy

[2] That is whether she might pull one down, i.e. masturbate. ['*Sich einen herunterreissen*' or '*ausreissen*' (literally, 'to pull one down' or 'out') are vulgar German terms equivalent to the English 'to toss oneself off'. Freud had already drawn attention to this symbolism at the end of his paper on 'Screen Memories' (1899*a*); see also below, p. 388 f.]

[3] The branch had long since come to stand for the male genital organ; incidentally it also made a plain allusion to her family name.

[4] This, as well as what next follows, related to marriage precautions.

[5] [This paragraph was added in 1925.—*Footnote added* (to the preceding paragraph) 1911:] A similar 'biographical' dream will be found below as the third of my examples of dream-symbolism [p. 364]. Another one has been recorded at length by Rank [1910], and another, which must be read 'in reverse', by Stekel (1909, 486).—[A reference to 'biographical' dreams will be found near the end of Freud's 'History of the Psycho-Analytic Movement' (1914*d*).]

I naturally have at my disposal[1] a superfluity of material of this kind, but to report it would involve us too deeply in a consideration of neurotic conditions. It all leads to the same conclusion, namely that there is no necessity to assume that any peculiar symbolizing activity of the mind is operating in the dream-work, but that dreams make use of any symbolizations which are already present in unconscious thinking, because they fit in better with the requirements of dream-construction on account of their representability and also because as a rule they escape censorship.

---

[1] [In the first three editions, 1900, 1909 and 1911, this paragraph was preceded by another, which was omitted from 1914 onwards. The deleted paragraph ran as follows: 'I must mention another circle of ideas which often serves as a disguise for sexual material both in dreams and in neuroses: namely ideas connected with changing house. "Changing house" may easily be replaced by the word "*Ausziehen*" [meaning both "moving house" and "undressing"], and is thus connected with the subject of "clothing". If there is also a lift or elevator in the dream, we shall be reminded of the English word "to lift", that is, "to lift one's clothes".']

REPRESENTATION BY SYMBOLS IN DREAMS
—SOME FURTHER TYPICAL DREAMS[1]

The analysis of this last, biographical, dream is clear evidence that I recognized the presence of symbolism in dreams from the very beginning. But it was only by degrees and as my experience increased that I arrived at a full appreciation of its extent and significance, and I did so under the influence of the contributions of Wilhelm Stekel (1911), about whom a few words will not be out of place here. [1925.]

That writer, who has perhaps damaged psycho-analysis as much as he has benefited it, brought forward a large number of unsuspected translations of symbols; to begin with they were met with scepticism, but later they were for the most part confirmed and had to be accepted. I shall not be belittling the value of Stekel's services if I add that the sceptical reserve with which his proposals were received was not without justification. For the examples by which he supported his interpretations were often unconvincing, and he made use of a method which must be rejected as scientifically untrustworthy. Stekel arrived at his interpretations of symbols by way of intuition, thanks to a peculiar gift for the direct understanding of them. But the existence of such a gift cannot be counted upon generally, its effectiveness is exempt from all criticism and consequently its findings have no claim to credibility. It is as though one sought

[1] [With the exception of two paragraphs (on p. 393 f.) none of Section E of this chapter appeared in the first edition of the book. As explained in the Editor's Introduction (p. xiii), much of the material was added in the 1909 and 1911 editions, but in them it was included in Chapter V under the heading of 'Typical Dreams' (Section D of that chapter). In the edition of 1914 the present section was first constituted, partly from the material previously added to Chapter V and partly from further new material. Still more material was added in subsequent editions. In view of these complications, in this section a date has been added in square brackets at the end of each paragraph. It will be understood from what has been said that material dated 1909 and 1911 originally appeared in Chapter V and was transferred to its present position in 1914.]

to base the diagnosis of infectious diseases upon olfactory impressions received at the patient's bedside—though there have undoubtedly been clinicians who could accomplish more than other people by means of the sense of smell (which is usually atrophied) and were really able to diagnose a case of enteric fever by smell. [1925.]

Advances in psycho-analytic experience have brought to our notice patients who have shown a direct understanding of dream-symbolism of this kind to a surprising extent. They were often sufferers from dementia praecox, so that for a time there was an inclination to suspect every dreamer who had this grasp of symbols of being a victim of that disease.[1] But such is not the case. It is a question of a personal gift or peculiarity which has no visible pathological significance. [1925.]

When we have become familiar with the abundant use made of symbolism for representing sexual material in dreams, the question is bound to arise of whether many of these symbols do not occur with a permanently fixed meaning, like the 'grammalogues' in shorthand; and we shall feel tempted to draw up a new 'dream-book' on the decoding principle [see p. 97 f.]. On that point there is this to be said: this symbolism is not peculiar to dreams, but is characteristic of unconscious ideation, in particular among the people, and it is to be found in folklore, and in popular myths, legends, linguistic idioms, proverbial wisdom and current jokes, to a more complete extent than in dreams. [1909.]

It would therefore carry us far beyond the sphere of dream-interpretation if we were to do justice to the significance of symbols and discuss the numerous, and to a large extent still unsolved, problems attaching to the concept of a symbol.[2] We must restrict ourselves here to remarking that representation by a symbol is among the indirect methods of representation, but that all kinds of indications warn us against lumping it in with other forms of indirect representation without being able to

[1] [Freud remarks elsewhere (1913a) that, just as the presence of dementia praecox facilitates the interpretation of symbols, so an obsessional neurosis makes it more difficult.]

[2] [Footnote 1911:] Cf. the works of Bleuler [1910] and of his Zürich pupils, Maeder [1908], Abraham [1909], etc., on symbolism, and the non-medical writers to whom they refer (Kleinpaul, etc.). [Added 1914:] What is most to the point on this subject will be found in Rank and Sachs (1913, Chapter I). [Added 1925:] See further Jones (1916).

form any clear conceptual picture of their distinguishing features. In a number of cases the element in common between a symbol and what it represents is obvious; in others it is concealed and the choice of the symbol seems puzzling. It is precisely these latter cases which must be able to throw light upon the ultimate meaning of the symbolic relation, and they indicate that it is of a genetic character. Things that are symbolically connected to-day were probably united in prehistoric times by conceptual and linguistic identity.[1] The symbolic relation seems to be a relic and a mark of former identity. In this connection we may observe how in a number of cases the use of a common symbol extends further than the use of a common language, as was already pointed out by Schubert (1814).[2] A number of symbols are as old as language itself, while others (e.g. 'airship', 'Zeppelin') are being coined continuously down to the present time. [1914.]

Dreams make use of this symbolism for the disguised representation of their latent thoughts. Incidentally, many of the symbols are habitually or almost habitually employed to express the same thing. Nevertheless, the peculiar plasticity of the psychical material [in dreams] must never be forgotten. Often enough a symbol has to be interpreted in its proper meaning and not symbolically; while on other occasions a dreamer may derive from his private memories the power to employ as sexual symbols all kinds of things which are not ordinarily employed as such.[3] If a dreamer has a choice open to him between a number of symbols, he will decide in favour of the

[1] [Footnote added 1925:] This view would be powerfully supported by a theory put forward by Dr. Hans Sperber (1912). He is of the opinion that all primal words referred to sexual things but afterwards lost their sexual meaning through being applied to other things and activities which were compared with the sexual ones.

[2] [This last clause was added in 1919.—Footnote 1914:] For instance, according to Ferenczi [see Rank, 1912a, 100], a ship moving on the water occurs in dreams of micturition in Hungarian dreamers, though the term 'schiffen' ['to ship'; cf. vulgar English 'to pumpship'] is unknown in that language. (See also p. 367 f. below.) In dreams of speakers of French and other Romance languages a room is used to symbolize a woman, though these languages have nothing akin to the German expression 'Frauenzimmer'. [See p. 214 n.]

[3] [In the editions of 1909 and 1911 only, the following sentence appeared at this point: 'Moreover the ordinarily used sexual symbols are not invariably unambiguous.']

one which is connected in its subject-matter with the rest of the material of his thoughts—which, that is to say, has individual grounds for its acceptance in addition to the typical ones. [1909; last sentence 1914.]

Though the later investigations since the time of Scherner have made it impossible to dispute the existence of dream-symbolism—even Havelock Ellis [1911, 109] admits that there can be no doubt that our dreams are full of symbolism—yet it must be confessed that the presence of symbols in dreams not only facilitates their interpretation but also makes it more difficult. As a rule the technique of interpreting according to the dreamer's free associations leaves us in the lurch when we come to the symbolic elements in the dream-content. Regard for scientific criticism forbids our returning to the arbitrary judgement of the dream-interpreter, as it was employed in ancient times and seems to have been revived in the reckless interpretations of Stekel. We are thus obliged, in dealing with those elements of the dream-content which must be recognized as symbolic, to adopt a combined technique, which on the one hand rests on the dreamer's associations and on the other hand fills the gaps from the interpreter's knowledge of symbols. We must combine a critical caution in resolving symbols with a careful study of them in dreams which afford particularly clear instances of their use, in order to disarm any charge of arbitrariness in dream-interpretation. The uncertainties which still attach to our activities as interpreters of dreams spring in part from our incomplete knowledge, which can be progressively improved as we advance further, but in part from certain characteristics of dream-symbols themselves. They frequently have more than one or even several meanings, and, as with Chinese script, the correct interpretation can only be arrived at on each occasion from the context. This ambiguity of the symbols links up with the characteristic of dreams for admitting of 'over-interpretation' [see p. 279]—for representing in a single piece of content thoughts and wishes which are often widely divergent in their nature. [1914.]

Subject to these qualifications and reservations I will now proceed. The Emperor and Empress (or the King and Queen) as a rule really represent the dreamer's parents; and a Prince or Princess represents the dreamer himself or herself. [1909.]

But the same high authority is attributed to great men as to the Emperor; and for that reason Goethe, for instance, appears as a father-symbol in some dreams (Hitschmann, 1913). [1919.] —All elongated objects, such as sticks, tree-trunks and umbrellas (the opening of these last being comparable to an erection) may stand for the male organ [1909]—as well as all long, sharp weapons, such as knives, daggers and pikes [1911]. Another frequent though not entirely intelligible symbol of the same thing is a nail-file—possibly on account of the rubbing up and down. [1909.]—Boxes, cases, chests, cupboards and ovens represent the uterus [1909], and also hollow objects, ships, and vessels of all kinds [1919].—Rooms in dreams are usually women ('*Frauenzimmer*', [see p. 214 *n*.]); if the various ways in and out of them are represented, this interpretation is scarcely open to doubt. [1909.]¹ In this connection interest in whether the room is open or locked is easily intelligible. (Cf. Dora's first dream in my 'Fragment of an Analysis of a Case of Hysteria', 1905*e* [Footnote near the beginning of Section II].) There is no need to name explicitly the key that unlocks the room; in his ballad of Count Eberstein, Uhland has used the symbolism of locks and keys to construct a charming piece of bawdry. [1911.] —A dream of going through a suite of rooms is a brothel or harem dream. [1909.] But, as Sachs [1914] has shown by some neat examples, it can also be used (by antithesis) to represent marriage. [1914.]—We find an interesting link with the sexual researches of childhood when a dreamer dreams of two rooms which were originally one, or when he sees a familiar room divided into two in the dream, or *vice versa*. In childhood the female genitals and the anus are regarded as a single area—the

---

¹ [*Footnote added* 1919:] 'One of my patients, who was living in a boarding-house, dreamt that *he met one of the maid-servants and asked her what her number was. To his surprise she answered*: "14". He had in fact started a *liaison* with this girl and had paid several visits to her in her bedroom. She had not unnaturally been afraid that the landlady might become suspicious, and, on the day before the dream, she had proposed that they should meet in an unoccupied room. This room was actually "No. 14", while in the dream it was the woman herself who bore this number. It would hardly be possible to imagine clearer proof of an identification between a woman and a room.' (Jones, 1914*a*.) Cf. Artemidorus, *Oneirocritica*, Book II, Chapter X: 'Thus, for instance, a bedchamber stands for a wife, if such there be in the house.' (Trans. F. S. Krauss, 1881, 110.)

'bottom' (in accordance with the infantile 'cloaca theory')[1]; and it is not until later that the discovery is made that this region of the body comprises two separate cavities and orifices. [1919.] —Steps, ladders or staircases, or, as the case may be, walking up or down them, are representations of the sexual act.[2]— Smooth walls over which the dreamer climbs, the façades of houses, down which he lowers himself—often in great anxiety —correspond to erect human bodies, and are probably repeating in the dream recollections of a baby's climbing up his parents or nurse. The 'smooth' walls are men; in his fear the dreamer often clutches hold of 'projections' in the façades of houses. [1911.]—Tables, tables laid for a meal, and boards also stand for women—no doubt by antithesis, since the contours of their bodies are eliminated in the symbols. [1909.] 'Wood' seems, from its linguistic connections, to stand in general for female 'material'. The name of the Island of 'Madeira' means 'wood' in Portuguese. [1911.] Since 'bed and board' constitute marriage, the latter often takes the place of the former in dreams and the sexual complex of ideas is, so far as may be, transposed on to the eating complex. [1909.]—As regards articles of clothing, a woman's hat can very often be interpreted with certainty as a genital organ, and, moreover, as a

---

[1] [See the section on 'Theories of Birth' in the second of Freud's *Three Essays on the Theory of Sexuality* (1905d).]

[2] [*Footnote* 1911:] I will repeat here what I have written on this subject elsewhere (Freud, 1910d): 'A little time ago I heard that a psychologist whose views are somewhat different from ours had remarked to one of us that, when all was said and done, we did undoubtedly exaggerate the hidden sexual significance of dreams: his own commonest dream was of going upstairs, and surely there could not be anything sexual in *that*. We were put on the alert by this objection, and began to turn our attention to the appearance of steps, staircases and ladders in dreams, and were soon in a position to show that staircases (and analogous things) were unquestionably symbols of copulation. It is not hard to discover the basis of the comparison: we come to the top in a series of rhythmical movements and with increasing breathlessness and then, with a few rapid leaps, we can get to the bottom again. Thus the rhythmical pattern of copulation is reproduced in going upstairs. Nor must we omit to bring in the evidence of linguistic usage. It shows us that "mounting" [German "*steigen*"] is used as a direct equivalent for the sexual act. We speak of a man as a "*Steiger*" [a "mounter"] and of "*nachsteigen*" ["to run after", literally "to climb after"]. In French the steps on a staircase are called "*marches*" and "*un vieux marcheur*" has the same meaning as our "*ein alter Steiger*" ["an old rake"].' [Cf. also p. 285 ff.]

man's. The same is true of an overcoat [German '*Mantel*'], though in this case it is not clear to what extent the use of the symbol is due to a verbal assonance. In men's dreams a necktie often appears as a symbol for the penis. No doubt this is not only because neckties are long, dependent objects and peculiar to men, but also because they can be chosen according to taste— a liberty which, in the case of the object symbolized, is forbidden by Nature.[1] Men who make use of this symbol in dreams are often very extravagant in ties in real life and own whole collections of them. [1911.]—It is highly probable that all complicated machinery and apparatus occurring in dreams stand for the genitals (and as a rule male ones [1919])—in describing which dream-symbolism is as indefatigable as the 'joke-work'.[2] [1909.] Nor is there any doubt that all weapons and tools are used as symbols for the male organ: e.g. ploughs, hammers, rifles, revolvers, daggers, sabres, etc. [1919.]—In the same way many landscapes in dreams, especially any containing bridges or wooded hills, may clearly be recognized as descriptions of the genitals. [1911.] Marcinowski [1912*a*] has published a collection of dreams illustrated by their dreamers with drawings that ostensibly represent landscapes and other localities occurring in the dreams. These drawings bring out very clearly the distinction between a dream's manifest and latent meaning. Whereas to the innocent eye they appear as plans, maps, and so on, closer inspection shows that they represent the human body, the genitals, etc., and only then do the dreams become intelligible. (See in this connection Pfister's papers [1911–12 and 1913] on cryptograms and puzzle-pictures.) [1914.] In the case of unintelligible neologisms, too, it is worth considering whether they may not be put together from components with a sexual

---

[1] [*Footnote added* 1914:] Compare the drawing made by a nineteen-year-old manic patient reproduced in *Zbl. Psychoanal.*, **2**, 675. [Rohrschach, 1912.] It represents a man with a necktie consisting of a snake which is turning in the direction of a girl. See also the story of 'The Bashful Man' in *Anthropophyteia*, **6**, 334: A lady went into a bathroom, and there she came upon a gentleman who scarcely had time to put on his shirt. He was very much embarrassed, but hurriedly covering his throat with the front part of his shirt, he exclaimed: 'Excuse me, but I've not got my necktie on.'

[2] [See Freud's volume on jokes (1905*c*), in which he introduced the term 'joke-work' (on the analogy of 'dream-work') to designate the psychological processes involved in the production of jokes.]

meaning. [1911.]—Children in dreams often stand for the genitals; and, indeed, both men and women are in the habit of referring to their genitals affectionately as their 'little ones'. [1909.] Stekel [1909, 473] is right in recognizing a 'little brother' as the penis. [1925.] Playing with a little child, beating it, etc., often represent masturbation in dreams. [1911.]—To represent castration symbolically, the dream-work makes use of baldness, hair-cutting, falling out of teeth and decapitation. If one of the ordinary symbols for a penis occurs in a dream doubled or multiplied, it is to be regarded as a warding-off of castration.[1] The appearance in dreams of lizards—animals whose tails grow again if they are pulled off—has the same significance. (Cf. the lizard-dream on p. 11 f.)—Many of the beasts which are used as genital symbols in mythology and folk-lore play the same part in dreams: e.g. fishes, snails, cats, mice (on account of the pubic hair), and above all those most important symbols of the male organ—snakes. Small animals and vermin represent small children—for instance, undesired brothers and sisters. Being plagued with vermin is often a sign of pregnancy. [1919.]—A quite recent symbol of the male organ in dreams deserves mention: the airship, whose use in this sense is justified by its connection with flying as well as sometimes by its shape. [1911.]

A number of other symbols have been put forward, with supporting instances, by Stekel, but have not yet been sufficiently verified. [1911.] Stekel's writings, and in particular his *Die Sprache des Traumes* (1911), contain the fullest collection of interpretations of symbols. Many of these show penetration, and further examination has proved them correct: for instance, his section on the symbolism of death. But this author's lack of a critical faculty and his tendency to generalization at all costs throw doubts upon others of his interpretations or render them unusable; so that it is highly advisable to exercise caution in accepting his conclusions. I therefore content myself with drawing attention to only a few of his findings. [1914.]

According to Stekel, 'right' and 'left' in dreams have an ethical sense. 'The right-hand path always means the path of righteousness and the left-hand one that of crime. Thus "left"

---

[1] [This point is elaborated in Section II of Freud's paper on 'The Uncanny' (1919*h*). See also Freud's posthumously published paper (written in 1922) on Medusa's head (1940*c*), and below, p. 412.]

may represent homosexuality, incest or perversion, and "right" may represent marriage, intercourse with a prostitute and so on, always looked at from the subject's individual moral standpoint.' (Stekel, 1909, 466 ff.)—Relatives in dreams usually play the part of genitals (ibid., 473). I can only confirm this in the case of sons, daughters and younger sisters[1]—that is only so far as they fall into the category of 'little ones'. On the other hand I have come across undoubted cases in which 'sisters' symbolized the breasts and 'brothers' the larger hemispheres.—Stekel explains failing to catch up with a carriage as regret at a difference in age which cannot be caught up with (ibid., 479).— Luggage that one travels with is a load of sin, he says, that weighs one down (loc. cit.). [1911.] But precisely luggage often turns out to be an unmistakable symbol of the dreamer's own genitals. [1914.]—Stekel also assigns fixed symbolic meanings to numbers, such as often appear in dreams [ibid., 497 ff.]. But these explanations seem neither sufficiently verified nor generally valid, though his interpretations usually appear plausible in the individual cases. [1911.][2] In any case the number three has been confirmed from many sides as a symbol of the male genitals. [1914.][3]

One of the generalizations put forward by Stekel concerns the double significance of genital symbols. [1914.] 'Where', he asks, 'is there a symbol which—provided that the imagination by any means admits of it—cannot be employed both in a male and in a female sense?' [1911, 73.] In any case the clause in parenthesis removes much of the certainty from this assertion, since in fact the imagination does not always admit of it. But I think it is worth while remarking that in my experience Stekel's generalization cannot be maintained in the face of the greater complexity of the facts. In addition to symbols which can stand with equal frequency for the male and for the female genitals, there are some which designate one of the sexes predominantly or almost exclusively, and yet others which are known *only* with

[1] [And, apparently, younger brothers, see above, p. 357.]

[2] [At this point, in the 1911 edition only, the following sentence appeared: 'In Wilhelm Stekel's recently published volume, *Die Sprache des Traumes*, which appeared too late for me to notice it, there is to be found (1911, 72 f.) a list of the commonest sexual symbols which is intended to show that all sexual symbols can be employed bisexually.']

[3] [A discussion of the number nine will be found in Section 3 of Freud (1923*d*).]

a male or a female meaning. For it is a fact that the imagination does not admit of long, stiff objects and weapons being used as symbols of the female genitals, or of hollow objects, such as chests, cases, boxes, etc., being used as symbols for the male ones. It is true that the tendency of dreams and of unconscious phantasies to employ sexual symbols bisexually betrays an archaic characteristic; for in childhood the distinction between the genitals of the two sexes is unknown and the same kind of genitals are attributed to both of them. [1911.] But it is possible, too, to be misled into wrongly supposing that a sexual symbol is bisexual, if one forgets that in some dreams there is a general inversion of sex, so that what is male is represented as female and *vice versa*. Dreams of this kind may, for instance, express a woman's wish to be a man. [1925.]

The genitals can also be represented in dreams by other parts of the body: the male organ by a hand or a foot and the female genital orifice by the mouth or an ear or even an eye. The secretions of the human body—mucus, tears, urine, semen, etc. —can replace one another in dreams. This last assertion of Stekel's [1911, 49], which is on the whole correct, has been justifiably criticized by Reitler (1913*b*) as requiring some qualification: what in fact happens is that significant secretions, such as semen, are replaced by indifferent ones. [1919.]

It is to be hoped that these very incomplete hints may serve to encourage others to undertake a more painstaking general study of the subject. [1909.][1] I myself have attempted to give a more elaborate account of dream-symbolism in my *Introductory Lectures on Psycho-Analysis* (1916–17 [Lecture X]). [1919.]

I shall now append a few examples of the use of these symbols in dreams, with the idea of showing how impossible it becomes to arrive at the interpretation of a dream if one excludes dream-symbolism, and how irresistibly one is driven to accept it in many cases. [1911.] At the same time, however, I should like to utter an express warning against over-estimating

---

[1] [*Footnote added* 1911:] However much Scherner's view of dream-symbolism may differ from the one developed in these pages, I must insist that he is to be regarded as the true discoverer of symbolism in dreams, and that the investigations of psycho-analysis have at last brought recognition to his book, published as it was so many years ago (in 1861), and for so long regarded as fantastic.

the importance of symbols in dream-interpretation, against restricting the work of translating dreams merely to translating symbols and against abandoning the technique of making use of the dreamer's associations. The two techniques of dream-interpretation must be complementary to each other; but both in practice and in theory the first place continues to be held by the procedure which I began by describing and which attributes a decisive significance to the comments made by the dreamer, while the translation of symbols, as I have explained it, is also at our disposal as an auxiliary method. [1909.]

I

A Hat as a Symbol of a Man (or of Male Genitals) [1911][1]

(Extract from the dream of a young woman suffering from agoraphobia as a result of fears of seduction.)

'*I was walking in the street in the summer, wearing a straw hat of peculiar shape; its middle-piece was bent upwards and its side-pieces*

---

[1] [This dream and the two next ones were first published in a paper entitled 'Additions to the Interpretation of Dreams' (1911a). The paper was introduced by the following paragraphs, which have never been reprinted in German:

'*Some Instances of Dream-Symbols.*—Of the many objections that have been raised against the procedure of psycho-analysis, the strangest, and, perhaps, one might add, the most ignorant, seems to me to be doubt as to the existence of symbolism in dreams and the unconscious. For no one who carries out psycho-analyses can avoid assuming the presence of such symbolism, and the resolution of dreams by symbols has been practised from the earliest times. On the other hand, I am ready to admit that the occurrence of these symbols should be subject to particularly strict proof in view of their great multiplicity.

'In what follows I have put together some examples from my most recent experience: cases in which a solution by means of a particular symbol strikes me as especially revealing. By this means a dream acquires a meaning which it could otherwise never have found; it falls into place in the chain of the dreamer's thoughts and its interpretation is recognized by the subject himself.

'On a point of technique I may remark that a dreamer's associations are apt to fail precisely in connection with the symbolic elements of dreams. In my record of these few selected examples I have tried to draw a sharp line between the work of the patient (or dreamer) himself and my own interventions.'

The paper ended with some shorter examples, which will be found *hung downwards'* (the description became hesitant at this point) *'in such a way that one side was lower than the other. I was cheerful and in a self-confident frame of mind; and, as I passed a group of young officers, I thought: "None of you can do me any harm!"* '

. Since nothing occurred to her in connection with the hat in the dream, I said: 'No doubt the hat was a male genital organ, with its middle-piece sticking up and its two side-pieces hanging down. It may seem strange, perhaps, that a hat should be a man, but you will remember the phrase *"Unter die Haube kommen"* ["to find a husband" (literally "to come under the cap")].' I intentionally gave her no interpretation of the detail about the two side-pieces hanging down unevenly; though it is precisely details of this kind that must point the way in determining an interpretation. I went on to say that as she had a husband with such fine genitals there was no need for her to be afraid of the officers—no need, that is, for her to wish for anything from them, since as a rule she was prevented from going for a walk unprotected and unaccompanied owing to her phantasies of being seduced. I had already been able to give her this last explanation of her anxiety on several occasions upon the basis of other material.

The way in which the dreamer reacted to this material was most remarkable. She withdrew her description of the hat and maintained that she had never said that the two side-pieces hung down. I was too certain of what I had heard to be led astray, and stuck to my guns. She was silent for a while and then found enough courage to ask what was meant by one of her husband's testes hanging down lower than the other and whether it was the same in all men. In this way the remarkable detail of the hat was explained and the interpretation accepted by her.

At the time my patient told me this dream I had long been familiar with the hat-symbol. Other, less transparent cases

reprinted in Section F of this chapter (Nos. 2, 3 and 4 on p. 408 f.). In the original paper these were introduced as follows:

'*Some Rarer Forms of Representation.*—I have mentioned "considerations of representability" as one of the factors that influence the formation of dreams. In the process of transforming a thought into a visual image a peculiar faculty is revealed by dreamers, and an analyst is rarely equal to following it with his guesses. It will therefore give him real satisfaction if the intuitive perception of the dreamer—the creator of these representations—is able to explain their meaning.']

had led me to suppose that a hat can also stand for female genitals.[1]

II

A 'LITTLE ONE' AS THE GENITAL ORGAN— 'BEING RUN OVER' AS A SYMBOL OF SEXUAL INTERCOURSE [1911]

(Another dream of the same agoraphobic patient.)

Her mother sent her little daughter away, so that she had to go by herself. Then she went in a train with her mother and saw her little one walk straight on to the rails so that she was bound to be run over. She heard the cracking of her bones. (This produced an uncomfortable feeling in her but no real horror.) Then she looked round out of the window of the railway-carriage to see whether the parts could not be seen behind. Then she reproached her mother for having made the little one go by herself.

ANALYSIS.—It is no easy matter to give a complete interpretation of the dream. It formed part of a cycle of dreams and can only be fully understood if it is taken in connection with the others. There is difficulty in obtaining in sufficient isolation the material necessary for establishing the symbolism.—In the first place, the patient declared that the train journey was to be interpreted historically, as an allusion to a journey she had taken when she was leaving a sanatorium for nervous diseases, with whose director, needless to say, she had been in love. Her mother had fetched her away, and the doctor had appeared at the station and handed her a bouquet of flowers as a parting present. It had been very awkward that her mother should have witnessed this tribute. At this point, then, her mother figured as interfering with her attempts at a love affair; and this had in fact been the part played by that severe lady during the patient's girlhood.—Her next association related to the sentence: 'she looked round to see whether the parts could not be seen from behind.' The façade of the dream would of course lead one to think of the parts of her little daughter who had been run over and mangled. But her association led in quite another direction.

[1] [*Footnote* 1911:] Cf. an example of this in Kirchgraber (1912). Stekel (1909, 475) records a dream in which a hat with a feather standing up crooked in the middle of it symbolized an (impotent) man. [Freud suggested an explanation of hat symbolism in a later paper (1916c).]

She recollected having once seen her father naked in the bathroom from behind; she went on to talk of the distinctions between the sexes, and laid stress on the fact that a man's genitals can be seen even from behind but a woman's cannot. In this connection she herself interpreted 'the little one' as meaning the genitals and 'her little one'—she had a four-year-old daughter—as her own genitals. She reproached her mother with having expected her to live as though she had no genitals, and pointed out that the same reproach was expressed in the opening sentence of the dream: 'her mother sent her little one away, so that she had to go by herself.' In her imagination 'going by herself in the streets' meant not having a man, not having any sexual relations ('coire' in Latin [from which 'coitus' is derived] means literally 'to go with')—and she disliked that. Her accounts all went to show that when she was a girl she had in fact suffered from her mother's jealousy owing to the preference shown her by her father.[1]

The deeper interpretation of this dream was shown by another dream of the same night, in which the dreamer identified herself with her brother. She had actually been a boyish girl, and had often been told that she should have been a boy. This identification with her brother made it particularly clear that 'the little one' meant a genital organ. Her mother was threatening him (or her) with castration, which could only have been a punishment for playing with her penis; thus the identification also proved that she herself had masturbated as a child —a memory which till then she had only had as applied to her brother. The information supplied by the second dream showed that she must have come to know about the male organ at an early age and have afterwards forgotten it. Further, the second dream alluded to the infantile sexual theory according to which girls are boys who have been castrated. [Cf. Freud, 1908c.] When I suggested to her that she had had this childish belief, she at once confirmed the fact by telling me that she had heard the anecdote of the little boy's saying to the little girl: 'Cut off?' and of the little girl's replying: 'No, always been like that.'

---

[1] [In the 1911 edition only, the following sentence was added at this point: 'Stekel [1909, 473], basing himself on a very common idiomatic usage, has suggested that the "little one" is a symbol of the male or female genitals.']

Thus the sending away of the little one (of the genital organ) in the first dream was also related to the threat of castration. Her ultimate complaint against her mother was for not having given birth to her as a boy.

The fact that 'being run over' symbolizes sexual intercourse would not be obvious from this dream, though it has been confirmed from many other sources.

III

The Genitals Represented by Buildings, Stairs and Shafts [1911][1]

(The dream of a young man inhibited by his father-complex.)

He was going for a walk with his father in a place which must certainly have been the Prater,[2] since he saw the ROTUNDA, *with a* SMALL ANNEX IN FRONT OF IT *to which a* CAPTIVE BALLOON *was attached, though it looked rather* LIMP. *His father asked him what all this was for; he was surprised at his asking, but explained it to him. Then they came into a courtyard which had a large sheet of tin laid out in it. His father wanted* TO PULL OFF *a large piece of it, but first looked around to see if anyone was watching. He told him that he need only tell the foreman and he could take some without any bother. A* STAIRCASE *led down from this yard into* A SHAFT, *whose walls were cushioned in some soft material, rather like a leather armchair. At the end of the shaft was a longish platform and then another* SHAFT *started.* . . .

ANALYSIS.—This dreamer belonged to a type whose therapeutic prospects are not favourable: up to a certain point they offer no resistance at all to analysis, but from then onwards turn out to be almost inaccessible. He interpreted this dream almost unaided. 'The Rotunda,' he said, 'was my genitals and the captive balloon in front of it was my penis, whose limpness I have reason to complain of.' Going into greater detail, then, we may translate the Rotunda as the bottom (habitually regarded by children as part of the genitals) and the small annex in front of it as the scrotum. His father asked him in the dream what all this was, that is, what was the purpose and function of the genitals. It seemed plausible to reverse this situation and

---

[1] [This dream and its interpretation are reproduced in Freud's *Introductory Lectures* (1916–17), Lecture XII, No. 7.]

[2] [See footnote, p. 192.]

turn the dreamer into the questioner. Since he had in fact never questioned his father in this way, we had to look upon the dream-thought as a wish, or take it as a conditional clause, such as: 'If I had asked my father for sexual enlightenment . . .' We shall presently find the continuation of this thought in another part of the dream.

The courtyard in which the sheet of tin was spread out is not to be taken symbolically in the first instance. It was derived from the business premises of the dreamer's father. For reasons of discretion I have substituted 'tin' for another material in which his father actually dealt: but I have made no other change in the wording of the dream. The dreamer had entered his father's business and had taken violent objection to the somewhat dubious practices on which the firm's earnings in part depended. Consequently the dream-thought I have just interpreted may have continued in this way: '(If I had asked him), he would have deceived me just as he deceives his customers.' As regards the 'pulling off' which served to represent his father's dishonesty in business, the dreamer himself produced a second explanation—namely that it stood for masturbating. Not only was I already familiar with this interpretation (see p. 348 *n.* above), but there was something to confirm it in the fact that the secret nature of masturbation was represented by its reverse: it might be done openly. Just as we should expect, the masturbatory activity was once again displaced on to the dreamer's father, like the questioning in the first scene of the dream. He promptly interpreted the shaft as a vagina, having regard to the soft cushioning of its walls. I added from my own knowledge derived elsewhere that climbing down, like climbing up in other cases, described sexual intercourse in the vagina. (See my remarks [in Freud 1910*d*], quoted above, p. 355 *n.*)

The dreamer himself gave a biographical explanation of the fact that the first shaft was followed by a longish platform and then by another shaft. He had practised intercourse for a time but had then given it up on account of inhibitions, and he now hoped to be able to resume it by the help of the treatment. The dream became more indistinct, however, towards the end, and it must seem probable to anyone who is familiar with these things that the influence of another topic was already making itself felt in the second scene of the dream, and was hinted at by the father's business, by his deceitful conduct and by the interpretation of the first shaft as a vagina: all this pointed to a connection with the dreamer's mother.[1]

IV

The Male Organ Represented by Persons and the Female Organ by a Landscape [1911]

(The dream of an uneducated woman whose husband was a policeman, reported by B. Dattner.)

'. . . *Then someone broke into the house and she was frightened and called out for a policeman. But he had quietly gone into a church,*[2] *to which a number of steps*[3] *led up, accompanied by two tramps. Behind the church there was a hill*[4] *and above it a thick wood.*[5] *The policeman was dressed in a helmet, brass collar and cloak.*[6] *He had a brown beard. The two tramps, who went along peaceably with the policeman, had sack-like aprons tied round their middles.*[7] *In front of the church a path led up to the hill; on both sides of it there grew grass and brushwood, which became thicker and thicker and, at the top of the hill, turned into a regular wood.*'

V

Dreams of Castration in Children [1919]

(a) A boy aged three years and five months, who obviously disliked the idea of his father's returning from the front, woke up one morning in a disturbed and excited state. He kept on repeating: '*Why was Daddy carrying his head on a plate? Last night Daddy was carrying his head on a plate.*'

---

[1] [The following additional paragraph was appended to this dream on its first publication (in Freud, 1911a): 'This dream as a whole belongs to the not uncommon class of "biographical" dreams, in which the dreamer gives a survey of his sexual life in the form of a continuous narrative. (See the example [on p. 347 ff.].)—The frequency with which buildings, localities and landscapes are employed as symbolic representations of the body, and in particular (with constant reiteration) of the genitals, would certainly deserve a comprehensive study, illustrated by numerous examples.']

[2] 'Or chapel (= vagina).'   [3] 'Symbol of copulation.'
[4] '*Mons veneris*.'   [5] 'Pubic hair.'
[6] 'According to an expert, demons in cloaks and hoods are of a phallic character.'
[7] 'The two halves of the scrotum.'

(*b*) A student who is now suffering from a severe obsessional neurosis remembers having repeatedly had the following dream during his sixth year: *He went to the hairdresser's to have his hair cut. A big, severe-looking woman came up to him and cut his head off. He recognized the woman as his mother.*

VI

URINARY SYMBOLISM [1914]

The series of drawings reproduced [on p. 368] were found by Ferenczi in a Hungarian comic paper called *Fidibusz*, and he at once saw how well they could be used to illustrate the theory of dreams. Otto Rank has already reproduced them in a paper (1912*a*, [99]).

The drawings bear the title 'A French Nurse's Dream'; but it is only the last picture, showing the nurse being woken up by the child's screams, that tells us that the seven previous pictures represent the phases of a dream. The first picture depicts the stimulus which should have caused the sleeper to wake: the little boy has become aware of a need and is asking for help in dealing with it. But in the dream the dreamer, instead of being in the bedroom, is taking the child for a walk. In the second picture she has already led him to a street corner where he is micturating—and she can go on sleeping. But the arousal stimulus continues; indeed, it increases. The little boy, finding he is not being attended to, screams louder and louder. The more imperiously he insists upon his nurse waking up and helping him, the more insistent becomes the dream's assurance that everything is all right and that there is no need for her to wake up. At the same time, the dream translates the increasing stimulus into the increasing dimensions of its symbols. The stream of water produced by the micturating boy becomes mightier and mightier. In the fourth picture it is already large enough to float a rowing boat; but there follow a gondola, a sailing-ship and finally a liner. The ingenious artist has in this way cleverly depicted the struggle between an obstinate craving for sleep and an inexhaustible stimulus towards waking.

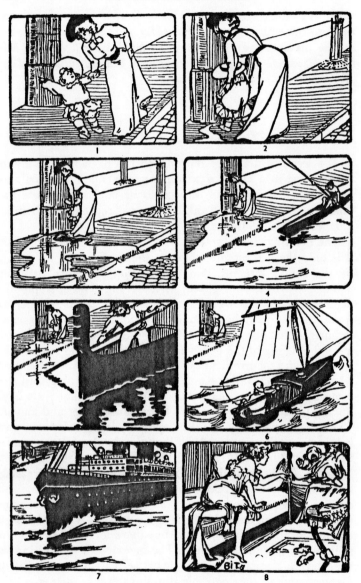

A French Nurse's Dream

VII

A STAIRCASE DREAM [1911]

(Reported and Interpreted by Otto Rank.)[1]

'I have to thank the same colleague to whom I owe the dream with a dental stimulus [recorded on p. 388 ff. below] for an equally transparent emission dream:

' "*I was running down the staircase [of a block of flats] in pursuit of a little girl who had done something to me, in order to punish her. At the foot of the stairs someone (a grown-up woman?) stopped the child for me. I caught hold of her; but I don't know whether I hit her, for I suddenly found myself on the middle of the staircase copulating with the child (as it were in the air). It was not a real copulation; I was only rubbing my genitals against her external genitals, and while I did so I saw them extremely distinctly, as well as her head, which was turned upwards and sideways. During the sexual act I saw hanging above me to my left (also as it were in the air) two small paintings—landscapes representing a house surrounded by trees. At the bottom of the smaller of these, instead of the painter's signature, I saw my own first name, as though it were intended as a birthday present for me. Then I saw a label in front of the two pictures, which said that cheaper pictures were also to be had. (I then saw myself very indistinctly as though I were lying in bed on the landing) and I was woken up by the feeling of wetness caused by the emission I had had.*"

'INTERPRETATION.—On the evening of the dream-day the dreamer had been in a book-shop, and as he was waiting to be attended to he had looked at some pictures which were on view there and which represented subjects similar to those in the dream. He went up close to one small picture which had particularly pleased him, to look at the artist's name—but it had been quite unknown to him.

'Later the same evening, when he was with some friends, he had heard a story of a Bohemian servant-girl who boasted that her illegitimate child had been "made on the stairs". The dreamer had enquired the details of this rather unusual event and had learnt that the servant-girl had gone home with her admirer to her parents' house, where there had been no opportunity for sexual intercourse, and in his excitement the man had copulated with her on the stairs. The dreamer had

[1] [Apparently not published elsewhere.]

made a joking allusion to a malicious expression used to describe adulterated wines, and had said that in fact the child came of a "cellar-stair vintage".

'So much for the connections with the previous day, which appeared with some insistence in the dream-content and were reproduced by the dreamer without any difficulty. But he brought up no less easily an old fragment of infantile recollection which had also found its use in the dream. The staircase belonged to the house where he had spent the greater part of his childhood and, in particular, where he had first made conscious acquaintance with the problems of sex. He had frequently played on this staircase and, among other things, used to slide down the banisters, riding astride on them—which had given him sexual feelings. In the dream, too, he rushed down the stairs extraordinarily fast—so fast, indeed, that, according to his own specific account, he did not put his feet down on the separate steps but "flew" down them, as people say. If the infantile experience is taken into account, the beginning part of the dream seems to represent the factor of sexual excitement.—But the dreamer had also often romped in a sexual way with the neighbours' children on this same staircase and in the adjacent building, and had satisfied his desires in just the same way as he did in the dream.

'If we bear in mind that Freud's researches into sexual symbolism (1910*d* [see above, p. 355 *n*.]) have shown that stairs and going upstairs in dreams almost invariably stand for copulation, the dream becomes quite transparent. Its motive force, as indeed was shown by its outcome—an emission—was of a purely libidinal nature. The dreamer's sexual excitement was awakened during his sleep—this being represented in the dream by his rushing down the stairs. The sadistic element in the sexual excitement, based on the romping in childhood, was indicated by the pursuit and overpowering of the child. The libidinal excitement increased and pressed towards sexual action —represented in the dream by his catching hold of the child and conveying it to the middle of the staircase. Up to that point the dream was only *symbolically* sexual and would have been quite unintelligible to any inexperienced dream-interpreter. But symbolic satisfaction of that kind was not enough to guarantee a restful sleep, in view of the strength of the libidinal excitation. The excitation led to an orgasm and thus revealed the fact that the whole staircase-symbolism represented copulation.—The present dream offers a specially clear confirmation of Freud's view that one of the reasons for the use of going upstairs as a sexual symbol is the rhythmical character of both activities: for the dreamer expressly stated that the most clearly defined element in the whole dream was the rhythm of the sexual act and its up and down motion.

'I must add a word with regard to the two pictures which, apart from their real meaning, also figured in a symbolic sense as "*Weibsbilder*".[1] This was shown at once by there being a large picture and a small picture, just as a large (or grown-up) girl and a small one appeared in the dream. The fact that "cheaper pictures were also to be had" led to the prostitute-complex; while on the other hand the appearance of the dreamer's first name on the small picture and the idea of its being intended as a birthday present for him were hints at the parental complex. ("Born on the stairs" = "begotten by copulation".)

'The indistinct final scene, in which the dreamer saw himself lying in bed on the landing and had a feeling of wetness, seems to have pointed the way beyond infantile masturbation still further back into childhood and to have had its prototype in similarly pleasurable scenes of bed-wetting.'

VIII

A Modified Staircase Dream [1911]

One of my patients, a man whose sexual abstinence was imposed on him by a severe neurosis, and whose [unconscious] phantasies were fixed upon his mother, had repeated dreams of going upstairs in her company. I once remarked to him that a moderate amount of masturbation would probably do him less harm than his compulsive self-restraint, and this provoked the following dream:

His piano-teacher reproached him for neglecting his piano-playing, and for not practising Moscheles' 'Études' and Clementi's 'Gradus ad Parnassum'.

By way of comment, he pointed out that '*Gradus*' are also

[1] [Literally 'pictures of women'—a common German idiom for 'women'.]

'steps'; and that the key-board itself is a staircase, since it contains scales [ladders].

It is fair to say that there is no group of ideas that is incapable of representing sexual facts and wishes.

IX

THE FEELING OF REALITY AND THE REPRESENTATION OF REPETITION [1919]

A man who is now thirty-five years old reported a dream which he remembered clearly and claimed to have had at the age of four. *The lawyer who had charge of his father's will*—he had lost his father when he was three—*brought two large pears. He was given one of them to eat; the other lay on the window-sill in the sitting-room.* He awoke with a conviction of the reality of what he had dreamt and kept obstinately asking his mother for the second pear, and insisted that it was on the window-sill. His mother had laughed at this.

ANALYSIS.—The lawyer was a jovial old gentleman who, the dreamer seemed to remember, had really once brought some pears along. The window-sill was as he had seen it in the dream. Nothing else occurred to him in connection with it—only that his mother had told him a dream shortly before. She had had two birds sitting on her head and had asked herself when they would fly away; they did not fly away, but one of them flew to her mouth and sucked at it.

The failure of the dreamer's associations gave us a right to attempt an interpretation by symbolic substitution. The two pears—'*pommes ou poires*'—were his mother's breasts which had given him nourishment; the window-sill was the projection formed by her bosom—like balconies in dreams of houses (see p. 355). His feeling of reality after waking was justified, for his mother had really suckled him, and had done so, in fact, for far longer than the usual time and his mother's breast was still available to him.[1] The dream must be translated: 'Give (or

---

[1] [Cf. p. 187. This point—the fact that a specially strong feeling after waking of the reality of the dream or of some part of it actually relates to the latent dream-thoughts—is insisted upon by Freud in a passage towards the end of Chapter II of his study on Jensen's *Gradiva* (1907*a*) and in the course of his first comments on the 'Wolf Man's' dream (Section IV of Freud, 1918*b*).]

show) me your breast again, Mother, that I used to drink from in the past.' 'In the past' was represented by his eating one of the pears; 'again' was represented by his longing for the other. The *temporal repetition* of an act is regularly shown in dreams by the *numerical multiplication* of an object.

It is most remarkable, of course, that symbolism should already be playing a part in the dream of a four-year-old child. But this is the rule and not the exception. It may safely be asserted that dreamers have symbolism at their disposal from the very first.

The following uninfluenced recollection by a lady who is now twenty-seven shows at what an early age symbolism is employed outside dream-life as well as inside it. *She was between three and four years old. Her nurse-maid took her to the lavatory along with a brother eleven months her junior and a girl cousin of an age between the other two, to do their small business before going out for a walk. Being the eldest, she sat on the seat, while the other two sat on chambers. She asked her cousin: 'Have you got a purse too? Walter's got a little sausage; I've got a purse.' Her cousin replied: 'Yes, I've got a purse too.' The nurse-maid heard what they said with much amusement and reported the conversation to the children's mother, who reacted with a sharp reprimand.*

I will here interpolate a dream (recorded in a paper by Alfred Robitsek, 1912) in which the beautifully chosen symbolism made an interpretation possible with only slight assistance from the dreamer.

x

'THE QUESTION OF SYMBOLISM IN THE DREAMS OF
NORMAL PERSONS' [1914]

'One objection which is frequently brought forward by opponents of psycho-analysis, and which has lately been voiced by Havelock Ellis (1911, 168), argues that though dream-symbolism may perhaps occur as a product of the neurotic mind, it is not to be found in normal persons. Now psycho-analytic research finds no fundamental, but only quantitative, distinctions between normal and neurotic life; and indeed the analysis of dreams, in which repressed complexes are operative alike in the healthy and the sick, shows a complete identity both in their mechanisms and in their symbolism. The naïve dreams of healthy people actually often contain a much simpler, more perspicuous and more characteristic symbolism than those of neurotics; for in the latter, as a result of the more powerful workings of the censorship and of the consequently more far-reaching dream-distortion, the symbolism may be obscure and hard to interpret. The dream recorded below will serve to illustrate this fact. It was dreamt by a girl who is not neurotic but is of a somewhat prudish and reserved character. In the course of conversation with her I learnt that she was engaged, but that there were some difficulties in the way of her marriage which were likely to lead to its postponement. Of her own accord she told me the following dream.

' "*I arrange the centre of a table with flowers for a birthday.*"[1] In reply to a question she told me that in the dream she seemed to be in her own home (where she was not at present living) and had "a feeling of happiness".

' "Popular" symbolism made it possible for me to translate the dream unaided. It was an expression of her bridal wishes: the table with its floral centre-piece symbolized herself and her genitals; she represented her wishes for the future as fulfilled, for her thoughts were already occupied with the birth of a baby; so her marriage lay a long way behind her.

'I pointed out to her that "*the 'centre' of a table*" was an unusual expression (which she admitted), but I could not of course question her further directly on that point. I carefully avoided suggesting the meaning of the symbols to her, and merely asked her what came into her head in connection with the separate parts of the dream. In the course of the analysis her reserve gave place to an evident interest in the interpretation and to an openness made possible by the seriousness of the conversation.

'When I asked what flowers they had been, her first reply was: "*expensive flowers; one has to pay for them*", and then that they had been "*lilies of the valley, violets and pinks or carnations*". I assumed that the word "lily" appeared in the dream in its popular sense as a symbol of chastity; she confirmed this assumption, for her association to "lily" was "*purity*". "*Valley*" is a frequent female symbol in dreams; so that the chance combination of the two symbols in the English name of the flower was

---

[1] [In the present analysis all the material printed in italics occurs in English in the original, exactly as here reproduced.]

used in the dream-symbolism to stress the preciousness of her virginity—"*expensive flowers, one has to pay for them*"—and to express her expectation that her husband would know how to appreciate its value. The phrase "*expensive flowers*, etc.", as will be seen, had a different meaning in the case of each of the three flower-symbols.

' "*Violets*" was ostensibly quite asexual; but, very boldly, as it seemed to me, I thought I could trace a secret meaning for the word in an unconscious link with the French word "*viol*" ["rape"]. To my surprise the dreamer gave as an association the English word "*violate*". The dream had made use of the great chance similarity between the words "*violet*" and "*violate*" —the difference in their pronunciation lies merely in the different stress upon their final syllables—in order to express "in the language of flowers" the dreamer's thoughts on the violence of defloration (another term that employs flower symbolism) and possibly also a masochistic trait in her character. A pretty instance of the "verbal bridges" [see p. 341 *n*.] crossed by the paths leading to the unconscious. The words "*one has to pay for them*" signified having to pay with her life for being a wife and a mother.

'In connection with "*pinks*", which she went on to call "*carnations*", I thought of the connection between that word and "carnal". But the dreamer's association to it was "*colour*". She added that "*carnations*" were the flowers which her *fiancé* gave her frequently and in great numbers. At the end of her remarks she suddenly confessed of her own accord that she had not told the truth: what had occurred to her had not been "*colour*" but "*incarnation*"—the word I had expected. Incidentally "*colour*" itself was not a very remote association, but was determined by the meaning of "*carnation*" (flesh-colour)—was determined, that is, by the same complex. This lack of straightforwardness showed that it was at this point that resistance was greatest, and corresponded to the fact that this was where the symbolism was most clear and that the struggle between libido and its repression was at its most intense in relation to this phallic theme. The dreamer's comment to the effect that her *fiancé* frequently gave her flowers of that kind was an indication not only of the double sense of the word "*carnations*" but also of their phallic meaning in the dream. The gift of flowers, an exciting factor of the dream derived from her current life, was used to express an exchange of sexual gifts: she was making a gift of her virginity and expected a full emotional and sexual life in return for it. At this point, too, the words "*expensive flowers, one has to pay for them*" must have had what was no doubt literally a financial meaning.—Thus the flower symbolism in this dream included virginal femininity, masculinity and an allusion to defloration by violence. It is worth pointing out in this connection that sexual flower symbolism, which, indeed, occurs very commonly in other connections, symbolizes the human organs of sex by blossoms, which are the sexual organs of plants. It may perhaps be true in general that gifts of flowers between lovers have this unconscious meaning.

'The birthday for which she was preparing in the dream meant, no doubt, the birth of a baby. She was identifying herself with her *fiancé*, and was representing him as "arranging" her for a birth—that is, as copulating with her. The latent thought may have run: "If I were he, I wouldn't wait—I would deflower my *fiancée* without asking her leave—I would use violence". This was indicated by the word "*violate*", and in this way the sadistic component of the libido found expression.

'In a deeper layer of the dream, the phrase "*I arrange . . .*" must no doubt have an auto-erotic, that is to say, an infantile, significance.

'The dreamer also revealed an awareness, which was only possible to her in a dream, of her physical deficiency: she saw herself like a table, without projections, and on that account laid all the more emphasis on the preciousness of the "*centre*"— on another occasion she used the words, "*a centre-piece of flowers*"—that is to say, on her virginity. The horizontal attribute of a table must also have contributed something to the symbol.

'The concentration of the dream should be observed: there was nothing superfluous in it, every word was a symbol.

'Later on the dreamer produced an addendum to the dream: "*I decorate the flowers with green crinkled paper*." She added that it was "*fancy paper*" of the sort used for covering common flower-pots. She went on: "*to hide untidy things, whatever was to be seen, which was not pretty to the eye; there is a gap, a little space in the flowers. The paper looks like velvet or moss*".—To "*decorate*" she gave the association "*decorum*", as I had expected. She said the green colour predominated, and her association to it was "*hope*"—

another link with pregnancy.—In this part of the dream the chief factor was not identification with a man; ideas of shame and self-revelation came to the fore. She was making herself beautiful for him and was admitting physical defects which she felt ashamed of and was trying to correct. Her associations *"velvet"* and *"moss"* were a clear indication of a reference to pubic hair.

'This dream, then, gave expression to thoughts of which the girl was scarcely aware in her waking life—thoughts concerned with sensual love and its organs. She was being "arranged for a birthday"—that is, she was being copulated with. The fear of being deflowered was finding expression, and perhaps, too, ideas of pleasurable suffering. She admitted her physical deficiencies to herself and overcompensated for them by an over-valuation of her virginity. Her shame put forward as an excuse for the signs of sensuality the fact that its purpose was the production of a baby. Material considerations, too, alien to a lover's mind, found their way to expression. The affect attaching to this simple dream—a feeling of happiness—indicated that powerful emotional complexes had found satisfaction in it.'

Ferenczi (1917)[1] has justly pointed out that the meaning of symbols and the significance of dreams can be arrived at with particular ease from the dreams of precisely those people who are uninitiated into psycho-analysis.

At this point I shall interpose a dream dreamt by a contemporary historical figure. I am doing so because in it an object that would in any case appropriately represent a male organ has a further attribute which established it in the clearest fashion as a phallic symbol. The fact of a riding whip growing to an endless length could scarcely be taken to mean anything but an erection. Apart from this, too, the dream is an excellent instance of the way in which thoughts of a serious kind, far removed from anything sexual, can come to be represented by infantile sexual material.

[1] [This paragraph was added in 1919.]

XI

A Dream of Bismarck's [1919][1]

'In his *Gedanken und Erinnerungen* [1898, 2, 194; English translation by A. J. Butler, *Bismarck, the Man and the Statesman*, 1898,
2, 209 f.] Bismarck quotes a letter written by him to the
Emperor William I on December 18th, 1881, in the course of
which the following passage occurs: "Your Majesty's communication encourages me to relate a dream which I had in the
Spring of 1863, in the hardest days of the Conflict, from which
no human eye could see any possible way out. I dreamt (as I
related the first thing next morning to my wife and other witnesses) that I was riding on a narrow Alpine path, precipice
on the right, rocks on the left. The path grew narrower, so that
the horse refused to proceed, and it was impossible to turn
round or dismount, owing to lack of space. Then, with my whip
in my left hand, I struck the smooth rock and called on God.
The whip grew to an endless length, the rocky wall dropped
like a piece of stage scenery and opened out a broad path, with
a view over hills and forests, like a landscape in Bohemia; there
were Prussian troops with banners, and even in my dream the
thought came to me at once that I must report it to your
Majesty. This dream was fulfilled, and I woke up rejoiced and
strengthened. . . ."

'The action of this dream falls into two sections. In the first
part the dreamer found himself in an *impasse* from which he was
miraculously rescued in the second part. The difficult situation
in which the horse and its rider were placed is an easily recognizable dream-picture of the statesman's critical position, which
he may have felt with particular bitterness as he thought over
the problems of his policy on the evening before the dream. In
the passage quoted above Bismarck himself uses the same simile
[of there being no possible "way out"] in describing the hope-
lessness of his position at the time. The meaning of the dream-
picture must therefore have been quite obvious to him. We are
at the same time presented with a fine example of Silberer's
"functional phenomenon" [cf. p. 503 ff.]. The process taking
place in the dreamer's mind—each of the solutions attempted
by his thoughts being met in turn by insuperable obstacles,

[1] From a paper by Hanns Sachs [1913].

while nevertheless he could not and might not tear himself free from the consideration of those problems—were most appropriately depicted by the rider who could neither advance nor retreat. His pride, which forbade his thinking of surrendering or resigning, was expressed in the dream by the words "it was impossible to turn round or dismount". In his quality of a man of action who exerted himself unceasingly and toiled for the good of others, Bismarck must have found it easy to liken himself to a horse; and in fact he did so on many occasions, for instance, in his well-known saying: "A good horse dies in harness." In this sense the words "the horse refused to proceed" meant nothing more nor less than that the over-tired statesman felt a need to turn away from the cares of the immediate present, or, to put it another way, that he was in the act of freeing himself from the bonds of the reality principle by sleeping and dreaming. The wish-fulfilment, which became so prominent in the second part of the dream, was already hinted at in the words "Alpine path". No doubt Bismarck already knew at that time that he was going to spend his next vacation in the Alps—at Gastein; thus the dream, by conveying him thither, set him free at one blow from all the burdens of State business.

'In the second part of the dream, the dreamer's wishes were represented as fulfilled in two ways: undisguisedly and obviously, and, in addition, symbolically. Their fulfilment was represented symbolically by the disappearance of the obstructive rock and the appearance in its place of a broad path—the "way out", which he was in search of, in its most convenient form; and, it was represented undisguisedly in the picture of the advancing Prussian troops. In order to explain this prophetic vision there is no need whatever for constructing mystical hypotheses; Freud's theory of wish-fulfilment fully suffices. Already at the time of this dream Bismarck desired a victorious war against Austria as the best escape from Prussia's internal conflicts. Thus the dream was representing this wish as fulfilled, just as is postulated by Freud, when the dreamer saw the Prussian troops with their banners in Bohemia, that is, in enemy country. The only peculiarity of the case was that the dreamer with whom we are here concerned was not content with the fulfilment of his wish in a *dream* but knew how to achieve it in *reality*. One feature which cannot fail to strike anyone familiar with the psycho-analytic technique of interpretation is the riding whip

—which grew to an "endless length". Whips, sticks, lances and similar objects are familiar to us as phallic symbols; but when a whip further possesses the most striking characteristic of a phallus, its extensibility, scarcely a doubt can remain. The exaggeration of the phenomenon, its growing to an "endless length", seems to hint at a hypercathexis[1] from infantile sources. The fact that the dreamer took the whip in his hand was a clear allusion to masturbation, though the reference was not, of course, to the dreamer's contemporary circumstances but to childish desires in the remote past. The interpretation discovered by Dr. Stekel [1909, 466 ff.] that in dreams "left" stands for what is wrong, forbidden and sinful is much to the point here, for it might very well be applied to masturbation carried out in childhood in the face of prohibition. Between this deepest infantile stratum and the most superficial one, which was concerned with the statesman's immediate plans, it is possible to detect an intermediate layer which was related to both the others. The whole episode of a miraculous liberation from need by striking a rock and at the same time calling on God as a helper bears a remarkable resemblance to the Biblical scene in which Moses struck water from a rock for the thirsting Children of Israel. We may unhesitatingly assume that this passage was familiar in all its details to Bismarck, who came of a Bible-loving Protestant family. It would not be unlikely that in this time of conflict Bismarck should compare himself with Moses, the leader, whom the people he sought to free rewarded with rebellion, hatred and ingratitude. Here, then, we should have the connection with the dreamer's contemporary wishes. But on the other hand the Bible passage contains some details which apply well to a masturbation phantasy. Moses seized the rod in the face of God's command and the Lord punished him for this transgression by telling him that he must die without entering the Promised Land. The prohibited seizing of the rod (in the dream an unmistakably phallic one), the production of fluid from its blow, the threat of death—in these we find all the principal factors of infantile masturbation united. We may observe with interest the process of revision which has welded together these two heterogeneous pictures (originating, the one from the

[1] [Sachs seems to be using the word simply to mean an 'additional cathexis' and not in the special sense in which Freud uses it below on pp. 594, 603, and 617.]

mind of a statesman of genius, and the other from the impulses of the primitive mind of a child) and which has by that means succeeded in eliminating all the distressing factors. The fact that seizing the rod was a forbidden and rebellious act was no longer indicated except symbolically by the "left" hand which performed it. On the other hand, God was called on in the manifest content of the dream as though to deny as ostentatiously as possible any thought of a prohibition or secret. Of the two prophecies made by God to Moses—that he should see the Promised Land but that he should not enter it—the first is clearly represented as fulfilled ("the view over hills and forests"), while the second, highly distressing one was not mentioned at all. The water was probably sacrificed to the requirements of secondary revision [cf. p. 488 ff.], which successfully endeavoured to make this scene and the former one into a single unity; instead of water, the rock itself fell.

'We should expect that at the end of an infantile masturbation phantasy, which included the theme of prohibition, the child would wish that the people in authority in his environment should learn nothing of what had happened. In the dream this wish was represented by its opposite, a wish to report to the King immediately what had happened. But this reversal fitted in excellently and quite unobtrusively into the phantasy of victory contained in the superficial layer of dream-thoughts and in a portion of the manifest content of the dream. A dream such as this of victory and conquest is often a cover for a wish to succeed in an *erotic* conquest; certain features of the dream, such as, for instance, that an obstacle was set in the way of the dreamer's advance but that after he had made use of the extensible whip a broad path opened out, might point in that direction, but they afford an insufficient basis for inferring that a definite trend of thoughts and wishes of that kind ran through the dream. We have here a perfect example of completely successful dream-distortion. Whatever was obnoxious in it was worked over so that it never emerged through the surface layer that was spread over it as a protective covering. In consequence of this it was possible to avoid any release of anxiety. The dream was an ideal case of a wish successfully fulfilled without infringing the censorship; so that we may well believe that the dreamer awoke from it "rejoiced and strengthened".'

As a last example, here is

XII

A CHEMIST'S DREAM [1909]

This was dreamt by a young man who was endeavouring to give up his habit of masturbating in favour of sexual relations with women.

PREAMBLE.—On the day before he had the dream he had been instructing a student on the subject of Grignard's reaction, in which magnesium is dissolved in absolutely pure ether through the catalytic action of iodine. Two days earlier, when the same reaction was being carried out, an explosion had occurred which had burnt the hand of one of the workers.

DREAM.—(I) *He was supposed to be making phenyl-magnesium-bromide. He saw the apparatus with particular distinctness, but had substituted himself for the magnesium. He now found himself in a singularly unstable state. He kept on saying to himself: 'This is all right, things are working, my feet are beginning to dissolve already, my knees are getting soft.' Then he put out his hands and felt his feet. Meanwhile (how, he could not tell) he pulled his legs out of the vessel and said to himself once more: 'This can't be right. Yes it is, though.' At this point he partly woke up and went through the dream to himself, so as to be able to report it to me. He was positively frightened of the solution*[1] *of the dream. He felt very much excited during this period of semi-sleep and kept repeating: 'Phenyl, phenyl.'*

(II) *He was at* ——*ing with his whole family and was due to be at the Schottentor*[2] *at half-past eleven to meet a particular lady. But he only woke at half-past eleven, and said to himself: 'It's too late. You can't get there before half-past twelve.' The next moment he saw the whole family sitting round the table; he saw his mother particularly clearly and the maid-servant carrying the soup-tureen. So he thought: 'Well, as we've started dinner, it's too late for me to go out.'*

ANALYSIS.—He had no doubt that even the first part of the dream had some connection with the lady whom he was to meet. (He had had the dream during the night before the expected *rendez-vous*.) He thought the student to whom he had

---

[1] [German '*Auflösung*'; also the word used above for 'dissolving'.]

[2] ['——ing', was presumably a suburb of Vienna (see p. 298); the Schottentor is near the middle of the town.]

given the instructions a particularly unpleasant person. He had said to him: 'That's not right', because the magnesium showed no signs of being affected. And the student had replied, as though he were quite unconcerned: 'No, nor it is.' The student must have stood for himself (the patient), who was just as indifferent about the analysis as the student was about the synthesis. The 'he' in the dream who carried out the operation stood for me. How unpleasant I must think him for being so indifferent about the result!

On the other hand, he (the patient) was the material which was being used for the analysis (or synthesis). What was in question was the success of the treatment. The reference to his legs in the dream reminded him of an experience of the previous evening. He had been having a dancing-lesson and had met a lady of whom he had been eager to make a conquest. He clasped her to himself so tightly that on one occasion she gave a scream. As he relaxed his pressure against her legs, he felt her strong responsive pressure against the lower part of his thighs as far down as his knees—the point mentioned in his dream. So that in this connection it was the woman who was the magnesium in the retort—things were working at last. He was feminine in relation to me, just as he was masculine in relation to the woman. If it was working with the lady it was working with him in the treatment. His feeling himself and the sensations in his knees pointed to masturbation and fitted in with his fatigue on the previous day.—His appointment with the lady had in fact been for half-past eleven. His wish to miss it by oversleeping and to stay with his sexual objects at home (that is, to keep to masturbation) corresponded to his resistance.

In connection with his repeating the word 'phenyl', he told me that he had always been very fond of all these radicals ending in '-yl', because they were so easy to use: benzyl, acetyl, etc. This explained nothing. But when I suggested *'Schlemihl'* to him as another radical in the series,[1] he laughed heartily and told me that in the course of the summer he had read a book by Marcel Prévost in which there was a chapter on *'Les exclus de l'amour'* which in fact included some remarks upon *'les Schlémiliés'*. When he read them he had said to himself: 'This is

[1] ['Schlemihl', which rhymes with the words ending in '-yl', is a word of Hebrew origin commonly used in German to mean an unlucky, incompetent person.]

just what I'm like.'—If he had missed the appointment it would have been another example of his 'Schlemihlness'.

It would seem that the occurrence of sexual symbolism in dreams has already been experimentally confirmed by some work carried out by K. Schrötter, on lines proposed by H. Swoboda. Subjects under deep hypnosis were given suggestions by Schrötter, and these led to the production of dreams a large part of whose content was determined by the suggestions. If he gave a suggestion that the subject should dream of normal or abnormal sexual intercourse, the dream, in obeying the suggestion, would make use of symbols familiar to us from psycho-analysis in place of the sexual material. For instance, when a suggestion was made to a female subject that she should dream of having homosexual intercourse with a friend, the friend appeared in the dream carrying a shabby hand-bag with a label stuck on to it bearing the words 'Ladies only'. The woman who dreamt this was said never to have had any knowledge of symbolism in dreams or of their interpretation. Difficulties are, however, thrown in the way of our forming an opinion of the value of these interesting experiments by the unfortunate circumstance that Dr. Schrötter committed suicide soon after making them. The only record of them is to be found in a preliminary communication published in the *Zentralblatt für Psychoanalyse* (Schrötter, 1912). [1914.]

Similar findings were published by Roffenstein in 1923. Some experiments made by Betlheim and Hartmann (1924) were of particular interest, since they made no use of hypnosis. These experimenters related anecdotes of a coarsely sexual character to patients suffering from Korsakoff's syndrome and observed the distortions which occurred when the anecdotes were reproduced by the patients in these confusional states. They found that the symbols familiar to us from the interpretation of dreams made their appearance (e.g. going upstairs, stabbing and shooting as symbols of copulation, and knives and cigarettes as symbols of the penis). The authors attached special importance to the appearance of the symbol of a staircase, for, as they justly observed, 'no conscious desire to distort could have arrived at a symbol of such a kind.' [1925.]

It is only now, after we have properly assessed the importance of symbolism in dreams, that it becomes possible for us to take up the theme of typical dreams, which was broken off on p. 276 above. [1914.] I think we are justified in dividing such dreams roughly into two classes: those which really always have the same meaning, and those which, in spite of having the same or a similar content, must nevertheless be interpreted in the greatest variety of ways. Among typical dreams of the first class I have already [p. 273 ff.] dealt in some detail with examination dreams. [1909.]

Dreams of missing a train deserve to be put alongside examination dreams on account of the similarity of their affect, and their explanation shows that we shall be right in doing so. They are dreams of consolation for another kind of anxiety felt in sleep—the fear of dying. 'Departing' on a journey is one of the commonest and best authenticated symbols of death. These dreams say in a consoling way: 'Don't worry, you won't die (depart)', just as examination dreams say soothingly: 'Don't be afraid, no harm will come to you this time either.' The difficulty of understanding both these kinds of dreams is due to the fact that the feeling of anxiety is attached precisely to the expression of consolation. [1911.][1]

The meaning of dreams 'with a dental stimulus' [cf. p. 227],[2] which I often had to analyse in patients, escaped me for a long time because, to my surprise, there were invariably too strong resistances against their interpretation. Overwhelming evidence left me at last in no doubt that in males the motive force of these dreams was derived from nothing other than the masturbatory desires of the pubertal period. I will analyse two dreams of this kind, one of which is also a 'flying dream'. They were both dreamt by the same person, a young man with strong homosexual leanings, which were, however, inhibited in real life.

He was attending a performance of 'Fidelio' and was sitting in the stalls at the Opera beside L., a man who was congenial to him and with whom he would have liked to make friends. Suddenly he flew through the

---

[1] [In the 1911 edition only, the following sentence appeared at this point: 'Death symbols are dealt with at length in the recently published volume by Stekel (1911).']

[2] [This and the following six paragraphs date from 1909.]

*air right across the stalls, put his hand in his mouth and pulled out two
of his teeth.*

He himself said of the flight that it was as though he was
being 'thrown' into the air. Since it was a performance of
Fidelio, the words:

> Wer ein holdes Weib errungen . . .

might have seemed appropriate. But the gaining of even the
loveliest woman was not among the dreamer's wishes. Two
other lines were more to the point:

> Wem der *grosse Wurf* gelungen,
> Eines Freundes Freund zu sein . . .[1]

The dream in fact contained this 'great throw', which, however,
was not only a wish-fulfilment. It also concealed the painful
reflection that the dreamer had often been unlucky in his
attempts at friendship, and had been 'thrown out'. It concealed,
too, his fear that this misfortune might be repeated in relation
to the young man by whose side he was enjoying the performance of *Fidelio*. And now followed what the fastidious dreamer
regarded as a shameful confession: that once, after being rejected by one of his friends, he had masturbated twice in
succession in the state of sensual excitement provoked by his
desire.

Here is the second dream: *He was being treated by two University
professors of his acquaintance instead of by me. One of them was doing
something to his penis. He was afraid of an operation. The other was
pushing against his mouth with an iron rod, so that he lost one or two
of his teeth. He was tied up with four silk cloths.*

It can scarcely be doubted that this dream had a sexual
meaning. The silk cloths identified him with a homosexual
whom he knew. The dreamer had never carried out coitus and

---

[1] [Wem der grosse Wurf gelungen,
Eines Freundes Freund zu sein,
Wer ein holdes Weib errungen. . .

'He who has won the *great throw* of becoming the friend of a friend, he
who has gained a lovely woman . . .!' These are the opening lines of the
second stanza of Schiller's *Hymn to Joy*, which was set to music by
Beethoven in his Choral Symphony. But the third of these lines (the one
first quoted above by Freud) is in fact also the opening line of the last
section of the final Chorus in Beethoven's opera *Fidelio*—his librettist
having apparently plagiarized Schiller.]

had never aimed at having sexual intercourse with men in real life; and he pictured sexual intercourse on the model of the pubertal masturbation with which he had once been familiar.

The many modifications of the typical dream with a dental stimulus (dreams, for instance, of a tooth being pulled out by someone else, etc.) are, I think, to be explained in the same way.[1] It may, however, puzzle us to discover how 'dental stimuli' have come to have this meaning. But I should like to draw attention to the frequency with which sexual repression makes use of transpositions from a lower to an upper part of the body.[2] Thanks to them it becomes possible in hysteria for all kinds of sensations and intentions to be put into effect, if not where they properly belong—in relation to the genitals, at least in relation to other, unobjectionable parts of the body. One instance of a transposition of this kind is the replacement of the genitals by the face in the symbolism of unconscious thinking. Linguistic usage follows the same line in recognizing the buttocks ['*Hinterbacken*', literally 'back-cheeks'] as homologous to the cheeks, and by drawing a parallel between the '*labia*' and the lips which frame the aperture of the mouth. Comparisons between nose and penis are common, and the similarity is made more complete by the presence of hair in both places. The one structure which affords no possibility of an analogy is the teeth; and it is precisely this combination of similarity and dissimilarity which makes the teeth so appropriate for representational purposes when pressure is being exercised by sexual repression.

I cannot pretend that the interpretation of dreams with a dental stimulus as dreams of masturbation—an interpretation whose correctness seems to me beyond doubt—has been entirely cleared up.[3] I have given what explanation I can and must

---

[1] [*Footnote added* 1914:] A tooth being pulled out by someone else in a dream is as a rule to be interpreted as castration (like having one's hair cut by a barber, according to Stekel). A distinction must in general be made between dreams with a dental stimulus and dentist dreams, such as those recorded by Coriat (1913).

[2] [Instances of this will be found in the case history of 'Dora' (Freud, 1905e). The comparison which follows had been drawn by Freud in a letter to Fliess of January 16, 1899 (Freud, 1950a, Letter 102).]

[3] [*Footnote added* 1909:] A communication by C. G. Jung informs us that dreams with a dental stimulus occurring in women have the meaning of birth dreams.—[*Added* 1919:] Ernest Jones [1914b] has brought forward clear confirmation of this. The element in common between

leave what remains unsolved. But I may draw attention to another parallel to be found in linguistic usage. In our part of the world the act of masturbation is vulgarly described as '*sich einen ausreissen*' or '*sich einen herunterreissen*' [literally, 'pulling one out' or 'pulling one down'].[1] I know nothing of the source of this terminology or of the imagery on which it is based; but 'a tooth' would fit very well into the first of the two phrases.

According to popular belief dreams of teeth being pulled out are to be interpreted as meaning the death of a relative, but psycho-analysis can at most confirm this interpretation only in the joking sense I have alluded to above. In this connection, however, I will quote a dream with a dental stimulus that has been put at my disposal by Otto Rank.[2]

'A colleague of mine, who has for some time been taking a lively interest in the problems of dream-interpretation, has sent me the following contribution to the subject of dreams with a dental stimulus.

' "A short time ago I had a dream that *I was at the dentist's and he was drilling a back tooth in my lower jaw. He worked on it so long that the tooth became useless. He then seized it with a forceps and pulled it out with an effortless ease that excited my astonishment. He told me not to bother about it, for it was not the tooth that he was really treating, and put it on the table, where the tooth (as it now seemed to me, an upper incisor) fell apart into several layers. I got up from the dentist's chair, went closer to it with a feeling of curiosity, and raised a medical question which interested me. The dentist explained to me, while he separated out the various portions of the strikingly white tooth and crushed them up (pulverized them) with an instrument, that it was connected with puberty and that it was only before puberty that teeth came out so easily, and that in the case of women the decisive factor was the birth of a child.*

' "I then became aware (while I was half asleep, I believe) that the dream had been accompanied by an emission, which I could not attach with certainty, however, to any particular part of the dream; I was most inclined to think that it had already occurred while the tooth was being pulled out.

this interpretation and the one put forward above lies in the fact that in both cases (castration and birth) what is in question is the separation of a part of the body from the whole.

[1] [*Footnote added* 1911:] Cf. the 'biographical' dream on p. 348, *n.* 2.

[2] [This paragraph and the quotation from Rank which follows were first included in 1911. The quotation is from Rank 1911*c*. Cf. the same dreamer's staircase dream on p. 369.]

' "I then went on to dream of an occurrence which I can no longer recall, but which ended *with my leaving my hat and coat somewhere (possibly in the dentist's cloak-room) in the hope that someone would bring them after me, and with my hurrying off, dressed only in my overcoat, to catch a train which was starting. I succeeded at the last moment in jumping on to the hindmost carriage where someone was already standing. I was not able, though, to make my way into the inside of the carriage, but was obliged to travel in an uncomfortable situation from which I tried, successfully in the end, to escape. We entered a big tunnel and two trains, going in the opposite direction to us, passed through our train as if it were the tunnel. I was looking into a carriage window as though I were outside.*

' "The following experiences and thoughts from the previous day provide material for an interpretation of the dream:

' "(I.) I had in fact been having dental treatment recently, and at the time of the dream I was having continual pain in the tooth in the lower jaw which was being drilled in the dream and at which the dentist had, again in reality, worked longer than I liked. On the morning of the dream-day I had once more been to the dentist on account of the pain; and he had suggested to me that I should have another tooth pulled out in the same jaw as the one he had been treating, saying that the pain probably came from this other one. This was a 'wisdom tooth' which I was cutting just then. I had raised a question touching his medical conscience in that connection.

' "(II.) On the afternoon of the same day, I had been obliged to apologize to a lady for the bad temper I was in owing to my toothache; whereupon she had told me she was afraid of having a root pulled out, the crown of which had crumbled away almost entirely. She thought that pulling out 'eye-teeth' was especially painful and dangerous, although on the other hand one of her acquaintances had told her that it was easier to pull out teeth in the upper jaw, which was where hers was. This acquaintance had also told her that he had once had the wrong tooth pulled out under an anaesthetic, and this had increased her dread of the necessary operation. She had then asked me whether 'eye-teeth' were molars or canines, and what was known about them. I pointed out to her on the one hand the superstitious element in all these opinions, though at the same time I emphasized the nucleus of truth in certain popular views. She was then able to repeat to me what she

believed was a very old and wide-spread popular belief—
that if a pregnant woman had toothache she would have a
boy.

' "(III.) This saying interested me in connection with what
Freud says in his *Interpretation of Dreams* on the typical meaning
of dreams with a dental stimulus as substitutes for masturbation,
since in the popular saying [quoted by the lady] a tooth and
male genitals (or a boy) were also brought into relation with
each other. On the evening of the same day, therefore, I read
through the relevant passage in the *Interpretation of Dreams* and
found there amongst other things the following statements
whose influence upon my dream may be observed just as
clearly as that of the other two experiences I have mentioned.
Freud writes of dreams with a dental stimulus that 'in males the
motive force of these dreams was derived from nothing other
than the masturbatory desires of the pubertal period' [p. 385].
And further: 'The many modifications of the typical dream
with a dental stimulus (dreams, for instance, of a tooth being
pulled out by someone else, etc.) are, I think, to be explained
in the same way. It may, however, puzzle us to discover how
"dental stimuli" should have come to have this meaning. But I
should like to draw attention to the frequency with which
sexual repression makes use of transpositions from a lower to an
upper part of the body.' (In the present dream from the lower
jaw to the upper jaw.) 'Thanks to them it becomes possible in
hysteria for all kinds of sensations and intentions to be put into
effect, if not where they properly belong—in relation to the
genitals, at least in relation to other, unobjectionable parts of
the body' [p. 387]. And again: 'But I may draw attention to
another parallel to be found in linguistic usage. In our part of
the world the act of masturbation is vulgarly described as
"*sich einen ausreissen*" or "*sich einen herunterreissen*" ' [p. 388]. I
was already familiar with this expression in my early youth as
a description of masturbation, and no experienced dream-
interpreter will have any difficulty in finding his way from here
to the infantile material underlying the dream. I will only add
that the ease with which the tooth in the dream, which after its
extraction turned into an upper incisor, came out, reminded me
of an occasion in my childhood on which I myself pulled out a
loose upper front tooth easily and without pain. This event,
which I can still remember clearly to-day in all its details,

occurred at the same early period to which my first conscious attempts at masturbation go back. (This was a screen memory.)

' "Freud's reference to a statement by C. G. Jung to the effect that 'dreams with a dental stimulus occurring in women have the meaning of birth dreams' [p. 387 footnote], as well as the popular belief in the significance of toothache in pregnant women, accounted for the contrast drawn in the dream between the decisive factor in the case of females and of males (puberty). In this connection I recall an earlier dream of mine which I had soon after a visit to the dentist and in which I dreamt that the gold crowns which had just been fixed fell out; this annoyed me very much in the dream on account of the considerable expense in which I had been involved and which I had not yet quite got over at the time. This other dream now became intelligible to me (in view of a certain experience of mine) as a recognition of the material advantages of masturbation over object-love: the latter, from an economic point of view, was in every respect less desirable (cf. the gold crowns)[1]; and I believe that the lady's remark about the significance of toothache in pregnant women had re-awakened these trains of thought in me."

'So much for the interpretation put forward by my colleague, which is most enlightening and to which, I think, no objections can be raised. I have nothing to add to it, except, perhaps, a hint at the probable meaning of the second part of the dream. This seems to have represented the dreamer's transition from masturbation to sexual intercourse, which was apparently accomplished with great difficulty—(cf. the tunnel through which the trains went in and out in various directions) as well as the danger of the latter (cf. pregnancy and the overcoat [see p. 186]). The dreamer made use for this purpose of the verbal bridges "*Zahn-ziehen* (*Zug*)" and "*Zahn-reissen* (*Reisen*)".[2]

'On the other hand, theoretically, the case seems to me interesting in two respects. In the first place, it brings evidence in favour of Freud's discovery that ejaculation in a dream accompanies the act of pulling out a tooth. In whatever form the emission may appear, we are obliged to regard it as a masturbatory satisfaction brought about without the assistance

---

[1] [The crown (*Krone*) was at this time the Austrian monetary unit.]

[2] ['*Zahn-ziehen*' = 'to pull out a tooth'; '*Zug*' (from the same root as '*ziehen*') = 'train' or 'pull'. '*Zahn-reissen*' = 'to pull out a tooth'; '*Reisen*' (pronounced not much unlike '*reissen*') = 'to travel'.]

of any mechanical stimulation. Moreover, in this case, the satisfaction accompanying the emission was not, as it usually is, directed to an object, even if only to an imaginary one, but had no object, if one may say so; it was completely auto-erotic, or at the most showed a slight trace of homosexuality (in reference to the dentist).

'The second point which seems to me to deserve emphasis is the following. It may plausibly be objected that there is no need at all to regard the present case as confirming Freud's view, since the events of the previous day would be sufficient in themselves to make the content of the dream intelligible. The dreamer's visit to the dentist, his conversation with the lady and his reading of the *Interpretation of Dreams* would quite sufficiently explain how he came to produce this dream, especially as his sleep was disturbed by toothache; they would even explain, if need be, how the dream served to dispose of the pain which was disturbing his sleep—by means of the idea of getting rid of the painful tooth and by simultaneously drowning with libido the painful sensation which the dreamer feared. But even if we make the greatest possible allowance for all this, it cannot be seriously maintained that the mere reading of Freud's explanations could have established in the dreamer the connection between pulling out a tooth and the act of masturbation, or could even have put that connection into operation, unless it had been laid down long since, as the dreamer himself admits it was (in the phrase "*sich einen ausreissen*"). This connection may have been revived not only by his conversation with the lady but by a circumstance which he reported subsequently. For in reading the *Interpretation of Dreams* he had been unwilling, for comprehensible reasons, to believe in this typical meaning of dreams with a dental stimulus, and had felt a desire to know whether that meaning applied to *all* dreams of that sort. The present dream confirmed the fact that this was so, at least as far as he was concerned, and thus showed him why it was that he had been obliged to feel doubts on the subject. In this respect too, therefore, the dream was the fulfilment of a wish—namely, the wish to convince himself of the range of application and the validity of this view of Freud's.'

The second group of typical dreams include those in which the dreamer flies or floats in the air, falls, swims, etc. What is the meaning of such dreams? It is impossible to give a general reply. As we shall hear, they mean something different in every instance; it is only the raw material of sensations contained in them which is always derived from the same source. [1909.]

The information provided by psycho-analyses forces me to conclude that these dreams, too, reproduce impressions of child-hood; they relate, that is, to games involving movement, which are extraordinarily attractive to children. There cannot be a single uncle who has not shown a child how to fly by rushing across the room with him in his outstretched arms, or who has not played at letting him fall by riding him on his knee and then suddenly stretching out his leg, or by holding him up high and then suddenly pretending to drop him. Children are delighted by such experiences and never tire of asking to have them repeated, especially if there is something about them that causes a little fright or giddiness. In after years they repeat these experiences in dreams; but in the dreams they leave out the hands which held them up, so that they float or fall un-supported. The delight taken by young children in games of this kind (as well as in swings and see-saws) is well known; when they come to see acrobatic feats in a circus their memory of such games is revived. Hysterical attacks in boys sometimes con-sist merely in reproductions of feats of this kind, carried out with great skill. It not uncommonly happens that these games of movement, though innocent in themselves, give rise to sexual feelings. Childish romping ['*Hetzen*'], if I may use a word which commonly describes all such activities, is what is being repeated in dreams of flying, falling, giddiness and so on; while the pleasur-able feelings attached to these experiences are transformed into anxiety. But, often enough, as every mother knows, romping among children actually ends in squabbling and tears. [1900.]

Thus I have good grounds for rejecting the theory that what provokes dreams of flying and falling is the state of our tactile feelings during sleep or sensations of the movement of our lungs, and so on. In my view these sensations are themselves repro-duced as part of the memory to which the dream goes back: that is to say, they are part of the *content* of the dream and not its source. [1900.][1]

[1] [*Footnote added* 1930:] These remarks on dreams of movement are repeated here, since the present context requires them. See above, p. 271 f. [where some additional footnotes will be found].

This material, then, consisting of sensations of movement of similar kinds and derived from the same source, is used to represent dream-thoughts of every possible sort. Dreams of flying or floating in the air (as a rule, pleasurably toned) require the most various interpretations; with some people these interpretations have to be of an individual character, whereas with others they may even be of a typical kind. One of my women patients used very often to dream that she was floating at a certain height over the street without touching the ground. She was very short, and she dreaded the contamination involved in contact with other people. Her floating dream fulfilled her two wishes, by raising her feet from the ground and lifting her head into a higher stratum of air. In other women I have found that flying dreams expressed a desire 'to be like a bird'; while other dreamers became angels during the night because they had not been called angels during the day. The close connection of flying with the idea of birds explains how it is that in men flying dreams usually have a grossly sensual meaning;[1] and we shall not be surprised when we hear that some dreamer or other is very proud of his powers of flight. [1909.]

Dr. Paul Federn (of Vienna [and later of New York]) has put forward[2] the attractive theory that a good number of these flying dreams are dreams of erection; for the remarkable phenomenon of erection, around which the human imagination has constantly played, cannot fail to be impressive, involving as it does an apparent suspension of the laws of gravity. (Cf. in this connection the winged phalli of the ancients.) [1911.]

It is a remarkable fact that Mourly Vold, a sober-minded investigator of dreams and one who is disinclined to interpretation of any kind, also supports the erotic interpretation of flying or floating dreams (Vold, 1910–12, **2**, 791). He speaks of the erotic factor as 'the most powerful motive for floating dreams', draws attention to the intense feeling of vibration in the body that accompanies such dreams and points to the frequency with which they are connected with erections or emissions. [1914.]

Dreams of falling, on the other hand, are more often characterized by anxiety. Their interpretation offers no difficulty in the case of women, who almost always accept the symbolic use

---

[1] [See p. 583, *n*. 3.]

[2] [At a meeting of the Vienna Psycho-Analytical Society. See his subsequent paper on the subject (Federn, 1914, 126).]

of falling as a way of describing a surrender to an erotic temptation. Nor have we yet exhausted the infantile sources of dreams
of falling. Almost every child has fallen down at one time or
other and afterwards been picked up and petted; or if he has
fallen out of his cot at night, has been taken into bed with his
mother or nurse. [1909.]

People who have frequent dreams of swimming and who feel
great joy in cleaving their way through the waves, and so on,
have as a rule been bed-wetters and are repeating in their
dreams a pleasure which they have long learnt to forgo. We
shall learn presently [p. 399 ff.] from more than one example
what it is that dreams of swimming are most easily used to
represent. [1909.]

The interpretation of dreams of fire justifies the nursery law
which forbids a child to 'play with fire'—so that he shall not
wet his bed at night. For in their case, too, there is an underlying recollection of the enuresis of childhood. In my 'Fragment
of an Analysis of a Case of Hysteria' [1905e, Part II, Dora's first
dream], I have given a complete analysis and synthesis of a fire-
dream of this kind in connection with the dreamer's case
history, and I have shown what impulses of adult years this
infantile material can be used to represent. [1911.]

It would be possible to mention a whole number of other
'typical' dreams if we take the term to mean that the same
manifest dream-content is frequently to be found in the dreams
of different dreamers. For instance we might mention dreams
of passing through narrow streets or of walking through whole
suites of rooms [cf. p. 214], and dreams of burglars—against
whom, incidentally, nervous people take precautions *before* they
go to sleep [cf. p. 403]; dreams of being pursued by wild
animals (or by bulls or horses) [cf. p. 410] or of being threatened
with knives, daggers or lances —these last two classes being characteristic of the manifest content of the dreams of people who
suffer from anxiety—and many more. An investigation specially devoted to this material would thoroughly repay the labour
involved. But instead of this I have two[1] observations to make,

[1] [This 'two' is a vestige of the 1909 and 1911 editions, in which the
whole discussion on 'typical' dreams was contained in Chapter V. The
first observation, introduced by a 'I', began with the paragraph which
now follows and continued to the end of the present Section E—to

though these do not apply exclusively to typical dreams. [1909.]

The more one is concerned with the solution of dreams, the more one is driven to recognize that the majority of the dreams of adults deal with sexual material and give expression to erotic wishes. A judgement on this point can be formed only by those who really analyse dreams, that is to say, who make their way through their manifest content to the latent dream-thoughts, and never by those who are satisfied with making a note of the manifest content alone (like Näcke, for instance, in his writings on sexual dreams). Let me say at once that this fact is not in the least surprising but is in complete harmony with the principles of my explanation of dreams. No other instinct has been subjected since childhood to so much suppression as the sexual instinct with its numerous components (cf. my *Three Essays on the Theory of Sexuality*, 1905*d*); from no other instinct are so many and such powerful unconscious wishes left over, ready to produce dreams in a state of sleep. In interpreting dreams we should never forget the significance of sexual complexes, though we should also, of course, avoid the exaggeration of attributing exclusive importance to them. [1909.]

We can assert of many dreams, if they are carefully interpreted, that they are bisexual, since they unquestionably admit of an 'over-interpretation' in which the dreamer's homosexual impulses are realized—impulses, that is, which are contrary to his normal sexual activities. To maintain, however, as do Stekel (1911, [71]) and Adler (1910, etc.), that *all* dreams are to be interpreted bisexually appears to me to be a generalization which is equally undemonstrable and unplausible and which I am not prepared to support. In particular, I cannot dismiss the obvious fact that there are numerous dreams which satisfy needs other than those which are erotic in the widest sense of the word: dreams of hunger and thirst, dreams of convenience, etc. So,

p. 404. The second observation, introduced by a 'II', immediately followed; it was the passage beginning on p. 351 with the words 'When we have become familiar' and continuing to the words 'another example of his "Schlemihlness"' on p. 384, with which, in those two editions, Chapter V ended. In later editions, of course, both these passages have become very greatly enlarged by the accretion of fresh material. In the 1909 edition the two observations together only occupied about five pages, as compared with forty-two in 1930.]

too, such statements as that 'the spectre of death is to be found behind every dream' (Stekel [1911, 34]), or that 'every dream shows an advance from the feminine to the masculine line' (Adler [1910]), appear to me to go far beyond anything that can be legitimately maintained in dream-interpretation. [1911.]

The assertion that all dreams require a sexual interpretation, against which critics rage so incessantly, occurs nowhere in my *Interpretation of Dreams*. It is not to be found in any of the numerous editions of this book and is in obvious contradiction to other views expressed in it. [1919.][1]

I have already shown elsewhere [p. 183 ff.] that strikingly innocent dreams may embody crudely erotic wishes, and I could confirm this by many new instances. But it is also true that many dreams which appear to be *indifferent* and which one would not regard as in any respect peculiar lead back on analysis to wishful impulses which are unmistakably sexual and often of an unexpected sort. Who, for instance, would have suspected the presence of a sexual wish in the following dream before it had been interpreted? The dreamer gave this account of it: *Standing back a little behind two stately palaces was a little house with closed doors. My wife led me along the piece of street up to the little house and pushed the door open; I then slipped quickly and easily into the inside of a court which rose in an incline.* Anyone, however, who has had a little experience in translating dreams will at once reflect that penetrating into narrow spaces and opening closed doors are among the commonest sexual symbols, and will easily perceive in this dream a representation of an attempt at *coitus a tergo* (between the two stately buttocks of the female body). The narrow passage rising in an incline stood, of course, for the vagina. The assistance attributed by the dreamer to his wife forces us to conclude that in reality it was only consideration for her that restrained the dreamer from making attempts of this kind. It turned out that on the dream-day a girl had come to live in the dreamer's household who had attracted him and had given him the impression that she would raise no great objections to an approach of that kind. The little house between the two palaces was a reminiscence of the Hradshin [Citadel] in Prague and was a further reference to the same girl, who came from that place. [1909.]

When I insist to one of my patients on the frequency of

[1] [This point is more fully dealt with on p. 160, footnote.]

Oedipus dreams, in which the dreamer has sexual intercourse with his own mother, he often replies: 'I have no recollection of having had any such dream.' Immediately afterwards, however, a memory will emerge of some other inconspicuous and indifferent dream, which the patient has dreamt repeatedly. Analysis then shows that this is in fact a dream with the same content—once more an Oedipus dream. I can say with certainty that *disguised* dreams of sexual intercourse with the dreamer's mother are many times more frequent than straightforward ones. [1909.][1]

[1] [*Footnote added* 1911:] I have published elsewhere a typical example of a disguised Oedipus dream of this kind. [Freud 1910*l*; now reprinted at the end of this footnote.] Another example, with a detailed analysis, has been published by Otto Rank (1911*a*).—[*Added* 1914:] For some other disguised Oedipus dreams, in which eye-symbolism is prominent, see Rank (1913). Other papers on eye-dreams and eye-symbolism, by Eder [1913], Ferenczi [1913] and Reitler [1913*a*] will be found in the same place. The blinding in the legend of Oedipus, as well as elsewhere, stands for castration.—[*Added* 1911:] Incidentally, the symbolic interpretation of undisguised Oedipus dreams was not unknown to the ancients. Rank (1910, 534) writes: 'Thus Julius Caesar is reported to have had a dream of sexual intercourse with his mother which was explained by the dream-interpreters as a favourable augury for his taking possession of the earth (Mother Earth). The oracle given to the Tarquins is equally well known, which prophesied that the conquest of Rome would fall to that one of them who should first kiss his mother ("*osculum matri tulerit*"). This was interpreted by Brutus as referring to Mother Earth. ("*Terram osculo contigit, scilicet quod ea communis mater omnium mortalium esset.*" ["He kissed the earth, saying it was the common mother of all mortals."] Livy, I, 56.)'—[*Added* 1914:] Compare in this connection the dream of Hippias reported by Herodotus (VI, 107) [*Trans.* 1922, 259]): 'As for the Persians, they were guided to Marathon by Hippias son of Pisistratus. Hippias in the past night had seen a vision in his sleep wherein he thought that he lay with his own mother; he interpreted this dream to signify that he should return to Athens and recover his power, and so die an old man in his own mother-country.' —[*Added* 1911:] These myths and interpretations reveal a true psychological insight. I have found that people who know that they are preferred or favoured by their mother give evidence in their lives of a peculiar self-reliance and an unshakeable optimism which often seem like heroic attributes and bring actual success to their possessors.

[This reprint of the short paper by Freud (1910*l*) which is mentioned at the beginning of the present footnote was added here in 1925:]

'TYPICAL EXAMPLE OF A DISGUISED OEDIPUS DREAM: A man dreamt that *he had a secret liaison with a lady whom someone else wanted to marry. He was worried in case this other man might discover the liaison and the proposed marriage come to nothing. He therefore behaved in a very affectionate way to the man.*

In some dreams of landscapes or other localities emphasis is laid in the dream itself on a convinced feeling of having been there once before. (Occurrences of '*déjà vu*' in dreams have a special meaning.[1]) These places are invariably the genitals of the dreamer's mother; there is indeed no other place about which one can assert with such conviction that one has been there once before. [1909.]

On one occasion only I was perplexed by an obsessional neurotic who told me a dream in which he was visiting a house that he had been in *twice* before. But this particular patient had told me a considerable time before of an episode during his sixth year. On one occasion he had been sharing his mother's bed and misused the opportunity by inserting his finger into her genitals while she was asleep. [1914.]

A large number of dreams,[2] often accompanied by anxiety and having as their content such subjects as passing through narrow spaces or being in water, are based upon phantasies of intra-uterine life, of existence in the womb and of the act of birth. What follows was the dream of a young man who, in his

---

He embraced him and kissed him.—There was only one point of contact between the content of this dream and the facts of the dreamer's life. He had a secret *liaison* with a married woman; and an ambiguous remark made by her husband, who was a friend of his, led him to suspect that the husband might have noticed something. But in reality there was something else involved, all mention of which was avoided in the dream but which alone provided a key to its understanding. The husband's life was threatened by an organic illness. His wife was prepared for the possibility of his dying suddenly, and the dreamer was consciously occupied with an intention to marry the young widow after her husband's death. This external situation placed the dreamer in the constellation of the Oedipus dream. His wish was capable of killing the man in order to get the woman as his wife. The dream expressed this wish in a hypocritically distorted form. Instead of her being married already, he made out that someone else wanted to marry her, which corresponded to his own secret intentions; and his hostile wishes towards her husband were concealed behind demonstrations of affection which were derived from his memory of his relations with his own father in childhood.' [Hypocritical dreams are discussed on pp. 145 n. and 471 ff.]

[1] [This last sentence was interpolated in 1914. The phenomenon of '*déjà vu*' in general is discussed by Freud in Chapter XII (D) of his *Psychopathology of Everyday Life* (1901*b*) and in another short paper (Freud, 1914*a*). See also below, p. 447.]

[2] [This paragraph and the three following ones date from 1909.]

imagination, had taken advantage of an intra-uterine opportunity of watching his parents copulating.

*He was in a deep pit with a window in it like the one in the Semmering
Tunnel.*[1] *At first he saw an empty landscape through the window, but
then invented a picture to fit the space, which immediately appeared and
filled in the gap. The picture represented a field which was being
ploughed up deeply by some implement; and the fresh air together with
the idea of hard work which accompanied the scene, and the blue-black
clods of earth, produced a lovely impression. He then went on further and
saw a book upon education open in front of him . . . and was surprised
that so much attention was devoted in it to the sexual feelings (of
children); and this led him to think of me.*

And here is a pretty water dream, dreamt by a woman
patient, which served a special purpose in the treatment. *At her
summer holiday resort, by the Lake of ——, she dived into the dark
water just where the pale moon was mirrored in it.*

Dreams like this one are birth dreams. Their interpretation
is reached by reversing the event reported in the manifest
dream; thus, instead of 'diving into the water' we have 'coming
out of the water', i.e. being born.[2] We can discover the locality
from which a child is born by calling to mind the slang use of
the word '*lune*' in French [viz. 'bottom']. The pale moon was
thus the white bottom which children are quick to guess that
they came out of. What was the meaning of the patient's wishing to be born at her summer holiday resort? I asked her and
she replied without hesitation: 'Isn't it just as though I had
been reborn through the treatment?' Thus the dream was
an invitation to me to continue treating her at the holiday
resort—that is, to visit her there. Perhaps there was a very
timid hint in it, too, of the patient's wish to become a mother
herself.[3]

---

[1] [A tunnel some 70 miles from Vienna on the main line to the south-
west.]

[2] [*Footnote added* 1914:] For the mythological significance of birth
from the water see Rank (1909).

[3] [*Footnote* 1909:] It was not for a long time that I learned to appreciate the importance of phantasies and unconscious thoughts about life
in the womb. They contain an explanation of the remarkable dread that
many people have of being buried alive; and they also afford the deepest
unconscious basis for the belief in survival after death, which merely
represents a projection into the future of this uncanny life before birth.
Moreover, the act of birth is the first experience of anxiety, and thus the source and

I will quote another birth-dream, together with its interpretation, from a paper by Ernest Jones [1910b].[1] '*She stood on the sea-shore watching a small boy, who seemed to be hers, wading into the water. This he did till the water covered him and she could only see his head bobbing up and down near the surface. The scene then changed into the crowded hall of an hotel. Her husband left her, and she "entered into conversation with" a stranger.* The second half of the dream revealed itself in the analysis as representing a flight from her husband and the entering into intimate relations with a third person. . . . The first part of the dream was a fairly evident birth-phantasy. In dreams as in mythology, the delivery of the child *from* the uterine waters is commonly presented by distortion as the entry of the child *into* water; among many others, the births of Adonis, Osiris, Moses and Bacchus are well-known illustrations of this. The bobbing up and down of the head into the water at once recalled to the patient the sensation of quickening she had experienced in her only pregnancy. Thinking of the boy going into the water induced a reverie in which she saw herself taking him out of the water, carrying him to a nursery, washing him and dressing him, and installing him in her household.

'The second half of the dream therefore represented thoughts concerning the elopement, that belonged to the first half of the underlying latent content; the first half of the dream corresponded with the second half of the latent content, the birth-phantasy. Besides this inversion in order, further inversions took place in each half of the dream. In the first half the child *entered* the water, and then his head bobbed; in the underlying dream-thoughts first the quickening occurred and then the child *left* the water (a double inversion). In the second half her husband left her; in the dream-thoughts she left her husband.'

Abraham (1909, 22 ff.) has reported another birth-dream, dreamt by a young woman who was facing her first confinement. A subterranean channel led direct into the water from a place in the floor of her room (genital canal—amniotic fluid). She raised a trap-door in the floor and a creature dressed in brown fur, very much resembling a seal, promptly appeared.

prototype of the affect of anxiety. [Cf. a much later discussion of this in a passage near the beginning of Chapter VIII of Freud's *Inhibitions, Symptoms and Anxiety* (1926d).]

[1] [This paragraph and the following one were added in 1914.]

This creature turned out to be the dreamer's younger brother, to whom she had always been like a mother. [1911.]

Rank [1912a] has shown from a series of dreams that birth-dreams make use of the same symbolism as dreams with a urinary stimulus. The erotic stimulus is represented in the latter as a urinary stimulus; and the stratification of meaning in these dreams corresponds to a change that has come over the meaning of the symbol since infancy. [1914.]

This is an appropriate point at which to return to a topic that was broken off in an earlier chapter (p. 237):[1] the problem of the part played in the formation of dreams by organic stimuli which disturb sleep. Dreams which come about under their influence openly exhibit not only the usual tendency to wish-fulfilment and to serving the end of convenience, but very often a perfectly transparent symbolism as well; for it not infrequently happens that a stimulus awakens a dreamer *after a vain attempt has been made to deal with it in a dream under a symbolic disguise.* This applies to dreams of emission or orgasm as well as to those provoked by a need to micturate or defaecate. 'The peculiar nature of emission dreams not only puts us in a position to reveal directly certain sexual symbols which are already known as being typical, but which have nevertheless been violently disputed; it also enables us to convince ourselves that some apparently innocent situations in dreams are no more than a symbolic prelude to crudely sexual scenes. The latter are as a rule represented undisguisedly in the relatively rare emission dreams, whereas they culminate often enough in anxiety dreams, which have the same result of awakening the sleeper.' [Rank, ibid., 55.]

The symbolism of dreams with a urinary stimulus is especially transparent and has been recognized from the earliest times. The view was already expressed by Hippocrates that dreams of fountains and springs indicate a disorder of the bladder (Havelock Ellis [1911, 164]). Scherner [1861, 189] studied the multiplicity of the symbolism of urinary stimuli and asserted that 'any urinary stimulus of considerable strength invariably passes over into stimulation of the sexual regions and symbolic representations of them. ... Dreams with a urinary stimulus are often at the same time representatives of sexual dreams.' [Ibid., 192.]

[1] [This paragraph and the three following ones date from 1919.]

Otto Rank, whose discussion in his paper on the stratification of symbols in arousal dreams [Rank, 1912a] I am here following, has made it seem highly probable that a great number of dreams with a urinary stimulus have in fact been caused by a *sexual* stimulus which has made a first attempt to find satisfaction regressively in the infantile form of urethral erotism. [Ibid., 78.] Those cases are particularly instructive in which the urinary stimulus thus set up leads to awakening and emptying the bladder, but in which the dream is nevertheless continued and the need then expressed in undisguisedly erotic imagery.[1]

Dreams with an intestinal stimulus throw light in an analogous fashion on the symbolism involved in them, and at the same time confirm the connection between gold and faeces which is also supported by copious evidence from social anthropology. (See Freud, 1908b; Rank, 1912a; Dattner, 1913; and Reik, 1915.) 'Thus, for instance, a woman who was receiving medical treatment for an intestinal disorder dreamt of someone who was burying a treasure in the neighbourhood of a little wooden hut which looked like a rustic out-door closet. There was a second part to the dream in which she was wiping the behind of her little girl who had dirtied herself.' [Rank, 1912a, 55.]

Rescue dreams are connected with birth dreams. In women's dreams, to rescue, and especially to rescue from the water, has the same significance as giving birth; but the meaning is modified if the dreamer is a man.[2] [1911.]

Robbers, burglars and ghosts, of whom some people feel frightened before going to bed, and who sometimes pursue their victims after they are asleep, all originate from one and the

[1] [*Footnote* 1919:] 'The same symbols which occur in their infantile aspect in bladder dreams, appear with an eminently sexual meaning in their "recent" aspects: Water = urine = semen = amniotic fluid; ship = "pump ship" (micturate) = uterus (box); to get wet = enuresis = copulation = pregnancy; to swim = full bladder = abode of the unborn; rain = micturate = symbol of fertility; travel (starting, getting out) = getting out of bed = sexual intercourse (honeymoon); micturate = emission.' (Rank, 1912a, 95.)

[2] [*Footnote* 1911:] A dream of this kind has been reported by Pfister (1909). For the symbolic meaning of rescuing see Freud, 1910d, and Freud, 1910h. [*Added* 1914:] See also Rank (1911b) and Reik (1911). [*Added* 1919:] See further, Rank (1914). [A dream of rescue from the water will be found in the second case discussed by Freud in his paper on 'Dreams and Telepathy' (1922a).]

same class of infantile reminiscence. They are the nocturnal visitors who rouse children and take them up to prevent their wetting their beds, or who lift the bed-clothes to make sure where they have put their hands in their sleep. Analyses of some of these anxiety-dreams have made it possible for me to identify these nocturnal visitors more precisely. In every case the robbers stood for the sleeper's father, whereas the ghosts corresponded to female figures in white night-gowns. [1909.]

SOME EXAMPLES.—CALCULATIONS AND
SPEECHES IN DREAMS[1]

Before assigning the fourth of the factors which govern the formation of dreams to its proper place [cf. p. 488 ff.], I propose to quote a number of examples from my collection. These will serve partly to illustrate the interplay between the three factors already known to us and partly to provide confirmatory evidence for what have hitherto been unsupported assertions or to indicate some conclusions which inevitably follow from them. In giving an account of the dream-work, I have found very great difficulty in backing my findings by examples. Instances in support of particular propositions carry conviction only if they are treated in the context of the interpretation of a dream as a whole. If they are torn from their context they lose their virtue; while, on the other hand, a dream-interpretation which is carried even a little way below the surface quickly becomes so voluminous as to make us lose the thread of the train of thought which it was designed to illustrate. This technical difficulty must serve as my excuse if in what follows I string together all sorts of things, whose only common bond is their connection with the contents of the preceding sections of this chapter. [1900.]

I will begin by giving a few instances of peculiar or unusual modes of representation in dreams.

A lady had the following dream: *A servant girl was standing on a ladder as if she were cleaning a window, and had a chimpanzee with her and a gorilla-cat* (the dreamer afterwards corrected this to *an angora cat*). *She hurled the animals at the dreamer; the chimpanzee*

---

[1] [As in the case of Section E, a large part of the first half of the present section was added to the work in its later editions. The date of the first inclusion of each paragraph will accordingly be found attached to it in square brackets. The second half of the section (from p. 414 onwards) dates from the first edition.—Another collection of examples of dream-analyses will be found in the twelfth of Freud's *Introductory Lectures* (1916–17).]

cuddled up to her, which was very disgusting.—This dream achieved its purpose by an extremely simple device: it took a figure of speech literally and gave an exact representation of its wording. 'Monkey', and animals' names in general, are used as invectives; and the situation in the dream meant neither more nor less than 'hurling invectives'. In the course of the present series of dreams we shall come upon a number of other instances of the use of this simple device during the dream-work. [1900.]

Another dream adopted a very similar procedure. *A woman had a child with a remarkably deformed skull. The dreamer had heard that the child had grown like that owing to its position in the uterus. The doctor said that the skull might be given a better shape by compression, but that that would damage the child's brain. She reflected that as he was a boy it would do him less harm.*—This dream contained a plastic representation of the abstract concept of 'impressions on children' which the dreamer had met with in the course of the explanations given her during her treatment. [1900.]

The dream-work adopted a slightly different method in the following instance. The dream referred to an excursion to the Hilmteich[1] near Graz. *The weather outside was fearful. There was a wretched hotel, water was dripping from the walls of the room, the bed-clothes were damp.* (The latter part of the dream was reported less directly than I have given it.) The meaning of the dream was 'superfluous'. This abstract idea, which was present in the dream-thoughts, was in the first instance given a somewhat forced twist and put into some such form as 'overflowing', 'flowing over' or 'fluid'—after which it was represented in a number of similar pictures: water outside, water on the walls inside, water in the dampness of the bed-clothes—everything flowing or 'overflowing'. [1900.]

We shall not be surprised to find that, for the purpose of representation in dreams, the spelling of words is far less important than their sound, especially when we bear in mind that the same rule holds good in rhyming verse. Rank (1910, 482) has recorded in detail, and analysed very fully, a girl's dream in which the dreamer described how she was walking through the fields and cutting off rich ears ['*Ähren*'] of barley and wheat. A friend of her youth came towards her, but she tried to avoid meeting him. The analysis showed that the dream was concerned with a kiss—an 'honourable kiss' ['*Kuss in Ehren*' pro-

[1] [A stretch of water in the outskirts of the town.]

nounced the same as '*Ähren*', literally, 'kiss in honour'].[1] In the dream itself the '*Ähren*', which had to be cut off, not pulled off, figured as ears of corn, while, condensed with '*Ehren*', they stood for a whole number of other [latent] thoughts. [1911.]

On the other hand, in other cases, the course of linguistic evolution has made things very easy for dreams. For language has a whole number of words at its command which originally had a pictorial and concrete significance, but are used to-day in a colourless and abstract sense. All that the dream need do is to give these words their former, full meaning or to go back a little way to an earlier phase in their development. A man had a dream, for instance, of his brother being in a *Kasten* ['box']. In the course of interpretation the *Kasten* was replaced by a *Schrank* ['cupboard'—also used abstractly for 'barrier', 'restriction']. The dream-thought had been to the effect that his brother ought to restrict himself ['*sich einschränken*']—instead of the dreamer doing so.[2] [1909.]

Another man dreamt that he climbed to the top of a mountain which commanded a quite unusually *extensive view*. Here he was identifying himself with a brother of his who was the editor of a *survey* which dealt with *far* Eastern affairs. [1911.]

In *Der Grüne Heinrich*[3] a dream is related in which a mettlesome horse was rolling about in a beautiful field of oats, each grain of which was 'a sweet almond, a raisin and a new penny piece . . . wrapped up together in red silk and tied up with a bit of pig's bristle.' The author (or dreamer) gives us an immediate interpretation of this dream-picture: the horse felt agreeably tickled and called out 'Der Hafer sticht mich!'[4] [1914.]

According to Henzen [1890] dreams involving puns and turns of speech occur particularly often in the old Norse sagas, in which scarcely a dream is to be found which does not contain an ambiguity or a play upon words. [1914.]

---

[1] [The reference is to a German proverb: '*Einen Kuss in Ehren kann niemand verwehren*' ('No one can refuse an honourable kiss'). The dreamer had in reality been given her first kiss as she was walking through a cornfield—a kiss among the ears of corn.]

[2] [This instance and the next are also quoted (with somewhat different comments) in respectively the seventh and eighth of Freud's *Introductory Lectures* (1916–17).]

[3] [Part IV, Chapter 6, of Gottfried Keller's novel.]

[4] [Literally: 'The oats are pricking me', but with the idiomatic meaning of 'Prosperity has spoiled me'.]

It would be a work in itself to collect these modes of representation and to classify them according to their underlying
principles. [1909.] Some of these representations might almost
be described as jokes, and they give one a feeling that one
would never have understood them without the dreamer's help.
[1911.]

(1) A man dreamt that *he was asked someone's name, but could
not think of it.* He himself explained that what this meant was
that 'he would never dream of such a thing'. [1911.]

(2)[1] A woman patient told me a dream in which *all the people
were especially big.* 'That means', she went on, 'that the dream
must be to do with events in my early childhood, for at that
time, of course, all grown-up people seemed to me enormously
big.' [Cf. p. 30 *n.*] She herself did not appear in the content of
this dream.—The fact of a dream referring to childhood may
also be expressed in another way, namely by a translation of
time into space. The characters and scenes are seen as though
they were at a great distance, at the end of a long road, or as
though they were being looked at through the wrong end of a
pair of opera-glasses. [1911.]

(3) A man who in his working life tended to use abstract and
indefinite phraseology, though he was quite sharp-witted in
general, dreamt on one occasion that *he arrived at a railway
station just as a train was coming in. What then happened was that the
platform moved towards the train, while the train stopped still*—an
absurd reversal of what actually happens. This detail was no
more than an indication that we should expect to find another
reversal in the dream's content. [Cf. p. 326.] The analysis of
the dream led to the patient's recollecting some picture-books
in which there were illustrations of men standing on their heads
and walking on their hands. [1911.]

(4) Another time the same dreamer told me a short dream
which was almost reminiscent of the technique of a rebus. He
dreamt that *his uncle gave him a kiss in an automobile.* He went on
at once to give me the interpretation, which I myself would

---

[1] [This and the two following examples were first published in a short
paper, '*Nachträge zur Traumdeutung*' (Freud, 1911a). See above, p. 360 *n.*]

never have guessed: namely that it meant auto-erotism. The content of this dream might have been produced as a joke in waking life.[1] [1911.]

(5) A man dreamt that *he was pulling a woman out from behind a bed*. The meaning of this was that he was giving her preference.[2] [1914.]

(6) A man dreamt that *he was an officer sitting at a table opposite the Emperor*. This meant that he was putting himself in opposition to his father. [1914.]

(7) A man dreamt that *he was treating someone for a broken limb*. The analysis showed that the broken bone ['*Knochenbruch*'] stood for a broken marriage ['*Ehebruch*', properly 'adultery'].[3] [1914.]

(8) The time of day in dreams very often stands for the age of the dreamer at some particular period in his childhood. Thus, in one dream, 'a quarter past five in the morning' meant the age of five years and three months, which was significant, since that was the dreamer's age at the time of the birth of his younger brother. [1914.]

(9) Here is another method of representing ages in a dream. A woman dreamt that *she was walking with two little girls whose ages differed by fifteen months*. She was unable to recall any family of her acquaintance to whom this applied. She herself put forward the interpretation that the two children both represented herself and that the dream was reminding her that the two traumatic events of her childhood were separated from each other by precisely that interval. One had occurred when she

---

[1] ['*Auto*' is the ordinary German word for 'motor-car'.—This dream is reported in slightly different terms in Freud's *Introductory Lectures* (1916–17), Lecture XV.]

[2] [The point here is a purely verbal one, depending on the similarity of the German words for 'pulling out' ('*hervorziehen*') and 'giving preference to' ('*vorziehen*'). This dream is also quoted in Freud, *Introductory Lectures* (1916–17), Lecture VII. Nos. 5, 6, 8 and 9 of the present set of examples were published first in Freud, 1913*h*.]

[3] [This example is also quoted in Freud's *Introductory Lectures* (1916–17), Lecture XI, where, in a footnote, a 'symptomatic act' is reported, which confirms this particular interpretation.]

was three and a half, the other when she was four and three-quarters. [1914.]

(10) It is not surprising that a person undergoing psycho-analytic treatment should often dream of it and be led to give expression in his dreams to the many thoughts and expectations to which the treatment gives rise. The imagery most frequently chosen to represent it is that of a journey, usually by motor-car, as being a modern and complicated vehicle. The speed of the car will then be used by the patient as an opportunity for giving vent to ironical comments.—If 'the unconscious', as an element in the subject's waking thoughts, has to be represented in a dream, it may be replaced very appropriately by subterranean regions.—These, where they occur *without* any reference to analytic treatment, stand for the female body or the womb.—'Down below' in dreams often relates to the genitals, 'up above', on the contrary, to the face, mouth or breast.—Wild beasts are as a rule employed by the dream-work to represent passionate impulses of which the dreamer is afraid, whether they are his own or those of other people. (It then needs only a slight dis-placement for the wild beasts to come to represent the people who are possessed by these passions. We have not far to go from here to cases in which a dreaded father is represented by a beast of prey or a dog or wild horse—a form of representation recall-ing totemism.)[1] It might be said that the wild beasts are used to represent the libido, a force dreaded by the ego and combated by means of repression. It often happens, too, that the dreamer separates off his neurosis, his 'sick personality', from himself and depicts it as an independent person. [1919.]

(11) Here is an example recorded by Hanns Sachs (1911): 'We know from Freud's *Interpretation of Dreams* that the dream-work makes use of different methods for giving a sensory form to words or phrases. If, for instance, the expression that is to be represented is an ambiguous one, the dream-work may exploit the fact by using the ambiguity as a switch-point: where one of the meanings of the word is present in the dream-thoughts the other one can be introduced into the manifest dream. This was the case in the following short dream in which ingenious use

[1] [See Freud, *Totem and Taboo* (1912–13), Chapter IV, Section 3.]

was made for representational purposes of appropriate impressions of the previous day. I was suffering from a cold on the "dream-day", and I had therefore decided in the evening that, if I possibly could, I would avoid getting out of bed during the night. I seemed in the dream merely to be continuing what I had been doing during the day. I had been engaged in sticking press-cuttings into an album and had done my best to put each one in the place where it belonged. I dreamt that *I was trying to paste a cutting into the album. But it wouldn't go on to the page* ["*er geht nicht auf die Seite*"], *which caused me much pain.* I woke up and became aware that the pain in the dream persisted in the form of a pain in my inside, and I was compelled to abandon the decision I had made before going to bed. My dream, in its capacity of guardian of my sleep, had given me the illusion of a fulfilment of my wish to stop in bed, by means of a plastic representation of the ambiguous phrase "*er geht nicht auf die Seite*" ["he isn't going to the lavatory"].' [1914.]

We can go so far as to say that the dream-work makes use, for the purpose of giving a visual representation of the dream-thoughts, of any methods within its reach, whether waking criticism regards them as legitimate or illegitimate. This lays the dream-work open to doubt and derision on the part of everyone who has only *heard* of dream-interpretation but never practised it. Stekel's book, *Die Sprache des Traumes* (1911), is particularly rich in examples of this kind. I have, however, avoided quoting instances from it, on account of the author's lack of critical judgement and of the arbitrariness of his technique, which give rise to doubts even in unprejudiced minds. [Cf. p. 350.] [1919.]

(12) [1914.] The following examples are taken from a paper by V. Tausk (1914) on the use of clothes and colours in dreaming.

(*a*) A. dreamt of *seeing a former governess of his in a dress of black lustre* ['*Lüster*'] *which fitted very tight across her buttocks.*—This was explained as meaning that the governess was lustful ['*lüstern*'].

(*b*) C. dreamt of *seeing a girl on the ―― Road, who was bathed in white light and was wearing a white blouse.*—The dreamer had had intimate relations with a Miss White for the first time on this road.

(c) Frau D. dreamt of *seeing the eighty-year-old Viennese actor Blasel lying on a sofa in full armour* ['*in voller Rüstung*']. *He began jumping over tables and chairs, drew a dagger, looked at himself in the looking-glass and brandished the dagger in the air as though he was fighting an imaginary enemy.*—Interpretation: The dreamer suffered from a long-standing affection of the bladder ['*Blase*']. She lay on a sofa for her analysis; when she looked at herself in a looking-glass, she thought privately that in spite of her age and illness she still looked hale and hearty ['*rüstig*'].

(13) [1919.] A 'GREAT ACHIEVEMENT' IN A DREAM.—A man dreamt that *he was a pregnant woman lying in bed. He found the situation very disagreeable. He called out: 'I'd rather be . . .'* (during the analysis, after calling to mind a nurse, he completed the sentence with the words 'breaking stones'). *Behind the bed there was hanging a map, the bottom edge of which was kept stretched by a strip of wood. He tore the strip of wood down by catching hold of its two ends. It did not break across but split into two halves lengthways. This action relieved him and at the same time helped on delivery.*

Without any assistance he interpreted tearing down the strip ['*Leiste*'] as a great achievement ['*Leistung*']. He was escaping from his uncomfortable situation (in the treatment) by tearing himself out of his feminine attitude. . . . The absurd detail of the strip of wood not simply breaking but splitting lengthways was explained thus: the dreamer recalled that this combination of doubling and destroying was an allusion to castration. Dreams very often represent castration by the presence of two penis symbols as the defiant expression of an antithetical wish [cf. p. 357]. Incidentally, the '*Leiste*' ['groin'] is a part of the body in the neighbourhood of the genitals. The dreamer summed up the interpretation of the dream as meaning that he had got the better of the threat of castration which had led to his adopting a feminine attitude.[1]

[1] [This example was first published as a separate paper (1914*e*). In reprinting it here, Freud omitted a passage, which occurred originally after the words 'by tearing himself out of his feminine attitude'. The omitted passage (which has never been reprinted) deals with Silberer's 'functional phenomenon', discussed below, on p. 503 ff. It ran as follows: 'No objection can be made to this interpretation of the patient's; but I would not describe it as "functional" simply because his dream-thoughts related to his attitude in the treatment. Thoughts of that kind serve as "material" for the construction of dreams like anything else. It is hard to

(14) [1919.] In an analysis which I was conducting in French a dream came up for interpretation in which I appeared as an elephant. I naturally asked the dreamer why I was represented in that form. '*Vous me trompez*' ['you are deceiving me'] was his reply ('*trompe*' = 'trunk').

The dream-work can often succeed in representing very refractory material, such as proper names, by a far-fetched use of out-of-the-way associations. In one of my dreams *old Brücke* [1] *had set me the task of making a dissection; . . . I fished something out that looked like a piece of crumpled silver-paper.* (I shall return to this dream later [see p. 452 ff.].) The association to this (at which I arrived with some difficulty) was 'stanniol'.[2] I then perceived that I was thinking of the name of Stannius, the author of a dissertation on the nervous system of fish, which I had greatly admired in my youth. The first scientific task which my teacher [Brücke] set me was in fact concerned with the nervous system of a fish, Ammocoetes [Freud, 1877a]. It was clearly impossible to make use of the name of this fish in a picture puzzle. [1900].

At this point I cannot resist recording a very peculiar dream, which also deserves to be noticed as having been dreamt by a child, and which can easily be explained analytically. 'I remember having often dreamt when I was a child', said a lady, '*that God wore a paper cocked-hat on his head.* I used very often to have a hat of that sort put on my head at meals, to prevent my being able to look at the other children's plates, to see how big their helpings were. As I had heard that God was omniscient, the

see why the thoughts of a person under analysis should not be concerned with his behaviour during treatment. [Cf. also p. 214, n. 4.] The distinction between "material" and "functional" phenomena in Silberer's sense is of significance only where—as was the case in Silberer's well-known self-observations as he was falling asleep [see p. 344 ff.]—there is an *alternative* between the subject's attention being directed *either* to some piece of thought-content present in his mind *or* to his own actual psychical state, and not where that state itself constitutes the content of his thoughts.' Freud also remarked in parenthesis that in any case the 'absurd detail of the strip of wood not simply breaking but splitting lengthways' could not be 'functional'.]

[1] [See footnote, p. 482.]
[2] [Silver-paper = tin-foil; stanniol is a derivative of tin (stannium).]

meaning of the dream was that I knew everything—even in spite of the hat that had been put on my head.'[1] [1909.]

The nature of the dream-work[2] and the way in which it plays about with its material, the dream-thoughts, are instructively shown when we come to consider numbers and calculations that occur in dreams. Moreover, numbers in dreams are regarded superstitiously as being especially significant in regard to the future.[3] I shall therefore select a few instances of this kind from my collection.

I

Extract from a dream dreamt by a lady shortly before her treatment came to an end: *She was going to pay for something. Her daughter took 3 florins and 65 kreuzers from her (the mother's) purse. The dreamer said to her: 'What are you doing? It only costs 21 kreuzers.'*[4] Owing to my knowledge of the dreamer's circumstances, this bit of dream was intelligible to me without any further explanation on her part. The lady came from abroad and her daughter was at school in Vienna. She was in a position to carry on her treatment with me as long as her daughter remained in Vienna. The girl's school year was due to end in three weeks and this also meant the end of the lady's treatment. The day before the dream, the headmistress had asked her whether she would not consider leaving her daughter at school for another year. From this suggestion she had evidently gone on to reflect that in that case she might also continue her treatment. This was what the

---

[1] [This dream is also discussed in Freud, *Introductory Lectures* (1916–17), Lecture VII.]

[2] [The remainder of the present section (F), with the exception of Example IV on p. 417, appeared in the original edition (1900).]

[3] [This point is discussed by Freud in Chapter XII (7) of his *Psychopathology of Everyday Life* (1901b) and in Section II of his paper on 'The Uncanny' (1919h).]

[4] [The old Austrian currency in florins and kreuzers was not replaced until after the first publication of this book. 1 florin (= 100 kreuzers) was at that time approximately equivalent to an English 1s. 10d. or an American 40 cents. Accordingly, of the sums mentioned in this dream and the next, 3 fl. 65 would have been about 6s. or $1.25; 21 kr. about 4d. or 7½ cents; 1 fl. 50 about 2s. 6d. or 62½ cents; and 150 fl. about £12 10s. or $62.50.]

dream referred to. One year is equal to 365 days. The three weeks which remained both of the school-year and of the treatment were equivalent to 21 days (though the hours of treatment would be less than this). The numbers, which in the dream-thoughts referred to periods of time, were attached in the dream itself to sums of money—not but what there was a deeper meaning involved, for 'time is money'. 365 kreuzer only amount to 3 florins and 65 kreuzers; and the smallness of the sums that occurred in the dream was obviously the result of wish-fulfilment. The dreamer's wish reduced the cost both of the treatment and of the year's school-fees.

II

The numbers which occurred in another dream involved more complicated circumstances. A lady who, though she was still young, had been married for a number of years, received news that an acquaintance of hers, Elise L., who was almost exactly her contemporary, had just become engaged. Thereupon she had the following dream. *She was at the theatre with her husband. One side of the stalls was completely empty. Her husband told her that Elise L. and her fiancé had wanted to go too, but had only been able to get bad seats—three for 1 florin 50 kreuzers[1]—and of course they could not take those. She thought it would not really have done any harm if they had.*

What was the origin of the 1 florin 50 kreuzers? It came from what was in fact an indifferent event of the previous day. Her sister-in-law had been given a present of 150 florins by her husband and had been in a hurry to get rid of them by buying a piece of jewellery. It is to be noticed that 150 florins is a *hundred* times as much as 1 florin 50 kreuzers. Where did the *three* come from which was the number of the theatre tickets? The only connection here was that her newly-engaged friend was the same number of months—*three*—her junior. The solution of the dream was arrived at with the discovery of the meaning of the empty stalls. They were an unmodified allusion to a small incident which had given her husband a good excuse for teasing her. She had planned to go to one of the plays that had been announced for the coming week and had taken the trouble to buy tickets several days ahead, and had therefore had to pay a booking fee. When they got to the theatre they found that one

[1] [See previous footnote.]

side of the house was almost empty. There had been *no need for her to be in such a hurry.*

Let me now put the dream-thoughts in place of the dream. 'It was *absurd* to marry so early. There was *no need for me to be in such a hurry.* I see from Elise L.'s example that I should have got a husband in the end. Indeed, I should have got one *a hundred times* better' (a *treasure*) 'if I had only *waited*' (in antithesis to her sister-in-law's *hurry*). 'My money' (or dowry) 'could have bought *three* men just as good.'

It will be observed that the meaning and context of the numbers have been altered to a far greater extent in this dream than in the former one. The processes of modification and distortion have gone further here; and this is to be explained by the dream-thoughts in this case having to overcome a specially high degree of endopsychic resistance before they could obtain representation. Nor should we overlook the fact that there was an element of absurdity in the dream, namely the *three* seats being taken by *two* people. I will anticipate my discussion of absurdity in dreams [p. 426 ff.] by pointing out that this absurd detail in the content of the dream was intended to represent the most strongly emphasized of the dream-thoughts, viz., 'it was *absurd* to marry so early'. The absurdity which had to find a place in the dream was ingeniously supplied by the number 3, which was itself derived from a quite immaterial point of distinction between the two people under comparison—the 3 months' difference between their ages. The reduction of the actual 150 florins to 1 florin 50 corresponded to the *low value* assigned by the dreamer to her husband (or treasure), in her suppressed thoughts.[1]

III

The next example exhibits the methods of calculation employed by dreams, which have brought them into so much disrepute. A man had a dream that *he was settled in a chair at the B.'s*—a family with which he had been formerly acquainted—*and said to them: 'It was a great mistake your not letting me have*

[1] [This dream is more elaborately analysed at various points in Freud's *Introductory Lectures* (1916–17), particularly at the end of Lecture VII and in two places in Lecture XIV. It and the preceding dream are also recorded in Section VII of Freud's work *On Dreams* (1901a), *Standard Ed.*, **5**, 669.]

Mali.'—'How old are you?' he then went on to ask the girl.—'I was born in 1882,' she replied.—'Oh, so you're 28, then.'

Since the dream dates from 1898 this was evidently a miscalculation, and the dreamer's inability to do sums would deserve to be compared with that of a general paralytic unless it could be explained in some other way. My patient was one of those people who, whenever they happen to catch sight of a woman, cannot let her alone in their thoughts. The patient who for some months used regularly to come next after him in my consulting room, and whom he thus ran into, was a young lady; he used constantly to make enquiries about her and was most anxious to create a good impression with her. It was she whose age he estimated at 28 years. So much by way of explanation of the result of the ostensible calculation. 1882, incidentally, was the year in which the dreamer had married.—I may add that he was unable to resist entering into conversation with the two other members of the female sex whom he came across in my house—the two maids (neither of them by any means youthful), one or other of whom used to open the door to him; he explained their lack of response as being due to their regarding him as an elderly gentleman of *settled* habits.

IV[1]

Here is another dream dealing with figures, which is characterized by the clarity of the manner in which it was determined, or rather, overdetermined. I owe both the dream and its interpretation to Dr. B. Dattner. 'The landlord of my block of flats, who is a police-constable, dreamt that *he was on street duty.* (This was a wish-fulfilment.) *An inspector came up to him, who had the number 22 followed by 62 or 26, on his collar. At any rate there were several twos on it.*

'The mere fact that in reporting the dream the dreamer broke up the number 2262 showed that its components had separate meanings. He recalled that the day before there had been some talk at the police station about the men's length of service. The occasion for it was an inspector who had retired on his pension at the age of 62. The dreamer had only served for 22 years, and it would be 2 years and 2 months before he would be eligible for a 90 per cent pension. The dream represented

[1] [This example was added in 1911.]

in the first place the fulfilment of a long-cherished wish of the dreamer's to reach the rank of inspector. The superior officer with "2262" on his collar was the dreamer himself. He was on street duty—another favourite wish of his—he had served his remaining 2 years and 2 months and now, like the 62-year-old inspector, he could retire on a full pension.'[1]

When we take together these and some other examples which I shall give later [p. 448 ff.], we may safely say that the dream-work does not in fact carry out any calculations at all, whether correctly or incorrectly; it merely throws into the *form* of a calculation numbers which are present in the dream-thoughts and can serve as allusions to matter that cannot be represented in any other way. In this respect the dream-work is treating numbers as a medium for the expression of its purpose in precisely the same way as it treats any other idea, including proper names and speeches that occur recognizably as verbal presentations. [See next paragraph but one.]

For the dream-work cannot actually *create* speeches. [See above, pp. 183 f. and 304.] However much speeches and conversations, whether reasonable or unreasonable in themselves, may figure in dreams, analysis invariably proves that all that the dream has done is to extract from the dream-thoughts fragments of speeches which have really been made or heard. It deals with these fragments in the most arbitrary fashion. Not only does it drag them out of their context and cut them in pieces, incorporating some portions and rejecting others, but it often puts them together in a new order, so that a speech which appears in the dream to be a connected whole turns out in analysis to be composed of three or four detached fragments. In producing this new version, a dream will often abandon the meaning that the words originally had in the dream-thoughts and give them a fresh one.[2] If we look closely into a speech that

[1] [*Footnote added* 1914:] For analyses of other dreams containing numbers, see Jung [1911], Marcinowski [1912b] and others. These often imply very complicated operations with numbers, which have been carried out by the dreamer with astonishing accuracy. See also Jones (1912a).

[2] [*Footnote added* 1909:] In this respect neuroses behave exactly like dreams. I know a patient one of whose symptoms is that, involuntarily and against her will, she hears—i.e. hallucinates—songs or fragments of songs, without being able to understand what part they play in her

occurs in a dream, we shall find that it consists on the one hand of relatively clear and compact portions and on the other hand of portions which serve as connecting matter and have probably been filled in at a later stage, just as, in reading, we fill in any letters or syllables that may have been accidentally omitted. Thus speeches in dreams have a structure similar to that of breccia, in which largish blocks of various kinds of stone are cemented together by a binding medium. [Cf. p. 449.]

Strictly speaking, this description applies only to such speeches in dreams as possess something of the sensory quality of speech, and which are described by the dreamer himself as being speeches. Other sorts of speeches, which are not, as it

mental life. (Incidentally, she is certainly not paranoic.) Analysis has shown that, by allowing herself a certain amount of licence, she puts the text of these songs to false uses. For instance in the lines [from Agathe's aria in Weber's *Freischütz*] '*Leise, leise, Fromme Weise!*' [literally, 'Softly, softly, devout melody'] the last word was taken by her unconscious as though it was spelt '*Waise*' [= 'orphan', thus making the lines read 'Softly, softly, pious orphan'], the orphan being herself. Again '*O du selige, o du fröhliche*' ['Oh thou blessèd and happy . . .'] is the opening of a Christmas carol; by not continuing the quotation to the word 'Christmastide' she turned it into a bridal song.—The same mechanism of distortion can also operate in the occurrence of an idea *unaccompanied* by hallucination. Why was it that one of my patients was pestered by the recollection of a poem that he had had to learn in his youth: '*Nächtlich am Busento lispeln . . .*' ['By night on the Busento whispering . . .']? Because his imagination went no further than the first part of this quotation: '*Nächtlich am Busen*' ['By night on the bosom']. [See p. 714.]

We are familiar with the fact that this same technical trick is used by parodists. Included in a series of 'Illustrations to the German Classics' published in *Fliegende Blätter* [the well-known comic paper] was one which illustrated Schiller's '*Siegesfest*', with the following quotation attached to it:

> Und des frisch erkämpften Weibes
> Freut sich der Atrid und strickt . .
>
> [The conqu'ring son of Atreus sits
> At his fair captive's side and knits. . . .]

Here the quotation broke off. In the original the lines continue:

> . . . Um den Reiz des schönen Leibes
> Seine Arme hochbeglückt.
>
> [. . . . His joyful and triumphant arms
> About her body's lovely charms.]

were, felt by him as having been heard or spoken (that is, which have no acoustic or motor accompaniments in the dream), are merely thoughts such as occur in our waking thought-activity and are often carried over unmodified into our dreams. Another copious source of undifferentiated speeches of this kind, though one which it is difficult to follow up, seems to be provided by material that has been *read*. But whatever stands out markedly in dreams as a speech can be traced back to real speeches which have been spoken or heard by the dreamer.

Instances showing that speeches in dreams have this origin have already been given by me in the course of analysing dreams which I have quoted for quite other purposes. Thus, in the 'innocent' market dream reported on p. 183, the spoken words 'that's not obtainable any longer' served to identify me with the butcher, while one portion of the other speech, 'I don't recognize that; I won't take it', was actually responsible for making the dream an 'innocent' one. The dreamer, it will be remembered, having had some suggestion made to her on the previous day by her cook, had replied with the words: 'I don't recognize that; behave yourself properly!' The innocent-sounding *first* part of this speech was taken into the dream by way of allusion to its *second* part, which fitted excellently into the phantasy underlying the dream, but would at the same time have betrayed it.

Here is another example, which will serve instead of many, all of them leading to the same conclusion.

The dreamer was in a big courtyard in which some dead bodies were being burnt. 'I'm off,' he said, 'I can't bear the sight of it.' (This was not definitely a speech.) *He then met two butcher's boys. 'Well,' he asked, 'did it taste nice?' 'No,' one of them answered, 'not a bit nice' —as though it had been human flesh.*

The innocent occasion of the dream was as follows. The dreamer and his wife had paid a visit after supper to their neighbours, who were excellent people but not precisely *appetizing*. The hospitable old lady was just having her supper and had tried to *force* him (there is a phrase with a sexual sense used jokingly among men to render this idea[1]) to taste some of it. He

---

[1] ['*Notzüchtigen*', 'to force sexually', 'to rape', is so used in place of '*nötigen*', 'to force' (in the ordinary sense).]

had declined, saying he had no appetite left: 'Get along!' she
had replied, 'you can manage it', or words to that effect. He had
therefore been obliged to taste it and had complimented her on
it, saying: 'That was very nice.' When he was once more alone
with his wife he had grumbled at his neighbour's insistence and
also at the quality of the food. The thought, 'I can't bear the
sight of it', which in the dream too failed to emerge as a speech
in the strict sense, was an allusion to the physical charms of the
lady from which the invitation had come, and it must be taken
as meaning that he had no desire to look at them.

More instruction can be derived from another dream, which
I shall report in this connection on account of the very distinct
speech which formed its centre-point, although I shall have to
put off explaining it fully till I come to discuss affect in dreams
[p. 460 ff.]. I had a very clear dream. *I had gone to Brücke's
laboratory at night, and, in response to a gentle knock on the door, I
opened it to* (the late) *Professor Fleischl,*[1] *who came in with a number
of strangers and, after exchanging a few words, sat down at his table.*
This was followed by a second dream. *My friend Fl.* [Fliess]
*had come to Vienna unobtrusively in July. I met him in the street in
conversation with my* (deceased) *friend P., and went with them to
some place where they sat opposite each other as though they were at a
small table. I sat in front at its narrow end. Fl. spoke about his sister
and said that in three-quarters of an hour she was dead, and added some
such words as 'that was the threshold'. As P. failed to understand him,*[2]
*Fl. turned to me and asked me how much I had told P. about his affairs.
Whereupon, overcome by strange emotions, I tried to explain to Fl. that
P. (could not understand anything at all, of course, because he) was not
alive. But what I actually said—and I myself noticed the mistake—
was, 'NON VIXIT.' I then gave P. a piercing look. Under my gaze he
turned pale; his form grew indistinct and his eyes a sickly blue—and
finally he melted away. I was highly delighted at this and I now realized that Ernst Fleischl, too, had been no more than an apparition, a
'revenant'* ['ghost'—literally, 'one who returns']; *and it seemed to
me quite possible that people of that kind only existed as long as one
liked and could be got rid of if someone else wished it.*
This fine specimen includes many of the characteristics of

---

[1] [See footnote on p. 482 for an explanation of the persons concerned.]
[2] [This detail is analysed below on p. 513.]

dreams—the fact that I exercised my critical faculties during
the dream and myself noticed my mistake when I said '*Non
vixit*' instead of '*Non vivit*' [that is, 'he did not live' instead of 'he
is not alive'], my unconcerned dealings with people who were
dead and were recognized as being dead in the dream itself,
the absurdity of my final inference and the great satisfaction
it gave me. This dream exhibits so many of these puzzling
features, indeed, that I would give a great deal to be able to
present the complete solution of its conundrums. But in point
of fact I am incapable of doing so—of doing, that is to say, what
I did in the dream, of sacrificing to my ambition people whom
I greatly value. Any concealment, however, would destroy
what I know very well to be the dream's meaning; and I shall
therefore content myself, both here and in a later context
[p. 480 ff.], with selecting only a few of its elements for interpretation.

The central feature of the dream was a scene in which I
annihilated P. with a look. His eyes changed to a strange and
uncanny blue and he melted away. This scene was unmistakably copied from one which I had actually experienced. At the
time I have in mind I had been a demonstrator at the Physiological Institute and was due to start work early in the morning.
It came to Brücke's ears that I sometimes reached the students'
laboratory late. One morning he turned up punctually at the
hour of opening and awaited my arrival. His words were brief
and to the point. But it was not they that mattered. What over-
whelmed me were the terrible blue eyes with which he looked
at me and by which I was reduced to nothing—just as P. was
in the dream, where, to my relief, the roles were reversed. No
one who can remember the great man's eyes, which retained
their striking beauty even in his old age, and who has ever seen
him in anger, will find it difficult to picture the young sinner's
emotions.

It was a long time, however, before I succeeded in tracing
the origin of the '*Non vixit*' with which I passed judgement in the
dream. But at last it occurred to me that these two words
possessed their high degree of clarity in the dream, not as
words heard or spoken, but as words *seen*. I then knew at once
where they came from. On the pedestal of the Kaiser Josef
Memorial in the Hofburg [Imperial Palace] in Vienna the
following impressive words are inscribed:

Saluti patriae vixit
non diu sed totus.[1]

I extracted from this inscription just enough to fit in with a hostile train of ideas among the dream-thoughts, just enough to imply that 'this fellow has no say in the matter—he isn't even alive'. And this reminded me that I had the dream only a few days after the unveiling of the memorial to Fleischl in the cloisters of the University.[2] At that time I had seen the Brücke memorial once again and must have reflected (unconsciously) with regret on the fact that the premature death of my brilliant friend P., whose whole life had been devoted to science, had robbed him of a well-merited claim to a memorial in these same precincts. Accordingly, I gave him this memorial in my dream; and, incidentally, as I remembered, his first name was Josef.[3]

By the rules of dream-interpretation I was even now not entitled to pass from the *Non vixit* derived from my recollection of the Kaiser Josef Memorial to the *Non vivit* required by the sense of the dream-thoughts. There must have been some other element in the dream-thoughts which would help to make the transition possible. It then struck me as noticeable that in the scene in the dream there was a convergence of a hostile and an affectionate current of feeling towards my friend P., the former being on the surface and the latter concealed, but both of them being represented in the single phrase *Non vixit*. As he had deserved well of science I built him a memorial; but as he was guilty of an evil wish[4] (which was expressed at the end of the dream) I annihilated him. I noticed that this last sentence had a quite special cadence, and I must have had some model in my mind. Where was an antithesis of this sort to be found, a

---

[1] ['For the well-being of his country he lived not long but wholly.'—*Footnote added* 1925:] The actual wording of the inscription is:

Saluti publicae vixit
non diu sed totus.

The reason for my mistake in putting '*patriae*' for '*publicae*' has probably been rightly guessed by Wittels [1924, 86; Engl. trans. (1924), 100 f.].

[2] [This ceremony took place on October 16, 1898.]

[3] I may add as an example of over-determination that my excuse for arriving too late at the laboratory lay in the fact that after working far into the night I had in the morning to cover the long distance between the *Kaiser Josef* Strasse and the Währinger Strasse.

[4] [This detail is further explained below, on p. 484.]

juxtaposition like this of two opposite reactions towards a single person, both of them claiming to be completely justified and yet not incompatible? Only in one passage in literature—but a passage which makes a profound impression on the reader: in Brutus's speech of self-justification in Shakespeare's *Julius Caesar* [iii, 2], 'As Caesar loved me, I weep for him; as he was fortunate, I rejoice at it; as he was valiant, I honour him; but, as he was ambitious, I slew him.' Were not the formal structure of these sentences and their antithetical meaning precisely the same as in the dream-thought I had uncovered? Thus I had been playing the part of Brutus in the dream. If only I could find one other piece of evidence in the content of the dream to confirm this surprising collateral connecting link! A possible one occurred to me. '*My friend Fl. came to Vienna in July.*' There was no basis in reality for this detail of the dream. So far as I knew, my friend Fl. had never been in Vienna in July. But the month of July was named after Julius Caesar and might therefore very well represent the allusion I wanted to the intermediate thought of my playing the part of Brutus.[1]

Strange to say, I really did once play the part of Brutus. I once acted in the scene between Brutus and Caesar from Schiller[2] before an audience of children. I was fourteen years old at the time and was acting with a nephew who was a year my senior. He had come to us on a visit from England; and he, too, was a *revenant*, for it was the playmate of my earliest years who had returned in him. Until the end of my third year we had been inseparable. We had loved each other and fought with each other; and this childhood relationship, as I have already hinted above [pp. 198 and 231], had a determining influence on all my subsequent relations with contemporaries. Since that time my nephew John has had many reincarnations which revived now one side and now another of his personality, unalterably fixed as it was in my unconscious memory. There must have been times when he treated me very badly and I must have shown courage in the face of my tyrant; for in my later years I have often been told of a short speech made by me in my own defence when my father, who was at the same time John's grandfather, had said to me accusingly: 'Why are you

[1] There was the further connection between 'Caesar' and 'Kaiser'.
[2] [This is in fact a lyric in dialogue form recited by Karl Moor in Act IV, Scene 5, of the earlier version of Schiller's play *Die Räuber*.]

hitting John?' My reply—I was not yet two years old at the time—was 'I hit him 'cos he hit me'. It must have been this scene from my childhood which diverted '*Non vivit*' into '*Non vixit*', for in the language of later childhood the word for to hit is '*wichsen*' [pronounced like the English 'vixen']. The dream-work is not ashamed to make use of links such as this one. There was little basis in reality for my hostility to my friend P., who was very greatly my superior and for that reason was well fitted to appear as a new edition of my early playmate. This hostility must therefore certainly have gone back to my complicated childhood relations to John. [See further p. 483 f.] [1]

As I have said, I shall return to this dream later.

[1] [Freud discusses his relations with his nephew John in a letter to Fliess of October 3, 1897. (Freud, 1950a, Letter 70.) A further, somewhat disguised account of an early episode, in which John and his younger sister Pauline (referred to below on p. 486) figured, is no doubt to be seen in the latter part of Freud's paper on 'Screen Memories' (1899a).— The subject of speeches in dreams is also mentioned on pp. 184, 304, 313 and 465.]

(G)

ABSURD DREAMS—INTELLECTUAL ACTIVITY IN DREAMS[1]

In the course of our dream-interpretations we have so often come across the element of absurdity that we cannot postpone any longer the moment of investigating its source and significance, if it has any. For it will be remembered that the absurdity of dreams has provided those who deny the value of dreams with one of their principal arguments in favour of regarding them as the meaningless product of a reduced and fragmentary mental activity [see p. 55 ff.].

I shall begin by giving a few examples in which the absurdity is only an apparent one and disappears as soon as the meaning of the dream is more closely examined. Here are two or three dreams which deal (by chance, as it may seem at first sight) with the dreamer's dead father.

I

This is the dream of a patient who had lost his father six years earlier. *His father had met with a grave calamity. He had been travelling by the night train, which had been derailed. The carriage seats were forced together and his head was compressed from side to side. The dreamer then saw him lying in bed with a wound over his left eyebrow which ran in a vertical direction. He was surprised at his father's having met with a calamity (since he was already dead,* as he added in telling me the dream). *How clear his eyes were!*

According to the ruling theory of dreams we should have to explain the content of this dream as follows. To begin with, we should suppose, while the dreamer was imagining the accident, he must have forgotten that his father had been in his grave for several years; but, as the dream proceeded, the recollection must have emerged, and led to his astonishment at his own dream while he was still asleep. Analysis teaches us, however, that it is eminently useless to look for explanations of this kind. The dreamer had commissioned a bust of his father from a sculptor

---

[1] [Henceforward, until the end of the book, it is to be assumed once more that the whole of the matter appeared in the first (1900) edition, except for passages to which a later date is specifically assigned.]

and had seen it for the first time two days before the dream. It was this that he had thought of as a calamity. The sculptor had never seen his father and had worked from photographs. On the day immediately before the dream the dreamer, in his filial piety, had sent an old family servant to the studio to see whether he would form the same opinion of the marble head, namely, that it was too narrow from side to side at the temples. He now proceeded to recall from his memory the material which had gone to the construction of the dream. Whenever his father was tormented by business worries or family difficulties, he had been in the habit of pressing his hands to the sides of his forehead, as though he felt that his head was too wide and wanted to compress it.—When the patient was four years old he had been present when a pistol, which had been accidentally loaded, had been discharged and had blackened his father's eyes. ('*How clear his eyes were!*')—At the spot on his forehead at which the dream located his father's injury, a deep furrow showed during his lifetime whenever he was thoughtful or sad. The fact that this furrow was replaced in the dream by a wound led back to the second exciting cause of the dream. The dreamer had taken a photograph of his little daughter. The plate had slipped through his fingers, and when he picked it up showed a crack which ran perpendicularly down the little girl's forehead as far as her eyebrow. He could not help feeling superstitious about this, since a few days before his mother's death he had broken a photographic plate with her portrait on it.

The absurdity of this dream was thus no more than the result of a piece of carelessness in verbal expression which failed to distinguish the bust and the photograph from the actual person. We might any of us say [looking at a picture]: 'There's something wrong with Father, don't you think?' The appearance of absurdity in the dream could easily have been avoided; and if we were to judge from this single example, we should be inclined to think that the apparent absurdity had been permitted or even designed.

II

Here is another, almost exactly similar, example from a dream of my own. (I lost my father in 1896.) *After his death my father played a political part among the Magyars and brought them together politically.* Here I saw a small and indistinct picture: *a*

*crowd of men as though they were in the Reichstag; someone standing
on one or two chairs, with other people round him. I remembered how
like Garibaldi he had looked on his death-bed, and felt glad that that
promise had come true.*

What could be more absurd than this? It was dreamt at a
time at which the Hungarians had been driven by parliamentary
obstruction into a state of lawlessness and were plunged into the
crisis from which they were rescued by Koloman Széll.[1] The
trivial detail of the scene in the dream appearing in pictures of
such a small size was not without relevance to its interpretation.
Our dream-thoughts are usually represented in visual pictures
which appear to be more or less life-size. The picture which I
saw in my dream, however, was a reproduction of a woodcut
inserted in an illustrated history of Austria, which showed
Maria Theresa at the Reichstag [Diet] of Pressburg in the
famous episode of '*Moriamur pro rege nostro*'.[2] Like Maria Theresa
in the picture, so my father stood in the dream surrounded by
the crowd. But he was *standing on one or two chairs* ['chair'
= '*Stuhl*']. He had *brought them together*, and was thus a presiding
judge ['*Stuhlrichter*', literally 'chair-judge']. (A connecting link
was provided by the common [German] phrase 'we shall need
no judge.')—Those of us who were standing round had in fact
remarked how like Garibaldi my father looked on his death-
bed. He had had a *post-mortem* rise of temperature, his cheeks
had been flushed more and more deeply red. . . . As I recalled
this, my thoughts involuntarily ran on:

> Und hinter ihm in wesenlosem Scheine
> Lag, was uns alle bändigt, das Gemeine.[3]

[1] [An acute political crisis in Hungary in 1898–9 had been solved by
the formation of a coalition government under Széll.]

[2] ['We will die for our king!' The response of the Hungarian nobles to
Maria Theresa's plea for support, after her accession in 1740, in the War
of the Austrian Succession.]—I cannot remember where I read an account
of a dream which was filled with unusually small figures, and the source
of which turned out to be one of Jacques Callot's etchings seen by the
dreamer during the day. These etchings do in fact contain a large number of very small figures. One series of them depicts the horrors of the
Thirty Years' War.

[3] [These lines are rom the Epilogue to Schiller's 'Lied von der
Glocke' written by Goethe a few months after his friend's death. He
speaks of Schiller's spirit moving forward into the eternity of truth,
goodness and beauty, while 'behind him, a shadowy illusion, lay what
holds us all in bondage—the things that are common'.]

These elevated thoughts prepared the way [in the analysis] for the appearance of something that was common ['*gemein*'] in another sense. My father's *post-mortem* rise of temperature corresponded to the words 'after his death' in the dream. His most severe suffering had been caused by a complete paralysis (*obstruction*) of the intestines during his last weeks. Disrespectful thoughts of all kinds followed from this. One of my contemporaries who lost his father while he was still at his secondary school—on that occasion I myself had been deeply moved and had offered to be his friend—once told me scornfully of how one of his female relatives had had a painful experience. Her father had fallen dead in the street and had been brought home; when his body was undressed it was found that at the moment of death, or *post mortem*, he had passed a stool ['*Stuhl*']. His daughter had been so unhappy about this that she could not prevent this ugly detail from disturbing her memory of her father. Here we have reached the wish that was embodied in this dream. 'To stand before one's children's eyes, after one's death, great and unsullied'—who would not desire this? What has become of the absurdity of the dream? Its apparent absurdity is due only to the fact that it gave a literal picture of a figure of speech which is itself perfectly legitimate and in which we habitually overlook any absurdity involved in the contradiction between its parts. In this instance, once again, it is impossible to escape an impression that the apparent absurdity is intentional and has been deliberately produced.[1]

The frequency with which dead people appear in dreams[2] and act and associate with us as though they were alive has caused unnecessary surprise and has produced some remarkable explanations which throw our lack of understanding of dreams into strong relief. Yet the explanation of these dreams is a very obvious one. It often happens that we find ourselves thinking: 'If my father were alive, what would he say to this?' Dreams are unable to express an 'if' of this kind except by representing the person concerned as present in some particular situation. Thus, for instance, a young man who had been left a large

[1] [This dream is further discussed on p. 447 f.]
[2] [This paragraph was added as a footnote in 1909 and included in the text in 1930.]

legacy by his grandfather, dreamt, at a time when he was feeling self-reproaches for having spent a considerable sum of money, that his grandfather was alive again and calling him to account. And when, from our better knowledge, we protest that after all the person in question is dead, what we look upon as a criticism of the dream is in reality either a consoling thought that the dead person has not lived to witness the event, or a feeling of satisfaction that he can no longer interfere in it.

There is another kind of absurdity, which occurs in dreams of dead relatives but which does not express ridicule and derision.[1] It indicates an extreme degree of repudiation, and so makes it possible to represent a repressed thought which the dreamer would prefer to regard as utterly unthinkable. It seems impossible to elucidate dreams of this kind unless one bears in mind the fact that dreams do not differentiate between what is wished and what is real. For instance, a man who had nursed his father during his last illness and had been deeply grieved by his death, had the following senseless dream some time afterwards. *His father was alive once more and was talking to him in his usual way, but* (the remarkable thing was that) *he had really died, only he did not know it.* This dream only becomes intelligible if, after the words 'but he had really died' we insert 'in consequence of the dreamer's wish', and if we explain that what 'he did not know' was that the dreamer had had this wish. While he was nursing his father he had repeatedly wished his father were dead; that is to say, he had had what was actually a merciful thought that death might put an end to his sufferings. During his mourning, after his father's death, even this sympathetic wish became a subject of unconscious self-reproach, as though by means of it he had really helped to shorten the sick man's life. A stirring up of the dreamer's earliest infantile impulses against his father made it possible for this self-reproach to find expression as a dream; but the fact

[1] [This paragraph was added as a footnote in 1911 and included in the text in 1930. The first sentence of the paragraph implies that Freud has already explained absurdity in dreams as being due to the presence of 'ridicule and derision' in the dream-thoughts. Actually he has not yet done so, and this conclusion is only explicitly stated in the paragraph below (on p. 444 f.) in which he sums up his theory of absurd dreams. It seems possible that the present paragraph, in its original footnote form, may by some oversight have been introduced here instead of at the later point.]

that the instigator of the dream and the daytime thoughts were such worlds apart was precisely what necessitated the dream's absurdity.[1]

It is true that dreams of dead people whom the dreamer has loved raise difficult problems in dream-interpretation and that these cannot always be satisfactorily solved. The reason for this is to be found in the particularly strongly marked emotional ambivalence which dominates the dreamer's relation to the dead person. It very commonly happens that in dreams of this kind the dead person is treated to begin with as though he were alive, that he then suddenly turns out to be dead and that in a subsequent part of the dream he is alive once more. This has a confusing effect. It eventually occurred to me that this alternation between death and life is intended to represent *indifference* on the part of the dreamer. ('It's all the same to me whether he's alive or dead.') This indifference is, of course, not real but merely desired; it is intended to help the dreamer to repudiate his very intense and often contradictory emotional attitudes and it thus becomes a dream-representation of his *ambivalence.*—In other dreams in which the dreamer associates with dead people, the following rule often helps to give us our bearings. If there is no mention in the dream of the fact that the dead man is dead, the dreamer is equating himself with him: he is dreaming of his own death. If, in the course of the dream, the dreamer suddenly says to himself in astonishment, 'why, he died ever so long ago', he is repudiating this equation and is denying that the dream signifies his own death.[2]—But I willingly confess to a feeling that dream-interpretation is far from having revealed all the secrets of dreams of this character.

III

In the example which I shall next bring forward I have been able to catch the dream-work in the very act of intentionally fabricating an absurdity for which there was absolutely no

[1] [*Footnote* 1911:] Cf. my paper on the two principles of mental functioning (1911*b*) [at the end of which this same dream is discussed.—A very similar dream is analysed as No. 3 in the twelfth of Freud's *Introductory Lectures* (1916–17).—The next paragraph was added as a footnote in 1919 and included in the text in 1930.]

[2] [This point was first made in Freud (1913*h*).]

occasion in the material. It is taken from the dream which arose from my meeting with Count Thun as I was starting for my holidays. [See p. 208 ff.] *I was driving in a cab and ordered the driver to drive me to a station. 'Of course I can't drive with you along the railway line itself,' I said, after he had raised some objection, as though I had overtired him. It was as if I had already driven with him for some of the distance one normally travels by train.* The analysis produced the following explanations of this confused and sense-less story. The day before, I had hired a cab to take me to an out-of-the-way street in Dornbach.[1] The driver, however, had not known where the street was and, as these excellent people are apt to do, had driven on and on until at last I had noticed what was happening and had told him the right way, adding a few sarcastic comments. A train of thought, to which I was later in the analysis to return, led from this cab-driver to aristocrats. For the moment it was merely the passing notion that what strikes us bourgeois plebs about the aristocracy is the preference they have for taking the driver's seat. Count Thun, indeed, was the driver of the State Coach of Austria. The next sentence in the dream, however, referred to my brother, whom I was thus identifying with the cab-driver. That year I had called off a trip I was going to make with him to Italy. ('*I can't drive with you along the railway line itself.*') And this cancellation had been a kind of punishment for the complaints he used to make that I was in the habit of overtiring him on such trips (this appeared in the dream unaltered) by insisting upon moving too rapidly from place to place and seeing too many beautiful things in a single day. On the evening of the dream my brother had accom-panied me to the station; but he had jumped out shortly before we got there, at the suburban railway station adjoining the main line terminus, in order to travel to Purkersdorf[2] by the suburban line. I had remarked to him that he might have stayed with me a little longer by travelling to Purkersdorf by the main line instead of the suburban one. This led to the passage in the dream in which I drove in the cab *for some of the distance one normally travels by train.* This was an inversion of what had happened in reality—a kind of '*tu quoque*' argument. What I had said to my brother was: 'you can travel on the main line in my company for the distance you would travel by the suburban

---

[1] [On the outskirts of Vienna.]
[2] [Seven or eight miles outside Vienna.]

line.' I brought about the whole confusion in the dream by putting 'cab' instead of 'suburban line' (which, incidentally, was of great help in bringing together the figures of the cab-driver and my brother). In this way I succeeded in producing something senseless in the dream, which it seems scarcely possible to disentangle and which was almost a direct contradiction of an earlier remark of mine in the dream ('*I can't drive with you along the railway line itself*'). Since, however, there was no necessity whatever for me to confuse the suburban railway and a cab, I must have arranged the whole of this enigmatic business in the dream on purpose.

But for *what* purpose? We are now to discover the significance of absurdity in dreams and the motives which lead to its being admitted or even created. The solution of the mystery in the present dream was as follows. It was necessary for me that there should be something absurd and unintelligible in this dream in connection with the word '*fahren*'[1] because the dream-thoughts included a particular judgement which called for representation. One evening, while I was at the house of the hospitable and witty lady who appeared as the 'housekeeper' in one of the other scenes in the same dream, I had heard two riddles which I had been unable to solve. Since they were familiar to the rest of the company, I cut a rather ludicrous figure in my vain attempts to find the answers. They depended upon puns on the words '*Nachkommen*' and '*Vorfahren*' and, I believe, ran as follows:

> Der Herr befiehlt's,
> Der Kutscher tut's.
> Ein jeder hat's,
> Im Grabe ruht's.

> [With the master's request
> The driver complies:
> By all men possessed
> In the graveyard it lies.]

(Answer: '*Vorfahren*' ['Drive up' and 'Ancestry'; more literally 'go in front' and 'predecessors'].)

[1] [The German word '*fahren*', which has already been used repeatedly in the dream and the analysis, is used for the English 'drive' (in a cab) and 'travel' (in a train) and has had to be translated by both of those words in different contexts. See also p. 210 *n.*]

It was particularly confusing that the first half of the second riddle was identical with that of the first:

> Der Herr befiehlt's,
> Der Kutscher tut's.
> Nicht jeder hat's,
> In der Wiege ruht's.
>
> [With the master's request
> The driver complies:
> Not by all men possessed
> In the cradle it lies.]

(Answer: '*Nachkommen*' ['Follow after' and 'Progeny'; more literally 'come after' and 'successors'].)

When I saw Count Thun *drive up* so impressively and when I thereupon fell into the mood of Figaro, with his remarks on the goodness of great gentlemen in having taken the trouble to be born (to become *progeny*), these two riddles were adopted by the dream-work as intermediate thoughts. Since aristocrats could easily be confused with drivers and since there was a time in our part of the world when a driver was spoken of as '*Schwager*' ['coachman' and 'brother-in-law'], the work of condensation was able to introduce my brother into the same picture. The dream-thought, however, which was operating behind all this ran as follows: 'It is absurd to be proud of one's ancestry; it is better to be an ancestor oneself.' This judgement, that something 'is absurd', was what produced the absurdity in the dream. And this also clears up the remaining enigma in this obscure region of the dream, namely why it was that I thought I had already driven with the driver *before* [*vorhergefahren* ('driven before')—*vorgefahren* ('driven up')—'*Vorfahren*' ('ancestry')].

A dream is made absurd, then, if a judgement that something 'is absurd' is among the elements included in the dream-thoughts—that is to say, if any one of the dreamer's unconscious trains of thought has criticism or ridicule as its motive. Absurdity is accordingly one of the methods by which the dream-work represents a contradiction—alongside such other methods as the reversal in the dream-content of some material relation in the dream-thoughts [p. 326 f.], or the exploitation of the sensation of motor inhibition [p. 337 f.]. Absurdity in a dream, however, is not to be translated by a simple 'no'; it is intended to reproduce the *mood* of the dream-thoughts, which combines derision or laughter with the contradiction. It is only with such an aim in view that the dream-work produces anything ridiculous. Here once again *it is giving a manifest form to a portion of the latent content.*[1]

Actually we have already come across a convincing example of an absurd dream with this kind of meaning: the dream—I interpreted it without any analysis—of the performance of a Wagner opera which lasted till a quarter to eight in the morning and in which the orchestra was conducted from a tower, and so on (see p. 342 f.). It evidently meant to say: 'This is a *topsy-turvy* world and a *crazy* society; the person who deserves something doesn't get it, and the person who doesn't care about something *does* get it'—and there the dreamer was comparing her fate with her cousin's.—Nor is it by any means a matter of chance that our first examples of absurdity in dreams related to a dead father. In such cases, the conditions for creating absurd dreams are found together in characteristic fashion. The authority wielded by a father provokes criticism from his children at an early age, and the severity of the demands he makes upon them leads them, for their own relief, to keep their eyes open to any weakness of their father's; but the filial piety called up in our minds by the figure of a father, particularly after his death, tightens the censorship which prohibits any such criticism from being consciously expressed.

IV

Here is another absurd dream about a dead father. *I received a communication from the town council of my birthplace concerning the*

[1] The dream-work is thus parodying the thought that has been presented to it as something ridiculous, by the method of creating something ridiculous in connection with that thought. Heine adopted the same line when he wanted to ridicule some wretched verses written by the King of Bavaria. He did so in still more wretched ones:

> Herr Ludwig ist ein grosser Poet,
> Und singt er, so stürzt Apollo
> Vor ihm auf die Kniee und bittet und fleht,
> 'Halt ein! ich werde sonst toll, o!'

> [Sir Ludwig is a magnificent bard
> And, as soon as he utters, Apollo
> Goes down on his knees and begs him: 'Hold hard!
> Or I'll shortly become a clod-poll oh!'
> *Lobgesänge auf König Ludwig*, I.]

fees due for someone's maintenance in the hospital in the year 1851, *which had been necessitated by an attack he had had in my house. I was amused by this since, in the first place, I was not yet alive in* 1851 *and, in the second place, my father, to whom it might have related, was already dead. I went to him in the next room, where he was lying on his bed, and told him about it. To my surprise, he recollected that in* 1851 *he had once got drunk and had had to be locked up or detained. It was at a time at which he had been working for the firm of T———. 'So you used to drink as well?' I asked; 'did you get married soon after that?' I calculated that, of course, I was born in* 1856, *which seemed to be the year which immediately followed the year in question.*

We should conclude from the preceding discussion that the insistence with which this dream exhibited its absurdities could only be taken as indicating the presence in the dream-thoughts of a particularly embittered and passionate polemic. We shall therefore be all the more astonished to observe that in this dream the polemic was carried on in the open and that my father was the explicit object of the ridicule. Openness of this kind seems to contradict our assumptions as regards the working of the censorship in connection with the dream-work. The position will become clearer, however, when it is realized that in this instance my father was merely put forward as a show-figure, and that the dispute was really being carried on with someone else, who only appeared in the dream in a single allusion. Whereas normally a dream deals with rebellion against someone else, behind whom the dreamer's father is concealed, the opposite was true here. My father was made into a man of straw, in order to screen someone else; and the dream was allowed to handle in this undisguised way a figure who was as a rule treated as sacred, because at the same time I knew with certainty that it was not he who was really meant. That this was so was shown by the exciting cause of the dream. For it occurred after I had heard that a senior colleague of mine, whose judgement was regarded as beyond criticism, had given voice to disapproval and surprise at the fact that the psycho-analytic treatment of one of my patients had already entered its *fifth year.*[1] The first sentences of the dream alluded under a

---

[1] [This was the patient frequently referred to in Freud's letters to Fliess (Freud, 1950a) as 'E'. The present dream is referred to in Letter 126 (December 21, 1899) and the very satisfactory termination of the treatment is announced in Letter 133 (April 16, 1900).]

transparent disguise to the fact that for some time this colleague had taken over the duties which my father could no longer fulfil ('*fees due*', '*maintenance in the hospital*'), and that, when our relations began to be less friendly, I became involved in the same kind of emotional conflict which, when a misunderstanding arises between a father and son, is inevitably produced owing to the position occupied by the father and the assistance formerly given by him. The dream-thoughts protested bitterly against the reproach that I was *not getting on faster*—a reproach which, applying first to my treatment of the patient, extended later to other things. Did he know anyone, I thought, who could get on more quickly? Was he not aware that, apart from my methods of treatment, conditions of that kind are altogether incurable and last a life-time? What were *four or five years* in comparison with a whole life-time, especially considering that the patient's existence had been so very much eased during the treatment?

A great part of the impression of absurdity in this dream was brought about by running together sentences from different parts of the dream-thoughts without any transition. Thus the sentence '*I went to him in the next room*', etc., dropped the subject with which the preceding sentences had been dealing and correctly reproduced the circumstances in which I informed my father of my having become engaged to be married without consulting him. This sentence was therefore reminding me of the admirable unselfishness displayed by the old man on that occasion, and contrasting it with the behaviour of someone else —of yet another person. It is to be observed that the dream was allowed to ridicule my father because in the dream-thoughts he was held up in unqualified admiration as a model to other people. It lies in the very nature of every censorship that of forbidden things it allows those which are *untrue* to be said rather than those which are *true*. The next sentence, to the effect that he recollected '*having once got drunk and been locked up for it*', was no longer concerned with anything that related to my father in reality. Here the figure for whom he stood was no less a person than the great Meynert[1], in whose footsteps I had trodden with such deep veneration and whose behaviour towards me, after a short period of favour, had turned to undisguised hostility.

[1] [Theodor Meynert (1833–1892) had been Professor of Psychiatry at the Vienna University.]

The dream reminded me that he himself had told me that at one time in his youth he had indulged in the habit of making himself *intoxicated with chloroform* and that on account of it he had had to go into a *home*. It also reminded me of another incident with him shortly before his death. I had carried on an embittered controversy with him in writing, on the subject of male hysteria, the existence of which he denied.[1] When I visited him during his fatal illness and asked after his condition, he spoke at some length about his state and ended with these words: 'You know, I was always one of the clearest cases of male hysteria.' He was thus admitting, to my satisfaction and astonishment, what he had for so long obstinately contested. But the reason why I was able in this scene of the dream to use my father as a screen for Meynert did not lie in any analogy that I had discovered between the two figures. The scene was a concise but entirely adequate representation of a conditional sentence in the dream-thoughts, which ran in full: 'If only I had been the second generation, the son of a professor or Hofrat, I should certainly have *got on faster*.' In the dream I made my father into a Hofrat and professor.—The most blatant and disturbing absurdity in the dream resides in its treatment of the date 1851, which seemed to me not to differ from 1856, *just as though a difference of five years was of no significance whatever.* But this last was precisely what the dream-thoughts sought to express. *Four or five years* was the length of time during which I enjoyed the support of the colleague whom I mentioned earlier in this analysis; but it was also the length of time during which I made my *fiancée* wait for our marriage; and it was also, by a chance coincidence which was eagerly exploited by the dream-thoughts, the length of time during which I made my patient of longest standing wait for a complete recovery. '*What are five years?*' asked the dream-thoughts; '*that's no time at all, so far as I'm concerned; it doesn't count.* I have time enough in front of me. And just as I succeeded in the end in *that*, though you would not believe it, so I shall achieve *this*, too.' Apart from this, however, the number 51 by itself, without the number of the century, was determined in another, and indeed, in an opposite sense; and this, too, is why it appeared in the dream several times. 51 is the age which seems to be a particularly dangerous

[1] [This controversy is described in some detail in the first chapter of Freud's *Autobiographical Study* (1925d).]

one to men; I have known colleagues who have died suddenly at that age, and amongst them one who, after long delays, had been appointed to a professorship only a few days before his death.[1]

V

Here is yet another absurd dream which plays about with numbers. *One of my acquaintances, Herr M., had been attacked in an essay with an unjustifiable degree of violence, as we all thought—by no less a person than Goethe. Herr M. was naturally crushed by the attack. He complained of it bitterly to some company at table; his veneration for Goethe had not been affected, however, by this personal experience. I tried to throw a little light on the chronological data, which seemed to me improbable. Goethe died in 1832. Since his attack on Herr M. must naturally have been made earlier than that, Herr M. must have been quite a young man at the time. It seemed to be a plausible notion that he was eighteen. I was not quite sure, however, what year we were actually in, so that my whole calculation melted into obscurity. Incidentally, the attack was contained in Goethe's well-known essay on 'Nature'.*

We shall quickly find means of justifying the nonsense in this dream. Herr M., whom I had got to know among some *company at table*, had not long before asked me to examine his brother, who was showing signs of *general paralysis*. The suspicion was correct; on the occasion of this visit an awkward episode occurred, for in the course of his conversation the patient for no accountable reason gave his brother away by talking of his *youthful follies*. I had asked the patient the year of his birth and made him do several small sums so as to test the weakness of his memory—though, incidentally, he was still able to meet the tests quite well. I could already see that I myself behaved like a paralytic in the dream. (*I was not quite sure what year we were in.*) Another part of the material of the dream was derived from another recent source. The editor of a medical journal,[2] with whom I was on friendly terms, had printed a highly unfavourable, a '*crushing*' criticism of my Berlin friend Fl.'s [Fliess's] last

---

[1] [This is no doubt a reference to Fliess's theory of periodicity. 51 = 28 + 23, the male and female periods respectively. Cf. Sections I and IV of Kris's introduction to Freud's correspondence with Fliess (Freud, 1950a). See also above, p. 166 ff.—The fact that the number 51 occurs several times is referred to on p. 513. The analysis of the dream is continued below on p. 449 ff.]   [2] [See p. 714.]

book. The criticism had been written by a very *youthful* reviewer who possessed small judgement. I thought I had a right to intervene and took the editor to task over it. He expressed lively regret at having published the criticism but would not undertake to offer any redress. I therefore severed my connection with the journal, but in my letter of resignation expressed a hope that *our personal relations would not be affected by the event*. The third source of the dream was an account I had just heard from a woman patient of her brother's mental illness, and of how he had broken out in a frenzy with cries of '*Nature! Nature!*' The doctors believed that his exclamation came from his having read *Goethe's* striking essay on that subject and that it showed he had been overworking at his studies in natural philosophy. I myself preferred to think of the sexual sense in which the word is used even by the less educated people here. This idea of mine was at least not disproved by the fact that the unfortunate young man subsequently mutilated his own genitals. *He was eighteen* at the time of his outbreak.

I may add that my friend's book which had been so severely criticized ('one wonders whether it is the author or oneself who is crazy', another reviewer had said) dealt with the *chronological data* of life and showed that the length of *Goethe's* life was a multiple of a number [of days] that has a significance in biology. So it is easy to see that in the dream I was putting myself in my friend's place. (*I tried to throw a little light on the chronological data.*) But I behaved like a paralytic, and the dream was a mass of absurdities. Thus the dream-thoughts were saying ironically: '*Naturally*, it's *he* [my friend F.] who is the crazy fool, and it's *you* [the critics] who are the men of genius and know better. Surely it can't by any chance be the reverse?' There were plenty of examples of this *reversal* in the dream. For instance, Goethe attacked the young man, which is absurd, whereas it is still easy for quite a young man to attack Goethe, who is immortal. And again, I calculated from the year of Goethe's *death*, whereas I had made the paralytic calculate from the year of his *birth*. [See p. 327, where this dream has already been mentioned.]

But I have also undertaken to show that no dream is prompted by motives other than egoistic ones. [See p. 267 ff.] So I must explain away the fact that in the present dream I made my friend's cause my own and put myself in his place. The strength of my critical conviction in waking life is not enough to account for this. The story of the eighteen-year-old patient, however, and the different interpretations of his exclaiming '*Nature!*' were allusions to the opposition in which I found myself to most doctors on account of my belief in the sexual aetiology of the psychoneuroses. I could say to myself: 'The kind of criticism that has been applied to your friend will be applied to you—indeed, to some extent it already *has* been.' The 'he' in the dream can therefore be replaced by 'we': 'Yes, you're quite right, it's *we* who are the fools.' There was a very clear reminder in the dream that '*mea res agitur*', in the allusion to Goethe's short but exquisitely written essay; for when at the end of my school-days I was hesitating in my choice of a career, it was hearing that essay read aloud at a public lecture that decided me to take up the study of natural science.[1]

VI

Earlier in this volume I undertook to show that another dream in which my own ego did not appear was nevertheless egoistic. On p. 269 I reported a short dream to the effect that Professor M. said: '*My son, the Myops . . .*', and I explained that the dream was only an introductory one, preliminary to another in which I *did* play a part. Here is the missing main dream, which introduces an absurd and unintelligible verbal form which requires an explanation.

On account of certain events which had occurred in the city of Rome, it had become necessary to remove the children to safety, and this was done. The scene was then in front of a gateway, double doors in the ancient style (the 'Porta Romana' at Siena, as I was aware during the dream itself). I was sitting on the edge of a fountain and was greatly depressed and almost in tears. A female figure—an attendant or nun—brought two boys out and handed them over to their father, who was not myself. The elder of the two was clearly my eldest son; I did not see the other one's face. The woman who brought out the boy asked him to kiss her good-bye. She was noticeable for having a red nose. The boy refused to kiss her, but, holding out his hand in farewell, said 'AUF GESERES'

[1] [This dream is further discussed on p. 448 f.; it is also analysed at length, and with a few additional details, in Part VI of Freud's short study *On Dreams* (1901*a*), *Standard Ed.*]., 5, 662—An English translation of Goethe's '*Fragment über die Natur*' will be found in Wittels, 1931, 31. See also p. 714.]

to her, and then 'AUF UNGESERES' *to the two of us (or to one of us).
I had a notion that this last phrase denoted a preference.*[1]

This dream was constructed on a tangle of thoughts provoked by a play which I had seen, called *Das neue Ghetto* [*The New Ghetto*]. The Jewish problem, concern about the future of one's children, to whom one cannot give a country of their own, concern about educating them in such a way that they can move freely across frontiers—all of this was easily recognizable among the relevant dream-thoughts.

'*By the waters of Babylon we sat down and wept.*' Siena, like Rome, is famous for its beautiful fountains. If Rome occurred in one of my dreams, it was necessary for me to find a substitute for it from some locality known to me (see p. 193 f.). Near the Porta Romana in Siena we had seen a large and brightly lighted building. We learned that it was the *Manicomio*, the insane asylum. Shortly before I had the dream I had heard that a man of the same religious persuasion as myself had been obliged to resign the position which he had painfully achieved in a State asylum.

Our interest is aroused by the phrase '*Auf Geseres*' (at a point at which the situation in the dream would have led one to expect '*Auf Wiedersehen*') as well as its quite meaningless opposite '*Auf Ungeseres*'. According to information I have received from philologists, '*Geseres*' is a genuine Hᴏrew word derived from a verb '*goiser*', and is best translated by 'imposed sufferings' or 'doom'. The use of the word in slang would incline one to suppose that it meant 'weeping and wailing'. '*Ungeseres*' was a private neologism of my own and was the first word to catch my attention, but to begin with I could make nothing of it. But the short remark at the end of the dream to the effect that '*Ungeseres*' denoted a preference over '*Geseres*' opened the door to associations and at the same time to an elucidation of the word. An analogous relationship occurs in the case of caviare; *unsalted* ['*ungesalzen*'] caviare is esteemed more highly than *salted* ['*gesalzen*']. 'Caviare to the general', aristocratic pretensions; behind this lay a joking allusion to a member of my household who, since she was younger than I, would, I hoped, look after my children in the future. This tallied with the fact that another member of my household, our excellent nurse, was

[1] [The words '*Geseres*' and '*Ungeseres*', neither of them German, are discussed below.]

recognizably portrayed in the female attendant or nun in the dream. There was still, however, no transitional idea between '*salted—unsalted*' and '*Geseres—Ungeseres*'. This was provided by '*leavened—unleavened*' ['*gesäuert—ungesäuert*']. In their flight out of Egypt the Children of Israel had not time to allow their dough to rise and, in memory of this, they eat unleavened bread to this day at Easter. At this point I may insert a sudden association that occurred to me during this portion of the analysis. I remembered how, during the previous Easter, my Berlin friend and I had been walking through the streets of Breslau, a town in which we were strangers. A little girl asked me the way to a particular street, and I was obliged to confess that I did not know; and I remarked to my friend: 'It is to be hoped that when she grows up that little girl will show more discrimination in her choice of the people whom she gets to direct her.' Shortly afterwards, I caught sight of a door-plate bearing the words 'Dr. Herodes. Consulting hours: . . .' 'Let us hope,' I remarked, 'that our colleague does not happen to be a children's doctor.' At this same time my friend had been telling me his views on the biological significance of *bilateral symmetry* and had begun a sentence with the words 'If we had an eye in the middle of our foreheads like a Cyclops . . .' This led to the Professor's remark in the introductory dream, '*My son, the Myops* . . .'[1] and I had now been led to the principal source of '*Geseres*'. Many years before, when this son of Professor M.'s, to-day an independent thinker, was still sitting at his school-desk, he was attacked by a disease of the eyes which, the doctor declared, gave cause for anxiety. He explained that so long as it remained *on one side* it was of no importance, but that if it passed over to the *other eye* it would be a serious matter. The affection cleared up completely in the one eye; but shortly afterwards signs in fact appeared of the other one being affected. The boy's mother, terrified, at once sent for the doctor to the remote spot in the country where they were staying. The doctor, however, now went over *to the other side*. 'Why are you making such a "*Geseres*"?' he shouted at the mother, 'if *one* side has got well, so will the *other*.' And he was right.

And now we must consider the relation of all this to me and my family. The school-desk at which Professor M.'s son took his

[1] [The German '*Myop*' is an *ad hoc* form constructed on the pattern of '*Zyklop*'.]

first steps in knowledge was handed over by his mother as a gift to my eldest son, into whose mouth I put the farewell phrases in the dream. It is easy to guess one of the wishes to which this transference gave rise. But the construction of the desk was also intended to save the child from being *short-sighted* and *one-sided*. Hence the appearance in the dream of '*Myops*' (and, behind it, '*Cyclops*') and the reference to *bilaterality*. My concern about one-sidedness had more than one meaning: it could refer not only to physical one-sidedness but also to one-sidedness of intellectual development. May it not even be that it was precisely this concern which, in its crazy way, the scene in the dream was contradicting? After the child had turned to *one side* to say farewell words, he turned to the *other side* to say the contrary, as though to restore the balance. *It was as though he was acting with due attention to bilateral symmetry!*

Dreams, then, are often most profound when they seem most crazy. In every epoch of history those who have had something to say but could not say it without peril have eagerly assumed a fool's cap. The audience at whom their forbidden speech was aimed tolerated it more easily if they could at the same time laugh and flatter themselves with the reflection that the unwelcome words were clearly nonsensical. The Prince in the play, who had to disguise himself as a madman, was behaving just as dreams do in reality; so that we can say of dreams what Hamlet said of himself, concealing the true circumstances under a cloak of wit and unintelligibility: 'I am but mad north-north-west: when the wind is southerly, I know a hawk from a hand-saw!'[1]

Thus I have solved the problem of absurdity in dreams by showing that the dream-thoughts are never absurd—never, at all events, in the dreams of sane people—and that the dream-work produces absurd dreams and dreams containing individual absurd elements if it is faced with the necessity of representing

---

[1] [*Hamlet*, II, 2.] This dream also provides a good example of the generally valid truth that dreams which occur during the same night, even though they are recollected as separate, spring from the ground-work of the same thoughts. [See above, p. 333 f.] Incidentally, the situation in the dream of my removing my children to safety from the City of Rome was distorted by being related back to an analogous event that occurred in my own childhood: I was envying some relatives who, many years earlier, had had an opportunity of removing their children to another country.

any criticism, ridicule or derision which may be present in the dream-thoughts.[1]

My next task is to show that the dream-work consists in nothing more than a combination of the three factors I have mentioned[2]—and of a fourth which I have still to mention [see p. 488]; that it carries out no other function than the translation of dream-thoughts in accordance with the four conditions to which it is subject; and that the question whether the mind operates in dreams with all its intellectual faculties or with only a part of them is wrongly framed and disregards the facts. Since, however, there are plenty of dreams in whose content judgements are passed, criticisms made, and appreciations expressed, in which surprise is felt at some particular element of the dream, in which explanations are attempted and argumentations embarked upon, I must now proceed to meet the objections arising from facts of this kind by producing some chosen examples.

My reply [put briefly] is as follows: *Everything that appears in dreams as the ostensible activity of the function of judgement is to be regarded not as an intellectual achievement of the dream-work but as belonging to the material of the dream-thoughts and as having been lifted from them into the manifest content of the dream as a ready-made structure.* I can even carry this assertion further. Even the judgements made *after waking* upon a dream that has been remembered, and the feelings called up in us by the reproduction of such a dream, form part, to a great extent, of the latent content of the dream and are to be included in its interpretation.

I

I have already quoted a striking example of this [p. 332 f.].[3] A woman patient refused to tell me a dream of hers because 'it was not clear enough'. She had seen someone in the dream but

---

[1] [The subject of absurdity in dreams is also discussed in the course of Chapter VI of Freud's book on jokes (1905c).—Towards the end of Section I of the case history of the 'Rat Man' (1909d), Freud remarks in a footnote that the same mechanism is used in obsessional neuroses.]

[2] [Viz. condensation, displacement and consideration for representability.]

[3] [Another example was also quoted in the same passage, p. 331.]

did not know whether it was her husband or her father. There then followed a second piece of dream in which a dust-bin [*Misttrügerl*] appeared, and this gave rise to the following recollection. When she had first set up house she had jokingly remarked on one occasion in the presence of a young relative who was visiting in the house that her next job was to get hold of a new dust-bin. The next morning one arrived for her, but it was filled with lilies of the valley. This piece of the dream served to represent a common [German] phrase 'not grown on my own manure'.[1] When the analysis was completed, it turned out that the dream-thoughts were concerned with the after-effects of a story, which the dreamer had heard when she was young, of how a girl had had a baby and of how it was *not clear who the father really was*. Here, then, the dream-representation had overflowed into the waking thoughts: one of the elements of the dream-thoughts had found representation in a waking judgement passed upon the dream as a whole.

II

Here is a similar case. One of my patients had a dream which struck him as interesting, for immediately after waking he said to himself: '*I must tell the doctor that.*' The dream was analysed and produced the clearest allusions to a *liaison* which he had started during the treatment and which he had decided to himself *not to tell me about*.[2]

III

Here is a third example, one from my own experience. *I was going to the hospital with P. through a district in which there were houses and gardens. At the same time I had a notion that I had often seen this district before in dreams. I did not know my way about very well. He showed me a road that led round the corner to a restaurant (indoors, not a garden). There I asked for Frau Doni and was told that she lived at the back in a small room with three children. I went towards*

---

[1] ['*Nicht auf meinem eigenen Mist gewachsen*'—meaning 'I am not responsible for that', or 'It's not my baby'. The German word '*Mist*', properly meaning manure, is used in slang for 'rubbish' and occurs in this sense in the Viennese term for a dust-bin: '*Misttrügerl*'.]

[2] [*Footnote added* 1909:] If in the actual course of a dream dreamt during psycho-analytic treatment the dreamer says to himself: '*I must tell the doctor that*', it invariably implies the presence of a strong resistance against confessing the dream—which is not infrequently thereupon forgotten.

it, but before I got there met an indistinct figure with my two little girls;
I took them with me after I had stood with them for a little while.
Some sort of reproach against my wife, for having left them there.

When I woke up I had a feeling of great *satisfaction*, the
reason for which I explained to myself as being that I was going
to discover from this analysis the meaning of 'I've dreamt of
that before'.[1] In fact, however, the analysis taught me nothing
of the kind; what it did show me was that the satisfaction
belonged to the latent content of the dream and not to any
judgement upon it. My satisfaction was with the fact that my
marriage had brought me children. P. was a person whose
course in life lay for some time alongside mine, who then out-
distanced me both socially and materially, but whose marriage
was childless. The two events which occasioned the dream will
serve, instead of a complete analysis, to indicate its meaning.
The day before, I had read in a newspaper the announcement
of the death of Frau Dona A——y (which I turned into 'Doni'
in the dream), who had died in childbirth. My wife told me that
the dead woman had been looked after by the same midwife
who had attended her at the birth of our two youngest children.
The name 'Dona' had struck me because I had met it for the
first time a short while before in an English novel. The second
occasion for the dream was provided by the date on which it
occurred. It was on the night before the birthday of my eldest
boy—who seems to have some poetic gifts.

IV

I was left with the same feeling of satisfaction when I woke
from the absurd dream of my father having played a political
part among the Magyars after his death; and the reason I gave
myself for this feeling was that it was a continuation of the feeling that accompanied the last piece of the dream. [See p. 426.]
*I remembered how like Garibaldi he had looked on his death-bed and felt
glad that it had come true. . . . (There was a continuation which I had
forgotten).* The analysis enabled me to fill in this gap in the
dream. It was a mention of my second son, to whom I had
given the first name of a great historical figure [Cromwell]

---

[1] [See above, p. 399.] A protracted discussion on this subject has run
through recent volumes of the *Revue Philosophique* [1896–98] under the
title of 'Paramnesia in Dreams'.—[This dream is referred to again on
p. 478 f.]

who had powerfully attracted me in my boyhood, especially since my visit to England. During the year before the child's birth I had made up my mind to use this name if it were a son and I greeted the new-born baby with it with a feeling of high *satisfaction*. (It is easy to see how the suppressed megalomania of fathers is transferred in their thoughts on to their children, and it seems quite probable that this is one of the ways in which the suppression of that feeling, which becomes necessary in actual life, is carried out.) The little boy's right to appear in the context of this dream was derived from the fact that he had just had the same misadventure—easily forgivable both in a child and in a dying man—of soiling his bed-clothes. Compare in this connection *Stuhlrichter* ['presiding judge', literally 'chair-' or 'stool-judge'] and the wish expressed in the dream to stand before one's children's eyes *great* and *unsullied*. [See below, p. 478.]

v

I now turn to consider expressions of judgement passed in the dream itself but not continued into waking life or transposed into it. In looking for examples of these, my task will be greatly assisted if I may make use of dreams which I have already recorded with other aims in view. The dream of Goethe's attack on Herr M. [p. 439 ff.] appears to contain a whole number of acts of judgement. '*I tried to throw a little light on the chronological data, which seemed to me improbable.*' This has every appearance of being a criticism of the absurd idea that Goethe should have made a literary attack on a young man of my acquaintance. '*It seemed to be a plausible notion that he was eighteen.*' This, again, sounds exactly like the outcome of a calculation, though, it is true, of a feeble-minded one. Lastly, '*I was not quite sure what year we were in*' seems like an instance of uncertainty or doubt in a dream.

Thus all of these seemed to be acts of judgement made for the first time in the dream. But analysis showed that their wording can be taken in another way, in the light of which they become indispensable for the dream's interpretation, while at the same time every trace of absurdity is removed. The sentence '*I tried to throw a little light on the chronological data*' put me in the place of my friend [Fliess] who was in fact seeking to throw light on the chronological data of life. This deprives the sentence of its significance as a judgement protesting against the absurdity of the preceding sentences. The interpolated phrase, '*which seemed to me improbable*', belonged with the subsequent one, '*It seemed to be a plausible notion*'. I had used almost these precise words to the lady who had told her brother's case-history. '*It seems to me an improbable notion* that his cries of "Nature! Nature!" had anything to do with Goethe; *it seems to me far more plausible* that the words had the sexual meaning you are familiar with.' It is true that here a judgement was passed—not in the dream, however, but in reality, and on an occasion which was recollected and exploited by the dream-thoughts. The content of the dream took over this judgement just like any other fragment of the dream-thoughts. The number '18' to which the judgement in the dream was senselessly attached, retains a trace of the real context from which the judgement was torn. Lastly, '*I was not quite sure what year we were in*' was intended merely to carry further my identification with the paralytic patient in my examination of whom this point had really arisen.

The resolution of what are ostensibly acts of judgement in dreams may serve to remind us of the rules laid down at the beginning of this book [p. 103 f.] for carrying out the work of interpretation: namely, that we should disregard the apparent coherence between a dream's constituents as an unessential illusion, and that we should trace back the origin of each of its elements on its own account. A dream is a conglomerate which, for purposes of investigation, must be broken up once more into fragments. [Cf. p. 419.] On the other hand, however, it will be observed that a psychical force is at work in dreams which creates this apparent connectedness, which, that is to say, submits the material produced by the dream-work to a 'secondary revision'. This brings us face to face with the manifestations of a force whose importance we shall later [p. 488 ff.] assess as the fourth of the factors concerned in the construction of dreams.

VI

Here is a further instance of a process of judgement at work in a dream that I have already recorded. In the absurd dream of the communication from the town council [p. 435 ff.] I asked: '*Did you get married soon after that?*' I calculated that, of course, *I was born in* 1856, *which seemed to be the year which immediately followed the year in question.* All of this was clothed in the form of a set of logical conclusions. My father had married in 1851, immediately after his attack; I, of course, was the eldest of the family and had been born in 1856; Q.E.D. As we know, this false conclusion was drawn in the interests of wish-fulfilment; and the predominant dream-thought ran: *'Four or five years, that's no time at all; it doesn't count.'* Every step in this set of logical conclusions, however alike in their content and their form, could be explained in another way as having been determined by the dream-thoughts. It was the *patient*, of whose long analysis my colleague had fallen foul, who had decided to get married immediately the treatment was finished. The manner of my interview with my father in the dream was like an interrogation or examination, and reminded me too of a teacher at the University who used to take down exhaustive particulars from the students who were enrolling themselves for his lectures: 'Date of birth?'—'1856'.—'*Patre?*' In reply to this, one gave one's father's first name with a Latin termination; and we students assumed that the Hofrat *drew conclusions* from the first name of the father which could not always be drawn from that of the student himself. Thus the *drawing of the conclusion* in the dream was no more than a repetition of the *drawing of a conclusion* which appeared as a piece of the material of the dream-thoughts. Something new emerges from this. If a conclusion appears in the content of the dream there is no question that it is derived from the dream-thoughts; but it may either be present in these as a piece of recollected material or it may link a series of dream-thoughts together in a logical chain. In any case, however, a conclusion in a dream represents a conclusion in the dream-thoughts.[1]

At this point we may resume our analysis of the dream. The interrogation by the professor led to a recollection of the register of University Students (which in my time was drawn up in Latin). It led further to thoughts upon the course of my academic studies. The *five years* which are prescribed for medical studies were once again too few for me. I quietly went on with my work for several more years; and in my circle of acquaintances I was regarded as an idler and it was doubted whether I should ever get through. Thereupon I *quickly* decided to take my examinations and I got through them *in spite of the delay*.

[1] These findings are in some respects a correction of what I have said above (p. 312) on the representation of logical relations in dreams. This earlier passage describes the general behaviour of the dream-work but takes no account of the finer and more precise details of its functioning.

Here was a fresh reinforcement of the dream-thoughts with which I was defiantly confronting my critics: 'Even though you won't believe it because I've taken my time, I *shall* get through; I *shall* bring my medical training to a *conclusion*. Things have often turned out like that before.'

This same dream in its opening passage contained some sentences which could hardly be refused the name of an argument. This argument was not even absurd; it might just as well have occurred in waking thought: *I was amused in the dream at the communication from the town council since, in the first place, I was not yet in the world in 1851 and, in the second place, my father, to whom it might have related, was already dead.* Both of these statements were not only correct in themselves but agreed precisely with the real arguments that I should bring up if I were actually to receive a communication of that kind. My earlier analysis of the dream showed that it grew out of deeply embittered and derisive dream-thoughts. If we may also assume that there were strong reasons present for the activity of the censorship, we shall understand that the dream-work had every motive for producing *a perfectly valid refutation of an absurd suggestion* on the model contained in the dream-thoughts. The analysis showed, however, that the dream-work did not have a free hand in framing this parallel but was obliged, for that purpose, to use material from the dream-thoughts. It was just as though there were an algebraic equation containing (in addition to numerals) plus and minus signs, indices and radical signs, and as though someone were to copy out the equation without understanding it, taking over both the operational symbols and the numerals into his copy but mixing them all up together. The two arguments [in the dream-content] could be traced back to the following material. It was distressing to me to think that some of the premises which underlay my psychological explanations of the psychoneuroses were bound to excite scepticism and laughter when they were first met with. For instance, I had been driven to assume that impressions from the second year of life, and sometimes even from the first, left a lasting trace on the emotional life of those who were later to fall ill, and that these impressions—though distorted and exaggerated in many ways by the memory—might constitute the first and deepest foundation for hysterical symptoms. Patients, to whom I explained this at some appropriate moment, used to parody this newly-gained knowledge by declaring that they were ready to look for recollections dating from a time *at which they were not yet alive.* My discovery of the unexpected part played by their *father* in the earliest sexual impulses of female patients might well be expected to meet with a similar reception (see the discussion on p. 257 f.). Nevertheless, it was my well-grounded conviction that both of these hypotheses were true. By way of confirmation I called to mind some instances in which the death of the father occurred while the child was at a very early age and in which later events, otherwise inexplicable, proved that the child had nevertheless retained unconsciously recollections of the figure which had disappeared so early in his life. I was aware that these two assertions of mine rested on *the drawing of conclusions* whose validity would be disputed. It was therefore an achievement of wish-fulfilment when the material of precisely *those conclusions which I was afraid would be contested* was employed by the dream-work for drawing *conclusions which it was impossible to contest.*

VII

At the beginning of a dream, which I have so far hardly touched upon [see p. 413], there was a clear expression of astonishment at the subject which had cropped up. *Old Brücke must have set me some task;* STRANGELY ENOUGH, *it related to a dissection of the lower part of my own body, my pelvis and legs, which I saw before me as though in the dissecting-room, but without noticing their absence in myself and also without a trace of any gruesome feeling. Louise N. was standing beside me and doing the work with me. The pelvis had been eviscerated, and it was visible now in its superior, now in its inferior, aspect, the two being mixed together. Thick flesh-coloured protuberances (which, in the dream itself, made me think of haemorrhoids) could be seen. Something which lay over it and was like crumpled silver-paper*[1] *had also to be carefully fished out. I was then once more in possession of my legs and was making my way through the town. But (being tired) I took a cab. To my astonishment the cab drove in through the door of a house, which opened and allowed it to pass along a passage which turned a corner at its end and finally led into the open air again.*[2]

[1] Stanniol, which was an allusion to the book by Stannius on the nervous system of fishes. (Cf. loc. cit.)

[2] It was the place on the ground-floor of my block of flats where the tenants keep their perambulators; but it was over-determined in several other ways.

Finally I was making a journey through a changing landscape with an Alpine guide who was carrying my belongings. Part of the way he carried me too, out of consideration for my tired legs. The ground was boggy; we went round the edge; people were sitting on the ground like Red Indians or gipsies—among them a girl. Before this I had been making my own way forward over the slippery ground with a constant feeling of surprise that I was able to do it so well after the dissection. At last we reached a small wooden house at the end of which was an open window. There the guide set me down and laid two wooden boards, which were standing ready, upon the window-sill, so as to bridge the chasm which had to be crossed over from the window. At that point I really became frightened about my legs, but instead of the expected crossing, I saw two grown-up men lying on wooden benches that were along the walls of the hut, and what seemed to be two children sleeping beside them. It was as though what was going to make the crossing possible was not the boards but the children. I awoke in a mental fright.

Anyone who has formed even the slightest idea of the extent of condensation in dreams will easily imagine what a number of pages would be filled by a full analysis of this dream. Fortunately, however, in the present context I need only take up one point in it, which provides an example of astonishment in dreams, as exhibited in the interpolation '*strangely enough*'. The following was the occasion of the dream. Louise N., the lady who was assisting me in my job in the dream, had been calling on me. 'Lend me something to read', she had said. I offered her Rider Haggard's *She*. 'A *strange* book, but full of hidden meaning', I began to explain to her; 'the eternal feminine, the immortality of our emotions . . .' Here she interrupted me: 'I know it already. Have you nothing of your own?'—'No, my own immortal works have not yet been written.'—'Well, when are we to expect these so-called ultimate explanations of yours which you've promised even *we* shall find readable?' she asked, with a touch of sarcasm. At that point I saw that someone else was admonishing me through her mouth and I was silent. I reflected on the amount of self-discipline it was costing me to offer the public even my book upon dreams—I should have to give away so much of my own private character in it.

> Das Beste was du wissen kannst,
> Darfst du den Buben doch nicht sagen.[1]

[1] [See footnote, p. 142.]

The task which was imposed on me in the dream of carrying out a dissection *of my own body* was thus my *self-analysis*[1] which was linked up with my giving an account of my dreams. Old Brücke came in here appropriately; even in the first years of my scientific work it happened that I allowed a discovery of mine to lie fallow until an energetic remonstrance on his part drove me into publishing it. The further thoughts which were started up by my conversation with Louise N. went too deep to become conscious. They were diverted in the direction of the material that had been stirred up in me by the mention of Rider Haggard's *She*. The judgement '*strangely enough*' went back to that book and to another one, *Heart of the World*, by the same author; and numerous elements of the dream were derived from these two imaginative novels. The boggy ground over which people had to be carried, and the chasm which they had to cross by means of boards brought along with them, were taken from *She*; the Red Indians, the girl and the wooden house were taken from *Heart of the World*. In both novels the guide is a woman; both are concerned with perilous journeys; while *She* describes an adventurous road that had scarcely ever been trodden before, leading into an undiscovered region. The tired feeling in my legs, according to a note which I find I made upon the dream, had been a real sensation during the day-time. It probably went along with a tired mood and a doubting thought: 'How much longer will my legs carry me?' The end of the adventure in *She* is that the guide, instead of finding immortality for herself and the others, perishes in the mysterious subterranean fire. A fear of that kind was unmistakably active in the dream-thoughts. The 'wooden house' was also, no doubt, a coffin, that is to say, the grave. But the dream-work achieved a masterpiece in its representation of this most unwished-for of all thoughts by a wish-fulfilment. For I had already been in a grave once, but it was an excavated Etruscan grave near Orvieto, a narrow chamber with two stone benches along its walls, on which the skeletons of two grown-up men were lying. The inside of the wooden house in the dream looked exactly like it, except that the stone was replaced by wood. The dream seems to have been saying: 'If you must rest in a grave, let it

[1] [Freud's self-analysis during the years before the publication of this book is one of the themes of his correspondence with Fliess (Freud, 1950*d*). Cf. Part III of Kris's introduction to the latter volume.]

be the Etruscan one.' And, by making this replacement, it transformed the gloomiest of expectations into one that was highly
desirable.[1] Unluckily, as we are soon to hear [p. 460 ff.], a
dream can turn into its opposite the *idea* accompanying an
affect but not always the affect itself. Accordingly, I woke up
in a *'mental fright'*, even after the successful emergence of the
idea that children may perhaps achieve what their father
has failed to—a fresh allusion to the strange novel in which a
person's identity is retained through a series of generations for
over two thousand years.[2]

VIII

Included in yet another of my dreams there was an expression
of surprise at something I had experienced in it; but the surprise was accompanied by such a striking, far-fetched and
almost brilliant attempt at an explanation that, if only on *its*
account, I cannot resist submitting the whole dream to analysis,
quite apart from the dream's possessing two other points to
attract our interest. I was travelling along the *Südbahn* railway-
line during the night of July 18–19th, and in my sleep I heard:
'Hollthurn,[3] *ten minutes' being called out. I at once thought of holothurians* [sea-slugs]—*of a natural history museum—that this was the
spot at which valiant men had fought in vain against the superior power
of the ruler of their country—yes, the Counter-Reformation in Austria—
it was as though it were a place in Styria or the Tyrol. I then saw indistinctly a small museum, in which the relics or belongings of these men
were preserved. I should have liked to get out, but hesitated to do so.
There were women with fruit on the platform. They were crouching on
the ground and holding up their baskets invitingly.—I hesitated because
I was not sure whether there was time, but we were still not moving.—
I was suddenly in another compartment, in which the upholstery and
seats were so narrow that one's back pressed directly against the back of
the carriage.*[4] *I was surprised by this, but I reflected that* I MIGHT HAVE
CHANGED CARRIAGES WHILE I WAS IN A SLEEPING STATE. *There*

---

[1] [This detail is used as an illustration in Chapter III of Freud's
Future of an Illusion (1927c).]

[2] [This dream is further discussed below on p. 477 f.]

[3] [Not the name of any real place.]

[4] This description was unintelligible even to myself; but I have followed the fundamental rule of reporting a dream in the words which
occurred to me as I was writing it down. The wording chosen is itself
part of what is represented by the dream. [Cf. p. 514.]

were several people, including an English brother and sister; a row of books were distinctly visible on a shelf on the wall. I saw 'The Wealth of Nations' and 'Matter and Motion' (by Clerk-Maxwell), a thick volume and bound in brown cloth. The man asked his sister about a book by Schiller, whether she had forgotten it. It seemed as though the books were sometimes mine and sometimes theirs. I felt inclined at that point to intervene in the conversation in a confirmatory or substantiating sense. . . . I woke up perspiring all over, because all the windows were shut. The train was drawn up at Marburg [in Styria].

While I was writing the dream down a new piece of it occurred to me, which my memory had tried to pass over. *I said* [in English] *to the brother and sister, referring to a particular work: 'It is from . . .', but corrected myself: 'It is by . . .' 'Yes,' the man commented to his sister, 'he said that right.'*[1]

The dream opened with the name of the station, which must no doubt have partly woken me up. I replaced its name, *Marburg*, by *Hollthurn*. The fact that I heard 'Marburg' when it was first called out, or perhaps later, was proved by the mentioning in the dream of Schiller, who was born at Marburg, though not at the one in Styria.[2] I was making my journey on that occasion, although I was travelling first class, under very uncomfortable conditions. The train was packed full, and in my compartment I had found a lady and gentleman who appeared to be very aristocratic and had not the civility, or did not think it worth the trouble, to make any disguise of their annoyance at my intrusion. My polite greeting met with no response. Although the man and his wife were sitting side by side (with their backs to the engine) the woman nevertheless made haste, under my very eyes, to engage the window-seat facing her by putting an umbrella on it. The door was shut immediately, and pointed remarks were exchanged between them on the subject of opening windows. They had probably seen at once that I was longing for some fresh air. It was a hot night and the atmosphere in the completely closed compartment soon became suffocating.

[1] [This piece of the dream is further considered on p. 519 f.]

[2] [*Footnote added* 1909:] Schiller was not born at any Marburg, but at Marbach, as every German school-boy knows, and as I knew myself. This was one more of those mistakes (see above, p. 197 *n.*) which slip in as a substitute for an intentional falsification at some other point, and which I have tried to explain in my *Psychopathology of Everyday Life.* [1901*b*, Chapter X, No. 1.]

My experiences of travelling have taught me that conduct of this ruthless and overbearing kind is a characteristic of people who are travelling on a free or half-price ticket. When the ticket-collector came and I showed him the ticket I had bought at such expense, there fell from the lady's mouth, in haughty and almost menacing tones, the words: 'My husband has a free pass.' She was an imposing figure with discontented features, of an age not far from the time of the decay of feminine beauty; the man uttered not a word but sat there motionless. I attempted to sleep. In my dream I took fearful vengeance on my disagreeable companions; no one could suspect what insults and humiliations lay concealed behind the broken fragments of the first half of the dream. When this need had been satisfied a second wish made itself felt—to change compartments. The scene is changed so often in dreams, and without the slightest objection being raised, that it would not have been in the least surprising if I had promptly replaced my travelling companions by more agreeable ones derived from my memory. But here was a case in which something resented the change of scene and thought it necessary to explain it. How did I suddenly come to be in another compartment? I had no recollection of having changed. There could be only one explanation: *I must have left the carriage while I was in a sleeping state*—a rare event, of which, however, examples are to be found in the experience of a neuropathologist. We know of people who have gone upon railway journeys in a twilight state, without betraying their abnormal condition by any signs, till at some point in the journey they have suddenly come to themselves completely and been amazed at the gap in their memory. In the dream itself, accordingly, I was declaring myself to be one of these cases of '*automatisme ambulatoire*'.

Analysis made it possible to find another solution. The attempt at an explanation, which seemed so striking when I was obliged to ascribe it to the dream-work, was not an original one of my own, but was copied from the neurosis of one of my patients. I have already spoken elsewhere [p. 260] of a highly educated and, in real life, soft-hearted man who, shortly after the death of his parents, began to reproach himself with having murderous inclinations, and then fell a victim to the precautionary measures which he was obliged to adopt as a safeguard. It was a case of severe obsessions accompanied by complete insight.

To begin with, walking through the streets was made a burden to him by a compulsion to make certain where every single person he met disappeared to; if anyone suddenly escaped his watchful eye, he was left with a distressing feeling and the idea that he might possibly have got rid of him. What lay behind this was, among other things, a 'Cain' phantasy—for 'all men are brothers'. Owing to the impossibility of carrying out this task, he gave up going for walks and spent his life incarcerated between his own four walls. But reports of murders which had been committed outside were constantly being brought into his room by the newspapers, and his conscience suggested to him, in the form of a doubt, that he might be the wanted murderer. The certainty that he had in fact not left his house for weeks protected him from these charges for a while, till one day the possibility came into his head that *he might have left his house while he was in an unconscious state* and have thus been able to commit the murder without knowing anything about it. From that time onwards he locked the front door of the house and gave the key to his old housekeeper with strict instructions never to let it fall into his hands even if he asked for it.

This, then, was the origin of my attempted explanation to the effect that I had changed carriages while I was in an unconscious state; it had been carried over ready-made into the dream from the material of the dream-thoughts, and was evidently intended in the dream to serve the purpose of identifying me with the figure of this patient. My recollection of him had been aroused by an easy association. My last night-journey, a few weeks earlier, had been made in the company of this very man. He was cured, and was travelling with me into the provinces to visit his relatives, who had sent for me. We had a compartment to ourselves; we left all the windows open all through the night and had a most entertaining time for as long as I stayed awake. I knew that the root of his illness had been hostile impulses against his father, dating from his childhood and involving a sexual situation. In so far, therefore, as I was identifying myself with him, I was seeking to confess to something analogous. And in fact the second scene of the dream ended in a somewhat extravagant phantasy that my two elderly travelling companions had treated me in such a stand-offish way because my arrival had prevented the affectionate exchanges which they had planned for the night. This phantasy went back, however, to a scene of early childhood in which the child, probably driven by sexual curiosity, had forced his way into his parents' bedroom and been turned out of it by his father's orders.

It is unnecessary, I think, to accumulate further examples. They would merely serve to confirm what we have gathered from those I have already quoted—that an act of judgement in a dream is only a repetition of some prototype in the dream-thoughts. As a rule, the repetition is ill-applied and interpolated into an inappropriate context, but occasionally, as in our last instances, it is so neatly employed that to begin with it may give the impression of independent intellectual activity in the dream. From this point we might turn our attention to the psychical activity which, though it does not appear to accompany the construction of dreams invariably, yet, whenever it does so, is concerned to fuse together elements in a dream which are of disparate origin into a whole which shall make sense and be without contradiction. Before approaching that subject, however, we are under an urgent necessity to consider the expressions of affect which occur in dreams and to compare them with the affects which analysis uncovers in the dream-thoughts.

AFFECTS IN DREAMS

A shrewd observation made by Stricker [1879, 51] has drawn our attention to the fact that the expression of affect in dreams cannot be dealt with in the same contemptuous fashion in which, after waking, we are accustomed to dismiss their *content*. 'If I am afraid of robbers in a dream, the robbers, it is true, are imaginary—but the fear is real.' [Cf. p. 74.] And this is equally true if I feel *glad* in a dream. Our feeling tells us that an affect experienced in a dream is in no way inferior to one of equal intensity experienced in waking life; and dreams insist with greater energy upon their right to be included among our real mental experiences in respect to their affective than in respect to their ideational content. In our waking state, however, we cannot in fact include them in this way, because we cannot make any psychical assessment of an affect unless it is linked to a piece of ideational material. If the affect and the idea are incompatible in their character and intensity, our waking judgement is at a loss.

It has always been a matter for surprise that in dreams the ideational content is not accompanied by the affective consequences that we should regard as inevitable in waking thought. Strümpell [1877, 27 f.] declared that in dreams ideas are denuded of their psychical values [cf. p. 53 f.]. But there is no lack in dreams of instances of a contrary kind, where an intense expression of affect appears in connection with subject-matter which seems to provide no occasion for any such expression. In a dream I may be in a horrible, dangerous and disgusting situation without feeling any fear or repulsion; while another time, on the contrary, I may be terrified at something harmless and delighted at something childish.

This particular enigma of dream-life vanishes more suddenly, perhaps, and more completely than any other, as soon as we pass over from the manifest to the latent content of the dream. We need not bother about the enigma, since it no longer exists. Analysis shows us that *the ideational material has undergone displacements and substitutions, whereas the affects have remained unaltered.*

It is small wonder that the ideational material, which has been changed by dream-distortion, should no longer be compatible with the affect, which is retained unmodified; nor is there anything left to be surprised at after analysis has put the right material back into its former position.[1]

In the case of a psychical complex which has come under the influence of the censorship imposed by resistance, the *affects* are the constituent which is least influenced and which alone can give us a pointer as to how we should fill in the missing thoughts. This is seen even more clearly in the psychoneuroses than in dreams. Their affects are always appropriate, at least in their *quality*, though we must allow for their intensity being increased owing to displacements of neurotic attention. If a hysteric is surprised at having to be so frightened of something trivial or if a man suffering from obsessions is surprised at such distressing self-reproaches arising out of a mere nothing, they have both gone astray, because they regard the ideational content—the triviality or the mere nothing—as what is essential; and they put up an unsuccessful fight because they take this ideational content as the starting-point of their thought-activity. Psycho-analysis can put them upon the right path by recognizing the affect as being, on the contrary, justified and by seeking out the idea which belongs to it but has been repressed and replaced by a substitute. A necessary premise to all this is that the release of affect and the ideational content do not constitute the indissoluble organic unity as which we are in the habit of treating

[1] [*Footnote added* 1919:] If I am not greatly mistaken, the first dream that I was able to pick up from my grandson, at the age of one year and eight months, revealed a state of affairs in which the dream-work had succeeded in transforming the *material* of the dream-thoughts into a wish-fulfilment, whereas the *affect* belonging to them persisted unchanged during the state of sleep. On the night before the day on which his father was due to leave for the front, the child cried out, sobbing violently: 'Daddy! Daddy!—baby!' This can only have meant that Daddy and baby were remaining together; whereas the tears recognized the approaching farewell. At that time the child was already quite well able to express the concept of separation. '*Fort*' ['gone'] (replaced by a long-drawn-out and peculiarly stressed 'o—o—o') had been one of his first words, and several months before this first dream he had played at 'gone' with all his toys. This game went back to a successful piece of self-discipline which he had achieved at an early age in allowing his mother to leave him and be 'gone'. [Cf. Chapter II of *Beyond the Pleasure Principle* (Freud, 1920g).]

them, but that these two separate entities may be merely *soldered* together and can thus be detached from each other by analysis. Dream-interpretation shows that this is in fact the case.

I shall begin by giving an example in which analysis explained the apparent absence of affect in a case where the ideational content should have necessitated its release.

I

She saw three lions in a desert, one of which was laughing; but she was not afraid of them. Afterwards, however, she must have run away from them, for she was trying to climb up a tree; but she found that her cousin, who was a French mistress, was up there already, etc.

The analysis brought up the following material. The indifferent precipitating cause of the dream was a sentence in her English composition: 'The mane is the ornament of the lion.' Her father wore a beard which framed his face like a mane. Her English mistress was called Miss Lyons. An acquaintance had sent her the ballads of Loewe [the German word for 'lion']. These, then, were the three lions; why should she be afraid of them?—She had read a story in which a negro, who had stirred up his companions to revolt, was hunted with bloodhounds and climbed up a tree to save himself. She went on, in the highest spirits, to produce a number of fragmentary recollections, such as the advice on how to catch lions from *Fliegende Blätter*: 'Take a desert and put it through a sieve and the lions will be left over.' And again, the highly amusing but not very proper anecdote of an official who was asked why he did not take more trouble to ingratiate himself with the head of his department and replied that he had tried to make his way in, but his superior *was up there already*. The whole material became intelligible when it turned out that the lady had had a visit on the dream-day from her husband's superior. He had been very polite to her and had kissed her hand and *she had not been in the least afraid of him*, although he was a very 'big bug' [in German, '*grosses Tier*' = 'big animal'], and played the part of a 'social *lion*' in the capital of the country she came from. So this lion was like the lion in *A Midsummer Night's Dream* that concealed the figure of Snug the joiner; and the same is true of all dream-lions of which the dreamer is not afraid.

II

As my second example I may quote the dream of the young girl who saw her sister's little son lying dead in his coffin [pp. 152 ff. and 248], but who, as I may now add, felt neither pain nor grief. We know from the analysis why this was. The dream merely disguised her wish to see the man she was in love with once more; and her affect had to be in tune with her wish and not with its disguise. There was thus no occasion for grief.

In some dreams the affect does at least remain in contact with the ideational material which has replaced that to which the affect was originally attached. In others, the dissolution of the complex has gone further. The affect makes its appearance completely detached from the idea which belongs to it and is introduced at some other point in the dream, where it fits in with the new arrangement of the dream-elements. The situation is then similar to the one we have found in the case of acts of judgement in dreams [p. 445 ff.]. If an important conclusion is drawn in the dream-thoughts, the dream also contains one; but the conclusion in the dream may be displaced on to quite different material. Such a displacement not infrequently follows the principle of antithesis.

This last possibility is exemplified in the following dream, which I have submitted to a most exhaustive analysis.

III

A castle by the sea; later it was no longer immediately on the sea, but on a narrow canal leading to the sea. The Governor was a Herr P. I was standing with him in a big reception room—with three windows in front of which there rose buttresses with what looked like crenellations. I had been attached to the garrison as something in the nature of a volunteer naval officer. We feared the arrival of enemy warships, since we were in a state of war. Herr P. intended to leave, and gave me instructions as to what was to be done if the event that we feared took place. His invalid wife was with their children in the threatened castle. If the bombardment began, the great hall was to be evacuated. He breathed heavily and turned to go; I held him back and asked him how I was to communicate with him in case of necessity. He added something in reply, but immediately fell down dead. No doubt I had put an unnecessary strain upon him with my questions. After his death, which made

*no further impression on me, I wondered whether his widow would remain
in the castle, whether I should report his death to the Higher Command
and whether I should take over command of the castle as being next in
order of rank. I was standing at the window, and observing the ships
as they went past. They were merchant vessels rushing past rapidly
through the dark water, some of them with several funnels and others
with bulging decks* (just like the station buildings in the introductory dream—not reported here). *Then my brother was standing beside me and we were both looking out of the window at the canal.
At the sight of one ship we were frightened and cried out: 'Here comes
the warship!' But it turned out that it was only the same ships that I
already knew returning. There now came a small ship, cut off short, in a
comic fashion, in the middle. On its deck some curious cup-shaped or
box-shaped objects were visible. We called out with one voice: 'That's
the breakfast-ship!'*

The rapid movements of the ships, the deep dark blue of the
water and the brown smoke from the funnels—all of this combined to create a tense and sinister impression.

The localities in the dream were brought together from
several trips of mine to the Adriatic (to Miramare, Duino,
Venice and Aquileia). A short but enjoyable Easter trip which
I had made to Aquileia with my brother a few weeks before the
dream was still fresh in my memory.[1] The dream also contained
allusions to the *maritime war* between America and Spain and to
anxieties to which it had given rise about the fate of my relatives in America. At two points in the dream affects were in
question. At one point an affect that was to be anticipated was
absent: attention was expressly drawn to the fact that the
Governor's death made no impression on me. At another point,
when I thought I saw the warship, I was *frightened* and felt all
the sensations of fright in my sleep. In this well-constructed
dream the affects were distributed in such a way that any
striking contradiction was avoided. There was no reason why I
should be frightened at the death of the Governor and it was
quite reasonable that as Commandant of the Castle I should be
frightened at the sight of the warship. The analysis showed,

[1] [This trip was described at length by Freud in a letter to Fliess of
April 14, 1898 (Freud, 1950a, Letter 88). Aquileia, ᴏ few miles inland, is
connected by a small canal with the lagoon, or ᴊe of whose islands
Grado is situated. These places, at the northeɪ ɪ end of the Adriatic,
formed part of Austria before 1918.]

however, that Herr P. was only a substitute for my own self. (In the dream *I* was the substitute for *him*.) *I* was the Governor who suddenly died. The dream-thoughts dealt with the future of my family after my premature death. This was the only distressing one among the dream-thoughts; and it must have been from it that the fright was detached and brought into connection in the dream with the sight of the warship. On the other hand, the analysis showed that the region of the dream-thoughts from which the warship was taken was filled with the most cheerful recollections. It was a year earlier, in Venice, and we were standing one magically beautiful day at the windows of our room on the Riva degli Schiavoni and were looking across the blue lagoon on which that day there was more movement than usual. English ships were expected and were to be given a ceremonial reception. Suddenly my wife cried out gaily as a child: '*Here comes the English warship!*' In the dream I was frightened at these same words. (We see once again that speeches in a dream are derived from speeches in real life [cf. p. 418 ff.]; I shall show shortly that the element 'English' in my wife's exclamation did not elude the dream-work either.) Here, then, in the process of changing the dream-thoughts into the manifest dream-content, I have transformed cheerfulness into fear, and I need only hint that this transformation was itself giving expression to a portion of the latent dream-content. This example proves, however, that the dream-work is at liberty to detach an affect from its connections in the dream-thoughts and introduce it at any other point it chooses in the manifest dream.

I take this opportunity of making a somewhat detailed analysis of the 'breakfast-ship', the appearance of which in the dream brought such a nonsensical conclusion to a situation which had up to then been kept at a rational level. When subsequently I called the dream-object more precisely to mind, it struck me that it was black and that, owing to the fact that it was cut off short where it was broadest in the middle, it bore a great resemblance at that end to a class of objects which had attracted our interest in the museums in the Etruscan towns. These were rectangular trays of black pottery, with two handles, on which there stood things like coffee- or tea-cups, not altogether unlike one of our modern *breakfast-sets*. In response to our enquiries we learned that this was the '*toilette*' [toilet-set] of an Etruscan lady, with receptacles for cosmetics and powder on it, and we had jokingly remarked that it would be a good idea to take one home with us for the lady of the house. The object in the dream meant, accordingly, a black 'toilette', i.e. mourning dress, and made a direct reference to a death. The other end of the dream-object reminded me of the funeral boats[1] in which in early times dead bodies were placed and committed to the sea for burial. This led on to the point which explained why the ships *returned* in the dream:

> Still, auf gerettetem Boot, treibt in den Hafen der Greis.[2]

It was the return after a shipwreck ['*Schiffbruch*', literally 'ship-break']—the breakfast-ship was broken off short in the middle. But what was the origin of the name 'breakfast'-ship? It was here that the word 'English' came in, which was left over from the warships. The English word 'breakfast' means 'breaking fast'. The 'breaking' related once more to the shipwreck ['ship-break'] and the fasting was connected with the black dress or *toilette*.

But it was only the *name* of the breakfast-ship that was newly constructed by the dream. The *thing* had existed and reminded me of one of the most enjoyable parts of my last trip. Mistrusting the food that would be provided at Aquileia, we had brought provisions with us from Gorizia and had bought a bottle of excellent Istrian wine at Aquileia. And while the little mail steamer made its way slowly through the '*Canale delle Mee*' across the empty lagoon to Grado we, who were the only passengers, ate our breakfast on deck in the highest spirits, and we had rarely tasted a better one. This, then, was the 'breakfast-ship', and it was precisely behind this memory of the most cheerful *joie de vivre* that the dream concealed the gloomiest thoughts of an unknown and uncanny future.[3]

The detachment of affects from the ideational material which

---

[1] '*Nachen*' [in German], a word which is derived, as a philological friend tells me, from the root '*νέκυς*' [corpse].

[2] [Safe on his ship, the old man quietly sails into port.
       (Part of an allegory of life and death.)
                    Schiller, *Nachträge zu den Xenien*,
                              'Erwartung und Erfüllung'.]

[3] [This dream is mentioned again on p. 547.]

generated them is the most striking thing which occurs to them during the formation of dreams; but it is neither the only nor the most essential alteration undergone by them on their path from the dream-thoughts to the manifest dream. If we compare the affects of the dream-thoughts with those in the dream, one thing at once becomes clear. Whenever there is an affect in the dream, it is also to be found in the dream-thoughts. But the reverse is not true. A dream is in general poorer in affect than the psychical material from the manipulation of which it has proceeded. When I have reconstructed the dream-thoughts, I habitually find the most intense psychical impulses in them striving to make themselves felt and struggling as a rule against others that are sharply opposed to them. If I then turn back to the dream, it not infrequently appears colourless, and without emotional tone of any great intensity. The dream-work has reduced to a level of indifference not only the content but often the emotional tone of my thoughts as well. It might be said that the dream-work brings about a *suppression of affects*. Let us, for instance, take the dream of the botanical monograph [p. 169 ff.]. The thoughts corresponding to it consisted of a passionately agitated plea on behalf of my liberty to act as I chose to act and to govern my life as seemed right to me and me alone. The dream that arose from them has an indifferent ring about it: 'I had written a monograph; it lay before me; it contained coloured plates; dried plants accompanied each copy.' This reminds one of the peace that has descended upon a battle-field strewn with corpses; no trace is left of the struggle which raged over it.

Things can be otherwise: lively manifestations of affect can make their way into the dream itself. For the moment, however, I will dwell upon the incontestible fact that large numbers of dreams appear to be indifferent, whereas it is never possible to enter into the dream-thoughts without being deeply moved.

No complete theoretical explanation can here be given of this suppression of affect in the course of the dream-work. It would require to be preceded by a most painstaking investigation of the theory of affects and of the mechanism of repression. [Cf. p. 604 ff.] I will only permit myself a reference to two points. I am compelled—for other reasons—to picture the release of affects as a centrifugal process directed towards the interior of the body and analogous to the processes of motor and secretory innervation.[1] Now just as in the state of sleep the sending out of motor impulses towards the external world appears to be suspended, so it may be that the centrifugal calling-up of affects by unconscious thinking may become more difficult during sleep. In that case the affective impulses occurring during the course of the dream-thoughts would from their very nature be weak impulses, and consequently those which found their way into the dream would be no less weak. On this view, then, the 'suppression of affect' would not in any way be the consequence of the dream-work but would result from the state of sleep. This may be true, but it cannot be the whole truth. We must also bear in mind that any relatively complex dream turns out to be a compromise produced by a conflict between psychical forces. For one thing, the thoughts constructing the wish are obliged to struggle against the opposition of a censoring agency; and for another thing, we have often seen that in unconscious thinking itself every train of thought is yoked with its contradictory opposite. Since all of these trains of thought are capable of carrying an affect, we shall by and large scarcely be wrong if we regard the suppression of affect as a consequence of the inhibition which these contraries exercise upon each other and which the censorship exercises upon the impulsions suppressed by it. *The inhibition of affect, accordingly, must be considered as the second consequence of the censorship of dreams, just as dream-distortion is its first consequence.*

I will here give as an instance a dream in which the indifferent feeling-tone of the content of the dream can be explained by the antithesis between the dream-thoughts. It is a short dream, which will fill every reader with disgust.

IV

A hill, on which there was something like an open-air closet: a very long seat with a large hole at the end of it. Its back edge was thickly

---

[1] [The release of affects is described as 'centrifugal' (though directed towards the interior of the body) from the point of view of the mental apparatus. The theory of the release of affects implicit in this passage is explained at some length in Section 12 ('The Experience of Pain') of Part I of Freud's 'Project for a Scientific Psychology' (in Freud, 1950a). See also p. 582 below.—For Freud's use of the term 'innervation' see footnote, p. 537.]

*covered with small heaps of faeces of all sizes and degrees of freshness.
There were bushes behind the seat. I micturated on the seat; a long stream
of urine washed everything clean; the lumps of faeces came away easily
and fell into the opening. It was as though at the end there was still some
left.*

Why did I feel no disgust during this dream?

Because, as the analysis showed, the most agreeable and satisfying thoughts contributed to bringing the dream about. What
at once occurred to me in the analysis were the Augean stables
which were cleansed by Hercules. This Hercules was I. The
hill and bushes came from Aussee, where my children were
stopping at the time. I had discovered the infantile aetiology
of the neuroses and had thus saved my own children from falling
ill. The seat (except, of course, for the hole) was an exact copy
of a piece of furniture which had been given to me as a present
by a grateful woman patient. It thus reminded me of how much
my patients honoured me. Indeed, even the museum of human
excrement could be given an interpretation to rejoice my heart.
However much I might be disgusted by it in reality, in the
dream it was a reminiscence of the fair land of Italy where, as
we all know, the W.C.s in the small towns are furnished in
precisely this way. The stream of urine which washed everything clean was an unmistakable sign of greatness. It was in that
way that Gulliver extinguished the great fire in Lilliput—
though incidentally this brought him into disfavour with its
tiny queen. But Gargantua, too, Rabelais' superman, revenged
himself in the same way on the Parisians by sitting astride on
Notre Dame and turning his stream of urine upon the city. It
was only on the previous evening before going to sleep that I
had been turning over Garnier's illustrations to Rabelais. And,
strangely enough, here was another piece of evidence that I was
the superman. The platform of Notre Dame was my favourite
resort in Paris; every free afternoon I used to clamber about
there on the towers of the church between the monsters and the
devils. The fact that all the faeces disappeared so quickly under
the stream recalled the motto: '*Afflavit et dissipati sunt*', which I
intended one day to put at the head of a chapter upon the
therapy of hysteria.[1]

And now for the true exciting cause of the dream. It had

[1] [*Footnote in 1925 edition only:*] For a correction of this quotation see
above, p. 214 *n.*

been a hot summer afternoon; and during the evening I had delivered my lecture on the connection between hysteria and the perversions, and everything I had had to say displeased me intensely and seemed to me completely devoid of any value. I was tired and felt no trace of enjoyment in my difficult work; I longed to be away from all this grubbing about in human dirt and to be able to join my children and afterwards visit the beauties of Italy. In this mood I went from the lecture room to a café, where I had a modest snack in the open air, since I had no appetite for food. One of my audience, however, went with me and he begged leave to sit by me while I drank my coffee and choked over my crescent roll. He began to flatter me: telling me how much he had learnt from me, how he looked at everything now with fresh eyes, how I had cleansed the *Augean stables* of errors and prejudices in my theory of the neuroses. He told me, in short, that I was a very great man. My mood fitted ill with this paean of praise; I fought against my feeling of disgust, went home early to escape from him, and before going to sleep turned over the pages of Rabelais and read one of Conrad Ferdinand Meyer's short stories, '*Die Leiden eines Knaben*' ['A Boy's Sorrows'].

Such was the material out of which the dream emerged. Meyer's short story brought up in addition a recollection of scenes from my childhood. (Cf. the last episode in the dream about Count Thun [p. 215 f.].) The day-time mood of revulsion and disgust persisted into the dream in so far as it was able to provide almost the entire material of its manifest content. But during the night a contrary mood of powerful and even exaggerated self-assertiveness arose and displaced the former one. The content of the dream had to find a form which would enable it to express both the delusions of inferiority and the megalomania in the same material. The compromise between them produced an ambiguous dream-content; but it also resulted in an indifferent feeling-tone owing to the mutual inhibition of these contrary impulses.

According to the theory of wish-fulfilment, this dream would not have become possible if the antithetical megalomanic train of thought (which, it is true, was suppressed, but had a pleasurable tone) had not emerged in addition to the feeling of disgust. For what is distressing may not be represented in a dream; nothing in our dream-thoughts which is distressing can force an entry into a dream unless it at the same time lends a disguise to the fulfilment of a wish. [Cf. p. 556 f.]

There is yet another alternative way in which the dream-work can deal with affects in the dream-thoughts, in addition to allowing them through or reducing them to nothing. It can *turn them into their opposite*. We have already become acquainted with the interpretative rule according to which every element in a dream can, for purposes of interpretation, stand for its opposite just as easily as for itself. [See p. 318.] We can never tell beforehand whether it stands for the one or for the other; only the context can decide. A suspicion of this truth has evidently found its way into popular consciousness: 'dream-books' very often adopt the principle of contraries in their interpretation of dreams. This turning of a thing into its opposite is made possible by the intimate associative chain which links the idea of a thing with its opposite in our thoughts. Like any other kind of displacement it can serve the ends of the censor-ship; but it is also frequently a product of wish-fulfilment, for wish-fulfilment consists in nothing else than a replacement of a disagreeable thing by its opposite. Just as ideas of things can make their appearance in dreams turned into their opposite, so too can the *affects* attaching to dream-thoughts; and it seems likely that this reversal of affect is brought about as a rule by the dream-censorship. In social life, which has provided us with our familiar analogy with the dream-censorship, we also make use of the suppression and reversal of affect, principally for purposes of dissimulation. If I am talking to someone whom I am obliged to treat with consideration while wishing to say something hostile to him, it is almost more important that I should conceal any expression of my *affect* from him than that I should mitigate the verbal form of my thoughts. If I were to address him in words that were not impolite, but accompanied them with a look or gesture of hatred and contempt, the effect which I should produce on him would not be very different from what it would have been if I had thrown my contempt openly in his face. Accordingly, the censorship bids me above all suppress my affects; and, if I am a master of dissimulation, I shall assume the *opposite* affect—smile when I am angry and seem affectionate when I wish to destroy.

We have already come across an excellent example of a

reversal of affect of this kind carried out in a dream on behalf of the dream-censorship. In the dream of 'my uncle with the yellow beard' [p. 137 ff.] I felt the greatest affection for my friend R., whereas and because the dream-thoughts called him a simpleton. It was from this example of reversal of affect that we derived our first hint of the existence of a dream-censorship. Nor is it necessary to assume, in such cases either, that the dream-work *creates* contrary affects of this kind out of nothing; it finds them as a rule lying ready to hand in the material of the dream-thoughts, and merely intensifies them with the psychical force arising from a motive of defence, till they can predominate for the purposes of dream-formation. In the dream of my uncle which I have just mentioned, the antithetical, affectionate affect probably arose from an infantile source (as was suggested by the later part of the dream), for the uncle-nephew relationship, owing to the peculiar nature of the earliest experiences of my childhood (cf. the analysis on p. 424 f. [and below, p. 483 f.]) had become the source of all my friendships and all my hatreds.

An excellent example of a reversal of affect of this kind[1] will be found in a dream recorded by Ferenczi (1916): 'An elderly gentleman was awakened one night by his wife, who had become alarmed because he was laughing so loudly and unrestrainedly in his sleep. Subsequently the man reported that he had had the following dream: *I was lying in bed and a gentleman who was known to me entered the room; I tried to turn on the light but was unable to: I tried over and over again, but in vain. Thereupon my wife got out of bed to help me, but she could not manage it either. But as she felt awkward in front of the gentleman owing to being 'en négligé', she finally gave it up and went back to bed. All of this was so funny that I couldn't help roaring with laughter at it. My wife said 'Why are you laughing? why are you laughing?' but I only went on laughing till I woke up.*—Next day the gentleman was very depressed and had a headache: so much laughing had upset him, he thought.

'The dream seems less amusing when it is considered analytically. The "gentleman known to him" who entered the room was, in the latent dream-thoughts, the picture of Death as the "great Unknown"—a picture which had been called up in his mind during the previous day. The old gentleman, who suffered

[1] [This paragraph and the next were added in 1919.]

from arterio-sclerosis, had had good reason the day before for thinking of dying. The unrestrained laughter took the place of sobbing and weeping at the idea that he must die. It was the light of life that he could no longer turn on. This gloomy thought may have been connected with attempts at copulation which he had made shortly before but which had failed even with the help of his wife *en négligé*. He realized that he was already going down hill. The dream-work succeeded in transforming the gloomy idea of impotence and death into a comic scene, and his sobs into laughter.'

There is one class of dreams which have a particular claim to be described as 'hypocritical' and which offer a hard test to the theory of wish-fulfilment.[1] My attention was drawn to them when Frau Dr. M. Hilferding brought up the following record of a dream of Peter Rosegger's for discussion by the Vienna Psycho-Analytical Society.

Rosegger writes in his story '*Fremd gemacht!*'[2]: 'As a rule I am a sound sleeper but many a night I have lost my rest—for, along with my modest career as a student and man of letters, I have for many years dragged around with me, like a ghost from which I could not set myself free, the shadow of a tailor's life.

'It is not as though in the day-time I had reflected very often or very intensely on my past. One who had cast off the skin of a Philistine and was seeking to conquer Earth and Heaven had other things to do. Nor would I, when I was a dashing young fellow, have given more than a thought to my nightly dreams. Only later, when the habit had come to me of reflecting upon everything, or when the Philistine within me began to stir a trifle, did I ask myself why it should be that, if I dreamt at all, I was always a journeyman tailor and that I spent so long a time as such with my master and worked without pay in his workshop. I knew well enough, as I sat like that beside him, sewing and ironing, that my right place was no longer there and that as a townsman I had other things to occupy me. But I was always on vacation, I was always having summer holidays, and

---

[1] [This paragraph and the following quotation from Rosegger, together with the discussion of it, were added in 1911. Rosegger (1843–1918) was a well-known Austrian writer who reached celebrity from very humble, peasant beginnings.]

[2] ['Dismissed!'] In the second volume of *Waldheimat*, p. 303.

so it was that I sat beside my master as his assistant. It often irked me and I felt sad at the loss of time in which I might well have found better and more useful things to do. Now and then, when something went awry, I had to put up with a scolding from my master, though there was never any talk of wages. Often, as I sat there with bent back in the dark workshop, I thought of giving notice and taking my leave. Once I even did so; but my master paid no heed and I was soon sitting beside him again and sewing.

'After such tedious hours, what a joy it was to wake! And I determined that if this persistent dream should come again I would throw it from me with energy and call aloud: "This is mere hocus-pocus, I am lying in bed and want to sleep. . . ." But next night I was once more sitting in the tailor's workshop.

'And so it went on for years with uncanny regularity. Now it happened once that my master and I were working at Alpelhofer's (the peasant in whose house I had worked when I was first apprenticed) and my master showed himself quite especially dissatisfied with my work. "I'd like to know where you're wool-gathering," he said, and looked at me darkly. The most reasonable thing to do, I thought, would be to stand up and tell him that I was only with him to please him and then go off. But I did not do so. I made no objection when my master took on an apprentice and ordered me to make room for him on the bench. I moved into the corner and sewed. The same day another journeyman was taken on as well, a canting hypocrite—he was a Bohemian—who had worked at our place nineteen years before, and had fallen into the brook once on his way back from the inn. When he looked for a seat there was no more room. I turned to my master questioningly, and he said to me: "You've no gift for tailoring, you can go! you're dismissed!" My fright at this was so overpowering that I awoke.

'The grey light of morning was glimmering through the uncurtained windows into my familiar home. Works of art surrounded me; there in my handsome book-case stood the eternal Homer, the gigantic Dante, the incomparable Shakespeare, the glorious Goethe—all the magnificent immortals. From the next room rang out the clear young voices of the awakening children joking with their mother. I felt as though I had found afresh this idyllically sweet, this peaceful, poetic, spiritual life in which I had so often and so deeply felt a meditative human happiness.

Yet it vexed me that I had not been beforehand with my master in giving him notice, but had been dismissed by him.

'And how astonished I was! From the night on which my master dismissed me, I enjoyed peace; I dreamt no more of the tailoring days which lay so far back in my past—days which had been so cheerfully unassuming but had thrown such a long shadow over my later years.'

In this series of dreams dreamt by an author who had been a journeyman tailor in his youth, it is hard to recognize the dominance of wish-fulfilment. All the dreamer's enjoyment lay in his day-time existence, whereas in his dreams he was still haunted by the shadow of an unhappy life from which he had at last escaped. Some dreams of my own of a similar kind have enabled me to throw a little light on the subject. As a young doctor I worked for a long time at the Chemical Institute without ever becoming proficient in the skills which that science demands; and for that reason in my waking life I have never liked thinking of this barren and indeed humiliating episode in my apprenticeship. On the other hand I have a regularly recurring dream of working in the laboratory, of carrying out analyses and of having various experiences there. These dreams are disagreeable in the same way as examination dreams and they are never very distinct. While I was interpreting one of them, my attention was eventually attracted by the word '*analysis*', which gave me a key to their understanding. Since those days I have become an 'analyst', and I now carry out analyses which are very highly spoken of, though it is true that they are '*psycho*-analyses'. It was now clear to me: if I have grown proud of carrying out analyses of that kind in my daytime life and feel inclined to boast to myself of how successful I have become, my dreams remind me during the night of those other, unsuccessful analyses of which I have no reason to feel proud. They are the punishment dreams of a *parvenu*, like the dreams of the journeyman tailor who had grown into a famous author. But how does it become possible for a dream, in the conflict between a *parvenu*'s pride and his self-criticism, to side with the latter, and choose as its content a sensible warning instead of an unlawful wish-fulfilment? As I have already said, the answer to this question raises difficulties. We may conclude that the foundation of the dream was formed in the first instance by an exaggeratedly ambitious phantasy, but that

humiliating thoughts that poured cold water on the phantasy
found their way into the dream instead. It may be remembered
that there are masochistic impulses in the mind, which may be
responsible for a reversal such as this. I should have no objection
to this class of dreams being distinguished from 'wish-fulfilment
dreams' under the name of 'punishment dreams'. I should not
regard this as implying any qualification of the theory of dreams
which I have hitherto put forward; it would be no more than a
linguistic expedient for meeting the difficulties of those who find
it strange that opposites should converge.[1] But a closer examination of some of these dreams brings something more to light.
In an indistinct part of the background of one of my laboratory
dreams I was of an age which placed me precisely in the
gloomiest and most unsuccessful year of my medical career. I
was still without a post and had no idea how I could earn my
living; but at the same time I suddenly discovered that I had
a choice open to me between several women whom I might
marry! So I was once more young, and, more than everything,
she was once more young—the woman who had shared all these
difficult years with me. The unconscious instigator of the dream
was thus revealed as one of the constantly gnawing wishes of a
man who is growing older. The conflict raging in other levels
of the mind between vanity and self-criticism had, it is true,
determined the content of the dream; but it was only the more
deeply-rooted wish for youth that had made it possible for that
conflict to appear as a dream. Even when we are awake we
sometimes say to ourselves: 'Things are going very well to-day
and times were hard in the old days; all the same, it was lovely
then—I was still young.'[2]

Another group of dreams,[3] which I have often come across

[1] [The last two sentences were added in 1919.]

[2] [*Footnote added* 1930:] Since psycho-analysis has divided the personality into an ego and a super-ego (Freud, 1921*c* [and 1923*b*]), it has
become easy to recognize in these punishment dreams fulfilments of the
wishes of the super-ego. [See below, p. 557 ff.—The Rosegger dreams are
also discussed in Section IX of Freud, 1923*c*.]

[3] [This paragraph was added in 1919, and seems to have been
wrongly interpolated at this point. It should probably have come *after*
the two next paragraphs. These date from 1911, like the preceding
Rosegger discussion, to which they are clearly related. What follows
them goes back once more to 1900.—Some further remarks on hypocritical dreams will be found near the end of Section III of Freud's
paper on a case of female homosexuality (1920*a*).]

in myself and recognized as hypocritical, have as their content a reconciliation with people with whom friendly relations have long since ceased. In such cases analysis habitually reveals some occasion which might urge me to abandon the last remnant of consideration for these former friends and to treat them as strangers or enemies. The dream, however, prefers to depict the opposite relationship. [Cf. p. 145 n.]

In forming any judgement upon dreams recorded by an imaginative writer it is reasonable to suppose that he may have omitted from his account details in the content of the dream which he regards as unessential or distracting. His dreams will in that case raise problems which would be quickly solved if their content were reported in full.

Otto Rank has pointed out to me that the Grimms' fairy tale of 'The Little Tailor, or Seven at a Blow' contains an exactly similar dream of a *parvenu*. The tailor, who has become a hero and the son-in-law of the King, dreams one night of his former handicraft, as he lies beside his wife, the Princess. She, becoming suspicious, posts armed guards the next night to listen to the dreamer's words and to arrest him. But the little tailor is warned, and sees to it that his dream is corrected.

The complicated process of elimination, diminution and reversal, by means of which the affects in the dream-thoughts are eventually turned into those in the dream, can be satisfactorily followed in suitable syntheses of dreams that have been completely analysed. I will quote a few more examples of affects in dreams where some of the possibilities I have enumerated will be found realized.

v

If we turn back to the dream about the strange task set me by old Brücke of making a dissection of my own pelvis [p. 452], it will be recalled that in the dream itself I missed the gruesome feeling ['*Grauen*'] appropriate to it. Now this was a wish-fulfilment in more than one sense. The dissection meant the self-analysis which I was carrying out, as it were, in the publication of this present book about dreams—a process which had been so distressing to me in reality that I had postponed the printing of the finished manuscript for more than a year. A wish then arose that I might get over this feeling of distaste; hence it was that I had no gruesome feeling ['*Grauen*'] in the dream. But I should also have been very glad to miss growing grey—'*Grauen*' in the other sense of the word. I was already growing quite grey, and the grey of my hair was another reminder that I must not delay any longer. And, as we have seen, the thought that I should have to leave it to my children to reach the goal of my difficult journey forced its way through to representation at the end of the dream.

Let us next consider the two dreams in which an expression of satisfaction was transposed to the moment after waking. In the one case the reason given for the satisfaction was an expectation that I should now discover what was meant by 'I've dreamt of that before', while the satisfaction really referred to the birth of my first children [p. 446 f.]. In the other case the ostensible reason was my conviction that something that had been 'prognosticated' was now coming true, while the real reference was similar to that in the former dream: it was the satisfaction with which I greeted the birth of my second son [p. 447 f.]. Here the affects which dominated the dream-thoughts persisted in the dreams; but it is safe to say that in *no* dream can things be as simple as all that. If we go a little more deeply into the two analyses we find that this satisfaction which had escaped censorship had received an accession from another source. This other source had grounds for fearing the censorship, and its affect would undoubtedly have aroused opposition if it had not covered itself by the similar, legitimate affect of satisfaction, arising from the permissible source, and slipped in, as it were, under its wing.

Unfortunately, I cannot demonstrate this in the actual case of these dreams, but an instance taken from another department of life will make my meaning clear. Let us suppose the following case. There is a person of my acquaintance whom I hate, so that I have a lively inclination to feel glad if anything goes wrong with him. But the moral side of my nature will not give way to this impulse. I do not dare to express a wish that he should be unlucky, and if he meets with some undeserved misfortune, I suppress my satisfaction at it and force myself to manifestations and thoughts of regret. Everyone must have found himself in this situation at some time or other. What now happens, however, is that the hated person, by a piece of misconduct of his own, involves himself in some well-deserved unpleasantness; when that happens, I may give free rein to my satisfaction that he has met with a just punishment and in this I find myself in agreement with many other people who are impartial. I may observe, however, that my satisfaction seems more intense than that of these other people; it has received an accession from the source of my hatred, which till then has been prevented from producing its affect, but in the altered circumstances is no longer hindered from doing so. In social life this occurs in general wherever antipathetic people or members of an unpopular minority put themselves in the wrong. Their punishment does not as a rule correspond to their wrongdoing but to their wrongdoing *plus* the ill-feeling directed against them which has previously been without any consequences. It is no doubt true that those who inflict the punishment are committing an injustice in this; but they are prevented from perceiving it by the satisfaction resulting from the removal of a suppression which has long been maintained within them. In cases such as this the affect is justified in its *quality* but not in its *amount*; and self-criticism which is set at rest on the one point is only too apt to neglect examination of the second one. When once a door has been opened, it is easy for more people to push their way through it than there had originally been any intention of letting in.

A striking feature in neurotic characters—the fact that a cause capable of releasing an affect is apt to produce in them a result which is qualitatively justified but quantitatively excessive—is to be explained along these same lines, in so far as it admits of any psychological explanation at all. The excess arises from sources of affect which had previously remained unconscious and suppressed. These sources have succeeded in setting up an associative link with the *real* releasing cause, and the desired path from the release of their own affect has been opened by the *other* source of affect, which is unobjectionable and legitimate. Our attention is thus drawn to the fact that in considering the suppressed and suppressing agencies, we must not regard their relation as being exclusively one of mutual inhibition. Just as much regard must be paid to cases in which the two agencies bring about a pathological effect by working side by side and by intensifying each other.

Let us now apply these hints upon psychical mechanisms to

an understanding of the expressions of affect in *dreams*. A satisfaction which is exhibited in a dream and can, of course, be immediately referred to its proper place in the dream-thoughts is not always completely elucidated by this reference alone. It is as a rule necessary to look for *another* source of it in the dream-thoughts, a source which is under the pressure of the censorship. As a result of that pressure, this source would normally have produced, not satisfaction, but the contrary affect. Owing to the presence of the first source of affect, however, the second source is enabled to withdraw its affect of satisfaction from repression and allow it to act as an intensification of the satisfaction from the first source. Thus it appears that affects in dreams are fed from a confluence of several sources and are over-determined in their reference to the material of the dream-thoughts. *During the dream-work, sources of affect which are capable of producing the same affect come together in generating it.*[1]

We can gain a little insight into these complications from the analysis of that fine specimen of a dream of which the words '*Non vixit*' formed the centre-point. (See p. 421 ff.) In that dream manifestations of affect of various qualities were brought together at two points in its manifest content. Hostile and distressing feelings—'overcome by strange emotions' were the words used in the dream itself—were piled up at the point at which I annihilated my opponent and friend with two words. And again, at the end of the dream, I was highly delighted, and I went on to approve the possibility, which in waking life I knew was absurd, of there being *revenants* who could be eliminated by a mere wish.

I have not yet related the exciting cause of the dream. It was of great importance and led deep into an understanding of the dream. I had heard from my friend in Berlin, whom I have referred to as 'Fl.' [i.e. Fliess], that he was about to undergo an operation and that I should get further news of his condition from some of his relatives in Vienna. The first reports I received after the operation were not reassuring and made me feel anxious. I should have much preferred to go to him myself, but just at that time I was the victim of a painful complaint

---

[1] [*Footnote added* 1909:] I have given an analogous explanation of the extraordinarily powerful pleasurable effect of tendentious jokes [Freud, 1905c, towards the end of Chapter IV].

which made movement of any kind a torture to me. The dream-thoughts now informed me that I feared for my friend's life. His only sister, whom I had never known, had, as I was aware, died in early youth after a very brief illness. (In the dream *Fl. spoke about his sister and said that in three-quarters of an hour she was dead.*) I must have imagined that his constitution was not much more resistant than his sister's and that, after getting some much worse news of him, I should make the journey after all—and arrive *too late*, for which I might never cease to reproach myself.[1] This reproach for coming too late became the central point of the dream but was represented by a scene in which Brücke, the honoured teacher of my student years, levelled this reproach at me with a terrible look from his blue eyes. It will soon appear what it was that caused the situation [in regard to Fl.] to be switched on to these lines. The scene [with Brücke] itself could not be reproduced by the dream in the form in which I experienced it. The other figure in the dream was allowed to keep the blue eyes, but the annihilating role was allotted to me—a reversal which was obviously the work of wish-fulfilment. My anxiety about my friend's recovery, my self-reproaches for not going to see him, the shame I felt about this—*he had come to Vienna* (to see me) *'unobtrusively'*—the need I felt to consider that I was excused by my illness—all of this combined to produce the emotional storm which was clearly perceived in my sleep and which raged in this region of the dream-thoughts.

But there was something else in the exciting cause of the dream, which had a quite opposite effect upon me. Along with the unfavourable reports during the first few days after the operation, I was given a warning not to discuss the matter with anyone. I had felt offended by this because it implied an unnecessary distrust of my discretion. I was quite aware that these instructions had not emanated from my friend but were due to tactlessness or over-anxiety on the part of the intermediary, but I was very disagreeably affected by the veiled reproach because it was—not wholly without justification. As we all know, it is

[1] It was this phantasy, forming part of the unconscious dream-thoughts, which so insistently demanded '*Non vivit*' instead of '*Non vixit*': 'You have come too late, he is no longer alive.' I have already explained on pp. 421–3 that '*Non vivit*' was also required by the *manifest* situation in the dream.

only reproaches which have something in them that 'stick'; it
is only they that upset us. What I have in mind does not relate,
it is true, to this friend, but to a much earlier period of my life.
On that occasion I caused trouble between two friends (both
of whom had chosen to honour me, too, with that name) by
quite unnecessarily telling one of them, in the course of conversation, what the other had said about him. At that time,
too, reproaches had been levelled at me, and they were still in
my memory. One of the two friends concerned was Professor
Fleischl; I may describe the other by his first name of 'Josef'
—which was also that of P., my friend and opponent in the
dream.[1]

The reproach of being unable to keep anything to myself was
attested in the dream by the element 'unobtrusive' and by Fl.'s
question as to *how much I had told P. about his affairs*. But it was
the intervention of this memory [of my early indiscretion and
its consequences] that transported the reproach against me for
coming too late from the present time to the period at which I
had worked in Brücke's laboratory. And, by turning the second
person in the scene of annihilation in the dream into a Josef,
I made the scene represent not only the reproach against me
for coming too late but also the far more strongly repressed
reproach that I was unable to keep a secret. Here the processes
of condensation and displacement at work in the dream, as
well as the reasons for them, are strikingly visible.

My present-day anger, which was only slight, over the
warning I had been given not to give anything away [about
Fl.'s illness] received reinforcements from sources in the depth
of my mind and thus swelled into a current of hostile feelings

---

[1] [What follows will be made more intelligible by some facts derived
from a paper by Bernfeld (1944). Freud worked at the Vienna Physiological Institute ('Brücke's laboratory') from 1876 to 1882. Ernst Brücke
(1819–92) was at its head; his two assistants in Freud's time were Sigmund Exner (1846–1925) and Ernst Fleischl von Marxow (1846–91),
both some ten years older than Freud. Fleischl suffered from a very
severe physical affliction during the later years of his life. It was at the
Physiological Institute that Freud met Josef Breuer (1842–1925), his
greatly senior collaborator in *Studies on Hysteria* (1895d) and the second
Josef in the present analysis. The first Josef—Freud's early deceased
'friend and opponent P.'—was Josef Paneth (1857–90), who succeeded
to Freud's position at the Institute.—See also the first volume of Ernest
Jones's Freud biography.]

against persons of whom I was in reality fond. The source of this reinforcement flowed from my childhood. I have already shown [p. 424 f.] how my warm friendships as well as my enmities with contemporaries went back to my relations in childhood with a nephew who was a year my senior; how he was my superior, how I early learned to defend myself against him, how we were inseparable friends, and how, according to the testimony of our elders, we sometimes fought with each other and—made complaints to them about each other. All my friends have in a certain sense been re-incarnations of this first figure who 'früh sich einst dem trüben Blick gezeigt'[1]: they have been *revenants*. My nephew himself re-appeared in my boyhood, and at that time we acted the parts of Caesar and Brutus together. My emotional life has always insisted that I should have an intimate friend and a hated enemy. I have always been able to provide myself afresh with both, and it has not infrequently happened that the ideal situation of childhood has been so completely reproduced that friend and enemy have come together in a single individual—though not, of course, both at once or with constant oscillations, as may have been the case in my early childhood.

I do not propose at this point to discuss how it is that in such circumstances as these a recent occasion for the generation of an affect can hark back to an infantile situation and be replaced by that situation as far as the production of affect is concerned. [See p. 546.] This question forms part of the psychology of unconscious thinking, and would find its proper place in a psychological elucidation of the neuroses. For the purposes of dream-interpretation let us assume that a childhood memory arose, or was constructed in phantasy, with some such content as the following. The two children had a dispute about some object. (What the object was may be left an open question, though the memory or pseudo-memory had a quite specific one in view.) Each of them claimed to have *got there before the other* and therefore to have a better right to it. They came to blows and might prevailed over right. On the evidence of the dream, I may myself have been aware that I was in the wrong ('*I myself noticed the mistake*'). However, this time I was the stronger and remained in possession of the field. The vanquished party

[1] [' . . . long since appeared before my troubled gaze' (Goethe, *Faust*, Dedication).]

hurried to his grandfather—my father—and complained about
me, and I defended myself in the words which I know from my
father's account: 'I hit him 'cos he hit me.' This memory, or
more probably phantasy, which came into my mind while I
was analysing the dream—without further evidence I myself
could not tell how[1]—constituted an intermediate element in the
dream-thoughts, which gathered up the emotions raging in
them as a well collects the water that flows into it. From this
point the dream-thoughts proceeded along some such lines as
these: 'It serves you right if you had to make way for me. Why
did you try to push *me* out of the way? I don't need you, I
can easily find someone else to play with,' and so on. These
thoughts now entered upon the paths which led to their representation in the dream. There had been a time when I had had
to reproach my friend Josef [P.] for an attitude of this same kind:
'*Ôte-toi que je m'y mette!*' He had followed in my footsteps as
demonstrator in Brücke's laboratory, but promotion there was
slow and tedious. Neither of Brücke's two assistants was inclined to budge from his place, and youth was impatient. My
friend, who knew that he could not expect to live long, and
whom no bonds of intimacy attached to his immediate superior,
sometimes gave loud expression to his impatience, and, since
this superior [Fleischl] was seriously ill, P.'s wish to have him
out of the way might have an uglier meaning than the mere
hope for the man's promotion. Not unnaturally, a few years
earlier, I myself had nourished a still livelier wish to fill a
vacancy. Wherever there is rank and promotion the way lies
open for wishes that call for suppression. Shakespeare's Prince
Hal could not, even at his father's sick-bed, resist the temptation of trying on the crown. But, as was to be expected, the
dream punished my friend, and not me, for this callous wish.[2]

'As he was ambitious, I slew him.' As he could not wait for
the removal of another man, he was himself removed. These
had been my thoughts immediately after I attended the unveiling at the University of the memorial—not to him but to the
other man. Thus a part of the satisfaction I felt in the dream

---

[1] [This point is discussed below on p. 513.]

[2] It will be noticed that the name Josef plays a great part in my
dreams (cf. the dream about my uncle [p. 137 ff.]). My own ego finds
it very easy to hide itself behind people of that name, since Joseph was
the name of a man famous in the Bible as an interpreter of dreams.

was to be interpreted: 'A just punishment! It serves you right!'

At my friend's [P.'s] funeral, a young man had made what seemed to be an inopportune remark to the effect that the speaker who had delivered the funeral oration had implied that without this one man the world would come to an end. He was expressing the honest feelings of someone whose pain was being interfered with by an exaggeration. But this remark of his was the starting-point of the following dream-thoughts: 'It's quite true that no one's irreplaceable. How many people I've followed to the grave already! But I'm still alive. I've survived them all; I'm left in possession of the field.' A thought of this kind, occurring to me at a moment at which I was afraid I might not find my friend [Fl.] alive if I made the journey to him, could only be construed as meaning that I was delighted because I had once more survived someone, because it was *he* and not I who had died, because I was left in possession of the field, as I had been in the phantasied scene from my childhood. This satisfaction, infantile in origin, at being in possession of the field constituted the major part of the affect that appeared in the dream. I was delighted to survive, and I gave expression to my delight with all the naïve egoism shown in the anecdote of the married couple one of whom said to the other: 'If one of us dies, I shall move to Paris.' So obvious was it to me that I should not be the one to die. [See p. 714]

It cannot be denied that to interpret and report one's dreams demands a high degree of self-discipline. One is bound to emerge as the only villain among the crowd of noble characters who share one's life. Thus it seemed to me quite natural that the *revenants* should only exist for just so long as one likes and should be removable at a wish. We have seen what my friend Josef was punished for. But the *revenants* were a series of re-incarnations of the friend of my childhood. It was therefore also a source of satisfaction to me that I had always been able to find successive substitutes for that figure; and I felt I should be able to find a substitute for the friend whom I was now on the point of losing: no one was irreplaceable.

But what had become of the dream-censorship? Why had it not raised the most energetic objections against this blatantly egoistic train of thought? And why had it not transformed the satisfaction attached to that train of thought into severe unpleasure? The explanation was, I think, that other, unobjection-able, trains of thought in connection with the same people found simultaneous satisfaction and screened with *their* affect the affect which arose from the forbidden infantile source. In another stratum of my thoughts, during the ceremonial unveiling of the memorial, I had reflected thus: 'What a number of valued friends I have lost, some through death, some through a breach of our friendship! How fortunate that I have found a substitute for them and that I have gained one who means more to me than ever the others could, and that, at a time of life when new friendships cannot easily be formed, I shall never lose his!' My satisfaction at having found a substitute for these lost friends could be allowed to enter the dream without interference; but there slipped in, along with it, the hostile satisfaction derived from the infantile source. It is no doubt true that infantile affection served to reinforce my contemporary and justified affection. But infantile hatred, too, succeeded in getting itself represented.

In addition to this, however, the dream contained a clear allusion to another train of thought which could legitimately lead to satisfaction. A short time before, after long expectation, a daughter had been born to my friend [Fl.]. I was aware of how deeply he had mourned the sister he had so early lost and I wrote and told him I was sure he would transfer the love he felt for her on to the child, and that the baby girl would allow him at last to forget his irreparable loss.

Thus this group of thoughts was connected once again with the intermediate thought in the latent content of the dream [cf. pp. 483–4] from which the associative paths diverged in contrary directions: 'No one is irreplaceable!' 'There are no-thing but *revenants*: all those we have lost come back!' And now the associative links between the contradictory components of the dream-thoughts were drawn closer by the chance fact that my friend's baby daughter had the same name as the little girl I used to play with as a child, who was of my age and the sister of my earliest friend and opponent. [See p. 425 *n.*] It gave me great *satisfaction* when I heard that the baby was to be called 'Pauline'. And as an allusion to this coincidence, I had replaced one Josef by another in the dream and found it impossible to suppress the similarity between the opening letters of the names 'Fleischl' and 'Fl.'. From here my thoughts went on to the subject of the names of my own children. I had insisted on their names being chosen, not according to the fashion of the moment, but in memory of people I have been fond of. Their names made the children into *revenants*. And after all, I reflected, was not having children our only path to immortality?

I have only a few more remarks to add on the subject of affect in dreams from another point of view. A dominating element in a sleeper's mind may be constituted by what we call a 'mood' —or *tendency* to some affect—and this may then have a determining influence upon his dreams. A mood of this kind may arise from his experiences or thoughts during the preceding day, or its sources may be somatic. [Cf. p. 237 f.] In either case it will be accompanied by the trains of thought appropriate to it. From the point of view of dream-construction it is a matter of indifference whether, as sometimes happens, these ideational contents of the dream-thoughts determine the mood in a primary fashion, or whether they are themselves aroused secondarily by the dreamer's emotional disposition which is in its turn to be explained on a somatic basis. In any case the construction of dreams is subject to the condition that it can only represent something which is the fulfilment of a wish and that it is only from wishes that it can derive its psychical motive force. A currently active mood is treated in the same way as a sensation arising and becoming currently active during sleep (cf. p. 235), which can be either disregarded or given a fresh interpretation in the sense of a wish-fulfilment. Distressing moods during sleep can become the motive force of a dream by arousing energetic wishes which the dream is supposed to fulfil. The material to which moods are attached is worked over until it can be used to express the fulfilment of a wish. The more intense and dominating a part is played in the dream-thoughts by the distressing mood, the more certain it becomes that the most strongly suppressed wishful impulses will make use of the opportunity in order to achieve representation. For, since the unpleasure which they would otherwise necessarily produce themselves is already present, they find the harder part of their task—the task of forcing their way through to representation—already accomplished for them. Here once more we are brought up against the problem of anxiety-dreams; and these, as we shall find, form a marginal case in the function of dreaming. [Cf. p. 579 ff.]

(I)

SECONDARY REVISION[1]

And now at last we can turn to the fourth of the factors concerned in the construction of dreams. If we pursue our investigation of the content of dreams in the manner in which we have
begun it—that is, by comparing conspicuous events in the
dream-content with their sources in the dream-thoughts, we
shall come upon elements the explanation of which calls for an
entirely new assumption. What I have in mind are cases in
which the dreamer is surprised, annoyed or repelled in the
dream, and, moreover, by a piece of the dream-content itself.
As I have shown in a number of instances [in the last section],
the majority of these critical feelings in dreams are not in fact
directed against the content of the dream, but turn out to be
portions of the dream-thoughts which have been taken over and
used to an appropriate end. But some material of this kind does
not lend itself to this explanation; its correlate in the material
of the dream-thoughts is nowhere to be found. What, for
instance, is the meaning of a critical remark found so often in
dreams: 'This is only a dream'? [See p. 338.] Here we have a
genuine piece of criticism of the dream, such as might be made
in waking life. Quite frequently, too, it is actually a prelude to
waking up; and still more frequently it has been preceded by
some distressing feeling which is set at rest by the recognition
that the state is one of dreaming. When the thought 'this is only
a dream' occurs during a dream, it has the same purpose in
view as when the words are pronounced on the stage by *la belle
Hélène* in Offenbach's comic opera of that name:[2] it is aimed at
reducing the importance of what has just been experienced and
at making it possible to tolerate what is to follow. It serves to
lull a particular agency to sleep which would have every reason
at that moment to bestir itself and forbid the continuance of the
dream—or the scene in the opera. It is more comfortable, how-

[1] ['*Sekundäre Bearbeitung.*' This term has previously been given the
somewhat misleading English rendering of 'secondary elaboration'.]

[2] [In the love duet between Paris and Helen in the second act, at the
end of which they are surprised by Menelaus.]

488

ver, to go on sleeping and tolerate the dream, because, after all, 'it *is* only a dream'. In my view the contemptuous critical judgement, 'it's only a dream', appears in a dream when the censorship, which is never quite asleep, feels that it has been taken unawares by a dream which has already been allowed through. It is too late to suppress it, and accordingly the censorship uses these words to meet the anxiety or the distressing feeling aroused by it. The phrase is an example of *esprit d'escalier* on the part of the psychical censorship.

This instance, however, provides us with convincing evidence that not everything contained in a dream is derived from the dream-thoughts, but that contributions to its content may be made by a psychical function which is indistinguishable from our waking thoughts. The question now arises whether this only occurs in exceptional cases, or whether the psychical agency which otherwise operates only as a censorship plays a *habitual* part in the construction of dreams.

We can have no hesitation in deciding in favour of the second alternative. There can be no doubt that the censoring agency, whose influence we have so far only recognized in limitations and omissions in the dream-content, is also responsible for inter-polations and additions in it. The interpolations are easy to recognize. They are often reported with hesitation, and intro-duced by an 'as though'; they are not in themselves particularly vivid and are always introduced at points at which they can serve as links between two portions of the dream-content or to bridge a gap between two parts of the dream. They are less easily retained in the memory than genuine derivatives of the material of the dream-thoughts; if the dream is to be forgotten they are the first part of it to disappear, and I have a strong suspicion that the common complaint of having dreamt a lot, but of having forgotten most of it and of having only retained fragments [p. 279], is based upon the rapid disappearance pre-cisely of these connecting thoughts. In a complete analysis these interpolations are sometimes betrayed by the fact that no material connected with them is to be found in the dream-thoughts. But careful examination leads me to regard this as the less frequent case; as a rule the connecting thoughts lead back nevertheless to material in the dream-thoughts, but to material which could have no claim to acceptance in the dream either on its own account or owing to its being over-determined.

Only in extreme cases, it seems, does the psychical function in dream-formation which we are now considering proceed to make new creations. So long as possible, it employs anything appropriate that it can find in the material of the dream-thoughts.

The thing that distinguishes and at the same time reveals this part of the dream-work[1] is its *purpose*. This function behaves in the manner which the poet maliciously ascribes to philosophers: it fills up the gaps in the dream-structure with shreds and patches.[2] As a result of its efforts, the dream loses its appearance of absurdity and disconnectedness and approximates to the model of an intelligible experience. But its efforts are not always crowned with success. Dreams occur which, at a superficial view, may seem faultlessly logical and reasonable; they start from a possible situation, carry it on through a chain of consistent modifications and—though far less frequently—bring it to a conclusion which causes no surprise. Dreams which are of such a kind have been subjected to a far-reaching revision by this psychical function that is akin to waking thought; they appear to have a meaning, but that meaning is as far removed as possible from their true significance. If we analyse them, we can convince ourselves that it is in these dreams that the secondary revision has played about with the material the most freely, and has retained the relations present in that material to the least extent. They are dreams which might be said to have been already interpreted once, before being submitted to waking interpretation.[3] In other dreams this tendentious revision has only partly succeeded; coherence seems to rule for a certain distance, but the dream then becomes senseless or confused, while perhaps later on in its course it may for a second time present an appearance of rationality. In yet other dreams the revision has failed altogether; we find ourselves helplessly face to face with a meaningless heap of fragmentary material.

[1] [Elsewhere Freud remarks that, strictly speaking, 'secondary revision' is *not* a part of the dream-work. Cf. his article on 'Psycho-Analysis' in Marcuse's *Handwörterbuch* (Freud, 1923a, end of paragraph on 'The Interpretation of Dreams'). This same point is also mentioned towards the end of Freud (1913a).]

[2] [An allusion to some lines in Heine's 'Die Heimkehr' (LVIII). The whole passage is quoted by Freud near the beginning of the last of his *New Introductory Lectures* (1933a).]

[3] [See, for instance, the dreams recorded on pp. 494 and 583.]

I do not wish to deny categorically that this fourth power in dream-construction—which we shall soon recognize as an old acquaintance, since in fact it is the only one of the four with which we are familiar in other connections—I do not wish to deny that this fourth factor has the capacity to create new contributions to dreams. It is certain, however, that, like the others, it exerts its influence principally by its preferences and selections from psychical material in the dream-thoughts that has already been formed. Now there is one case in which it is to a great extent spared the labour of, as it were, building up a façade for the dream—the case, namely, in which a formation of that kind already exists, available for use in the material of the dream-thoughts. I am in the habit of describing the element in the dream-thoughts which I have in mind as a 'phantasy'.[1] I shall perhaps avoid misunderstanding if I mention the 'day-dream' as something analogous to it in waking life.[2] The part played in our mental life by these structures has not yet been fully recognized and elucidated by psychiatrists, though M. Benedikt has made what seems to me a very promising start in that direction.[3] The importance of day-dreams has not escaped the unerring vision of imaginative writers; there is, for instance, a well-known account by Alphonse Daudet in *Le Nabab* of the day-dreams of one of the minor characters in that story. [Cf. p. 535.] The study of the psychoneuroses leads to the surprising discovery that these phantasies or day-dreams are the immediate forerunners of hysterical symptoms, or at least of a whole number of them. Hysterical symptoms are not attached to actual memories, but to phantasies erected on the basis of memories.[4] The frequent occurrence of conscious day-time

---

[1] ['*Phantasie.*' This German word was earlier used only to mean 'imagination'; '*Phantasiebildung*' ('imaginative formation') would have been used here.]

[2] '*Rêve*', '*petit roman*',—'day-dream', '[continuous] story'. [These last words are in English in the original. The term '*Tagtraum*', used in the text above, was unfamiliar to German readers and called for elucidation.]

[3] [Freud himself later devoted two papers to the subject of day-dreams: 1908*a* and 1908*e*. In 1921 *The Psychology of Day-Dreams* was published by J. Varendonck, to which Freud provided an introduction (Freud, 1921*b*).]

[4] [This was expressed by Freud more trenchantly in a memorandum accompanying his letter to Fliess of May 2, 1897 (Freud, 1950*a*, Draft L): 'Phantasies are psychical façades constructed in order to bar the way to these memories [of primal scenes].']

phantasies brings these structures to our knowledge; but just as there are phantasies of this kind which are conscious, so, too, there are unconscious ones in great numbers, which have to remain unconscious on account of their content and of their origin from repressed material. Closer investigation of the characteristics of these day-time phantasies shows us how right it is that these formations should bear the same name as we give to the products of our thought during the night—the name, that is, of 'dreams'. They share a large number of their properties with night-dreams, and their investigation might, in fact, have served as the shortest and best approach to an understanding of night-dreams.

Like dreams, they are wish-fulfilments; like dreams, they are based to a great extent on impressions of infantile experiences; like dreams, they benefit by a certain degree of relaxation of censorship. If we examine their structure, we shall perceive the way in which the wishful purpose that is at work in their production has mixed up the material of which they are built, has rearranged it and has formed it into a new whole. They stand in much the same relation to the childhood memories from which they are derived as do some of the Baroque palaces of Rome to the ancient ruins whose pavements and columns have provided the material for the more recent structures.

The function of 'secondary revision', which we have attributed to the fourth of the factors concerned in shaping the content of dreams, shows us in operation once more the activity which is able to find free vent in the creation of day-dreams without being inhibited by any other influences. We might put it simply by saying that this fourth factor of ours seeks to mould the material offered to it into something like a day-dream. If, however, a day-dream of this kind has already been formed within the nexus of the dream-thoughts, this fourth factor in the dream-work will prefer to take possession of the ready-made day-dream and seek to introduce it into the content of the dream. There are some dreams which consist merely in the repetition of a day-time phantasy which may perhaps have remained unconscious:[1] such, for instance, as the boy's dream of

[1] [Cf. the long footnote to the section on 'The Barrier against Incest' near the end of the third of Freud's *Three Essays on the Theory of Sexuality* (1905*d*). This footnote was added in the Fourth Edition of that book (1920).]

driving in a war-chariot with the heroes of the Trojan War [p. 129 f.]. In my 'Autodidasker' dream [p. 298 ff.] the second part at all events was a faithful reproduction of a day-time phantasy, innocent in itself, of a conversation with Professor N. In view of the complicated conditions which a dream has to satisfy when it comes into existence, it happens more frequently that the ready-made phantasy forms only a *portion* of the dream, or that only a portion of the phantasy forces its way into the dream. Thereafter, the phantasy is treated in general like any other portion of the latent material, though it often remains recognizable as an entity in the dream. There are often parts of my dreams which stand out as producing a different impression from the rest. They strike me as being, as it were, more fluent, more connected and at the same time more fleeting than other parts of the same dream. These, I know, are unconscious phantasies which have found their way into the fabric of the dream, but I have never succeeded in pinning down a phantasy of this kind. Apart from this, these phantasies, like any other component of the dream-thoughts, are compressed, condensed, superimposed on one another, and so on. There are, however, transitional cases, between the case in which they constitute the content (or at least the façade) of the dream unaltered and the extreme opposite, in which they are represented in the content of the dream only by *one* of their elements or by a distant allusion. What happens to phantasies present in the dream-thoughts is evidently also determined by any advantages they may have to offer the requirements of the censorship and of the urge towards condensation.

In selecting examples of dream-interpretation I have so far as possible avoided dreams in which unconscious phantasies play any considerable part, because the introduction of this particular psychical element would have necessitated lengthy discussions on the psychology of unconscious thinking. Nevertheless, I cannot completely escape a consideration of phantasies in this connection, since they often make their way complete into dreams and since still more often clear glimpses of them can be seen behind the dream. I will therefore quote one more dream, which seems to be composed of two different and opposing phantasies which coincide with each other at a few points and of which one is superficial while the second is, as it were, an interpretation of the first. [See above p. 490.][1]

The dream—it is the only one of which I possess no careful notes—ran roughly as follows. The dreamer, a young unmarried man, was sitting in the restaurant at which he usually ate and which was presented realistically in the dream. Several people then appeared, in order to fetch him away, and one of them wanted to arrest him. He said to his companions at table: 'I'll pay later; I'll come back.' But they exclaimed with derisive smiles: 'We know all about that; that's what they all say!' One of the guests called out after him: 'There goes another one!' He was then led into a narrow room in which he found a female figure carrying a child. One of the people accompanying him said: 'This is Herr Müller.' A police inspector, or some such official, was turning over a bundle of cards or papers and as he did so repeated 'Müller, Müller, Müller.' Finally he asked the dreamer a question, which he answered with an 'I will'. He then turned round to look at the female figure and observed that she was now wearing a big beard.

Here there is no difficulty in separating the two components. The superficial one was a *phantasy of arrest* which appears as though it had been freshly constructed by the dream-work. But behind it some material is visible which had been only slightly re-shaped by the dream-work: *a phantasy of marriage*. Those features which were common to both phantasies emerge with special clarity, in the same way as in one of Galton's composite photographs. The promise made by the young man (who up till then had been a bachelor) that he would come back and join his fellow-diners at their table, the scepticism of his boon-companions (whom experience had taught better), the exclama-

---

[1] [*Footnote added* 1909:] In my 'Fragment of an Analysis of a Case of Hysteria' (1905e [Part II]), I have analysed a good specimen of a dream of this sort, made up of a number of superimposed phantasies. Incidentally, I underestimated the importance of the part played by these phantasies in the formation of dreams so long as I was principally working on my own dreams, which are usually based on discussions and conflicts of thought and comparatively rarely on day-dreams. In the case of other people it is often much easier to demonstrate the complete analogy between night-dreams and day-dreams. With hysterical patients, a hysterical attack can often be replaced by a dream; and it is then easy to convince oneself that the immediate forerunner of *both* these psychical structures was a day-dream phantasy.

tion 'there goes another one (to get married)'—all of these features fitted in easily with the alternative interpretation. So, too, did the 'I will' with which he replied to the official's question. The turning over the bundle of papers, with the constant repetition of the same name, corresponded to a less important but recognizable feature of wedding festivities, namely the reading out of a bundle of telegrams of congratulation, all of them with addresses bearing the same names. The phantasy of marriage actually scored a victory over the covering phantasy of arrest in the fact of the bride's making a personal appearance in the dream. I was able to discover from an enquiry—the dream was not analysed—why it was that at the end of it the bride wore a beard. On the previous day the dreamer had been walking in the street with a friend who was as shy of marrying as he was himself, and he had drawn his friend's attention to a dark-haired beauty who had passed them. 'Yes,' his friend had remarked, 'if only women like that didn't grow beards like their fathers' in a few years' time.' This dream did not, of course, lack elements in which dream-distortion had been carried deeper. It may well be, for instance, that the words 'I'll pay later' referred to what he feared might be his father-in-law's attitude on the subject of a dowry. In fact, all kinds of qualms were evidently preventing the dreamer from throwing himself into the phantasy of marriage with any enjoyment. One of these qualms, a fear that marriage might cost him his freedom, was embodied in the transformation into a scene of arrest.

If we return for a moment to the point that the dream-work is glad to make use of a ready-made phantasy instead of putting one together out of the material of the dream-thoughts, we may perhaps find ourselves in a position to solve one of the most interesting puzzles connected with dreams. On p. 26 f. I told the well-known anecdote of how Maury, having been struck in his sleep on the back of his neck by a piece of wood, woke up from a long dream which was like a full-length story set in the days of the French Revolution. Since the dream, as reported, was a coherent one and was planned entirely with an eye to providing an explanation of the stimulus which woke him and whose occurrence he could not have anticipated, the only possible hypothesis seems to be that the whole elaborate dream must have been composed and must have taken place during the short period of time between the contact of the board with Maury's cervical vertebrae and his consequent awakening. We should never dare to attribute such rapidity to thought-activity in waking life, and we should therefore be driven to conclude that the dream-work possesses the advantage of accelerating our thought-processes to a remarkable degree.

Strong objections have been raised to what quickly became a popular conclusion by some more recent writers (Le Lorrain, 1894 and 1895, Egger, 1895, and others). On the one hand they throw doubts upon the accuracy of Maury's account of his dream; and on the other hand they attempt to show that the rapidity of the operations of our waking thoughts is no less than in this dream when exaggerations have been discounted. The discussion raised questions of principle which do not seem to me immediately soluble. But I must confess that the arguments brought forward (by Egger, for instance), particularly against Maury's guillotine dream, leave me unconvinced. I myself would propose the following explanation of this dream. Is it so highly improbable that Maury's dream represents a phantasy which had been stored up ready-made in his memory for many years and which was aroused—or I would rather say 'alluded to'—at the moment at which he became aware of the stimulus which woke him? If this were so, we should have escaped the whole difficulty of understanding how such a long story with all its details could have been composed in the extremely short period of time which was at the dreamer's disposal—for the story would have been composed already. If the piece of wood had struck the back of Maury's neck while he was awake, there would have been an opportunity for some such thought as: 'That's just like being guillotined.' But since it was in his sleep that he was struck by the board, the dream-work made use of the impinging stimulus in order rapidly to produce a wish-fulfilment; it was *as though* it thought (this is to be taken purely figuratively): 'Here's a good opportunity of realizing a wishful phantasy which was formed at such and such a time in the course of reading.' It can hardly be disputed, I think, that the dream-story was precisely of a sort likely to be constructed by a young man under the influence of powerfully exciting impressions. Who—least of all what Frenchman or student of the history of civilization—could fail to be gripped by narratives of the Reign of Terror, when the men and women of the aristocracy, the flower of the nation, showed that they could die with a cheerful mind and could retain the liveliness of their wit and the elegance of their manners till the very moment of the fatal summons? How tempting for a young man to plunge into all this in his imagination—to picture himself bidding a lady farewell—kissing her hand and mounting the scaffold unafraid! Or, if ambition were the prime motive of the phantasy, how tempting for him to take the place of one of those formidable figures who, by the power alone of their thoughts and flaming eloquence, ruled the city in which the heart of humanity beat convulsively in those days—who were led by their convictions to send thousands of men to their death and who prepared the way for the transformation of Europe, while all the time their own heads were insecure and destined to fall one day beneath the knife of the guillotine—how tempting to picture himself as one of the Girondists, perhaps, or as the heroic Danton! There is one feature in Maury's recollection of the dream, his being 'led to the place of execution, surrounded by an immense mob', which seems to suggest that his phantasy was in fact of this ambitious type.

Nor is it necessary that this long-prepared phantasy should have been gone through during sleep; it would have been sufficient for it to be merely touched on. What I mean is this. If a few bars of music are played and someone comments that it is from Mozart's *Figaro* (as happens in *Don Giovanni*) a number of recollections are roused in me all at once, none of which can enter my consciousness singly at the first moment. The key-phrase serves as a port of entry through which the whole network is simultaneously put in a state of excitation. It may well be the same in the case of unconscious thinking. The rousing stimulus excites the psychical port of entry which allows access to the whole guillotine phantasy. But the phantasy is not gone through during sleep but only in the recollection of the sleeper after his awakening. After waking he remembers in all its details the phantasy which was stirred up as a whole in his dream. One has no means of assuring oneself in such a case that one is really remembering something one has dreamt. This same explanation—that it is a question of ready-made phantasies which are brought into excitation as a whole by the rousing stimulus—can be applied to other dreams which are focused upon a rousing stimulus, such, for instance, as Napoleon's battle dream before the explosion of the infernal machine [pp. 26 and 233 f.].

Among the dreams[1] collected by Justine Tobowolska in her dissertation on the apparent passage of time in dreams, the most informative seems to me to be the one reported by Macario (1857, 46) as having been dreamt by a dramatic author, Casimir Bonjour. One evening Bonjour wanted to attend the first performance of one of his pieces; but he was so fatigued that as he was sitting behind the scenes he dozed off just at the moment the curtain went up. During his sleep he went through the whole five acts of the play, and observed all the various signs of emotion shown by the audience during the different scenes. At the end of the performance he was delighted to hear his name being shouted with the liveliest demonstrations of applause. Suddenly he woke up. He could not believe either his eyes or his ears, for the performance had not gone beyond the first few lines of the first scene; he could not have been asleep for longer than two minutes. It is surely not too rash to suppose in the case of this dream that the dreamer's going through all five acts of the play and observing the attitude of the public to different passages in it need not have arisen from any fresh production of material during his sleep, but may have reproduced a piece of phantasy-activity (in the sense I have described) which had already been completed. Tobowolska, like other writers, emphasizes the fact that dreams with an accelerated passage of ideas have the common characteristic of seeming specially coherent, quite unlike other dreams, and that the recollection of them is summary far more than detailed. This would indeed be a characteristic which ready-made phantasies of this kind, touched upon by the dream-work, would be bound to possess, though this is a conclusion which the writers in question fail to draw. I do not assert, however, that *all* arousal dreams admit of this explanation, or that the problem of the accelerated passage of ideas in dreams can be entirely dismissed in this fashion.

At this point it is impossible to avoid considering the relation between this secondary revision of the content of dreams and the remaining factors of the dream-work. Are we to

[1] [This paragraph was added in 1914 with the exception of the last sentence, which appeared in the original edition.]

suppose that what happens is that in the first instance the dream-constructing factors—the tendency towards condensation, the necessity for evading the censorship, and considerations of representability by the psychical means open to dreams —put together a provisional dream-content out of the material provided, and that this content is subsequently re-cast so as to conform so far as possible to the demands of a second agency? This is scarcely probable. We must assume rather that from the very first the demands of this second factor constitute one of the conditions which the dream must satisfy and that this condition, like those laid down by condensation, the censorship imposed by resistance, and representability, operates simultaneously in a conducive and selective sense upon the mass of material present in the dream-thoughts. In any case, however, of the four conditions for the formation of dreams, the one we have come to know last is the one whose demands appear to have the least cogent influence on dreams.

The following consideration makes it highly probable that the psychical function which carries out what we have described as the secondary revision of the content of dreams is to be identified with the activity of our waking thought. Our waking (preconscious[1]) thinking behaves towards any perceptual material with which it meets in just the same way in which the function we are considering behaves towards the content of dreams. It is the nature of our waking thought to establish order in material of that kind, to set up relations in it and to make it conform to our expectations of an intelligible whole. [Cf. pp. 28 f. and 46.] In fact, we go too far in that direction. An adept in sleight of hand can trick us by relying upon this intellectual habit of ours. In our efforts at making an intelligible pattern of the sense-impressions that are offered to us, we often fall into the strangest errors or even falsify the truth about the material before us.

The evidences of this are too universally known for there to be any need to insist upon them further. In our reading we pass over misprints which destroy the sense, and have the illusion that what we are reading is correct. The editor of a popular French periodical is said to have made a bet that he would

---

[1] [Freud's first published use of the term seems to occur on p. 338; it is explained below on p. 541. It appears as early as December 6, 1896, in his correspondence with Fliess (Freud, 1950a, Letter 52).]

have the words 'in front' or 'behind' inserted by the printer in every sentence of a long article without a single one of his readers noticing it. He won his bet. Many years ago I read in a newspaper a comic instance of a false connection. On one occasion during a sitting of the French Chamber a bomb thrown by an anarchist exploded in the Chamber itself and Dupuy subdued the consequent panic with the courageous words: '*La séance continue*'. The visitors in the gallery were asked to give their impressions as witnesses of the outrage. Among them were two men from the provinces. One of these said that it was true that he had heard a detonation at the close of one of the speeches but had assumed that it was a parliamentary usage to fire a shot each time a speaker sat down. The second one, who had probably already heard *several* speeches, had come to the same conclusion, except that he supposed that a shot was only fired as a tribute to a particularly successful speech.

There is no doubt, then, that it is our normal thinking that is the psychical agency which approaches the content of dreams with a demand that it must be intelligible, which subjects it to a first interpretation and which consequently produces a complete misunderstanding of it. [See p. 490.] For the purposes of *our* interpretation it remains an essential rule invariably to leave out of account the ostensible continuity of a dream as being of suspect origin, and to follow the same path back to the material of the dream-thoughts, no matter whether the dream itself is clear or confused.

We now perceive, incidentally, on what it is that the range in the quality of dreams between confusion and clarity which was discussed on p. 330 f. depends. Those parts of a dream on which the secondary revision has been able to produce some effect are clear, while those parts on which its efforts have failed are confused. Since the confused parts of a dream are so often at the same time the less vivid parts, we may conclude that the secondary dream-work is also to be held responsible for a contribution to the plastic intensity of the different dream-elements.

If I look around for something with which to compare the final form assumed by a dream as it appears after normal thought has made its contribution, I can think of nothing better than the enigmatic inscriptions with which *Fliegende Blätter* has for so long entertained its readers. They are intended to make the reader believe that a certain sentence—for the sake of contrast, a sentence in dialect and as scurrilous as possible—is a Latin inscription. For this purpose the letters contained in the words are torn out of their combination into syllables and arranged in a new order. Here and there a genuine Latin word appears; at other points we seem to see abbreviations of Latin words before us; and at still other points in the inscription we may allow ourselves to be deceived into overlooking the senselessness of isolated letters by parts of the inscription seeming to be defaced or showing lacunae. If we are to avoid being taken in by the joke, we must disregard everything that makes it seem like an inscription, look firmly at the letters, pay no attention to their ostensible arrangement, and so combine them into words belonging to our own mother tongue.[1]

Secondary revision[2] is the one factor in the dream-work which has been observed by the majority of writers on the subject and of which the significance has been appreciated. Havelock Ellis (1911, 10–11) has given an amusing account of its functioning: 'Sleeping consciousness we may even imagine as saying to itself in effect: "Here comes our master, Waking Consciousness, who attaches such mighty importance to reason and logic and so forth. Quick! gather things up, put them in order—any order will do—before he enters to take possession." '

The identity of its method of working with that of waking thought has been stated with particular clarity by Delacroix (1904, 926): 'Cette fonction d'interprétation n'est pas particulière au rêve; c'est le même travail de coordination logique que nous faisons sur nos sensations pendant la veille.'[3]   James Sully

---

[1] [An instance of the operation of the process of secondary revision in the case of a fairy-tale is given on p. 243 and in the case of *Oedipus Rex* on p. 264. Its application to obsessions and phobias is mentioned on p. 244, and to paranoia in Lecture XXIV of Freud's *Introductory Lectures* (1916–17). An example of secondary revision in a telegraphic error is recorded in Chapter VI (No. 19) of *The Psychopathology of Everyday Life* (1901*b*). The analogy between the secondary revision of dreams and the formation of 'systems' of thought is discussed at some length in Chapter III, Section 4, of *Totem and Taboo* (1912–13).]

[2] [The remainder of this chapter, with the exception of the last paragraph, which was in the original edition, was added in 1914.]

[3] ['This interpretative function is not peculiar to dreams. It is the same work of logical co-ordination which we carry out upon our sensations while we are awake.']

[1893, 355–6] is of the same opinion. So, too, is Tobowolska (1900, 93): 'Sur ces successions incohérentes d'hallucinations, l'esprit s'efforce de faire le même travail de coordination logique qu'il fait pendant la veille sur les sensations. Il relie entre elles par un lien imaginaire toutes ces images décousues et bouche les écarts trop grands qui se trouvaient entre elles.'[1]

According to some writers, this process of arranging and interpreting begins during the dream itself and is continued after waking. Thus Paulhan (1894, 546): 'Cependant j'ai souvent pensé qu'il pouvait y avoir une certaine déformation, ou plutôt reformation, du rêve dans le souvenir. . . . La tendence systématisante de l'imagination pourrait fort bien achever après le réveil ce qu'elle a ébauché pendant le sommeil. De la sorte, la rapidité réelle de la pensée serait augmentée en apparence par les perfectionnements dus à l'imagination éveillée.'[2] Bernard-Leroy and Tobowolska (1901, 592): 'Dans le rêve, au contraire, l'interprétation et la coordination se font non seulement à l'aide des données du rêve, mais encore à l'aide de celles de la veille. . . .'[3]

Inevitably, therefore, this one recognized factor in the formation of dreams has had its importance over-estimated, so that it has been credited with the whole achievement of the creation of dreams. This act of creation, as Goblot (1896, 288 f.) and still more Foucault (1906) suppose, is performed at the moment of waking; for these two writers attribute to waking thought an ability to construct a dream out of the thoughts that emerge during sleep. Bernard-Leroy and Tobowolska (1901) comment on this view: 'On a cru pouvoir placer le rêve au moment du réveil, et ils ont attribué à la pensée de la veille la

[1] ['The mind endeavours to carry out upon these incoherent trains of hallucinations the same work of logical co-ordination that it carries out upon sensations during the day-time. It connects up all these detached images by an imaginary link and stops up any excessively wide gaps between them.']

[2] ['I have often thought, however, that dreams may be to some extent misshaped, or rather reshaped, in memory. . . . The tendency of the imagination towards systematization might very well complete after waking what it had started upon in sleep. In that way the real speed of thought would be given an apparent increase by the improvements due to the waking imagination.']

[3] ['In a dream, on the contrary, interpretation and co-ordination are carried out by the help not only of the data presented in the dream, but of the data available in waking life. . . .']

fonction de construire le rêve avec les images présentes dans la pensée du sommeil.'[1]

From this discussion of secondary revision I will go on to consider a further factor in the dream-work which has recently been brought to light by some finely perceptive observations carried out by Herbert Silberer. As I have mentioned earlier (p. 344 ff.), Silberer has, as it were, caught in the very act the process of transforming thoughts into images, by forcing himself into intellectual activity while he was in a state of fatigue and drowsiness. At such moments the thought with which he was dealing vanished and was replaced by a vision which turned out to be a substitute for what were as a rule abstract thoughts. (Cf. the examples in the passage just referred to.) Now it happened during these experiments that the image which arose, and which might be compared to an element of a dream, sometimes represented something other than the thought that was being dealt with—namely, the fatigue itself, the difficulty and unpleasure involved in the work. It represented, that is to say, the subjective state and mode of functioning of the person making the effort instead of the object of his efforts. Silberer described occurrences of this kind, which were very frequent in his case, as a 'functional phenomenon' in contrast to the 'material phenomenon' which would have been expected.

For instance: 'One afternoon I was lying on my sofa feeling extremely sleepy; nevertheless I forced myself to think over a philosophical problem. I wanted to compare the views of Kant and Schopenhauer upon Time. As a result of my drowsiness I was unable to keep the arguments of both of them before my mind at once, which was necessary in order to make the comparison. After a number of vain attempts, I once more impressed Kant's deductions upon my mind with all the strength of my will, so that I might apply them to Schopenhauer's statement of the problem. I then directed my attention to the latter; but when I tried to turn back again to Kant, I found that his argument had once more escaped me and I tried vainly to pick it up once more. This vain effort at recovering the Kant *dossier* which

[1] ['It has been thought possible to locate dreams at the moment of waking, and [these authors] have ascribed to waking thought the function of constructing dreams out of the images present in sleeping thought.']

was stored away somewhere in my head was suddenly represented before my closed eyes as a concrete and plastic symbol, as though it were a dream-picture: *I was asking for information from a disobliging secretary who was bent over his writing-table and refused to put himself out at my insistent demand. He half straightened himself and gave me a disagreeable and uncomplying look.*' (Silberer, 1909, 513 f. [Freud's italics.])

Here are some other instances, which relate to the oscillation between sleeping and waking:

'Example No. 2.—Circumstances: In the morning, at waking. While I was at a certain depth of sleep (a twilight state) and reflecting over a previous dream and in a sort of way continuing to dream it, I felt myself approaching nearer to waking consciousness but wanted to remain in the twilight state.

'Scene: *I was stepping across a brook with one foot but drew it back again at once with the intention of remaining on this side.*' (Silberer, 1912, 625.)

'Example No. 6.—Conditions as in example No. 4' (in which he had wanted to lie in bed a little longer, though without oversleeping). 'I wanted to give way to sleep for a little longer.

'Scene: *I was saying good-bye to someone and was arranging with him (or her) to meet him (or her) again soon.*' (Ibid., 627.)

The 'functional' phenomenon, 'the representation of a state instead of an object', was observed by Silberer principally in the two conditions of falling asleep and waking up. It is obvious that dream-interpretation is only concerned with the latter case. Silberer has given examples which show convincingly that in many dreams the last pieces of the manifest content, which are immediately followed by waking, represent nothing more nor less than an intention to wake or the process of waking. The representation may be in terms of such images as crossing a threshold ('threshold symbolism'), leaving one room and entering another, departure, home-coming, parting with a companion, diving into water, etc. I cannot, however, refrain from remarking that I have come across dream-elements which can be related to threshold symbolism, whether in my own dreams or in those of subjects whom I have analysed, far less frequently than Silberer's communications would have led one to expect.

It is by no means inconceivable or improbable that this threshold symbolism might throw light upon some elements in the middle of the texture of dreams—in places, for instance, where there is a question of oscillations in the depth of sleep and of an inclination to break off the dream. Convincing instances of this, however, have not been produced.[1] What seem to occur more frequently are cases of overdetermination, in which a part of a dream which has derived its material content from the nexus of dream-thoughts is employed to represent *in addition* some state of mental activity.

This very interesting functional phenomenon of Silberer's has, through no fault of its discoverer's, led to many abuses; for it has been regarded as lending support to the old inclination to give abstract and symbolic interpretations to dreams. The preference for the 'functional category' is carried so far by some people that they speak of the functional phenomenon wherever intellectual activities or emotional processes occur in the dream-thoughts, although such material has neither more nor less right than any other kind to find its way into a dream as residues of the previous day. [Cf. pp. 214 *n.* 4, and 412 *n.*]

We are ready to recognize the fact that Silberer's phenomena constitute a second contribution on the part of waking thought to the construction of dreams; though it is less regularly present and less significant than the first one, which has already been introduced under the name of 'secondary revision'. It has been shown that a part of the attention which operates during the day continues to be directed towards dreams during the state of sleep, that it keeps a check on them and criticizes them and reserves the power to interrupt them. It has seemed plausible to recognize in the mental agency which thus remains awake the censor [2] to whom we have had to attribute such a powerful restricting influence upon the form taken by dreams. What Silberer's observations have added to this is the fact that in certain circumstances a species of self-observation plays a part in this and makes a contribution to the content of the dream. The probable relations of this self-observing agency, which may

[1] [See, however, a subsequent remark by Freud on p. 559 below.]

[2] [Freud almost always uses the German word '*Zensur*' ('censorship'); but here and a few lines lower down he uses the personal form '*Zensor*' ('censor'). Other instances of this very rare occurrence will be found in Section III of the paper on 'Narcissism' (Freud, 1914c) and in Lecture XXIX of the *New Introductory Lectures* (Freud, 1933a).]

be particularly prominent in philosophical minds, to endopsychic perception, to delusions of observation, to conscience
and to the censor of dreams can be more appropriately treated
elsewhere.[1]

I will now try to sum up this lengthy disquisition on the
dream-work. We were faced by the question whether the mind
employs the whole of its faculties without reserve in constructing
dreams or only a functionally restricted fragment of them. Our
investigations led us to reject entirely the form in which the
question was framed as being inadequate to the circumstances.
If, however, we had to reply to the question on the basis of the
terms in which it was stated, we should be obliged to reply in
the affirmative to *both* the alternatives, mutually exclusive
though they appear to be. Two separate functions may be distinguished in mental activity during the construction of a
dream: the production of the dream-thoughts, and their transformation into the content of the dream. The dream-thoughts
are entirely rational and are constructed with an expenditure
of all the psychical energy of which we are capable. They have
their place among thought-processes that have not become
conscious—processes from which, after some modification, our
conscious thoughts, too, arise. However many interesting and
puzzling questions the dream-thoughts may involve, such questions have, after all, no special relation to dreams and do not
call for treatment among the problems of dreams.[2] On the other

---

[1] [*Footnote added* 1914:] 'On Narcissism' (Freud, 1914c [Section III]).
—[The next paragraph appeared in the first edition.]

[2] [*Footnote added* 1925:] I used at one time to find it extraordinarily
difficult to accustom readers to the distinction between the manifest
content of dreams and the latent dream-thoughts. Again and again
arguments and objections would be brought up based upon some
uninterpreted dream in the form in which it had been retained in the
memory, and the need to interpret it would be ignored. But now that
analysts at least have become reconciled to replacing the manifest dream
by the meaning revealed by its interpretation, many of them have
become guilty of falling into another confusion which they cling to with
equal obstinacy. They seek to find the essence of dreams in their latent
content and in so doing they overlook the distinction between the latent
dream-thoughts and the dream-work. At bottom, dreams are nothing
other than a particular *form* of thinking, made possible by the conditions
of the state of sleep. It is the *dream-work* which creates that form, and it

hand, the second function of mental activity during dream-construction, the transformation of the unconscious thoughts into the content of the dream, is peculiar to dream-life and characteristic of it. This dream-work proper diverges further from our picture of waking thought than has been supposed even by the most determined depreciator of psychical functioning during the formation of dreams. The dream-work is not simply more careless, more irrational, more forgetful and more incomplete than waking thought; it is completely different from it qualitatively and for that reason not immediately comparable with it. It does not think, calculate or judge in any way at all; it restricts itself to giving things a new form. It is exhaustively described by an enumeration of the conditions which it has to satisfy in producing its result. That product, the dream, has above all to evade the censorship, and with that end in view the dream-work makes use of a *displacement of psychical intensities* to the point of a transvaluation of all psychical values. The thoughts have to be reproduced exclusively or predominantly in the material of visual and acoustic memory-traces, and this necessity imposes upon the dream-work *considerations of representability* which it meets by carrying out fresh displacements. Greater intensities have probably to be produced than are available in the dream-thoughts at night, and this purpose is served by the extensive *condensation* which is carried out with the constituents of the dream-thoughts. Little attention is paid to the logical relations between the thoughts; those relations are ultimately given a disguised representation in certain *formal* characteristics of dreams. Any affect attached to the dream-thoughts undergoes less modification than their ideational content. Such affects are as a rule suppressed; when they are retained, they are detached from the ideas that properly belong to them, affects of a similar character being brought together. Only a single portion of the dream-work and one which operates to an irregular degree, the working over of the material by partly

alone is the essence of dreaming—the explanation of its peculiar nature. I say this in order to make it possible to assess the value of the notorious 'prospective purpose' of dreams. [See below, p. 579 f. *n.*] The fact that dreams concern themselves with attempts at solving the problems by which our mental life is faced is no more strange than that our conscious waking life should do so; beyond this it merely tells us that that activity can also be carried on in the preconscious—and this we already knew.

aroused waking thought, tallies to some extent with the view
which other writers have sought to apply to the entire activity
of dream-construction.[1]

[1] [At this point there followed in the fourth, fifth, sixth and seventh
editions (from 1914 to 1922) two self-contained essays by Otto Rank,
bearing the titles 'Dreams and Creative Writing' and 'Dreams and
Myths'. These were omitted from the *Gesammelte Schriften*, 1924, with a
comment by Freud (3, 150) that they were 'naturally not included in a
collected edition of my works'. They were, however, not re-inserted in
the subsequent (eighth) edition of 1930. See the Editor's Introduction,
p. xxi.]

CHAPTER VII

THE PSYCHOLOGY OF THE DREAM-PROCESSES[1]

AMONG the dreams which have been reported to me by other people, there is one which has special claims upon our attention at this point. It was told to me by a woman patient who had herself heard it in a lecture on dreams: its actual source is still unknown to me. Its content made an impression on the lady, however, and she proceeded to 're-dream' it, that is, to repeat some of its elements in a dream of her own, so that, by taking it over in this way, she might express her agreement with it on one particular point.

The preliminaries to this model dream were as follows. A father had been watching beside his child's sick-bed for days and nights on end. After the child had died, he went into the next room to lie down, but left the door open so that he could see from his bedroom into the room in which his child's body was laid out, with tall candles standing round it. An old man had been engaged to keep watch over it, and sat beside the body murmuring prayers. After a few hours' sleep, the father had a dream that *his child was standing beside his bed, caught him by the arm and whispered to him reproachfully: 'Father, don't you see I'm burning?'* He woke up, noticed a bright glare of light from the next room, hurried into it and found that the old watchman had dropped off to sleep and that the wrappings and one of the arms of his beloved child's dead body had been burned by a lighted candle that had fallen on them.

The explanation of this moving dream is simple enough and, so my patient told me, was correctly given by the lecturer. The glare of light shone through the open door into the sleeping man's eyes and led him to the conclusion which he would have arrived at if he had been awake, namely that a candle had fallen over and set something alight in the neighbourhood of the body.

[1] [Some light has been thrown on the difficulties presented in the later sections of this chapter by Freud's early correspondence with Wilhelm Fliess (Freud, 1950a). Cf. the Editor's Introduction (p. xv ff.).]

It is even possible that he had felt some concern when he went to sleep as to whether the old man might not be incompetent to carry out his task.

Nor have I any changes to suggest in this interpretation except to add that the content of the dream must have been overdetermined and that the words spoken by the child must have been made up of words which he had actually spoken in his lifetime and which were connected with important events in the father's mind. For instance, '*I'm burning*' may have been spoken during the fever of the child's last illness, and '*Father, don't you see?*' may have been derived from some other highly emotional situation of which we are in ignorance.

But, having recognized that the dream was a process with a meaning, and that it can be inserted into the chain of the dreamer's psychical experiences, we may still wonder why it was that a dream occurred at all in such circumstances, when the most rapid possible awakening was called for. And here we shall observe that this dream, too, contained the fulfilment of a wish. The dead child behaved in the dream like a living one: he himself warned his father, came to his bed, and caught him by the arm, just as he had probably done on the occasion from the memory of which the first part of the child's words in the dream were derived. For the sake of the fulfilment of this wish the father prolonged his sleep by one moment. The dream was preferred to a waking reflection because it was able to show the child as once more alive. If the father had woken up first and then made the inference that led him to go into the next room, he would, as it were, have shortened his child's life by that moment of time.

There can be no doubt what the peculiar feature is which attracts our interest to this brief dream. Hitherto we have been principally concerned with the secret meaning of dreams and the method of discovering it and with the means employed by the dream-work for concealing it. The problems of dream-interpretation have hitherto occupied the centre of the picture. And now we come upon a dream which raises no problem of interpretation and the meaning of which is obvious, but which, as we see, nevertheless retains the essential characteristics that differentiate dreams so strikingly from waking life and consequently call for explanation. It is only after we have disposed of everything that has to do with the work of interpretation that we can begin to realize the incompleteness of our psychology of dreams.

But before starting off along this new path, it will be well to pause and look around, to see whether in the course of our journey up to this point we have overlooked anything of importance. For it must be clearly understood that the easy and agreeable portion of our journey lies behind us. Hitherto, unless I am greatly mistaken, all the paths along which we have travelled have led us towards the light—towards elucidation and fuller understanding. But as soon as we endeavour to penetrate more deeply into the mental process involved in dreaming, every path will end in darkness. There is no possibility of *explaining* dreams as a psychical process, since to explain a thing means to trace it back to something already known, and there is at the present time no established psychological knowledge under which we could subsume what the psychological examination of dreams enables us to infer as a basis for their explanation. On the contrary, we shall be obliged to set up a number of fresh hypotheses which touch tentatively upon the structure of the apparatus of the mind and upon the play of forces operating in it. We must be careful, however, not to pursue these hypotheses too far beyond their first logical links, or their value will be lost in uncertainties. Even if we make no false inferences and take all the logical possibilities into account, the probable incompleteness of our premises threatens to bring our calculation to a complete miscarriage. No conclusions upon the construction and working methods of the mental instrument can be arrived at or at least fully proved from even the most painstaking investigation of dreams or of any other mental function taken *in isolation*. To achieve this result, it will be necessary to correlate all the established implications derived from a comparative study of a whole series of such functions. Thus the psychological hypotheses to which we are led by an analysis of the processes of dreaming must be left, as it were, in suspense, until they can be related to the findings of other enquiries which seek to approach the kernel of the same problem from another angle.

THE FORGETTING OF DREAMS

I suggest, therefore, that we should first turn to a topic that raises a difficulty which we have not hitherto considered but which is nevertheless capable of cutting the ground from under all our efforts at interpreting dreams. It has been objected on more than one occasion that we have in fact no knowledge of the dreams that we set out to interpret, or, speaking more correctly, that we have no guarantee that we know them as they actually occurred. (See p. 45 ff.)

In the first place, what we remember of a dream and what we exercise our interpretative arts upon has been mutilated by the untrustworthiness of our memory, which seems quite especially incapable of retaining a dream and may well have lost precisely the most important parts of its content. It quite frequently happens that when we seek to turn our attention to one of our dreams we find ourselves regretting the fact that, though we dreamt far more, we can remember nothing but a single fragment which is itself recollected with peculiar uncertainty.

Secondly, there is every reason to suspect that our memory of dreams is not only fragmentary but positively inaccurate and falsified. On the one hand it may be doubted whether what we dreamt was really as disconnected and hazy as our recollection of it; and on the other hand it may also be doubted whether a dream was really as connected as it is in the account we give of it, whether in attempting to reproduce it we do not fill in what was never there, or what has been forgotten, with new and arbitrarily selected material, whether we do not add embellishments and trimmings and round it off so that there is no possibility of deciding what its original content may have been. Indeed one author, Spitta (1882, [338]),[1] goes to the point of suggesting that in so far as a dream shows any kind of order or coherence, these qualities are only introduced into it when we try to recall it to mind. [Cf. p. 47.] Thus there seems to be a

[1] [Added in text in 1914 and transferred to footnote in 1930:] So too Foucault [1906, 141 f.] and Tannery [1898]

danger that the very thing whose value we have undertaken to assess may slip completely through our fingers.

Hitherto in interpreting dreams we have disregarded such warnings. On the contrary, we have accepted it as being just as important to interpret the smallest, least conspicuous and most uncertain constituents of the content of dreams as those that are most clearly and certainly preserved. The dream of Irma's injection contained the phrase 'I *at once* called in Dr. M.' [p. 111]; and we assumed that even this detail would not have found its way into the dream unless it had had some particular origin. It was thus that we came upon the story of the unfortunate patient to whose bedside I had 'at once' called in my senior colleague. In the apparently absurd dream which treated the difference between 51 and 56 as a negligible quantity, the number 51 was mentioned several times. [See p. 435.] Instead of regarding this as a matter of course or as something indifferent, we inferred from it that there was a *second* line of thought in the latent content of the dream leading to the number 51; and along this track we arrived at my fears of 51 years being the limit of my life, in glaring contrast to the dream's dominant train of thought which was lavish in its boasts of a long life. In the '*Non vixit*' dream [p. 421 ff.] there was an inconspicuous interpolation which I overlooked at first: '*As P. failed to understand him, Fl. asked me*', etc. When the interpretation was held up, I went back to these words and it was they that led me on to the childhood phantasy which turned out to be an intermediate nodal point in the dream-thoughts. [See p. 483 f.] This was arrived at by way of the lines:

> Selten habt ihr mich *verstanden*,
> Selten auch verstand ich Euch,
> Nur wenn wir im *Kot* uns fander
> So verstanden wir uns gleich.[1]

Examples could be found in every analysis to show that precisely the most trivial elements of a dream are indispensable to its interpretation and that the work in hand is held up if attention is not paid to these elements until too late. We have

---

[1] [Literally: 'Rarely have you *understood* me, and rarely too have I understood you. Not until we both found ourselves in the *mud* did we promptly understand each other.' Heine, *Buch der Lieder*, 'Die Heimkehr', LXXVIII.]

attached no less importance in interpreting dreams to every shade of the form of words in which they were laid before us. And even when it happened that the text of the dream as we had it was meaningless or inadequate—as though the effort to give a correct account of it had been unsuccessful—we have taken this defect into account as well. In short, we have treated as Holy Writ what previous writers have regarded as an arbitrary improvisation, hurriedly patched together in the embarrassment of the moment. This contradiction stands in need of an explanation.

The explanation is in our favour, though without putting the other writers in the wrong. In the light of our newly-won understanding of the origin of dreams the contradiction disappears completely. It is true that we distort dreams in attempting to reproduce them; here we find at work once more the process which we have described as the secondary (and often ill-conceived) revision of the dream by the agency which carries out normal thinking [p. 488 ff.]. But this distortion is itself no more than a part of the revision to which the dream-thoughts are regularly subjected as a result of the dream-censorship. The other writers have at this point noticed or suspected the part of dream-distortion which operates manifestly; *we* are less interested, since we know that a much more far-reaching process of distortion, though a less obvious one, has already developed the dream out of the hidden dream-thoughts. The only mistake made by previous writers has been in supposing that the modification of the dream in the course of being remembered and put into words is an *arbitrary* one and cannot be further resolved and that it is therefore calculated to give us a misleading picture of the dream.[1] They have underestimated the extent to which psychical events are determined. There is nothing arbitrary about them. It can be shown quite generally that if an element is left undetermined by one train of thought, its determination is immediately effected by a second one. For instance, I may try to think of a number arbitrarily. But this is impossible: the number that occurs to me will be unambiguously and necessarily determined by thoughts of mine, though they may be

[1] [A misunderstanding in a contrary direction of the mportance of the text of dreams is discussed towards the end of Freud's paper on the technical uses of dream-interpretation in therapeutic analyses (1911*e*).]

remote from my immediate intention.[1] The modifications to which dreams are submitted under the editorship of waking life are just as little arbitrary. They are associatively linked to the material which they replace, and serve to show us the way to that material, which may in its turn be a substitute for something else.

In analysing the dreams of my patients I sometimes put this assertion to the following test, which has never failed me. If the first account given me by a patient of a dream is too hard to follow I ask him to repeat it. In doing so he rarely uses the same words. But the parts of the dream which he describes in different terms are by that fact revealed to me as the weak spot in the dream's disguise: they serve my purpose just as Hagen's was served by the embroidered mark on Siegfried's cloak.[2] That is the point at which the interpretation of the dream can be started. My request to the patient to repeat his account of the dream has warned him that I was proposing to take special pains in solving it; under pressure of the resistance, therefore, he hastily covers the weak spots in the dream's disguise by replacing any expressions that threaten to betray its meaning by other less revealing ones. In this way he draws my attention to the expression which he has dropped out. The trouble taken by the dreamer in preventing the solution of the dream gives me a basis for estimating the care with which its cloak has been woven.

Previous writers have had less justification in devoting so much space to the *doubt* with which our judgement receives accounts of dreams. For this doubt has no intellectual warrant. There is in general no guarantee of the correctness of our memory; and yet we yield to the compulsion to attach belief to its data far more often than is objectively justified. Doubt

---

[1] [*Footnote added* 1909:] See my *Psychopathology of Everyday Life* [1901*b*, Chapter XII(A), Nos. 2 to 7.—No. 2 relates to a letter written by Freud to Fliess on August 27, 1899 (Freud, 1950*a*, Letter 116), while he was correcting the proofs of the present volume, in which he prophesied that the book would contain 2,467 misprints. (See below, p. 532 *n*.)]

[2] [There was only one spot on Siegfried's body where he could be wounded. By a trick, Hagen persuaded Kriemhild, who alone knew where the spot was, to embroider a small cross on Siegfried's cloak at the vital point. It was there that Hagen later stabbed him. (*Nibelungenlied*, XV and XVI.)]

whether a dream or certain of its details have been correctly reported is once more a derivative of the dream-censorship, of resistance to the penetration of the dream-thoughts into consciousness.[1] This resistance has not been exhausted even by the displacements and substitutions it has brought about; it persists in the form of doubt attaching to the material which has been allowed through. We are especially inclined to misunderstand this doubt since it is careful never to attack the more intense elements of a dream but only the weak and indistinct ones. As we already know, however, a complete reversal of all psychical values takes place between the dream-thoughts and the dream [p. 330]. Distortion is only made possible by a withdrawal of psychical value; it habitually expresses itself by that means and is occasionally content to require nothing more. If, then, an indistinct element of a dream's content is in addition attacked by doubt, we have a sure indication that we are dealing with a comparatively direct derivative of one of the proscribed dream-thoughts. The state of things is what it was after some sweeping revolution in one of the republics of antiquity or the Renaissance. The noble and powerful families which had previously dominated the scene were sent into exile and all the high offices were filled by newcomers. Only the most impoverished and powerless members of the vanquished families, or their remote dependants, were allowed to remain in the city; and even so they did not enjoy full civic rights and were viewed with distrust. The distrust in this analogy corresponds to the doubt in the case we are considering. That is why in analysing a dream I insist that the whole scale of estimates of certainty shall be abandoned and that the faintest possibility that something of this or that sort may have occurred in the dream shall be treated as complete certainty. In tracing any element of a dream it will be found that unless this attitude is firmly adopted the analysis will come to a standstill. If any doubt is thrown upon the value of the element in question, the psychical result in the patient is that none of the involuntary ideas underlying that element comes into his head. This result is not a self-evident one. It would not make nonsense if someone were to say: 'I don't know for certain whether such and such a thing came into the dream, but here is what occurs to me in connection with it.' But in fact

[1] [For the same mechanism of doubt in cases of hysteria see a passage near the beginning of Part I of the case history of 'Dora' (1905*e*).]

no one ever does say this; and it is precisely the fact that doubt produces this interrupting effect upon an analysis that reveals it as a derivative and tool of psychical resistance. Psychoanalysis is justly suspicious. One of its rules is that *whatever interrupts the progress of analytic work is a resistance*.[1]

The *forgetting* of dreams, too, remains inexplicable unless the power of the psychical censorship is taken into account. In a number of cases the feeling of having dreamt a great deal during the night and of only having retained a little of it may in fact have some other meaning, such as that the dream-work has been perceptibly proceeding all through the night but has only left a short dream behind. [Cf. pp. 279 f., 489, and 576.] It is no doubt true that we forget dreams more and more as time passes after waking; we often forget them in spite of the most painstaking efforts to recall them. But I am of opinion that the extent of this forgetting is as a rule over-estimated; and there is a similar over-estimation of the extent to which the gaps in a dream limit our knowledge of it. It is often possible by means of analysis to restore all that has been lost by the forgetting of the dream's content; at least, in quite a number of cases one can reconstruct from a single remaining fragment not, it is true, the dream—which is in any case a matter of no importance—but all the dream-thoughts. This demands a certain amount of attention and self-discipline in carrying out the analysis; that is all—but it shows that there was no lack of a hostile [i.e. resistant] purpose at work in the forgetting of the dream.[2]

---

[1] [*Footnote added* 1925:] The proposition laid down in these peremptory terms—'whatever interrupts the progress of analytic work is a resistance'—is easily open to misunderstanding. It is of course only to be taken as a technical rule, as a warning to analysts. It cannot be disputed that in the course of an analysis various events may occur the responsibility for which cannot be laid upon the patient's intentions. His father may die without his having murdered him; or a war may break out which brings the analysis to an end. But behind its obvious exaggeration the proposition is asserting something both true and new. Even if the interrupting event is a real one and independent of the patient, it often depends on him how great an interruption it causes; and resistance shows itself unmistakably in the readiness with which he accepts an occurrence of this kind or the exaggerated use which he makes of it.

[2] [*Footnote added* 1919:] I may quote the following dream from my *Introductory Lectures* [Freud, 1916–17, Lecture VII] as an example of the meaning of doubt and uncertainty in a dream and of its content being

Convincing evidence of the fact that the forgetting of dreams is tendentious and serves the purpose of resistance[1] is afforded when it is possible to observe in analyses a preliminary stage of forgetting. It not infrequently happens that in the middle of the work of interpretation an omitted portion of the dream comes to light and is described as having been forgotten till that moment. Now a part of a dream that has been rescued from oblivion in this way is invariably the most important part; it always lies on the shortest road to the dream's solution and has for that reason at the same time shrunk down to a single element; in spite of this the dream was successfully analysed after a short delay:

'A sceptical woman patient had a longish dream in the course of which some people told her about my book on jokes and praised it highly. Something came in then about a *"channel"*, *perhaps it was another book that mentioned a channel, or something else about a channel . . . she didn't know . . . it was all so indistinct.*

'No doubt you will be inclined to expect that the element "channel", since it was so indistinct, would be inaccessible to interpretation. You are right in suspecting a difficulty; but the difficulty did not arise from the indistinctness: both the difficulty and the indistinctness arose from another cause. Nothing occurred to the dreamer in connection with "channel", and *I* could of course throw no light on it. A little later—it was the next day, in point of fact—she told me that she had thought of something that *might* have something to do with it. It was a joke, too,— a joke she had heard. On the steamer between Dover and Calais a well-known author fell into conversation with an Englishman. The latter had occasion to quote the phrase: "Du sublime au ridicule il n'y a qu'un pas. [It is only a step from the sublime to the ridiculous.]" Yes, replied the author, *"le Pas de Calais"*—meaning that he thought France sublime and England ridiculous. But the *Pas de Calais* is a channel—the English Channel. You will ask whether I think this had anything to do with the dream. Certainly I think so; and it provides the solution of the puzzling element of the dream. Can you doubt that this joke was already present before the dream occurred, as the unconscious thought behind the element "channel"? Can you suppose that it was introduced as a subsequent invention? The association betrayed the scepticism which lay concealed behind the patient's ostensible admiration; and her resistance against revealing this was no doubt the common cause both of her delay in producing the association and of the indistinctness of the dream-element concerned. Consider the relation of the dream-element to its unconscious background: it was, as it were, a fragment of that background, an allusion to it, but it was made quite incomprehensible by being isolated.'

[1] On the purposes of forgetting in general see my short paper on the psychical mechanism of forgetting (Freud, 1898*b*). [*Added* 1909:] Later included [with modifications] as the first chapter in my *Psychopathology of Everyday Life* (Freud, 1901*b*).

been exposed to resistance more than any other part. Among the specimen dreams scattered through this volume, there is one in which a part of its content was added like this as an after-thought.[1] It is the travel dream in which I revenged myself on two disagreeable fellow-travellers and which I had to leave almost uninterpreted on account of its gross indecency. [See p. 455 ff.] The omitted portion ran as follows: '*I said* [in English], *referring to one of Schiller's works: "It is from . . ." but, noticing the mistake, I corrected myself: "It is by . . ." "Yes", the man commented to his sister, "he said that right."* '[2]

Self-corrections in dreams, which seem so marvellous to some writers, need not occupy our attention. I will indicate instead the recollection which served as the model for my verbal error in this dream. When I was nineteen[3] years old I visited England for the first time and spent a whole day on the shore of the Irish Sea. I naturally revelled in the opportunity of collecting the marine animals left behind by the tide and I was occupied with a starfish—the words '*Hollthurn*' and '*holothurians* [sea-slugs]' occurred at the beginning of the dream—when a charming little girl came up to me and said: 'Is it a starfish? Is it alive?' 'Yes,' I replied, 'he is alive', and at once, embarrassed at my mistake, repeated the sentence correctly. The dream replaced the verbal error which I then made by another into which a German is equally liable to fall. '*Das Buch ist von Schiller*' should be translated not with a 'from' but with a 'by'. After all that we have heard of the purposes of the dream-work and its reckless choice of methods for attaining them, we shall not be surprised to hear that it effected this replacement because of the magnificent piece of condensation that was made possible by the identity of sound of the English 'from' and the German adjective '*fromm*' ['pious']. But how did my blameless memory of the sea-shore come to be in the dream? It served as the most innocent possible example of my using a word indicating gender

---

[1] [Another instance will be found on p. 155 *n*. Yet another occurs in the analysis of Dora's second dream (Freud, 1905*e*, Section III).]

[2] [*Footnote added* 1914:] Corrections such as this in the usages of foreign languages are not infrequent in dreams but are more often attributed to other people. Maury (1878, 143) once dreamt, at a time when he was learning English, that, in telling someone that he had visited him the day before, he used the words 'I called for you yesterday'. Whereupon the other answered correctly: 'You should have said "I called *on* you yesterday".'   [3] [See p. 714.]

or sex in the wrong place—of my bringing in sex (the word 'he') where it did not belong. This, incidentally, was one of the keys to the solution of the dream. No one who has heard, furthermore, the origin attributed to the title of Clerk-Maxwell's 'Matter and Motion' [mentioned in the dream, p. 456] will have any difficulty in filling in the gaps: Molière's 'Le Malade Imaginaire'—'La matière est-elle laudable?'[1]—A motion of the bowels.

Moreover I am in a position to offer an ocular demonstration of the fact that the forgetting of dreams is to a great extent a product of resistance. One of my patients will tell me he has had a dream but has forgotten every trace of it: it is therefore just as though it had never happened. We proceed with our work. I come up against a resistance; I therefore explain something to the patient and help him by encouragement and pressure to come to terms with some disagreeable thought. Hardly have I succeeded in this than he exclaims: 'Now I remember what it was I dreamt.' The same resistance which interfered with our work that day also made him forget the dream. By overcoming this resistance I have recalled the dream to his memory.

In just the same way, when a patient reaches some particular point in his work, he may be able to remember a dream which he had dreamt three or four or even more days before and which had hitherto remained forgotten.[2]

Psycho-analytic experience[3] has provided us with yet another proof that the forgetting of dreams depends far more upon resistance than upon the fact, stressed by the authorities, that the waking and sleeping states are alien to each other [p. 45]. It not infrequently happens to me, as well as to other analysts and to patients under treatment, that, having been woken up, as one might say, by a dream, I immediately afterwards, and in full possession of my intellectual powers, set about interpreting it. In such cases I have often refused to rest till I have arrived at a complete understanding of the dream; yet it has

[1] ['Is the matter laudable?'—Old medical terminology for 'Is the excretion healthy?'—The next phrase is in English in the original.]

[2] [Footnote added 1914:] Ernest Jones has described [1912b] an analogous case which often occurs: while a dream is being analysed the patient may recollect a second one which was dreamt during the same night but whose very existence had not been suspected.

[3] [This paragraph and the next were added in 1911.]

sometimes been my experience that after finally waking up in the morning I have entirely forgotten both my interpretative activity and the content of the dream, though knowing that I have had a dream and interpreted it.[1] It happens far more often that the dream draws the findings of my interpretative activity back with it into oblivion than that my intellectual activity succeeds in preserving the dream in my memory. Yet there is no such psychical gulf between my interpretative activity and my waking thoughts as the authorities suppose to account for the forgetting of dreams.

Morton Prince (1910 [141]) has objected to my explanation of the forgetting of dreams on the ground that that forgetting is only a special case of the amnesia attaching to dissociated mental states, that it is impossible to extend my explanation of this special amnesia to other types and that my explanation is consequently devoid of value even for its immediate purpose. His readers are thus reminded that in the course of all his descriptions of these dissociated states he has never attempted to discover a dynamic explanation of such phenomena. If he had, he would inevitably have found that repression (or, more precisely, the resistance created by it) is the cause both of the dissociations and of the amnesia attaching to their psychical content.

An observation which I have been able to make in the course of preparing this manuscript has shown me that dreams are no more forgotten than other mental acts and can be compared, by no means to their disadvantage, with other mental functions in respect of their retention in the memory. I had kept records of a large number of my own dreams which for one reason or another I had not been able to interpret completely at the time or had left entirely uninterpreted. And now, between one and two years later, I have attempted to interpret some of them for the purpose of obtaining more material in illustration of my views. These attempts have been successful in every instance; indeed the interpretation may be said to have proceeded more easily after this long interval than it did at the time when the dream was a recent experience. A possible explanation of this is that in the meantime I have overcome some of the internal resistances which previously obstructed me. When making these

[1] [Cf. Postscript to the 'Analysis of a Phobia in a Five-Year-Old Boy' (Freud, 1922c).]

subsequent interpretations I have compared the dream-thoughts that I elicited at the time of the dream with the present, usually far more copious, yield, and I have always found that the old ones are included among the new. My astonishment at this was quickly halted by the reflection that I had long been in the habit of getting my patients, who sometimes tell me dreams dating from earlier years, to interpret them—by the same procedure and with the same success—as though they had dreamt them the night before. When I come to discuss anxiety-dreams I shall give two examples of postponed interpretations like these. [See p. 583 ff.] I was led into making my first experiment of this kind by the justifiable expectation that in this as in other respects dreams would behave like neurotic symptoms. When I treat a psychoneurotic—a hysteric, let us say—by psycho-analysis, I am obliged to arrive at an explanation for the earliest and long since vanished symptoms of his illness no less than for the contemporary ones which brought him to me for treatment; and I actually find the earlier problem easier to solve than the immediate one. As long ago as in 1895 I was able to give an explanation in *Studies on Hysteria* [Breuer and Freud, 1895 (Frau Cäcilie M., in Case History V)] of the first hysterical attack which a woman of over forty had had in her fifteenth year.[1]

And here I will mention a number of further, somewhat disconnected, points on the subject of interpreting dreams, which may perhaps help to give readers their bearings should they feel inclined to check my statements by subsequent work upon their own dreams.

No one should expect that an interpretation of his dreams will fall into his lap like manna from the skies. Practice is needed even for perceiving endoptic phenomena or other sensa-

---

[1] [Added in the text in 1919 and transferred to a footnote in 1930:] Dreams which occur in the earliest years of childhood and are retained in the memory for dozens of years, often with complete sensory vividness, are almost always of great importance in enabling us to understand the history of the subject's mental development and of his neurosis. Analysis of such dreams protects the physician from errors and uncertainties which may lead, among other things, to theoretical confusion. [The example of the 'Wolf Man's' dream was no doubt especially in Freud's mind (1918b).]

tions from which our attention is normally withheld; and this is so even though there is no psychical motive fighting against such perceptions. It is decidedly more difficult to get hold of 'involuntary ideas'. Anyone who seeks to do so must familiarize himself with the expectations raised in the present volume and must, in accordance with the rules laid down in it, endeavour during the work to refrain from any criticism, any *parti pris*, and any emotional or intellectual bias. He must bear in mind Claude Bernard's[1] advice to experimenters in a physiological laboratory: 'travailler comme une bête'—he must work, that is, with as much persistence as an animal and with as much disregard of the result. If this advice is followed, the task will no longer be a hard one.

The interpretation of a dream cannot always be accomplished at a single sitting. When we have followed a chain of associations, it not infrequently happens that we feel our capacity exhausted; nothing more is to be learnt from the dream that day. The wisest plan then is to break off and resume our work another day: another part of the dream's content may then attract our attention and give us access to another stratum of dream-thoughts. This procedure might be described as 'fractional' dream-interpretation.

It is only with the greatest difficulty that the beginner in the business of interpreting dreams can be persuaded that his task is not at an end when he has a complete interpretation in his hands—an interpretation which makes sense, is coherent and throws light upon every element of the dream's content. For the same dream may perhaps have another interpretation as well, an 'over-interpretation', which has escaped him. It is, indeed, not easy to form any conception of the abundance of the unconscious trains of thought, all striving to find expression, which are active in our minds. Nor is it easy to credit the skill shown by the dream-work in always hitting upon forms of expression that can bear several meanings—like the Little Tailor in the fairy story who hit seven flies at a blow. My readers will always be inclined to accuse me of introducing an unnecessary amount of ingenuity into my interpretations; but actual experience would teach them better. [See p. 297 f. *n*.]

On the other hand,[2] I cannot confirm the opinion, first stated

---

[1] [The French physiologist (1813–78).]
[2] [This paragraph was added in 1919.]

by Silberer [e.g. 1914, Part II, Section 5], that all dreams (or many dreams, or certain classes of dreams) require two different interpretations, which are even stated to bear a fixed relation to each other. One of these interpretations, which Silberer calls the 'psycho-analytic' one, is said to give the dream some meaning or other, usually of an infantile-sexual kind; the other and more important interpretation, to which he gives the name of 'anagogic', is said to reveal the more serious thoughts, often of profound import, which the dream-work has taken as its material. Silberer has not given evidence in support of this opinion by reporting a series of dreams analysed in the two directions. And I must object that the alleged fact is non-existent. In spite of what he says, the majority of dreams require no 'over-interpretation' and, more particularly, are insusceptible to an anagogic interpretation. As in the case of many other theories put forward in recent years, it is impossible to overlook the fact that Silberer's views are influenced to some extent by a purpose which seeks to disguise the fundamental circumstances in which dreams are formed and to divert interest from their instinctual roots. In a certain number of cases I have been able to confirm Silberer's statements. Analysis showed that in such cases the dream-work found itself faced with the problem of transforming into a dream a series of highly abstract thoughts from waking life which were incapable of being given any direct representation. It endeavoured to solve the problem by getting hold of another group of intellectual material, somewhat loosely related (often in a manner which might be described as 'allegorical') to the abstract thoughts, and at the same time capable of being represented with fewer difficulties. The *abstract* interpretation of a dream that has arisen in this way is given by the dreamer without any difficulty; the *correct* interpretation of the material that has been interpolated must be looked for by the technical methods which are now familiar to us.[1]

The question whether it is possible to interpret *every* dream must be answered in the negative.[2] It must not be forgotten

[1] [Freud also discussed this point in a long footnote in his paper 'A Metapsychological Supplement to the Theory of Dreams' (1917*d*) and towards the end of his 'Dreams and Telepathy' (1922*a*).]

[2] [This question is considered at greater length in Freud, 1925*i*, Section A.]

that in interpreting a dream we are opposed by the psychical forces which were responsible for its distortion. It is thus a question of relative strength whether our intellectual interest, our capacity for self-discipline, our psychological knowledge and our practice in interpreting dreams enable us to master our internal resistances. It is always possible to go *some* distance: far enough, at all events, to convince ourselves that the dream is a structure with a meaning, and as a rule far enough to get a glimpse of what that meaning is. Quite often an immediately succeeding dream allows us to confirm and carry further the interpretation we have tentatively adopted for its predecessor. A whole series of dreams, continuing over a period of weeks or months, is often based upon common ground and must accordingly be interpreted in connection with one another. [Cf. pp. 193 and 362.] In the case of two consecutive dreams it can often be observed that one takes as its central point something that is only on the periphery of the other and *vice versa*, so that their interpretations too are mutually complementary. I have already given instances which show that different dreams dreamt on the same night are, as a quite general rule, to be treated in their interpretation as a single whole. [See p. 333 f.]

There is often a passage in even the most thoroughly interpreted dream which has to be left obscure; this is because we become aware during the work of interpretation that at that point there is a tangle of dream-thoughts which cannot be unravelled and which moreover adds nothing to our knowledge of the content of the dream. This is the dream's navel, the spot where it reaches down into the unknown. [Cf. p. 111 *n.*] The dream-thoughts to which we are led by interpretation cannot, from the nature of things, have any definite endings; they are bound to branch out in every direction into the intricate network of our world of thought. It is at some point where this meshwork is particularly close that the dream-wish grows up, like a mushroom out of its mycelium.

But we must return to the facts concerning the forgetting of dreams, for we have failed to draw one important conclusion from them. We have seen that waking life shows an unmistakable inclination to forget any dream that has been formed in the course of the night—whether as a whole directly after waking, or bit by bit in the course of the day; and we have recognized that the agent chiefly responsible for this forgetting is the mental resistance to the dream which has already done what it could against it during the night. But if all this is so, the question arises how it comes about that a dream can be formed at all in the face of this resistance. Let us take the most extreme case, in which waking life has got rid of a dream as though it had never occurred. A consideration of the interplay of psychical forces in this case must lead us to infer that the dream would in fact not have occurred at all if the resistance had been as strong during the night as during the day. We must conclude that during the night the resistance loses some of its power, though we know it does not lose the whole of it, since we have shown the part it plays in the formation of dreams as a distorting agent. But we are driven to suppose that its power may be diminished at night and that this makes the formation of dreams possible. This makes it easy to understand how, having regained its full strength at the moment of waking, it at once proceeds to get rid of what it was obliged to permit while it was weak. Descriptive psychology tells us that the principal *sine qua non* for the formation of dreams is that the mind shall be in a state of sleep; and we are now able to explain this fact: *the state of sleep makes the formation of dreams possible because it reduces the power of the endopsychic censorship.*

It is no doubt tempting to regard this as the only possible inference that can be drawn from the facts of the forgetting of dreams, and to make it the basis for further conclusions as to the conditions of energy prevailing during sleeping and waking. For the moment, however, we will stop at this point. When we have entered a little more deeply into the psychology of dreams we shall find that the factors making possible the formation of dreams can be viewed in another way as well. It may be that the resistance against the dream-thoughts becoming conscious can be evaded without any reduction having taken place in its power. And it seems a plausible idea that *both* of the two factors favouring the formation of dreams—the reduction and the evasion of the resistance—are simultaneously made possible by the state of sleep. I will break off here, though I shall pick up the argument again presently. [Cf. p. 573 f.]

There is another set of objections to our method of interpreting dreams with which we must now deal. Our procedure consists in abandoning all those purposive ideas which normally govern our reflections, in focusing our attention on a single element of the dream and in then taking note of whatever involuntary thoughts may occur to us in connection with it. We then take the next portion of the dream and repeat the process with *it*. We allow ourselves to be led on by our thoughts regardless of the direction in which they carry us and drift on in this way from one thing to another. But we cherish a confident belief that in the end, without any active intervention on our part, we shall arrive at the dream-thoughts from which the dream originated.

Our critics argue against this along the following lines. There is nothing wonderful in the fact that a single element of the dream should lead us *somewhere*; every idea can be associated with *something*. What *is* remarkable is that such an aimless and arbitrary train of thought should happen to bring us to the dream-thoughts. The probability is that we are deceiving ourselves. We follow a chain of associations from one element, till, for one reason or another, it seems to break off. If we then take up a second element, it is only to be expected that the originally unrestricted character of our associations will be narrowed. For we still have the earlier chain of thoughts in our memory, and for that reason, in analysing the second dream-idea, we are more likely to hit upon associations which have something in common with associations from the first chain. We then delude ourselves into thinking that we have discovered a thought which is a connecting point between two elements of the dream. Since we give ourselves complete liberty to connect thoughts as we please and since in fact the only transitions from one idea to another which we exclude are those which operate in normal thinking, we shall find no difficulty in the long run in concocting out of a number of 'intermediate thoughts' something which we describe as the dream-thoughts and which—though without any guarantee, since we have no other knowledge of what the dream-thoughts are—we allege to be the psychical substitute for the dream. But the whole thing is completely arbitrary; we are merely exploiting chance connections in a manner which gives an effect of ingenuity. In this way anyone who cares to take such useless pains can worry out any interpretation he pleases from any dream.

If we were in fact met by objections such as these, we might defend ourselves by appealing to the impression made by our interpretations, to the surprising connections with other elements of the dream which emerge in the course of our pursuing a single one of its ideas, and to the improbability that anything which gives such an exhaustive account of the dream could have been arrived at except by following up psychical connections which had already been laid down. We might also point out in our defence that our procedure in interpreting dreams is identical with the procedure by which we resolve hysterical symptoms; and there the correctness of our method is warranted by the coincident emergence and disappearance of the symptoms, or, to use a simile, the assertions made in the text are borne out by the accompanying illustrations. But we have no reason for evading the problem of how it is possible to reach a pre-existing goal by following the drift of an arbitrary and purposeless chain of thoughts; since, though we may not be able to solve the problem, we can completely cut the ground from under it.

For it is demonstrably untrue that we are being carried along a purposeless stream of ideas when, in the process of interpreting a dream, we abandon reflection and allow involuntary ideas to emerge. It can be shown that all that we can ever get rid of are purposive ideas that are *known* to us; as soon as we have done this, *unknown*—or, as we inaccurately say, 'unconscious'—purposive ideas take charge and thereafter determine the course of the involuntary ideas. No influence that we can bring to bear upon our mental processes can ever enable us to think without purposive ideas; nor am I aware of any states of psychical confusion which can do so.[1] Psychiatrists have been

---

[1] [*Footnote added* 1914:] It was not until later that my attention was drawn to the fact that Eduard von Hartmann takes the same view on this important matter of psychology: 'In discussing the part played by the unconscious in artistic creation, Eduard von Hartmann (1890, **1**, Section B, Chapter V) made a clear statement of the law in accordance with which the association of ideas is governed by unconscious purposive ideas, though he was unaware of the scope of the law. He set out to prove that "every combination of sensuous presentations, when it is not left purely to chance, but is led to a definite end, requires the help of the Unconscious" (ibid., **1**, 245; English translation, 1884, **1**, 283], and that the part played by conscious interest is to stimulate the unconscious to select the most appropriate idea among the countless possible ones. It is the unconscious which makes the appropriate selection of a purpose for the interest and this "holds good of the association of ideas in abstract

far too ready in this respect to abandon their belief in the connectedness of psychical processes. I know for a fact that trains of thought without purposive ideas no more occur in hysteria and paranoia than they do in the formation or resolution of dreams. It may be that they do not occur in any of the endogenous psychical disorders. Even the deliria of confusional states may have a meaning, if we are to accept Leuret's brilliant suggestion [1834, 131] that they are only unintelligible to us owing to the gaps in them. I myself have formed the same opinion when I have had the opportunity of observing them. Deliria are the work of a censorship which no longer takes the trouble to conceal its operation; instead of collaborating in producing a new version that shall be unobjectionable, it ruthlessly deletes whatever it disapproves of, so that what remains becomes quite disconnected. This censorship acts exactly like the censorship of newspapers at the Russian frontier, which allows foreign journals to fall into the hands of the readers whom it is its business to protect only after a quantity of passages have been blacked out.

It may be that free play of ideas with a fortuitous chain of

thinking as well as in sensuous imagining and artistic combination" and in the production of jokes [ibid., 1, 247; English translation, 1, 285 f.]. For this reason a limitation of the association of ideas to an exciting idea and an excited idea (in the sense of a pure association psychology) cannot be upheld. Such a limitation could be justified "only if there are conditions in human life in which man is free not only from every conscious purpose, but also from the sway or co-operation of every unconscious interest, every passing mood. This is, however, a condition hardly ever occurring, for even if one in appearance completely abandons his train of thought to accident, or if one abandons oneself entirely to the involuntary dreams of fancy, yet always other leading interests, dominant feelings and moods prevail at one time rather than at another, and these will always exert an influence on the association of ideas." [Ibid., 1, 246; English translation, 1, 284.] "In semi-conscious dreams always only such ideas as correspond to the main [unconscious] interest of the moment occur." [Loc. cit.] The emphasis thus laid upon the influence of feelings and moods on the free sequence of thoughts makes it possible to justify the methodological procedure of psycho-analysis completely from the standpoint of Hartmann's psychology.' (Pohorilles, 1913.)—Du Prel (1885, 107) refers to the fact that after we have vainly tried to recall a name, it often comes into our heads again suddenly and without any warning. He concludes from this that unconscious but none the less purposeful thinking has taken place and that its result has suddenly entered consciousness.

associations is to be found in destructive organic cerebral processes; what is regarded as such in the psychoneuroses can always be explained as an effect of the censorship's influence upon a train of thought which has been pushed into the foreground by purposive ideas that have remained hidden.[1] It has been regarded as an unfailing sign of an association being uninfluenced by purposive ideas if the associations (or images) in question seem to be interrelated in what is described as a 'superficial' manner—by assonance, verbal ambiguity, temporal coincidence without connection in meaning, or by any association of the kind that we allow in jokes or in play upon words. This characteristic is present in the chains of thought which lead from the elements of a dream to the intermediate thoughts and from these to the dream-thoughts proper; we have seen instances of this—not without astonishment—in many dream analyses. No connection was too loose, no joke too bad, to serve as a bridge from one thought to another. But the true explanation of this easy-going state of things is soon found. *Whenever one psychical element is linked with another by an objectionable or superficial association, there is also a legitimate and deeper link between them which is subjected to the resistance of the censorship.*[2]

The real reason for the prevalence of superficial associations is not the abandonment of purposive ideas but the pressure of the censorship. Superficial associations replace deep ones if the censorship makes the normal connecting paths impassable. We may picture, by way of analogy, a mountain region, where some general interruption of traffic (owing to floods, for instance) has blocked the main, major roads, but where communications are still maintained over inconvenient and steep footpaths normally used only by the hunter.

Two cases may here be distinguished, though in essence they are the same. In the first of these, the censorship is directed only against the *connection* between two thoughts, which are unobjectionable separately. If so, the two thoughts will enter consciousness in succession; the connection between them will

[1] [*Footnote added* 1909:] This assertion has received striking confirmation from C. G. Jung's analyses in cases of dementia praecox. (Jung, 1907.)

[2] [Everywhere else in this work Freud speaks of 'the censorship of the resistance'. A later clarification of the relation between the concepts of 'resistance' and 'censorship' will be found in Lecture XXIX of the *New Introductory Lectures* (1933a).]

remain concealed, but, instead, a superficial link between them will occur to us, of which we should otherwise never have thought. This link is usually attached to some part of the complex of ideas quite other than that on which the suppressed and essential connection is based. The second case is where the two thoughts are in themselves subject to censorship on account of their content. If so, neither of them appears in its true shape but only in a modified one which replaces it; and the two replacing thoughts are chosen in such a way that they have a superficial association that repeats the essential connection which relates the two thoughts that have been replaced. *In both these cases the pressure of the censorship has resulted in a displacement from a normal and serious association to a superficial and apparently absurd one.*

Since we are aware that displacements of this kind occur, we have no hesitation when we are interpreting dreams in relying upon superficial associations as much as upon others.[1]

In the psycho-analysis of neuroses the fullest use is made of these two theorems—that, when conscious purposive ideas are abandoned, concealed purposive ideas assume control of the current of ideas, and that superficial associations are only substitutes by displacement for suppressed deeper ones. Indeed, these theorems have become basic pillars of psycho-analytic technique. When I instruct a patient to abandon reflection of any kind and to tell me whatever comes into his head, I am relying firmly on the presumption that he will not be able to abandon the purposive ideas inherent in the treatment and I feel justified in inferring that what seem to be the most innocent and arbitrary things which he tells me are in fact related to his illness. There is another purposive idea of which the patient

---

[1] The same considerations apply equally, of course, to cases in which the superficial associations appear openly in the content of the dream, as, for instance, in the two dreams of Maury's quoted above on page 59. (*Pèlerinage — Pelletier — pelle; kilomètre — kilogramme — Gilolo — Lobelia —Lopez—lotto.*) My work with neurotic patients has taught me the nature of the memories of which this is a favourite method of representation. They are occasions on which the subject has turned over the pages of encyclopaedias or dictionaries in order (like most people at the inquisitive age of puberty) to satisfy their craving for an answer to the riddles of sex.—[An example of this will be found in the analysis of 'Dora's' second dream (Freud, 1905e, Section III).]

has no suspicion—one relating to myself. The full estimate of the importance of these two theorems, as well as more detailed information about them, fall within the province of an account of the technique of psycho-analysis. Here, then, we have reached one of the frontier posts at which, in accordance with our programme, we must drop the subject of dream-interpretation.[1]

There is one true conclusion that we may glean from these objections, namely that we need not suppose that every association that occurs during the work of interpretation had a place in the dream-work during the night. [Cf. pp. 280 and 311.] It is true that in carrying out the interpretation in the waking state we follow a path which leads back from the elements of the dream to the dream-thoughts and that the dream-work followed one in the contrary direction. But it is highly improbable that these paths are passable both ways. It appears, rather, that in the daytime we drive shafts which follow along fresh chains of thought and that these shafts make contact with the intermediate thoughts and the dream-thoughts now at one point and now at another. We can see how in this manner fresh daytime material inserts itself into the interpretative chains. It is probable, too, that the increase in resistance that has set in since the night makes new and more devious detours necessary. The number and nature of the collaterals [see p. 311 n.] that we spin in this way during the day is of no psychological importance whatever, so long as they lead us to the dream-thoughts of which we are in search.

[1] [Footnote added 1909:] These two theorems, which sounded most unplausible at the time they were made, have since been experimentally employed and confirmed by Jung and his pupils in their studies in word-association. [Jung, 1906.—A most interesting argument on the allied topic of the validity of chains of association starting from numbers selected 'by chance' (see above, p. 514 f.) is developed by Freud in the long footnote added in 1920 to Chapter XII (A, No. 7) of The Psychopathology of Everyday Life (1901b).]

REGRESSION

Having now repelled the objections that have been raised against us, or having at least indicated where our defensive weapons lie, we must no longer postpone the task of setting about the psychological investigations for which we have so long been arming ourselves. Let us summarize the principal findings of our enquiry so far as it has gone. Dreams are psychical acts of as much significance as any others; their motive force is in every instance a wish seeking fulfilment; the fact of their not being recognizable as wishes and their many peculiarities and absurdities are due to the influence of the psychical censorship to which they have been subjected during the process of their formation; apart from the necessity of evading this censorship, other factors which have contributed to their formation are a necessity for the condensation of their psychical material, a regard for the possibility of its being represented in sensory images and—though not invariably—a demand that the structure of the dream shall have a rational and intelligible exterior. Each of these propositions opens a way to fresh psychological postulates and speculations; the mutual relation between the wish which is the dream's motive force and the four conditions to which the dream's formation is subject, as well as the interrelations between the latter, require to be investigated; and the place of dreams in the nexus of mental life has to be assigned.

It was with a view to reminding us of the problems which have still to be solved that I opened the present chapter with an account of a dream. There was no difficulty in interpreting that dream—the dream of the burning child—even though its interpretation was not given fully in our sense. I raised the question of why the dreamer dreamt it at all instead of waking up, and recognized that one of his motives was a wish to represent his child as still alive. Our further discussions will show us that yet another wish also played a part. [See below, pp. 570-1.] Thus it was in the first instance for the sake of fulfilling a wish that the process of thought during sleep was transformed into a dream.

If we eliminate the wish-fulfilment, we shall see that only one feature is left to distinguish the two forms of psychical event. The dream-thought would have run: 'I see a glare coming from the room where the dead body is lying. Perhaps a candle has fallen over and my child may be burning.' The dream repeated these reflections unaltered, but it represented them in a situation which was actually present and which could be perceived through the senses like a waking experience. Here we have the most general and the most striking psychological characteristic of the process of dreaming: a thought, and as a rule a thought of something that is wished, is objectified in the dream, is represented as a scene, or, as it seems to us, is experienced.

How, then, are we to explain this characteristic peculiarity of the dream-work, or, to put the question more modestly, how are we to find a place for it in the nexus of psychical processes?

If we look into the matter more closely we shall observe that two almost independent features stand out as characteristic of the form taken by this dream. One is the fact that the thought is represented as an immediate situation with the 'perhaps' omitted, and the other is the fact that the thought is transformed into visual images and speech.

In this particular dream the change made in the thoughts by the conversion of the expectation expressed by them into the present tense may not seem particularly striking. This is because of what can only be described as the unusually subordinate part played in this dream by wish-fulfilment. Consider instead another one, in which the dream-wish was not detached from the waking thoughts that were carried over into sleep—for instance, the dream of Irma's injection [p. 106 ff.]. There the dream-thought that was represented was in the optative: 'If only Otto were responsible for Irma's illness!' The dream repressed the optative and replaced it by a straightforward present: 'Yes, Otto is responsible for Irma's illness.' This, then, is the first of the transformations which is brought about in the dream-thoughts even by a distortionless dream. We need not linger long over this first peculiarity of dreams. We can deal with it by drawing attention to conscious phantasies—to day-dreams—which treat their ideational content in just the same manner.

While Daudet's Monsieur Joyeuse[1] was wandering, out of work, through the streets of Paris (though his daughters believed that he had a job and was sitting in an office), he was dreaming of developments that might bring him influential help and lead to his finding employment—and he was dreaming in the present tense. Thus dreams make use of the present tense in the same manner and by the same right as day-dreams. The present tense is the one in which wishes are represented as fulfilled.

But dreams differ from day-dreams in their second characteristic: namely, in the fact of their ideational content being transformed from thoughts into sensory images, to which belief is attached and which appear to be experienced. I must add at once that not every dream exhibits this transformation from idea into sensory image. There are dreams which consist only of thoughts but which cannot on that account be denied the essential nature of dreams. My 'Autodidasker' dream [p. 298 ff.] was of that kind; it included scarcely more sensory elements than if I had thought its content in the daytime. And in every dream of any considerable length there are elements which have not, like the rest, been given a sensory form, but which are simply thought or known, in the kind of way in which we are accustomed to think or know things in waking life. It should also be remembered here that it is not only in dreams that such transformations of ideas into sensory images occur: they are also found in hallucinations and visions, which may appear as independent entities, so to say, in health or as symptoms in the psychoneuroses. In short, the relation which we are examining now is not in any respect an exclusive one. Nevertheless it remains true that this characteristic of dreams, when it is present, strikes us as being their most notable one; so that it would be impossible for us to imagine the dream-world without it. But in order to arrive at an understanding of it we must embark upon a discussion that will take us far afield.

As the starting-point for our enquiry, I should like to pick out one from among many remarks made upon the theory of dreaming by those who have written on the subject. In the course of a

[1] [In *Le Nabab* (cf. p. 491). A slip made by Freud over this name in his first draft of this sentence is discussed by him in his *Psychopathology of Everyday Life* (1901b), Chapter VII, towards the end of Section A.]

short discussion on the topic of dreams, the great Fechner (1889, **2**, 520–1) puts forward the idea that *the scene of action of dreams is different from that of waking ideational life.* [Cf. above, p. 48.] This is the only hypothesis that makes the special peculiarities of dream-life intelligible.[1]

What is presented to us in these words is the idea of *psychical locality.* I shall entirely disregard the fact that the mental apparatus with which we are here concerned is also known to us in the form of an anatomical preparation, and I shall carefully avoid the temptation to determine psychical locality in any anatomical fashion. I shall remain upon psychological ground, and I propose simply to follow the suggestion that we should picture the instrument which carries out our mental functions as resembling a compound microscope or a photographic apparatus, or something of the kind. On that basis, psychical locality will correspond to a point inside the apparatus at which one of the preliminary stages of an image comes into being. In the microscope and telescope, as we know, these occur in part at ideal points, regions in which no tangible component of the apparatus is situated. I see no necessity to apologize for the imperfections of this or of any similar imagery. Analogies of this kind are only intended to assist us in our attempt to make the complications of mental functioning intelligible by dissecting the function and assigning its different constituents to different component parts of the apparatus. So far as I know, the experiment has not hitherto been made of using this method of dissection in order to investigate the way in which the mental instrument is put together, and I can see no harm in it. We are justified, in my view, in giving free rein to our speculations so long as we retain the coolness of our judgement and do not mistake the scaffolding for the building. And since at our first approach to something unknown all that we need is the assistance of provisional ideas, I shall give preference in the first instance to hypotheses of the crudest and most concrete description.

Accordingly, we will picture the mental apparatus as a compound instrument, to the components of which we will give the

[1] [In a letter to Fliess of February 9, 1898 (Freud, 1950*a*, Letter 83), Freud writes that this passage in Fechner is the only sensible remark he has found in the literature on dreams.]

name of 'agencies',[1] or (for the sake of greater clarity) 'systems'. It is to be anticipated, in the next place, that these systems may perhaps stand in a regular spatial relation to one another, in the same kind of way in which the various systems of lenses in a telescope are arranged behind one another. Strictly speaking, there is no need for the hypothesis that the psychical systems are actually arranged in a *spatial* order. It would be sufficient if a fixed order were established by the fact that in a given psychical process the excitation passes through the systems in a particular *temporal* sequence. In other processes the sequence may perhaps be a different one; that is a possibility that we shall leave open. For the sake of brevity we will in future speak of the components of the apparatus as 'ψ-systems'.

The first thing that strikes us is that this apparatus, compounded of ψ-systems, has a sense or direction. All our psychical activity starts from stimuli (whether internal or external) and ends in innervations.[2] Accordingly, we shall ascribe a sensory and a motor end to the apparatus. At the sensory end there lies a system which receives perceptions; at the motor end there lies another, which opens the gateway to motor activity. Psychical processes advance in general from the perceptual end to the motor end. Thus the most general schematic picture of the psychical apparatus may be represented thus (Fig. 1):

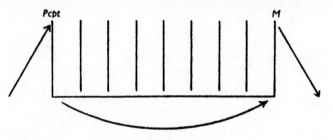

FIG. 1.

[1] ['*Instanzen*', literally 'instances', in a sense similar to that in which the word occurs in the phrase 'a Court of First Instance'.]

[2] ['Innervation' is a highly ambiguous term. It is very frequently used in a structural sense, to mean the anatomical distribution of nerves in some organism or bodily region. Freud uses it more often (though not invariably) to mean the transmission of energy into a system of nerves, or (as in the present instance) specifically into an *efferent* system—to indicate, that is to say, a process tending towards discharge.]

This, however, does no more than fulfil a requirement with which we have long been familiar, namely that the psychical apparatus must be constructed like a reflex apparatus. Reflex processes remain the model of every psychical function.

Next, we have grounds for introducing a first differentiation at the sensory end. A trace is left in our psychical apparatus of the perceptions which impinge upon it. This we may describe as a 'memory-trace'; and to the function relating to it we give the name of 'memory'. If we are in earnest over our plan of attaching psychical processes to systems, memory-traces can only consist in permanent modifications of the elements of the systems. But, as has already been pointed out elsewhere,[1] there are obvious difficulties involved in supposing that one and the same system can accurately retain modifications of its elements and yet remain perpetually open to the reception of fresh occasions for modification. In accordance, therefore, with the principle which governs our experiment, we shall distribute these two functions on to different systems. We shall suppose that a system in the very front of the apparatus receives the perceptual stimuli but retains no trace of them and thus has no memory, while behind it there lies a second system which transforms the momentary excitations of the first system into permanent traces. The schematic picture of our psychical apparatus would then be as follows (Fig. 2):

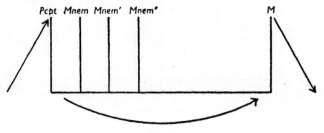

Pcpt Mnem Mnem' Mnem"   M

FIG. 2.

It is a familiar fact that we retain permanently something more than the mere *content* of the perceptions which impinge

[1] [By Breuer in a footnote to Section I of his theoretical contribution to Breuer and Freud, 1895, where, among other things, he writes: 'The mirror of a reflecting telescope cannot at the same time be a photographic plate.']

upon the system *Pcpt.* Our perceptions are linked with one another in our memory—first and foremost according to simultaneity of occurrence. We speak of this fact as 'association'. It is clear, then, that, if the *Pcpt.* system has no memory whatever, it cannot retain any associative traces; the separate *Pcpt.* elements would be intolerably obstructed in performing their function if the remnant of an earlier connection were to exercise an influence upon a fresh perception. We must therefore assume the basis of association lies in the mnemic systems. Association would thus consist in the fact that, as a result of a diminution in resistances and of the laying down of facilitating paths, an excitation is transmitted from a given *Mnem.* element more readily to one *Mnem.* element than to another.

Closer consideration will show the necessity for supposing the existence not of one but of several such *Mnem.* elements, in which one and the same excitation, transmitted by the *Pcpt.* elements, leaves a variety of different permanent records. The first of these *Mnem.* systems will naturally contain the record of association in respect to *simultaneity in time*; while the same perceptual material will be arranged in the later systems in respect to other kinds of coincidence, so that one of these later systems, for instance, will record relations of similarity, and so on with the others. It would of course be a waste of time to try to put the psychical significance of a system of this kind into words. Its character would lie in the intimate details of its relations to the different elements of the raw material of memory, that is—if we may hint at a theory of a more radical kind—in the degrees of conductive resistance which it offered to the passage of excitation from those elements.

At this point I will interpolate a remark of a general nature which may perhaps have important implications. It is the *Pcpt.* system, which is without the capacity to retain modifications and is thus without memory, that provides our consciousness with the whole multiplicity of sensory qualities. On the other hand, our memories—not excepting those which are most deeply stamped on our minds—are in themselves unconscious. They can be made conscious; but there can be no doubt that they can produce all their effects while in an unconscious condition. What we describe as our 'character' is based on the memory-traces of our impressions; and, moreover, the impressions which have had the greatest effect on us—those of our earliest youth—are precisely the ones which scarcely ever become conscious. But if memories become conscious once more, they exhibit no sensory quality or a very slight one in comparison with perceptions. A most promising light would be thrown on the conditions governing the excitation of neurones if it could be confirmed that *in the ψ-systems memory and the quality that characterizes consciousness are mutually exclusive.*[1]

The assumptions we have so far put forward as to the construction of the psychical apparatus at its sensory end have been made without reference to dreams or to the psychological information that we have been able to infer from them. Evidence afforded by dreams will, however, help us towards understanding another portion of the apparatus. We have seen [see p. 143 ff.] that we were only able to explain the formation of dreams by venturing upon the hypothesis of there being two psychical agencies, one of which submitted the activity of the other to a criticism which involved its exclusion from consciousness. The critical agency, we concluded, stands in a closer relation to consciousness than the agency criticized: it stands like a screen between the latter and consciousness. Further, we found reasons [p. 489] for identifying the critical agency with the agency which directs our waking life and determines our voluntary, conscious actions. If, in accordance with our assumptions, we replace these agencies by systems, then our last conclusion must lead us to locate the critical system at the motor end of the apparatus. We will now introduce the two systems

---

[1] [*Footnote added* 1925:] I have since suggested that consciousness actually arises *instead of* the memory-trace. See my 'Note upon the "Mystic Writing-Pad"' (1925a). [Cf. also Chapter IV of *Beyond the Pleasure Principle* (1920g), where the same point is made.—The whole of the present discussion on memory will be made more intelligible by a study of these two passages from Freud's later writings. But still more light is thrown on it by some of his earlier reflections on the subject revealed in the Fliess correspondence (Freud, 1950a). See, for instance, Section 3 of Part I of the 'Project for a Scientific Psychology' (written in the autumn of 1895) and Letter 52 (written on December 6, 1896). This letter, incidentally, contains what is evidently an early version of the 'schematic picture' represented above as well as the first appearance of the abbreviations by which the various systems are here distinguished. The equivalent English symbols are self-explanatory: '*Cs.*' for the 'conscious' system, '*Pcs.*' for the 'preconscious', '*Ucs.*' for the 'unconscious', '*Pcpt.*' for the 'perceptual' and '*Mnem.*' for the 'mnemic' systems.]

into our schematic picture and give them names to express their relation to consciousness (Fig. 3):

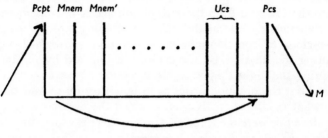

FIG. 3.

We will describe the last of the systems at the motor end as 'the preconscious', to indicate that the excitatory processes occurring in it can enter consciousness without further impediment provided that certain other conditions are fulfilled: for instance, that they reach a certain degree of intensity, that the function which can only be described as 'attention' is distributed in a particular way [see p. 593], and so on. This is at the same time the system which holds the key to voluntary movement. We will describe the system that lies behind it as 'the unconscious', because it has no access to consciousness *except via the preconscious*, in passing through which its excitatory process is obliged to submit to modifications.[1]

In which of these systems, then, are we to locate the impetus to the construction of dreams? For simplicity's sake, in the system *Ucs.* It is true that in the course of our future discussion we shall learn that this is not entirely accurate, and that the process of forming dreams is obliged to attach itself to dream-thoughts belonging to the preconscious system [p. 562]. But when we consider the dream-wish, we shall find that the motive force for producing dreams is supplied by the *Ucs.* [p. 561]; and

[1] [*Footnote added* 1919:] If we attempted to proceed further with this schematic picture, in which the systems are set out in linear succession, we should have to reckon with the fact that the system next beyond the *Pcs.* is the one to which consciousness must be ascribed—in other words, that *Pcpt.* = *Cs.* [See below, p. 615 ff. For a fuller discussion of this see Freud, 1917d.—Freud's later 'schematic picture' of the mind, first given in *The Ego and the Id* (1923b), Chapter II, and repeated (with some modifications) in the *New Introductory Lectures* (1933a), Lecture XXXI, lays more stress on structure than on function.]

owing to this latter factor we shall take the unconscious system as the starting-point of dream-formation. Like all other thought-structures, this dream-instigator will make an effort to advance into the *Pcs.* and from there to obtain access to consciousness.

Experience shows us that this path leading through the pre-conscious to consciousness is barred to the dream-thoughts during the daytime by the censorship imposed by resistance. During the night they are able to obtain access to conscious-ness; but the question arises as to how they do so and thanks to what modification. If what enabled the dream-thoughts to achieve this were the fact that at night there is a lowering of the resistance which guards the frontier between the unconscious and the preconscious, we should have dreams which were in the nature of ideas and which were without the hallucinatory quality in which we are at the moment interested. Thus the lowering of the censorship between the two systems *Ucs.* and *Pcs.* can only explain dreams formed like 'Autodidasker' and not dreams like that of the burning child which we took as the starting-point of our investigations.

The only way in which we can describe what happens in hallucinatory dreams is by saying that the excitation moves in a *backward* direction. Instead of being transmitted towards the *motor* end of the apparatus it moves towards the *sensory* end and finally reaches the perceptual system. If we describe as 'pro-gressive' the direction taken by psychical processes arising from the unconscious during waking life, then we may speak of dreams as having a 'regressive' character.[1]

This regression, then, is undoubtedly one of the psychological characteristics of the process of dreaming; but we must re-member that it does not occur only in dreams. Intentional

---

[1] [*Footnote added* 1914:] The first hint at the factor of regression is to be found as far back as in Albertus Magnus [the thirteenth century Schol-astic writer]. The *'imaginatio'*, he tells us, constructs dreams out of the stored-up images of sensory objects; and the process is carried out in a reverse direction to that in waking life. (Quoted by Diepgen, 1912, 14.) —Hobbes writes in the *Leviathan* (1651, Pt. I, Chapter 2): 'In sum, our dreams are the reverse of our waking imaginations, the motion, when we are awake, beginning at one end, and when we dream at another.' (Quoted by Havelock Ellis, 1911, 109.)—[Breuer, in Section I of Chap-ter III of Breuer and Freud, 1895, speaks (in connection with hallucina-tions) of 'a "retrogressive" excitation, emanating from the organ of memory, and acting upon the perceptual apparatus by means of ideas'.]

recollection and other constituent processes of our normal thinking involve a retrogressive movement in the psychical apparatus from a complex ideational act back to the raw material of the memory-traces underlying it. In the waking state, however, this backward movement never extends beyond the mnemic images; it does not succeed in producing a hallucinatory revival of the *perceptual* images. Why is it otherwise in dreams? When we were considering the work of condensation in dreams we were driven to suppose that the intensities attaching to ideas can be completely transferred by the dream-work from one idea to another [p. 330]. It is probably this alteration in the normal psychical procedure which makes possible the cathexis of the system *Pcpt.* in the reverse direction, starting from thoughts, to the pitch of complete sensory vividness.

We must not delude ourselves into exaggerating the importance of these considerations. We have done no more than give a name to an inexplicable phenomenon. We call it 'regression' when in a dream an idea is turned back into the sensory image from which it was originally derived. But even this step requires justification. What is the point of this nomenclature if it teaches us nothing new? I believe the name 'regression' is of help to us in so far as it connects a fact that was already known to us with our schematic picture, in which the mental apparatus was given a sense or direction. And it is at this point that that picture begins to repay us for having constructed it. For an examination of it, without any further reflection, reveals a further characteristic of dream-formation. If we regard the process of dreaming as a regression occurring in our hypothetical mental apparatus, we at once arrive at the explanation of the empirically established fact that all the logical relations belonging to the dream-thoughts disappear during the dream-activity or can only find expression with difficulty [p. 312]. According to our schematic picture, these relations are contained not in the *first Mnem.* systems but in *later* ones; and in case of regression they would necessarily lose any means of expression except in perceptual images. *In regression the fabric of the dream-thoughts is resolved into its raw material.*

What modification is it that renders possible a regression which cannot occur in daytime? We must be content with some conjectures on this point. No doubt it is a question of changes in the cathexes of energy attaching to the different systems, changes which increase or diminish the facility with which those systems can be passed through by the excitatory process. But in any apparatus of this kind the same results upon the passage of excitations might be produced in more than one way. Our first thoughts will of course be of the state of sleep and the changes in cathexis which it brings about at the sensory end of the apparatus. During the day there is a continuous current from the *Pcpt.* system flowing in the direction of motor activity; but this current ceases at night and could no longer form an obstacle to a current of excitation flowing in the opposite sense. Here we seem to have the 'shutting-out of the external world', which some authorities regard as the theoretical explanation of the psychological characteristics of dreams. (See p. 51.)

In explaining regression in dreams, however, we must bear in mind the regressions which also occur in pathological waking states; and here the explanation just given leaves us in the lurch. For in those cases regression occurs in spite of a sensory current flowing without interruption in a forward direction. My explanation of hallucinations in hysteria and paranoia and of visions in mentally normal subjects is that they are in fact regressions —that is, thoughts transformed into images—but that the only thoughts that undergo this transformation are those which are intimately linked with memories that have been suppressed or have remained unconscious.

For instance, one of my youngest hysterical patients, a twelve-year-old boy, was prevented from falling asleep by *'green faces with red eyes'* which terrified him. The source of this phenomenon was a suppressed, though at one time conscious, memory of a boy whom he had often seen four years earlier. This boy had presented him with an alarming picture of the consequences of bad habits in children, including masturbation —a habit with which my patient was now reproaching himself in retrospect. His mother had pointed out at the time that the ill-behaved boy had a *greenish face* and *red* (i.e. red-rimmed) *eyes*. Here was the origin of his bogey, whose only purpose, incidentally, was to remind him of another of his mother's predictions—that boys of that sort grow into idiots, can learn nothing at school and die young. My little patient had fulfilled one part of the prophecy, for he was making no progress at his school, and, as was shown from his account of the involuntary thoughts that occurred to him, he was terrified of the other part.

I may add that after a short time the treatment resulted in his being able to sleep, in his nervousness disappearing and his being awarded a mark of distinction at the end of his school-year.

In the same connection I will give the explanation of a vision that was described to me by another hysterical patient (a woman of forty) as having happened before she fell ill. One morning she opened her eyes and saw her brother in the room, though, as she knew, he was in fact in an insane asylum. Her small son was sleeping in the bed beside her. To save the child from having a *fright* and *falling into convulsions* when he saw his *uncle*, she pulled the *sheet* over his face, whereupon the apparition vanished. This vision was a modified version of a memory from the lady's childhood; and, though it was conscious, it was intimately related to all the unconscious material in her mind. Her nurse had told her that her mother (who had died very young, when my patient was only eighteen months old) had suffered from epileptic or hysterical *convulsions*, which went back to a *fright* caused by her brother (my patient's *uncle*) appearing to her disguised as a ghost with a *sheet* over his head. Thus the vision contained the same elements as the memory: the brother's appearance, the sheet, the fright and its results. But the elements had been arranged in a different context and transferred on to other figures. The obvious motive of the vision, or of the thoughts which it replaced, was her concern lest her little boy might follow in the footsteps of his uncle, whom he greatly resembled physically.

The two instances that I have quoted are neither of them entirely devoid of connection with the state of sleep and for that reason are perhaps not well chosen for what I want them to prove. I will therefore refer the reader to my analysis of a woman suffering from hallucinatory paranoia (Freud, 1896b [Part III]) as well as to the findings in my still unpublished studies on the psychology of the psychoneuroses,[1] for evidence that in such instances of the regressive transformation of thoughts we must not overlook the influence of memories, mostly from childhood, which have been suppressed or have remained unconscious. The thoughts which are connected with a memory of this kind and which are forbidden expression by the censorship are, as it were, attracted by the memory into regression as being the form of representation in which the memory itself

[1] [Never published under any such title.]

is couched. I may also recall that one of the facts arrived at in the *Studies on Hysteria* [Breuer and Freud, 1895—e.g. in Breuer's first case history] was that when it was possible to bring infantile scenes (whether they were memories or phantasies) into consciousness, they were seen like hallucinations and lost that characteristic only in the process of being reported. It is moreover a familiar observation that, even in those whose memory is not normally of a visual type, the earliest recollections of childhood retain far into life the quality of sensory vividness.

If we now bear in mind how great a part is played in the dream-thoughts by infantile experiences or by phantasies based upon them, how frequently portions of them re-emerge in the dream-content and how often the dream-wishes themselves are derived from them, we cannot dismiss the probability that in dreams too the transformation of thoughts into visual images may be in part the result of the attraction which memories couched in visual form and eager for revival bring to bear upon thoughts cut off from consciousness and struggling to find expression. On this view a dream might be described as *a substitute for an infantile scene modified by being transferred on to a recent experience*. The infantile scene is unable to bring about its own revival and has to be content with returning as a dream.

This indication of the way in which infantile scenes (or their reproductions as phantasies) function in a sense as models for the content of dreams, removes the necessity for one of the hypotheses put forward by Scherner and his followers in regard to internal sources of stimulation. Scherner [1861] supposes that, when dreams exhibit particularly vivid or particularly copious visual elements, there is present a state of 'visual stimulation', that is, of internal excitation in the organ of vision [cf. p. 227]. We need not dispute this hypothesis, but can content ourselves with assuming that this state of excitation applies merely to the *psychical* perceptual system of the visual organ; we may, however, further point out that the state of excitation has been set up by a *memory*, that it is a *revival* of a visual excitation which was originally an immediate one. I cannot produce any good example from my own experience of an *infantile* memory producing this kind of result. My dreams are in general less rich in sensory elements than I am led to suppose is the case in other people. But in the case of my most vivid and beautiful dream of the last few years I was easily able to trace back the hallucinatory clarity of the dream's content to the sensory qualities of recent or fairly recent impressions. On p. 463 ff. I recorded a dream in which the deep blue colour of the water, the brown of the smoke coming from the ship's funnels, and the dark brown and red of the buildings left behind a profound impression on me. This dream, if any, should be traceable to a visual stimulus. What was it that had brought my visual organ into this state of stimulation? A recent impression, which attached itself to a number of earlier ones. The colours which I saw were in the first instance those of a box of toy bricks with which, on the day before the dream, my children had put up a fine building and shown it off for my admiration. The big bricks were of the same dark red and the small ones were of the same blue and brown. This was associated with colour impressions from my last travels in Italy: the beautiful blue of the Isonzo and the lagoons and the brown of the Carso.[1] The beauty of the colours in the dream was only a repetition of something seen in my memory.

Let us bring together what we have found out about the peculiar propensity of dreams to recast their ideational content into sensory images. We have not explained this feature of the dream-work, we have not traced it back to any known psychological laws; but we have rather picked it out as something that suggests unknown implications and we have characterized it with the word 'regressive'. We have put forward the view that in all probability this regression, wherever it may occur, is an effect of a resistance opposing the progress of a thought into consciousness along the normal path, and of a simultaneous attraction exercised upon the thought by the presence of memories possessing great sensory force.[2] In the case of dreams, regression may perhaps be further facilitated by the cessation of the progressive current which streams in during the daytime from the sense organs; in other forms of regression, the absence

---

[1] [The limestone plateau behind Trieste.]

[2] [*Footnote added* 1914:] In any account of the theory of repression it would have to be laid down that a thought becomes repressed as a result of the combined influence upon it of *two* factors. It is pushed from the one side (by the censorship of the *Cs.*) and pulled from the other (by the *Ucs.*), in the same kind of way in which people are conveyed to the top of the Great Pyramid. [*Added* 1919:] Cf. [the opening pages of] my paper on repression (Freud, 1915d).

of this accessory factor must be made up for by a greater intensity of the other motives for regression. Nor must we forget to observe that in these pathological cases of regression as well as in dreams the process of transference of energy must differ from what it is in regressions occurring in normal mental life, since in the former cases that process makes possible a complete hallucinatory cathexis of the perceptual systems. What we have described, in our analysis of the dream-work, as 'regard for representability' might be brought into connection with the *selective attraction* exercised by the visually recollected scenes touched upon by the dream-thoughts.

It is further to be remarked[1] that regression plays a no less important part in the theory of the formation of neurotic symptoms than it does in that of dreams. Three kinds of regression are thus to be distinguished: (*a*) *topographical* regression, in the sense of the schematic picture of the ψ-systems which we have explained above; (*b*) *temporal* regression, in so far as what is in question is a harking back to older psychical structures; and (*c*) *formal* regression, where primitive methods of expression and representation take the place of the usual ones. All these three kinds of regression are, however, one at bottom and occur together as a rule; for what is older in time is more primitive in form and in psychical topography lies nearer to the perceptual end. [Cf. Freud, 1917*d*.]

Nor can we leave the subject of regression in dreams[2] without setting down in words a notion by which we have already repeatedly been struck and which will recur with fresh intensity when we have entered more deeply into the study of the psychoneuroses: namely that dreaming is on the whole an example of regression to the dreamer's earliest condition, a revival of his childhood, of the instinctual impulses which dominated it and of the methods of expression which were then available to him. Behind this childhood of the individual we are promised a picture of a phylogenetic childhood—a picture of the development of the human race, of which the individual's development is in fact an abbreviated recapitulation influenced by the chance circumstances of life. We can guess how much to the

---

[1] [This paragraph was added in 1914.]
[2] [This paragraph was added in 1919.]

point is Nietzsche's assertion that in dreams 'some primaeval relic of humanity is at work which we can now scarcely reach any longer by a direct path'; and we may expect that the analysis of dreams will lead us to a knowledge of man's archaic heritage, of what is psychically innate in him. Dreams and neuroses seem to have preserved more mental antiquities than we could have imagined possible; so that psycho-analysis may claim a high place among the sciences which are concerned with the reconstruction of the earliest and most obscure periods of the beginnings of the human race.

It may well be that this first portion of our psychological study of dreams will leave us with a sense of dissatisfaction. But we can console ourselves with the thought that we have been obliged to build our way out into the dark. If we are not wholly in error, other lines of approach are bound to lead us into much the same region and the time may then come when we shall find ourselves more at home in it.

(C)

WISH-FULFILMENT

The dream of the burning child at the beginning of this chapter gives us a welcome opportunity of considering the difficulties with which the theory of wish-fulfilment is faced. It will no doubt have surprised all of us to be told that dreams are nothing other than fulfilments of wishes, and not only on account of the contradiction offered by anxiety-dreams. When analysis first revealed to us that a meaning and a psychical value lay concealed behind dreams, we were no doubt quite unprepared to find that that meaning was of such a uniform character. According to Aristotle's accurate but bald definition, a dream is thinking that persists (in so far as we are asleep) in the state of sleep. [Cf. p. 2.] Since, then, our daytime thinking produces psychical acts of such various sorts—judgements, inferences, denials, expectations, intentions, and so on—why should it be obliged during the night to restrict itself to the production of wishes alone? Are there not, on the contrary, numerous dreams which show us psychical acts of other kinds—worries, for instance—transformed into dream-shape? And was not the dream with which we began this chapter (a quite particularly transparent one) precisely a dream of this sort? When the glare of light fell on the eyes of the sleeping father, he drew the worrying conclusion that a candle had fallen over and might have set the dead body on fire. He turned this conclusion into a dream by clothing it in a sensory situation and in the present tense. What part was played in this by wish-fulfilment? can we fail to see in it the predominating influence of a thought persisting from waking life or stimulated by a new sense-impression? All this is quite true and compels us to enter more closely into the part played by wish-fulfilment in dreams and into the importance of waking thoughts which persist into sleep.

We have already been led by wish-fulfilment itself to divide dreams into two groups. We have found some dreams which appeared openly as wish-fulfilments, and others in which the wish-fulfilment was unrecognizable and often disguised by every possible means. In the latter we have perceived the dream-censorship at work. We found the undistorted wishful dreams principally in children; though *short*, frankly wishful dreams *seemed* (and I lay emphasis upon this qualification) to occur in adults as well.

We may next ask where the wishes that come true in dreams originate. What contrasting possibilities or what alternatives have we in mind in raising this question? It is the contrast, I think, between the consciously perceived life of daytime and a psychical activity which has remained unconscious and of which we can only become aware at night. I can distinguish three possible origins for such a wish. (1) It may have been aroused during the day and for external reasons may not have been satisfied; in that case an acknowledged wish which has not been dealt with is left over for the night. (2) It may have arisen during the day but been repudiated; in that case what is left over is a wish which has not been dealt with but has been suppressed. (3) It may have no connection with daytime life and be one of those wishes which only emerge from the suppressed part of the mind and become active in us at night. If we turn again to our schematic picture of the psychical apparatus, we shall localize wishes of the first kind in the system *Pcs.*; we shall suppose that wishes of the second kind have been driven out of the system *Pcs.* into the *Ucs.*, where, if at all, they continue to exist; and we shall conclude that wishful impulses of the third kind are altogether incapable of passing beyond the system *Ucs.* The question then arises whether wishes derived from these different sources are of equal importance for dreams and have equal power to instigate them.

If we cast our minds over the dreams that are at our disposal for answering this question, we shall at once be reminded that we must add a fourth source of dream-wishes, namely the current wishful impulses that arise during the night (e.g. those stimulated by thirst or sexual needs). In the next place, we shall form the opinion that the place of origin of a dream-wish probably has no influence on its capacity for instigating dreams. I may recall the little girl's dream which prolonged a trip on the lake that had been interrupted during the day and the other children's dreams which I have recorded. [See p. 127 ff.] They were explained as being due to unfulfilled, but unsuppressed, wishes from the previous day. Instances of a wish that has been suppressed in the daytime finding its way out in a dream are exceedingly numerous. I will add a further very simple example of this class. The dreamer was a lady who was rather fond of making fun of people and one of whose friends, a woman younger than herself, had just become engaged. All day long she had been asked by her acquaintances whether she knew the young man and what she thought of him. She had replied with nothing but praises, with which she had silenced her real judgement; for she would have liked to tell the truth—that he was a '*Dutzendmensch*' [literally a 'dozen man', a very commonplace sort of person—people like him are turned out by the *dozen*]. She dreamt that night that she was asked the same question, and replied with the formula: '*In the case of repeat orders it is sufficient to quote the number.*' We have learnt, lastly, from numerous analyses that wherever a dream has undergone distortion the wish has arisen from the unconscious and was one which could not be perceived during the day. Thus it seems at a first glance as though all wishes are of equal importance and equal power in dreams.

I cannot offer any proof here that the truth is nevertheless otherwise; but I may say that I am strongly inclined to suppose that dream-wishes are more strictly determined. It is true that children's dreams prove beyond a doubt that a wish that has not been dealt with during the day can act as a dream-instigator. But it must not be forgotten that it is a *child's* wish, a wishful impulse of the strength proper to children. I think it is highly doubtful whether in the case of an adult a wish that has not been fulfilled during the day would be strong enough to produce a dream. It seems to me, on the contrary, that, with the progressive control exercised upon our instinctual life by our thought-activity, we are more and more inclined to renounce as unprofitable the formation or retention of such intense wishes as children know. It is possible that there are individual differences in this respect, and that some people retain an infantile type of mental process longer than others, just as there are similar differences in regard to the diminution of visual imagery, which is so vivid in early years. But in general, I think, a wish that has been left over unfulfilled from the previous day is insufficient to produce a dream in the case of an adult. I readily admit that a wishful impulse originating in the conscious will *contribute* to the instigation of a dream, but it will probably not do more than that. The dream would not materialize if the pre-conscious wish did not succeed in finding reinforcement from elsewhere.

From the unconscious, in fact. *My supposition is that a conscious wish can only become a dream-instigator if it succeeds in awakening an unconscious wish with the same tenor and in obtaining reinforcement from it.* From indications derived from the psycho-analysis of the neuroses, I consider that these unconscious wishes are always on the alert, ready at any time to find their way to expression when an opportunity arises for allying themselves with an impulse from the conscious and for transferring their own great intensity on to the latter's lesser one.[1] It will then *appear* as though the conscious wish alone had been realized in the dream; only some small peculiarity in the dream's configuration will serve as a finger-post to put us on the track of the powerful ally from the unconscious. These wishes in our unconscious, ever on the alert and, so to say, immortal, remind one of the legendary Titans, weighed down since primaeval ages by the massive bulk of the mountains which were once hurled upon them by the victorious gods and which are still shaken from time to time by the convulsion of their limbs. But these wishes, held under repression, are themselves of infantile origin, as we are taught by psychological research into the neuroses. I would propose, therefore, to set aside the assertion made just now [p. 551], that the place of origin of dream-wishes is a matter of indifference and replace it by another one to the following effect: *a wish which is represented in a dream must be an infantile one.* In the case of adults it originates from the *Ucs.*, in the case of children, where there is as yet no division or censorship between the *Pcs.* and the *Ucs.*, or where that division is only gradually being set up, it is an unfulfilled, unrepressed wish from waking

---

[1] They share this character of indestructibility with all other mental acts which are truly unconscious, i.e. which belong to the system *Ucs.* only. These are paths which have been laid down once and for all, which never fall into disuse and which, whenever an unconscious excitation re-cathects them, are always ready to conduct the excitatory process to discharge. If I may use a simile, they are only capable of annihilation in the same sense as the ghosts in the underworld of the *Odyssey* —ghosts which awoke to new life as soon as they tasted blood. Processes which are dependent on the preconscious system are destructible in quite another sense. The psychotherapy of the neuroses is based on this distinction. [See below, p. 577 f.]

life. I am aware that this assertion cannot be proved to hold universally; but it can be proved to hold frequently, even in unsuspected cases, and it cannot be *contradicted* as a general proposition.

In my view, therefore, wishful impulses left over from conscious waking life must be relegated to a secondary position in respect to the formation of dreams. I cannot allow that, as contributors to the content of dreams, they play any other part than is played, for instance, by the material of sensations which become currently active during sleep. (See pp. 228–9.) I shall follow the same line of thought in now turning to consider those psychical instigations to dreaming, left over from waking life, which are *other* than wishes. When we decide to go to sleep, we may succeed in temporarily bringing to an end the cathexes of energy attaching to our waking thoughts. Anyone who can do this easily is a good sleeper; the first Napoleon seems to have been a model of this class. But we do not always succeed in doing so, nor do we always succeed completely. Unsolved problems, tormenting worries, overwhelming impressions—all these carry thought-activity over into sleep and sustain mental processes in the system that we have named the preconscious. If we wish to classify the thought-impulses which persist in sleep, we may divide them into the following groups: (1) what has not been carried to a conclusion during the day owing to some chance hindrance; (2) what has not been dealt with owing to the insufficiency of our intellectual power—what is unsolved; (3) what has been rejected and suppressed during the daytime. To these we must add (4) a powerful group consisting of what has been set in action in our *Ucs.* by the activity of the preconscious in the course of the day; and finally (5) the group of daytime impressions which are indifferent and have for that reason not been dealt with.

There is no need to underestimate the importance of the psychical intensities which are introduced into the state of sleep by these residues of daytime life, and particularly of those in the group of unsolved problems. It is certain that these excitations continue to struggle for expression during the night; and we may assume with equal certainty that the state of sleep makes it impossible for the excitatory process to be pursued in the habitual manner in the preconscious and brought to an end by becoming conscious. In so far as our thought-processes are able to become conscious in the normal way at night, we are simply not asleep. I am unable to say what modification in the system *Pcs.* is brought about by the state of sleep;[1] but there can be no doubt that the psychological characteristics of sleep are to be looked for essentially in modifications in the cathexis of this particular system—a system that is also in control of access to the power of movement, which is paralysed during sleep. On the other hand, nothing in the psychology of dreams gives me reason to suppose that sleep produces any modifications other than secondary ones in the state of things prevailing in the *Ucs.* No other course, then, lies open to excitations occurring at night in the *Pcs.* than that followed by wishful excitations arising from the *Ucs.*; the preconscious excitations must find reinforcement from the *Ucs.* and must accompany the unconscious excitations along their circuitous paths. But what is the relation of the preconscious residues of the previous day to *dreams?* There is no doubt that they find their way into dreams in great quantity, and that they make use of the content of dreams in order to penetrate into consciousness even during the night. Indeed they occasionally dominate the content of a dream and force it to carry on the activity of daytime. It is certain, too, that the day's residues may be of any other character just as easily as wishes; but it is highly instructive in this connection, and of positively decisive importance for the theory of wish-fulfilment, to observe the condition to which they must submit in order to be received into a dream.

Let us take one of the dreams I have already recorded—for instance, the one in which my friend Otto appeared with the signs of Graves' disease. (See p. 269 ff.) I had been worried during the previous day by Otto's looks; and, like everything else concerned with him, this worry affected me closely. And it pursued me, as I may assume, into my sleep. I was probably anxious to discover what could be wrong with him. This worry found expression during the night in the dream I have described, the content of which was in the first place nonsensical and in the second place was in no respect the fulfilment of a

[1] [*Footnote added* 1919:] I have tried to penetrate further into an understanding of the state of things prevailing during sleep and of the determining conditions of hallucination in a paper entitled 'A Metapsychological Supplement to the Theory of Dreams' [Freud, 1917*d*].

wish. I then began to investigate the origin of this inappropriate expression of the worry I had felt during the day, and by means of analysis I found a connection through the fact of my having identified my friend with a certain Baron L. and myself with Professor R. There was only one explanation of my having been obliged to choose this particular substitute for my daytime thought. I must have been prepared at all times in my *Ucs.* to identify myself with Professor R., since by means of that identification one of the immortal wishes of childhood—the megalomaniac wish—was fulfilled. Ugly thoughts hostile to my friend, which were certain to be repudiated during the day, had seized the opportunity of slipping through with the wish and getting themselves represented in the dream; but my daytime worry had also found some sort of expression in the content of the dream by means of a substitute. [Cf. p. 267.] The daytime thought, which was not in itself a wish but on the contrary a worry, was obliged to find a connection in some way or other with an infantile wish which was now unconscious and suppressed, and which would enable it—suitably decocted, it is true—to 'originate' in consciousness. The more dominating was the worry, the more far-fetched a link could be established; there was no necessity for there being any connection whatever between the content of the wish and that of the worry, and in fact no such connection existed in our example.

It may perhaps be useful[1] to continue our examination of the same question by considering how a dream behaves when the dream-thoughts present it with material which is the complete reverse of a wish-fulfilment—well-justified worries, painful reflections, distressing realizations. The many possible outcomes can be classed under the two following groups. (A) The dream-work may succeed in replacing all the distressing ideas by contrary ones and in suppressing the unpleasurable affects attaching to them. The result will be a straightforward dream of satisfaction, a palpable 'wish-fulfilment', about which there seems no more to be said. (B) The distressing ideas may make their way, more or less modified but none the less quite recognizable, into the manifest content of the dream. This is the case which raises doubts as to the validity of the wish theory of dreams and needs further investigation. Dreams of this sort with a distressing

[1] [This paragraph and the two following ones were added in 1919.]

content may either be experienced with indifference, or they may be accompanied by the whole of the distressing affect which their ideational content seems to justify, or they may even lead to the development of anxiety and to awakening.

Analysis is able to demonstrate that these unpleasurable dreams are wish-fulfilments no less than the rest. An unconscious and repressed wish, whose fulfilment the dreamer's ego could not fail to experience as something distressing, has seized the opportunity offered to it by the persisting cathexis of the distressing residues of the previous day; it has lent them its support and by that means rendered them capable of entering a dream. But whereas in Group A the unconscious wish coincided with the conscious one, in Group B the gulf between the unconscious and the conscious (between the repressed and the ego) is revealed and the situation in the fairy tale of the three wishes which were granted by the fairy to the husband and wife is realized. (See below, p. 580 f. *n*.) The satisfaction at the fulfilment of the repressed wish may turn out to be so great that it counterbalances the distressing feelings attaching to the day's residues [cf. p. 470]; in that case the feeling-tone of the dream is indifferent, in spite of its being on the one hand the fulfilment of a wish and on the other the fulfilment of a fear. Or it may happen that the sleeping ego takes a still larger share in the constructing of the dream, that it reacts to the satisfying of the repressed wish with violent indignation and itself puts an end to the dream with an outburst of anxiety. Thus there is no difficulty in seeing that unpleasurable dreams and anxiety-dreams are just as much wish-fulfilments in the sense of our theory as are straightforward dreams of satisfaction.

Unpleasurable dreams may also be 'punishment-dreams'. [See p. 473 ff.] It must be admitted that their recognition means in a certain sense a new addition to the theory of dreams. What is fulfilled in them is equally an unconscious wish, namely a wish that the dreamer may be punished for a repressed and forbidden wishful impulse. To that extent dreams of this kind fall in with the condition that has been laid down here that the motive force for constructing a dream must be provided by a wish belonging to the unconscious. A closer psychological analysis, however, shows how they differ from other wishful dreams. In the cases forming Group B the dream-constructing wish is an unconscious one and belongs to the repressed, while in punishment-dreams, though it is equally an unconscious one, it must be reckoned as belonging not to the repressed but to the 'ego'. Thus punishment-dreams indicate the possibility that the ego may have a greater share than was supposed in the construction of dreams. The mechanism of dream-formation would in general be greatly clarified if instead of the opposition between 'conscious' and 'unconscious' we were to speak of that between the 'ego' and the 'repressed'. This cannot be done, however, without taking account of the processes underlying the psycho-neuroses, and for that reason it has not been carried out in the present work. I will only add that punishment-dreams are not in general subject to the condition that the day's residues shall be of a distressing kind. On the contrary, they occur most easily where the opposite is the case—where the day's residues are thoughts of a satisfying nature but the satisfaction which they express is a forbidden one. The only trace of these thoughts that appears in the manifest dream is their diametric opposite, just as in the case of dreams belonging to Group A. The essential characteristic of punishment-dreams would thus be that in their case the dream-constructing wish is not an unconscious wish derived from the repressed (from the system *Ucs.*), but a punitive one reacting against it and belonging to the ego, though at the same time an unconscious (that is to say, preconscious) one.[1]

I will report a dream of my own[2] in order to illustrate what I have just said, and in particular the way in which the dream-work deals with a residue of distressing anticipations from the previous day.

'Indistinct beginning. *I said to my wife that I had a piece of news for her, something quite special. She was alarmed and refused to listen. I assured her that on the contrary it was something that she would be very glad to hear, and began to tell her that our son's officers' mess had sent a sum of money* (5000 *Kronen?*) . . . *something about distinction . . . distribution. . . . Meanwhile I had gone with her into a small*

---

[1] [*Footnote added* 1930:] This would be the appropriate point for a reference to the 'super-ego', one of the later findings of psycho-analysis. [Cf. p. 476, *n.* 2.—A class of dreams which are an exception to the 'wish-theory' (those which occur in traumatic neuroses) is discussed in Chapter II of *Beyond the Pleasure Principle* (1920g) and in the last pages of Lecture XXIX in the *New Introductory Lectures* (1933a).]

[2] [This paragraph and the two following ones were added as a footnote in 1919, and incorporated in the text in 1930.]

*room, like a store-room, to look for something. Suddenly I saw my son
appear. He was not in uniform but in tight-fitting sports clothes (like a
seal?), with a little cap. He climbed up on to a basket that was standing
beside a cupboard, as though he wanted to put something on the cupboard. I called out to him: no reply. It seemed to me that his face or
forehead was bandaged. He was adjusting something in his mouth, pushing something into it. And his hair was flecked with grey. I thought:
"Could he be as exhausted as all that? And has he got false teeth?"*
Before I could call out again I woke up, feeling no anxiety but
with my heart beating rapidly. My bedside clock showed that
it was two thirty.'

Once again it is impossible for me to present a complete
analysis. I must restrict myself to bringing out a few salient
points. Distressing anticipations from the previous day were
what gave rise to the dream: we had once more been without
news of our son at the front for over a week. It is easy to see
that the content of the dream expressed a conviction that he
had been wounded or killed. Energetic efforts were clearly
being made at the beginning of the dream to replace the distressing thoughts by their contrary. I had some highly agreeable
news to communicate—something about money being sent . . .
distinction . . . distribution. (The sum of money was derived
from an agreeable occurrence in my medical practice; it was an
attempt at a complete diversion from the topic.) But these
efforts failed. My wife suspected something dreadful and refused
to listen to me. The disguises were too thin and references to
what it was sought to repress pierced through them everywhere.
If my son had been killed, his fellow-officers would send back
his belongings and I should have to distribute what he left
among his brothers and sisters and other people. A 'distinction'
is often awarded to an officer who has fallen in battle. Thus the
dream set about giving direct expression to what it had first
sought to deny, though the inclination towards wish-fulfilment
was still shown at work in the distortions. (The change of
locality during the dream is no doubt to be understood as what
Silberer [1912] has described as 'threshold symbolism'. [Cf.
above, p. 504 f.]) We cannot tell, it is true, what it was that provided the dream with the motive force for thus giving expression
to my distressing thoughts. My son did not appear as someone
'falling' but as someone 'climbing'. He had in fact been a keen
mountaineer. He was not in uniform but in sports clothes; this

meant that the place of the accident that I *now* feared had been taken by an *earlier*, sporting one; for he had had a fall during a ski-ing expedition and broken his thigh. The way in which he was dressed, on the other hand, which made him look like a seal, at once recalled someone younger—our funny little grandson; while the grey hair reminded me of the latter's father, our son-in-law, who had been hard hit by the war. What could this mean? . . . but I have said enough of it.—The locality in a store-closet and the cupboard from which he wanted to take something ('on which he wanted to put something' in the dream)—these allusions reminded me unmistakably of an accident of my own which I had brought on myself when I was between two and three years old.[1] I had climbed up on to a stool in the store-closet to get something nice that was lying on a cupboard or table. The stool had tipped over and its corner had struck me behind my lower jaw; I might easily, I reflected, have knocked out all my teeth. The recollection was accompanied by an admonitory thought: 'that serves you right'; and this seemed as though it was a hostile impulse aimed at the gallant soldier. Deeper analysis at last enabled me to discover what the concealed impulse was which might have found satisfaction in the dreaded accident to my son: it was the envy which is felt for the young by those who have grown old, but which they believe they have completely stifled. And there can be no question that it was precisely the *strength* of the painful emotion which would have arisen if such a misfortune had really happened that caused that emotion to seek out a repressed wish-fulfilment of this kind in order to find some consolation.[2]

I am now in a position to give a precise account of the part played in dreams by the unconscious wish. I am ready to admit that there is a whole class of dreams the *instigation* to which arises principally or even exclusively from the residues of daytime life; and I think that even my wish that I might at long last become a Professor Extraordinarius might have allowed me to sleep through the night in peace if my worry over my friend's health had not still persisted from the previous day [p. 271]. But the worry alone could not have made a dream. The *motive*

[1] [Cf. p. 17, footnote.]

[2] [This dream is discussed briefly in its possible telepathic aspect at the beginning of Freud's paper on 'Dreams and Telepathy' (1922a)].

force which the dream required had to be provided by a wish; it was the business of the worry to get hold of a wish to act as the motive force of the dream.

The position may be explained by an analogy. A daytime thought may very well play the part of *entrepreneur* for a dream; but the *entrepreneur*, who, as people say, has the idea and the initiative to carry it out, can do nothing without capital; he needs a *capitalist* who can afford the outlay, and the capitalist who provides the psychical outlay for the dream is invariably and indisputably, whatever may be the thoughts of the previous day, *a wish from the unconscious*.[1]

Sometimes the capitalist is himself the *entrepreneur*, and indeed in the case of dreams this is the commoner event: an unconscious wish is stirred up by daytime activity and proceeds to construct a dream. So, too, the other possible variations in the economic situation that I have taken as an analogy have their parallel in dream-processes. The *entrepreneur* may himself make a small contribution to the capital; several *entrepreneurs* may apply to the same capitalist; several capitalists may combine to put up what is necessary for the *entrepreneur*. In the same way, we come across dreams that are supported by more than one dream-wish; and so too with other similar variations, which could easily be run through, but which would be of no further interest to us. We must reserve until later what remains to be said of the dream-wish.

The *tertium comparationis* [third element of comparison] in the analogy that I have just used—the quantity[2] put at the disposal of the *entrepreneur* in an appropriate amount—is capable of being applied in still greater detail to the purpose of elucidating the structure of dreams. In most dreams it is possible to detect a central point which is marked by peculiar sensory intensity, as I have shown on pp. 305 [and 329 f.]. This central point is as a rule the direct representation of the wish-fulfilment, for, if we undo the displacements brought about by the dream-work, we find that the *psychical* intensity of the elements in the dream-thoughts has been replaced by the *sensory* intensity of the

[1] [These last two paragraphs are quoted in full by Freud at the end of his analysis of Dora's first dream (1905*e*, Part II), which, he comments, is a complete confirmation of their correctness.]

[2] [Of capital in the case of the analogy, and of psychical energy in the case of a dream.]

elements in the content of the actual dream. The elements in the *neighbourhood* of the wish-fulfilment often have nothing to do with its meaning, but turn out to be derivatives of distressing thoughts that run contrary to the wish. But owing to their being in what is often an artificially established connection with the central element, they have acquired enough intensity to become capable of being represented in the dream. Thus the wish-fulfilment's power of bringing about representation is diffused over a certain sphere surrounding it, within which all the elements— including even those possessing no means of their own—become empowered to obtain representation. In the case of dreams that are actuated by *several* wishes, it is easy to delimit the spheres of the different wish-fulfilments, and gaps in the dream may often be understood as frontier zones between those spheres.[1]

Though the preceding considerations have reduced the importance of the part played by the day's residues in dreams, it is worth while devoting a little more attention to them. It must be that they are essential ingredients in the formation of dreams, since experience has revealed the surprising fact that in the content of every dream some link with a recent daytime impression —often of the most insignificant sort—is to be detected. We have not hitherto been able to explain the necessity for this addition to the mixture that constitutes a dream (see p. 181). And it is only possible to do so if we bear firmly in mind the part played by the unconscious wish and then seek for information from the psychology of the neuroses. We learn from the latter that an unconscious idea is as such quite incapable of entering the preconscious and that it can only exercise any effect there by establishing a connection with an idea which already belongs to the preconscious, by transferring its intensity on to it and by getting itself 'covered' by it. Here we have the fact of 'transference',[2] which provides an explanation of so many striking

[1] [A particularly clear summary of the part played by the 'day's residues' in the construction of dreams will be found in the course of Freud's short paper, 1913a.]

[2] [In his later writings Freud regularly used this same word 'transference' ('*Übertragung*') to describe a somewhat different, though not unrelated, psychological process, first discovered by him as occurring in the course of psycho-analytic treatment—namely, the process of 'transferring' on to a contemporary object feelings which originally applied, and still unconsciously apply, to an infantile object. (See, e.g., Freud, 1905e,

phenomena in the mental life of neurotics. The preconscious idea, which thus acquires an undeserved degree of intensity, may either be left unaltered by the transference, or it may have a modification forced upon it, derived from the content of the idea which effects the transference. I hope I may be forgiven for drawing analogies from everyday life, but I am tempted to say that the position of a repressed idea resembles that of an American dentist in this country: he is not allowed to set up in practice unless he can make use of a legally qualified medical practitioner to serve as a stalking-horse and to act as a 'cover' in the eyes of the law. And just as it is not exactly the physicians with the largest practices who form alliances of this kind with dentists, so in the same way preconscious or conscious ideas which have already attracted a sufficient amount of the attention that is operating in the preconscious will not be the ones to be chosen to act as covers for a repressed idea. The unconscious prefers to weave its connections round preconscious impressions and ideas which are either indifferent and have thus had no attention paid to them, or have been rejected and have thus had attention promptly withdrawn from them. It is a familiar article in the doctrine of association, and one that is entirely confirmed by experience, that an idea which is bound by a very intimate tie in one direction, tends, as it were, to repel whole groups of new ties. I once attempted to base a theory of hysterical paralyses on this proposition.[1]

If we assume that the same need for transference on the part of repressed ideas which we have discovered in analysing the neuroses is also at work in dreams, two of the riddles of the dream are solved at a blow: the fact, namely, that every analysis of a dream shows some recent impression woven into its texture and that this recent element is often of the most trivial kind [p. 180]. I may add that (as we have already found elsewhere [p. 177]) the reason why these recent and indifferent elements so frequently find their way into dreams as substitutes for the most ancient of all the dream-thoughts is that they have least to fear from the censorship imposed by resistance. But while the

Section IV, and Freud, 1915a.) The word occurs also in this other sense in the present volume—e.g. on pp. 184 and 200—and had already been so used by Freud in the last pages of Chapter IV of *Studies on Hysteria* (Breuer and Freud, 1895).]

[1] [See Section IV of Freud 1893c.]

fact that *trivial* elements are preferred is explained by their free-dom from censorship, the fact that *recent* elements occur with such regularity points to the existence of a need for transference. Both groups of impressions satisfy the demand of the repressed for material that is still clear of associations—the indifferent ones because they have given no occasion for the formation of many ties, and the recent ones because they have not yet had time to form them.

It will be seen, then, that the day's residues, among which we may now class the indifferent impressions, not only *borrow* something from the *Ucs.* when they succeed in taking a share in the formation of a dream—namely the instinctual force which is at the disposal of the repressed wish—but that they also *offer* the unconscious something indispensable—namely the neces-sary point of attachment for a transference. If we wished to penetrate more deeply at this point into the processes of the mind, we should have to throw more light upon the interplay of excitations between the preconscious and the unconscious—a subject towards which the study of the psychoneuroses draws us, but upon which, as it happens, dreams have no help to offer.

I have only one thing more to add about the day's residues. There can be no doubt that it is they that are the true disturbers of sleep and not dreams, which, on the contrary are concerned to guard it. I shall return to this point later. [See p. 577 ff.]

We have so far been studying dream-wishes: we have traced them from their origin in the region of the *Ucs.* and have analysed their relations to the day's residues, which in their turn may either be wishes or psychical impulses of some other kind or simply recent impressions. In this way we have allowed room for every claim that may be raised by any of the multifarious waking thought-activities on behalf of the importance of the part played by them in the process of constructing dreams. It is not impossible, even, that our account may have provided an explanation of the extreme cases in which a dream, pursuing the activities of daytime, arrives at a happy solution of some unsolved problem of waking life.[1] All we need is an example of this kind, so that we might analyse it and trace the source of the infantile or repressed wishes whose help has been enlisted and

[1] [See above, p. 64 f. An instance of this is mentioned in a footnote at the end of Section II of *The Ego and the Id* (Freud, 1923b).]

has reinforced the efforts of preconscious activity with such success. But all this has not brought us a step nearer to solving the riddle of why it is that the unconscious has nothing else to offer during sleep but the motive force for the fulfilment of a *wish*. The answer to this question must throw light upon the psychical nature of wishes, and I propose to give the answer by reference to our schematic picture of the psychical apparatus.

There can be no doubt that that apparatus has only reached its present perfection after a long period of development. Let us attempt to carry it back to an earlier stage of its functioning capacity. Hypotheses, whose justification must be looked for in other directions, tell us that at first the apparatus's efforts were directed towards keeping itself so far as possible free from stimuli; [1] consequently its first structure followed the plan of a reflex apparatus, so that any sensory excitation impinging on it could be promptly discharged along a motor path. But the exigencies of life interfere with this simple function, and it is to them, too, that the apparatus owes the impetus to further development. The exigencies of life confront it first in the form of the major somatic needs. The excitations produced by internal needs seek discharge in movement, which may be described as an 'internal change' or an 'expression of emotion'. A hungry baby screams or kicks helplessly. But the situation remains unaltered, for the excitation arising from an internal need is not due to a force producing a *momentary* impact but to one which is in continuous operation. A change can only come about if in some way or other (in the case of the baby, through outside help) an 'experience of satisfaction' can be achieved which puts an end to the internal stimulus. An essential component of this experience of satisfaction is a particular perception (that of nourishment, in our example) the mnemic image of which remains associated thenceforward with the memory trace of the excitation produced by the need. As a result of the link that has thus been established, next time this need arises a psychical

---

[1] [This is the so-called 'Principle of Constancy' which is discussed in the opening pages of *Beyond the Pleasure Principle* (1920*g*). But it was already a fundamental assumption in some of Freud's earliest psychological writings, e.g. in his posthumously published 'Letter to Josef Breuer' of June 29, 1892 (Freud, 1941*a*). The whole gist of the present paragraph is already stated in Sections 1, 2, 11 and 16 of Part I of his 'Project for a Scientific Psychology' written in the autumn of 1895 (Freud, 1950*a*). Cf. Editor's Introduction, p. xv ff.]

impulse will at once emerge which will seek to re-cathect the mnemic image of the perception and to re-evoke the perception itself, that is to say, to re-establish the situation of the original satisfaction. An impulse of this kind is what we call a wish; the reappearance of the perception is the fulfilment of the wish; and the shortest path to the fulfilment of the wish is a path leading direct from the excitation produced by the need to a complete cathexis of the perception. Nothing prevents us from assuming that there was a primitive state of the psychical apparatus in which this path was actually traversed, that is, in which wishing ended in hallucinating. Thus the aim of this first psychical activity was to produce a 'perceptual identity'[1]— a repetition of the perception which was linked with the satisfaction of the need.

The bitter experience of life must have changed this primitive thought-activity into a more expedient secondary one. The establishment of a perceptual identity along the short path of regression within the apparatus does not have the same result elsewhere in the mind as does the cathexis of the same perception from without. Satisfaction does not follow; the need persists. An internal cathexis could only have the same value as an external one if it were maintained unceasingly, as in fact occurs in hallucinatory psychoses and hunger phantasies, which exhaust their whole psychical activity in clinging to the object of their wish. In order to arrive at a more efficient expenditure of psychical force, it is necessary to bring the regression to a halt before it becomes complete, so that it does not proceed beyond the mnemic image, and is able to seek out other paths which lead eventually to the desired perceptual identity being established from the direction of the external world.[2] This inhibition of the regression and the subsequent diversion of the excitation become the business of a second system, which is in control of voluntary movement—which for the first time, that is, makes use of movement for purposes remembered in advance. But all the complicated thought-activity which is spun out from the mnemic image to the moment at which the perceptual identity

---

[1] [I.e. something perceptually identical with the 'experience of satisfaction'.]

[2] [*Footnote added* 1919:] In other words, it becomes evident that there must be a means of 'reality-testing' [i.e. of testing things to see whether they are real or not].

is established by the external world—all this activity of thought merely constitutes a roundabout path to wish-fulfilment which has been made necessary by experience.[1] Thought is after all nothing but a substitute for a hallucinatory wish; and it is self-evident that dreams must be wish-fulfilments, since nothing but a wish can set our mental apparatus at work. Dreams, which fulfil their wishes along the short path of regression, have merely preserved for us in that respect a sample of the psychical apparatus's primary method of working, a method which was abandoned as being inefficient. What once dominated waking life, while the mind was still young and incompetent, seems now to have been banished into the night—just as the primitive weapons, the bows and arrows, that have been abandoned by adult men, turn up once more in the nursery. *Dreaming is a piece of infantile mental life that has been superseded.* These methods of working on the part of the psychical apparatus, which are normally suppressed in waking hours, become current once more in psychosis and then reveal their incapacity for satisfying our needs in relation to the external world.[2]

The unconscious wishful impulses clearly try to make themselves effective in daytime as well, and the fact of transference, as well as the psychoses, show us that they endeavour to force their way by way of the preconscious system into consciousness and to obtain control of the power of movement. Thus the censorship between the *Ucs.* and the *Pcs.*, the assumption of whose existence is positively forced upon us by dreams, deserves to be recognized and respected as the watchman of our mental health. Must we not regard it, however, as an act of carelessness on the part of that watchman that it relaxes its activities during the night, allows the suppressed impulses in the *Ucs.* to find expression, and makes it possible for hallucinatory regression to

[1] The wish-fulfilling activity of dreams is justly extolled by Le Lorrain, who speaks of it as 'sans fatigue sérieuse, sans être obligé de recourir à cette lutte opiniâtre et longue qui use et corrode les jouissances poursuivies [incurring no serious fatigue and not being obliged to embark upon the long and obstinate struggle that wears away and spoils enjoyments that have to be pursued]'.

[2] [*Footnote added* 1914:] I have elsewhere carried this train of thought further in a paper on the two principles of mental functioning (Freud, 1911*b*)—the pleasure principle and the reality principle, as I have proposed calling them. [The argument is in fact developed further below, on p. 598 ff.]

occur once more? I think not. For even though this critical watchman goes to rest—and we have proof that its slumbers are not deep—it also shuts the door upon the power of movement. No matter what impulses from the normally inhibited *Ucs.* may prance upon the stage, we need feel no concern; they remain harmless, since they are unable to set in motion the motor apparatus by which alone they might modify the external world. The state of sleep guarantees the security of the citadel that must be guarded. The position is less harmless when what brings about the displacement of forces is not the nightly relaxation in the critical censorship's output of force, but a pathological reduction in that force or a pathological intensification of the unconscious excitations while the preconscious is still cathected and the gateway to the power of movement stands open. When this is so, the watchman is overpowered, the unconscious excitations overwhelm the *Pcs.*, and thence obtain control over our speech and actions; or they forcibly bring about hallucinatory regression and direct the course of the apparatus (which was not designed for their use) by virtue of the attraction exercised by perceptions on the distribution of our psychical energy. To this state of things we give the name of psychosis.

We are now well on the way to proceeding further with the erection of the psychological scaffolding, which we stopped at the point at which we introduced the two systems *Ucs.* and *Pcs.* But there are reasons for continuing a little with our consideration of wishes as the sole psychical motive force for the construction of dreams. We have accepted the idea that the reason why dreams are invariably wish-fulfilments is that they are products of the system *Ucs.*, whose activity knows no other aim than the fulfilment of wishes and which has at its command no other forces than wishful impulses. If we insist, for even a moment longer, upon our right to base such far-reaching psychological speculations upon the interpretation of dreams, we are in duty bound to prove that those speculations have enabled us to insert dreams into a nexus which can include other psychical structures as well. If such a thing as a system *Ucs.* exists (or something analogous to it for the purposes of our discussion), dreams cannot be its only manifestation; every dream may be a wish-fulfilment, but apart from dreams there must be other forms of abnormal wish-fulfilments. And it is a fact that the theory governing all psychoneurotic symptoms culminates in a single proposition, which asserts that *they too are to be regarded as fulfilments of unconscious wishes*.[1] Our explanation makes the dream only the first member of a class which is of the greatest significance to psychiatrists and an understanding of which implies the solution of the purely psychological side of the problem of psychiatry.[2]

The other members of this class of wish-fulfilments—hysterical symptoms, for instance—possess one essential characteristic, however, which I cannot discover in dreams. I have learnt from the researches which I have mentioned so often in the course of this work that in order to bring about the formation of a hysterical symptom *both* currents of our mind must converge. A symptom is not merely the expression of a realized unconscious wish; a wish from the preconscious which is fulfilled by the same symptom must also be present. So that the symptom will have *at least* two determinants, one arising from each of the systems involved in the conflict. As in the case of dreams, there are no limits to the further determinants that may be present—to the 'overdetermination' of the symptoms.[3] The determinant which does not arise from the *Ucs.* is invariably, so far as I know, a train of thought reacting against the unconscious wish—a self-punishment, for instance. I can therefore make the quite general assertion that *a hysterical symptom develops only where the fulfilments of two opposing wishes, arising each from a different psychical system, are able to converge in a single expression.* (Compare in this connection my most recent formulations on the origin of hysterical symptoms in my paper on hysterical phantasies and their relation to bisexuality. [Freud, 1908a.][4]) Examples would serve very little purpose here, since nothing but an exhaustive elucidation of the complications involved

[1] [*Footnote added* 1914:] Or more correctly, one portion of the symptom corresponds to the unconscious wish-fulfilment and another portion to the mental structure reacting against the wish.

[2] [*Footnote added* 1914:] As Hughlings Jackson said: 'Find out all about dreams and you will have found out all about insanity.' [Quoted by Ernest Jones (1911), who had heard it at first hand from Hughlings Jackson.]

[3] [Cf. Freud in Breuer and Freud, 1895, Chapter IV, Section 1, Observation 3.]

[4] [This sentence was added in 1909.]

could carry conviction. I will therefore leave my assertion to stand for itself and only quote an example in order to make the point clear, and not to carry conviction. In one of my women patients, then, hysterical vomiting turned out to be on the one hand the fulfilment of an unconscious phantasy dating from her puberty—of a wish, that is, that she might be continuously pregnant and have innumerable children, with a further wish, added later, that she might have them by as many men as possible. A powerful defensive impulse had sprung up against this unbridled wish. And, since the patient might lose her figure and her good looks as a result of her vomiting, and so might cease to be attractive to anyone, the symptom was acceptable to the punitive train of thought as well; and since it was permitted by both sides it could become a reality. This was the same method of treating a wish-fulfilment as was adopted by the Parthian queen towards the Roman triumvir Crassus. Believing that he had embarked on his expedition out of love of gold, she ordered molten gold to be poured down his throat when he was dead: 'Now', she said, 'you have what you wanted.' But all that we so far know about dreams is that they express the fulfilment of a wish from the unconscious; it seems as though the dominant, preconscious system acquiesces in this after insisting upon a certain number of distortions. Nor is it possible as a general rule to find a train of thought opposed to the dream-wish and, like its counterpart, realized in the dream. Only here and there in dream analyses do we come upon signs of reactive creations, like, for instance, my affectionate feelings for my friend R. in the dream of my uncle [with the yellow beard] (cf. p. 140 ff.). But we can find the missing ingredient from the preconscious elsewhere. Whereas the wish from the *Ucs.* is able to find expression in the dream after undergoing distortions of every kind, the dominant system withdraws into a *wish to sleep*, realizes that wish by bringing about the modifications which it is able to produce in the cathexes within the psychical apparatus, and persists in that wish throughout the whole duration of sleep.[1]

This determined wish on the part of the preconscious to sleep exercises a generally facilitating effect on the formation of dreams. Let me recall the dream dreamt by the man who was

[1] I have borrowed this idea from the theory of sleep put forward by Liébeault (1889), to whom is due the revival in modern times of research into hypnotism.

led to infer from the glare of light coming out of the next room that his child's body might be on fire [p. 509 ff.]. The father drew this inference in a dream instead of allowing himself to be woken up by the glare; and we have suggested that one of the psychical forces responsible for this result was a wish which prolonged by that one moment the life of the child whom he pictured in the dream. Other wishes, originating from the repressed, probably escape us, since we are unable to analyse the dream. But we may assume that a further motive force in the production of the dream was the father's need to sleep; his sleep, like the child's life, was prolonged by one moment by the dream. 'Let the dream go on'—such was his motive—'or I shall have to wake up.' In every other dream, just as in this one, the wish to sleep lends its support to the unconscious wish. On p. 125 f. I described some dreams which appeared openly as dreams of convenience. But in fact all dreams can claim a right to the same description. The operation of the wish to continue sleeping is most easily to be seen in arousal dreams, which modify external sensory stimuli in such a way as to make them compatible with a continuance of sleep; they weave them into a dream in order to deprive them of any possibility of acting as reminders of the external world. That same wish must, however, play an equal part in allowing the occurrence of all other dreams, though it may only be from *within* that they threaten to shake the subject out of his sleep. In some cases, when a dream carries things too far, the *Pcs.* says to consciousness: 'Never mind! go on sleeping! after all it's only a dream!' [See p. 488 f.] But this describes in general the attitude of our dominant mental activity towards dreams, though it may not be openly expressed. I am driven to conclude that *throughout our whole sleeping state we know just as certainly that we are dreaming as we know that we are sleeping.* We must not pay too much attention to the counterargument that our consciousness is never brought to bear on the latter piece of knowledge and that it is only brought to bear on the former on particular occasions when the censorship feels that it has, as it were, been taken off its guard.

On the other hand,[1] there are some people who are quite clearly aware during the night that they are asleep and dreaming and who thus seem to possess the faculty of consciously directing their dreams. If, for instance, a dreamer of this kind

[1] [This paragraph was added in 1909.]

is dissatisfied with the turn taken by a dream, he can break it off without waking up and start it again in another direction—just as a popular dramatist may under pressure give his play a happier ending. Or another time, if his dream has led him into a sexually exciting situation, he can think to himself: 'I won't go on with this dream any further and exhaust myself with an emission; I'll hold it back for a real situation instead.'

The Marquis d'Hervey de Saint-Denys [1867, 268ff.],[1] quoted by Vaschide (1911, 139), claimed to have acquired the power of accelerating the course of his dreams just as he pleased, and of giving them any direction he chose. It seems as though in his case the wish to sleep had given place to another preconscious wish, namely to observe his dreams and enjoy them. Sleep is just as compatible with a wish of this sort as it is with a mental reservation to wake up if some particular condition is fulfilled (e.g. in the case of a nursing mother or wet-nurse) [p. 223 f.]. Moreover, it is a familiar fact that anyone who takes an interest in dreams remembers a considerably greater number of them after waking.

Ferenczi (1911),[2] in the course of a discussion of some other observations upon the directing of dreams, remarks: 'Dreams work over the thoughts which are occupying the mind at the moment from every angle; they will drop a dream-image if it threatens the success of a wish-fulfilment and will experiment with a fresh solution, till at last they succeed in constructing a wish-fulfilment which satisfies both agencies of the mind as a compromise.'

[1] [This paragraph was added in 1914.]
[2] [This paragraph was added as a footnote in 1914 and included in the text in 1930.]

(D)

AROUSAL BY DREAMS—THE FUNCTION OF
DREAMS—ANXIETY-DREAMS

Now that we know that all through the night the preconscious is concentrated upon the wish to sleep, we are in a position to carry our understanding of the process of dreaming a stage further. But first let us summarize what we have learnt so far.

The situation is this. Either residues of the previous day have been left over from the activity of waking life and it has not been possible to withdraw the whole cathexis of energy from them; or the activity of waking life during the course of the day has led to the stirring up of an unconscious wish; or these two events have happened to coincide. (We have already discussed the various possibilities in this connection.) The unconscious wish links itself up with the day's residues and effects a transference on to them; this may happen either in the course of the day or not until a state of sleep has been established. A wish now arises which has been transferred on to the recent material; or a recent wish, having been suppressed, gains fresh life by being reinforced from the unconscious. This wish seeks to force its way along the normal path taken by thought-processes, through the *Pcs.* (to which, indeed, it in part belongs) to consciousness. But it comes up against the censorship, which is still functioning and to the influence of which it now submits. At this point it takes on the distortion for which the way has already been paved by the transference of the wish on to the recent material. So far it is on the way to becoming an obsessive idea or a delusion or something of the kind—that is, *a thought* which has been intensified by transference and distorted in its expression by censorship. Its further advance is halted, however, by the sleeping state of the preconscious. (The probability is that that system has protected itself against the invasion by diminishing its own excitations.) The dream-process consequently enters on a regressive path, which lies open to it precisely owing to the peculiar nature of the state of sleep, and it is led along that path by the attraction exercised on it by groups of memories; some of these memories themselves exist only in the form of visual cathexes and not as translations into the terminology of the later systems. [Cf. p. 546.] In the course of its regressive path the dream-process acquires the attribute of representability. (I shall deal later with the question of compression [p. 595].) It has now completed the second portion of its zigzag journey. The first portion was a progressive one, leading from the unconscious scenes or phantasies to the preconscious; the second portion led from the frontier of the censorship back again to perceptions. But when the content of the dream-process has become perceptual, by that fact it has, as it were, found a way of evading the obstacle put in its way by the censorship and the state of sleep in the *Pcs.* [Cf. p. 526.] It succeeds in drawing attention to itself and in being noticed by consciousness.

For consciousness, which we look upon in the light of a sense organ for the apprehension of psychical qualities, is capable in waking life of receiving excitations from two directions. In the first place, it can receive excitations from the periphery of the whole apparatus, the perceptual system; and in addition to this, it can receive excitations of pleasure and unpleasure, which prove to be almost the only psychical quality attaching to transpositions of energy in the inside of the apparatus. All other processes in the ψ-systems, including the *Pcs.*, are lacking in any psychical quality and so cannot be objects of consciousness, except in so far as they bring pleasure or unpleasure to perception. We are thus driven to conclude that *these releases of pleasure and unpleasure automatically regulate the course of cathectic processes.* But, in order to make more delicately adjusted performances possible, it later became necessary to make the course of ideas less dependent upon the presence or absence of unpleasure. For this purpose the *Pcs.* system needed to have qualities of its own which could attract consciousness; and it seems highly probable that it obtained them by linking the preconscious processes with the mnemic system of indications of speech, a system not without quality. [See p. 611 *n.*] By means of the qualities of that system, consciousness, which had hitherto been a sense organ for perceptions alone, also became a sense organ for a portion of our thought-processes. Now, therefore, there are, as it were, *two* sensory surfaces, one directed towards perception and the other towards the preconscious thought-processes.

I must assume that the state of sleep makes the sensory surface of consciousness which is directed towards the *Pcs.* far more insusceptible to excitation than the surface directed towards the *Pcpt.* systems. Moreover, this abandonment of interest in thought-processes during the night has a purpose: thinking is to come to a standstill, for the *Pcs.* requires sleep. Once, however, a dream has become a *perception*, it is in a position to excite consciousness, by means of the qualities it has now acquired. This sensory excitation proceeds to perform what is its essential function: it directs a part of the available cathectic energy in the *Pcs.* into attention to what is causing the excitation. [See p. 593.] It must therefore be admitted that every dream has an *arousing* effect, that it sets a part of the quiescent force of the *Pcs.* in action. The dream is then submitted by this force to the influence which we have described as secondary revision with an eye to consecutiveness and intelligibility. That is to say, the dream is treated by it just like any other perceptual content; it is met by the same anticipatory ideas, in so far as its subject-matter allows [p. 499]. So far as this third portion of the dream-process has any direction it is once again a progressive one.

To avoid misunderstandings, a word about the chronological relations of these dream-processes will not be out of place. A very attractive conjecture has been put forward by Goblot [1896, 289 f.], suggested, no doubt, by the riddle of Maury's guillotine dream [p. 26 f.]. He seeks to show that a dream occupies no more than the transition period between sleeping and waking. The process of awakening takes a certain amount of time, and during that time the dream occurs. We imagine that the final dream-image was so powerful that it compelled us to wake; whereas in fact it was only so powerful because at that moment we were already on the point of waking. 'Un rêve c'est un réveil qui commence.'[1]

It has already been pointed out by Dugas [1897*b*] that Goblot would have to disregard many facts before he could assert his thesis generally. Dreams occur from which we do not awaken—for instance, some in which we dream that we are dreaming. With our knowledge of the dream-work, we could not possibly agree that it only covers the period of awakening. It seems probable, on the contrary, that the first portion of the dream-work has already begun during the day, under the control of

[1] ['A dream is an awakening that is beginning.']

the preconscious. Its second portion—the modification imposed by the censorship, the attraction exercised by unconscious scenes, and the forcing of its way to perception—no doubt proceeds all through the night; and in this respect we may perhaps always be right when we express a feeling of having been dreaming all night long, though we cannot say what. [See p. 517.]

But it seems to me unnecessary to suppose that dream-processes really maintain, up to the moment of becoming conscious, the chronological order in which I have described them: that the first thing to appear is the transferred dream-wish, that distortion by the censorship follows, then the regressive change in direction, and so on. I have been obliged to adopt this order in my description; but what happens in reality is no doubt a simultaneous exploring of one path and another, a swinging of the excitation now this way and now that, until at last it accumulates in the direction that is most opportune and one particular grouping becomes the permanent one. Certain personal experiences of my own lead me to suspect that the dream-work often requires more than a day and a night in order to achieve its result; and if this is so, we need no longer feel any amazement at the extraordinary ingenuity shown in the construction of the dream. In my opinion even the demand for the dream to be made intelligible as a perceptual event may be put into effect before the dream attracts consciousness to itself. From then onwards, however, the pace is accelerated, for at that point a dream is treated in the same fashion as anything else that is perceived. It is like a firework, which takes hours to prepare but goes off in a moment.

The dream-process has by now either acquired sufficient intensity through the dream-work to attract consciousness to itself and arouse the preconscious, irrespectively of the time and depth of sleep; or its intensity is insufficient to achieve this and it must remain in a state of readiness until, just before waking, attention becomes more mobile and comes to meet it. The majority of dreams appear to operate with comparatively low psychical intensities, for they mostly wait until the moment of waking. But this also explains the fact that, if we are suddenly woken from deep sleep, we usually perceive something that we have dreamt. In such cases, just as when we wake of our own accord, the first thing we see is the perceptual content that has been constructed by the dream-work and immediately afterwards we see the perceptual content that is offered to us from outside ourselves.

Greater theoretical interest, however, attaches to the dreams which have the power to rouse us in the middle of our sleep. Bearing in mind the expediency which is everywhere else the rule, we may ask why a dream, that is, an unconscious wish, is given the power to interfere with sleep, that is, with the fulfilment of the preconscious wish. The explanation no doubt lies in relations of energy of which we have no knowledge. If we possessed such knowledge, we should probably find that allowing the dream to take its course and expending a certain amount of more or less detached attention on it is an economy of energy compared with holding the unconscious as tightly under control at night as in the daytime. [Cf. p. 578.] Experience shows that dreaming is compatible with sleeping, even if it interrupts sleep several times during the night. One wakes up for an instant and then falls asleep again at once. It is like brushing away a fly in one's sleep: a case of *ad hoc* awakening. If one falls asleep again, the interruption has been disposed of. As is shown by such familiar examples as the sleep of a nursing mother or wetnurse [p. 223 f.], the fulfilment of the wish to sleep is quite compatible with maintaining a certain expenditure of attention in some particular direction.

At this point an objection arises, which is based on a better knowledge of unconscious processes. I myself have asserted that unconscious wishes are always active. But in spite of this they seem not to be strong enough to make themselves perceptible during the day. If, however, while a state of sleep prevails, an unconscious wish has shown itself strong enough to construct a dream and arouse the preconscious with it, why should this strength fail after the dream has been brought to knowledge? Should not the dream continue to recur perpetually, precisely as the vexatious fly keeps on coming back after it has been driven away? What right have we to assert that dreams get rid of the disturbance of sleep?

It is perfectly true that unconscious wishes always remain active. They represent paths which can always be traversed, whenever a quantity of excitation makes use of them. [Cf. p. 553 *n*.] Indeed it is a prominent feature of unconscious processes that they are indestructible. In the unconscious nothing can be brought to an end, nothing is past or forgotten. This is brought most vividly home to one in studying the neuroses, and especially hysteria. The unconscious path of thoughts, which leads to discharge in a hysterical attack, immediately becomes traversable once more, when sufficient excitation has accumulated. A humiliation that was experienced thirty years ago acts exactly like a fresh one throughout the thirty years, as soon as it has obtained access to the unconscious sources of emotion. As soon as the memory of it is touched, it springs into life again and shows itself cathected with excitation which finds a motor discharge in an attack. This is precisely the point at which psychotherapy has to intervene. Its task is to make it possible for the unconscious processes to be dealt with finally and be forgotten. For the fading of memories and the emotional weakness of impressions which are no longer recent, which we are inclined to regard as self-evident and to explain as a primary effect of time upon mental memory-traces, are in reality secondary modifications which are only brought about by laborious work. What performs this work is the preconscious, and *psychotherapy can pursue no other course than to bring the Ucs. under the domination of the Pcs.*[1]

Thus there are two possible outcomes for any particular unconscious excitatory process. Either it may be left to itself, in which case it eventually forces its way through at some point and on this single occasion finds discharge for its excitation in movement; or it may come under the influence of the preconscious, and its excitation, instead of being *discharged*, may be *bound* by the preconscious. *This second alternative is the one which occurs in the process of dreaming.* [See p. 601 *n*.] The cathexis from the *Pcs.* which goes halfway to meet the dream after it has become perceptual, having been directed on to it by the excitation in consciousness, binds the dream's unconscious excitation and makes it powerless to act as a disturbance. If it is true that the dreamer wakes for an instant, yet he really *has* brushed away the fly that was threatening to disturb his sleep. It begins to dawn on us that it actually *is* more expedient and economical to allow the unconscious wish to take its course, to leave the path to regression open to it so that it can construct a dream, and then to bind the dream and dispose of it with a small expenditure of preconscious work—rather than to continue

[1] [The last clause of this sentence was printed in spaced type only from 1919 onwards. Cf. p. 553 *n*.]

keeping a tight rein on the unconscious throughout the whole period of sleep. [Cf. p. 577.] It was indeed to be expected that dreaming, even though it may originally have been a process without a useful purpose, would have procured itself some function in the interplay of mental forces. And we can now see what that function is. Dreaming has taken on the task of bringing back under control of the preconscious the excitation in the *Ucs.* which has been left free; in so doing, it discharges the *Ucs.* excitation, serves it as a safety valve and at the same time preserves the sleep of the preconscious in return for a small expenditure of waking activity. Thus, like all the other psychical structures in the series of which it is a member, it constitutes a compromise; it is in the service of both of the two systems, since it fulfils the two wishes in so far as they are compatible with each other. If we turn back to the 'excretion theory' of dreams put forward by Robert [1886], which I explained on p. 78 ff., we shall see at a glance that in its essence we must accept his account of the *function* of dreams, though differing from him in his premises and in his view of the dream-process itself. [See p. 177 f.][1]

The qualification 'in so far as the two wishes are compatible

[1] [*Footnote added* 1914:] Is this the only function that can be assigned to dreams? I know of no other. It is true that Maeder [1912] has attempted to show that dreams have other, 'secondary', functions. He started out from the correct observation that some dreams contain attempts at solving conflicts, attempts which are later carried out in reality and which thus behave as though they were trial practices for waking actions. He therefore drew a parallel between dreams and the play of animals and children, which may be regarded as practice in the operation of innate instincts and as preparation for serious activity later on, and put forward the hypothesis that dreams have a *'fonction ludique'* ['play function']. Shortly before Maeder, Alfred Adler [1911, 215 *n.*], too, had insisted that dreams possessed a function of 'thinking ahead'. (In an analysis which I published in 1905 ['Fragment of an Analysis of a Case of Hysteria', Part II (1905*e*)], a dream, which could only be regarded as expressing an intention, was repeated every night until it was carried out. [Cf. above, p. 190.])

A little reflection will convince us, however, that this 'secondary' function of dreams has no claim to be considered as a part of the subject of dream-interpretation. Thinking ahead, forming intentions, framing attempted solutions which may perhaps be realized later in waking life, all these, and many other similar things, are products of the unconscious and preconscious activity of the mind; they may persist in the state of with each other' implies a hint at the possible case in which the function of dreaming may come to grief. The dream-process is allowed to begin as a fulfilment of an unconscious wish; but if this attempted wish-fulfilment jars upon the preconscious so violently that it is unable to continue sleeping, then the dream has made a breach in the compromise and has failed to carry out the second half of its task. In that case the dream is immediately broken off and replaced by a state of complete waking. Here again it is not really the fault of the dream if it has now to appear in the role of a *disturber* of sleep instead of in its normal one of a *guardian* of sleep; and this fact need not prejudice us against its having a useful purpose. This is not the only instance in the organism of a contrivance which is normally useful becoming useless and disturbing as soon as the conditions that give rise to it are somewhat modified; and the disturbance at least serves the new purpose of drawing attention to the modification and of setting the organism's regulative machinery in motion against it. What I have in mind is of course the case of anxiety-dreams, and in order that I may not be thought to be evading this evidence against the theory of wish-fulfilment whenever I come across it, I will at all events give some hints of their explanation.

There is no longer anything contradictory to us in the notion that a psychical process which develops anxiety can nevertheless be the fulfilment of a wish. We know that it can be explained by the fact that the wish belongs to one system, the *Ucs.*, while it has been repudiated and suppressed by the other system, the *Pcs.*[1] Even where psychical health is perfect, the subjugation of

sleep as 'the day's residues' and combine with an unconscious wish (cf. p. 550 ff.) in forming a dream. Thus the dream's function of 'thinking ahead' is rather a function of preconscious waking thought, the products of which may be revealed to us by the analysis of dreams or of other phenomena. It has long been the habit to regard dreams as identical with their manifest content; but we must now beware equally of the mistake of confusing dreams with latent dream-thoughts. [Cf. p. 506 f. *n.* above and a passage at the end of the discussion of Case I in Freud's paper on 'Dreams and Telepathy' (1922a).]

[1] [*Footnote added* 1919:] 'A second factor, which is much more important and far-reaching, but which is equally overlooked by laymen is the following. No doubt a wish-fulfilment must bring pleasure; but the question then arises "To whom?" To the person who has the wish, of course. But, as we know, a dreamer's relation to his wishes is a quite peculiar one. He repudiates them and censors them—he has no liking for them,

the *Ucs.* by the *Pcs.* is not complete; the measure of suppression indicates the degree of our psychical normality. Neurotic symptoms show that the two systems are in conflict with each other; they are the products of a compromise which brings the conflict to an end for the time being. On the one hand, they allow the *Ucs.* an outlet for the discharge of its excitation, and provide it with a kind of sally-port, while, on the other hand, they make it possible for the *Pcs.* to control the *Ucs.* to some extent. It is instructive to consider, for instance, the significance of a hysterical phobia or an agoraphobia. Let us suppose that a neurotic patient is unable to cross the street alone—a condition which we rightly regard as a 'symptom'. If we remove this symptom by compelling him to carry out the act of which he believes himself incapable, the consequence will be an attack of anxiety; and indeed the occurrence of an anxiety-attack in the street is often the precipitating cause of the onset of an agoraphobia. We see, therefore, that the symptom has been constructed in order to avoid an outbreak of anxiety; the phobia is erected like a frontier fortification against the anxiety.

Our discussion cannot be carried any further without ex-

in short. So that their fulfilment will give him no pleasure, but just the opposite; and experience shows that this opposite appears in the form of anxiety, a fact which has still to be explained. Thus a dreamer in his relation to his dream-wishes can only be compared to an amalgamation of two separate people who are linked by some important common element. Instead of enlarging on this, I will remind you of a familiar fairy tale [referred to above on p. 557] in which you will find the same situation repeated. A good fairy promised a poor married couple to grant them the fulfilment of their first three wishes. They were delighted, and made up their minds to choose their three wishes carefully. But a smell of sausages being fried in the cottage next door tempted the woman to wish for a couple of them. They were there in a flash; and this was the first wish-fulfilment. But the man was furious, and in his rage wished that the sausages were hanging on his wife's nose. This happened too; and the sausages were not to be dislodged from their new position. This was the second wish-fulfilment; but the wish was the man's, and its fulfilment was most disagreeable for his wife. You know the rest of the story. Since after all they were in fact one—man and wife—the third wish was bound to be that the sausages should come away from the woman's nose. This fairy tale might be used in many other connections; but here it serves only to illustrate the possibility that if two people are not at one with each other the fulfilment of a wish of one of them may bring nothing but unpleasure to the other.' (*Introductory Lectures on Psycho-Analysis* [Freud, 1916–17], Lecture XIV.)

amining the part played by the affects in these processes; but we can only do so imperfectly in the present connection. Let us assume, then, that the suppression of the *Ucs.* is necessary above all because, if the course of ideas in the *Ucs.* were left to itself, it would generate an affect which was originally of a pleasurable nature, but became unpleasurable after the process of 'repression' occurred. The purpose, and the result too, of suppression is to prevent this release of unpleasure. The suppression extends over the ideational content of the *Ucs.*, since the release of unpleasure might start from that content. This presupposes a quite specific assumption as to the nature of the generation of affect.[1] It is viewed as a motor or secretory function, the key to whose innervation lies in the ideas in the *Ucs.* Owing to the domination established by the *Pcs.* these ideas are, as it were, throttled, and inhibited from sending out impulses which would generate affect. If, therefore, the cathexis from the *Pcs.* ceases, the danger is that the unconscious excitations may release affect of a kind which (as a result of the repression which has already occurred) can only be experienced as unpleasure, as anxiety.

This danger materializes if the dream-process is allowed to take its course. The conditions which determine its realization are that repressions must have occurred and that the suppressed wishful impulses shall be able to grow sufficiently strong. These determinants are thus quite outside the psychological framework of dream-formation. If it were not for the fact that our topic is connected with the subject of the generation of anxiety by the single factor of the liberation of the *Ucs.* during sleep, I should be able to omit any discussion of anxiety-dreams and avoid the necessity for entering in these pages into all the obscurities surrounding them.

The theory of anxiety-dreams, as I have already repeatedly declared, forms part of the psychology of the neuroses.[2] We have nothing more to do with it when once we have indicated its point of contact with the topic of the dream-process. There is only one thing more that I can do. Since I have asserted that neurotic anxiety arises from sexual sources, I can submit some

[1] [For this assumption cf. p. 468 and footnote.]

[2] [The following sentence was added at this point in 1911, but omitted again in 1925 and subsequently: 'Anxiety in dreams, I should like to insist, is an anxiety problem and not a dream problem.']

anxiety-dreams to analysis in order to show the sexual material present in their dream-thoughts.[1]

I have good reasons for leaving on one side in the present discussion the copious examples afforded by my neurotic patients, and for preferring to quote some anxiety-dreams dreamt by young people.

It is dozens of years since I myself had a true anxiety-dream. But I remember one from my seventh or eighth year, which I submitted to interpretation some thirty years later. It was a very vivid one, and in it I saw *my beloved mother, with a peculiarly peaceful, sleeping expression on her features, being carried into the room by two (or three) people with birds' beaks and laid upon the bed.* I awoke in tears and screaming, and interrupted my parents' sleep. The strangely draped and unnaturally tall figures with birds' beaks were derived from the illustrations to Philippson's Bible.[2] I fancy they must have been gods with falcons' heads from an ancient Egyptian funerary relief. Besides this, the analysis brought to mind an ill-mannered boy, a son of a *concierge*, who used to play with us on the grass in front of the house when we were children, and who I am inclined to think was called Philipp. It seems to me that it was from this boy that I first heard the vulgar term for sexual intercourse, instead of which educated people always use a latin word, 'to copulate', and which was clearly enough indicated by the choice of the falcons' heads.[3] I must have guessed the sexual significance of the word from the face of my young instructor, who was well acquainted with the facts of life. The expression on my mother's features in the dream was copied from the view I had had of my grandfather a few days before his death as he lay snoring in a coma. The interpretation carried out in the dream by the 'secondary revision' [p. 490] must therefore have been that my mother was dying; the funerary relief fitted in with this. I awoke in anxiety, which did not cease till I had woken my

[1] [Some of the comments in what follows would require revision in the light of Freud's later views on anxiety. See also pp. 160 ff., 236 and 337.]

[2] [*Die israelitische Bibel*, an edition of the Old Testament in Hebrew and German, Leipzig, 1839–54 (Second ed. 1858). A footnote to the fourth chapter of Deuteronomy shows a number of woodcuts of Egyptian gods, several with birds' heads.]

[3] [The German slang term referred to is '*vögeln*', from '*Vogel*' the ordinary word for 'bird'.]

parents up. I remember that I suddenly grew calm when I saw my mother's face, as though I had needed to be reassured that she was not dead. But this 'secondary' interpretation of the dream had already been made under the influence of the anxiety which had developed. I was not anxious because I had dreamt that my mother was dying; but I interpreted the dream in that sense in my preconscious revision of it because I was already under the influence of the anxiety. The anxiety can be traced back, when repression is taken into account, to an obscure and evidently sexual craving that had found appropriate expression in the visual content of the dream.

A twenty-seven-year-old man, who had been seriously ill for a year, reported that when he was between eleven and thirteen he had repeatedly dreamt (to the accompaniment of severe anxiety) that *a man with a hatchet was pursuing him; he tried to run away, but seemed to be paralysed and could not move from the spot.* This is a good example of a very common sort of anxiety-dream, which would never be suspected of being sexual. In analysis, the dreamer first came upon a story (dating from a time later than the dream) told him by his uncle, of how he had been attacked in the street one night by a suspicious-looking individual; the dreamer himself concluded from this association that he may have heard of some similar episode at the time of the dream. In connection with the hatchet, he remembered that at about that time he had once injured his hand with a hatchet while he was chopping up wood. He then passed immediately to his relations with his younger brother. He used to ill-treat this brother and knock him down; and he particularly remembered an occasion when he had kicked him on the head with his boot and had drawn blood, and how his mother had said: 'I'm afraid he'll be the death of him one day.' While he still seemed to be occupied with the subject of violence, a recollection from his ninth year suddenly occurred to him. His parents had come home late and had gone to bed while he pretended to be asleep; soon he had heard sounds of panting and other noises which had seemed to him uncanny, and he had also been able to make out their position in the bed. Further thoughts showed that he had drawn an analogy between this relation between his parents and his own relation to his younger brother. He had subsumed what happened between his parents under the concept of violence and struggling; and he had found evidence in favour of this view in the fact that he had often noticed blood in his mother's bed.

It is, I may say, a matter of daily experience that sexual intercourse between adults strikes any children who may observe it as something uncanny and that it arouses anxiety in them. I have explained this anxiety by arguing that what we are dealing with is a sexual excitation with which their understanding is unable to cope and which they also, no doubt, repudiate because their parents are involved in it, and which is therefore transformed into anxiety. At a still earlier period of life sexual excitations directed towards a parent of the opposite sex have not yet met with repression and, as we have seen, are freely expressed. (See p. 256 ff.)

I should have no hesitation in giving the same explanation of the attacks of night terrors accompanied by hallucinations (*pavor nocturnus*) which are so frequent in children. In this case too it can only be a question of sexual impulses which have not been understood and which have been repudiated. Investigation would probably show a periodicity in the occurrence of the attacks, since an increase in sexual libido can be brought about not only by accidental exciting impressions but also by successive waves of spontaneous developmental processes.

I lack a sufficiency of material based upon observation to enable me to confirm this explanation.[1]

Paediatricians, on the other hand, seem to lack the only line of approach which can make this whole class of phenomena intelligible, whether from the somatic or from the psychical aspect. I cannot resist quoting an amusing instance of the way in which the blinkers of medical mythology can cause an observer to miss an understanding of such cases by a narrow margin. My instance is taken from a thesis on *pavor nocturnus* by Debacker (1881, 66):

A thirteen-year-old boy in delicate health began to be apprehensive and dreamy. His sleep became disturbed and was interrupted almost once a week by severe attacks of anxiety accompanied by hallucinations. He always retained a very clear recollection of these dreams. He said that the Devil had shouted at him: 'Now we've got you, now we've got you!' There was then a smell of pitch and brimstone and his skin was burnt by

---

[1] [*Footnote added* 1919:] Since I wrote this a great quantity of such material has been brought forward in psycho-analytic literature.

flames. He woke up from the dream in terror, and at first could not cry out. When he had found his voice he was clearly heard to say: 'No, no, not me; I've not done anything!' or 'Please not! I won't do it again!' or sometimes: 'Albert never did that!' Later, he refused to undress 'because the flames only caught him when he was undressed'. While he was still having these devil-dreams, which were a threat to his health, he was sent into the country. There he recovered in the course of eighteen months, and once, when he was fifteen, he confessed: 'Je n'osais pas l'avouer, mais j'éprouvais continuellement des picotements et des surexcitations aux *parties*[1]; à la fin, cela m'énervait tant que plusieurs fois j'ai pensé me jeter par la fenêtre du dortoir.'[2]

There is really very little difficulty in inferring: (1) that the boy had masturbated when he was younger, that he had probably denied it, and that he had been threatened with severe punishment for his bad habit (cf. his admission: 'Je ne le ferais plus', and his denial: 'Albert n'a jamais fait ça'); (2) that with the onset of puberty the temptation to masturbate had revived with the tickling in his genitals; but (3) that a struggle for repression had broken out in him, which had suppressed his libido and transformed it into anxiety, and that the anxiety had taken over the punishments with which he had been threatened earlier.

And now let us see the inferences drawn by our author (ibid., 69): 'The following conclusions can be drawn from this observation:

'(1) The influence of puberty upon a boy in delicate health can lead to a condition of great weakness and can result in a considerable degree of *cerebral anaemia*.[3]

'(2) This cerebral anaemia produces character changes, demonomanic hallucinations and very violent nocturnal (and perhaps also diurnal) anxiety-states.

'(3) The boy's demonomania and self-reproaches go back to the influences of his religious education, which affected him as a child.

'(4) All the symptoms disappeared in the course of a some-

---

[1] I have italicized this word, but it is impossible to misunderstand it.
[2] ['I didn't dare admit it; but I was continually having prickly feelings and overexcitement in my parts; in the end it got on my nerves so much that I often thought of jumping out of the dormitory window.']
[3] The italics are mine.

what protracted visit to the country, as the result of physical exercise and the regaining of strength with the passage of puberty.

'(5) A predisposing influence upon the origin of the child's brain condition may perhaps be attributed to heredity and to a past syphilitic infection in his father.'

And here is the final conclusion: 'Nous avons fait entrer cette observation dans le cadre des délires apyrétiques d'inanition, car c'est à l'ischémie cérébrale que nous rattachons cet état particulier.'[1]

[1] ['We have classified this case among the apyretic deliria of inanition, for we attribute this particular state to cerebral ischaemia.']

THE PRIMARY AND SECONDARY PROCESSES— REPRESSION

In venturing on an attempt to penetrate more deeply into the psychology of dream-processes, I have set myself a hard task, and one to which my powers of exposition are scarcely equal. Elements in this complicated whole which are in fact simultaneous can only be represented successively in my description of them, while, in putting forward each point, I must avoid appearing to anticipate the grounds on which it is based: difficulties such as these it is beyond my strength to master. In all this I am paying the penalty for the fact that in my account of dream-psychology I have been unable to follow the historical development of my own views. Though my own line of approach to the subject of dreams was determined by my previous work on the psychology of the neuroses, I had not intended to make use of the latter as a basis of reference in the present work. Nevertheless I am constantly being driven to do so, instead of proceeding, as I should have wished, in the contrary direction and using dreams as a means of approach to the psychology of the neuroses. I am conscious of all the trouble in which my readers are thus involved, but I can see no means of avoiding it. [See p. 104 *n.*]

In my dissatisfaction at this state of things, I am glad to pause for a little over another consideration which seems to put a higher value on my efforts. I found myself faced by a topic on which, as has been shown in my first chapter, the opinions of the authorities were characterized by the sharpest contradictions. My treatment of the problems of dreams has found room for the majority of these contradictory views. I have only found it necessary to give a categorical denial of two of them—the view that dreaming is a meaningless process [p. 55 ff.] and the view that it is a somatic one [p. 77 f.]. Apart from this, I have been able to find a justification for all these mutually contradictory opinions at one point or other of my complicated thesis and to show that they had lighted upon some portion of the truth.

The view that dreams carry on the occupations and interests of waking life [p. 7 f.] has been entirely confirmed by the discovery of the concealed *dream-thoughts*. These are only concerned with what seems important to us and interests us greatly. Dreams are never occupied with minor details. But we have also found reason for accepting the contrary view, that dreams pick up indifferent refuse left over from the previous day [p. 18 ff.] and that they cannot get control of any major daytime interest until it has been to some extent withdrawn from waking activity [p. 18]. We have found that this holds good of the dream's *content*, which gives expression to the dream-thoughts in a form modified by distortion. For reasons connected with the mechanism of association, as we have seen, the dream-process finds it easier to get control of recent or indifferent ideational material which has not yet been requisitioned by waking thought-activity; and for reasons of censorship it transfers psychical intensity from what is important but objectionable on to what is indifferent.

The fact that dreams are hypermnesic [p. 11 ff.] and have access to material from childhood [p. 15 ff.] has become one of the corner-stones of our teaching. Our theory of dreams regards wishes originating in infancy as the indispensable motive force for the formation of dreams.

It has naturally not occurred to us to throw any doubt on the significance, which has been experimentally demonstrated, of external sensory stimuli during sleep [p. 23 ff.]; but we have shown that such material stands in the same relation to the dream-wish as do the residues of thought left over from daytime activity. Nor have we seen any reason to dispute the view that dreams interpret objective sensory stimuli just as illusions do [p. 28 f.]; but we have found the motive which provides the reason for that interpretation, a reason which has been left unspecified by other writers. Interpretation is carried out in such a way that the object perceived shall not interrupt sleep and shall be usable for purposes of wish-fulfilment. As regards subjective states of excitation in the sense organs during sleep, the occurrence of which seems to have been proved by Trumbull Ladd [1892; see above, p. 32 f.], it is true that we have not accepted them as a particular source of dreams; but we have been able to explain them as resulting from the regressive revival of memories that are in operation behind the dream.

Internal organic sensations, which have commonly been taken as a cardinal point in explanations of dreaming [p. 33 ff.], have retained a place, though a humbler one, in our theory. Such sensations—sensations of falling, for instance, or floating, or being inhibited—provide a material which is accessible at any time and of which the dream-work makes use, whenever it has need of it, for expressing the dream-thoughts.

The view that the dream-process is a rapid or instantaneous one [p. 64] is in our opinion correct as regards the perception by consciousness of the preconstructed dream-content; it seems probable that the preceding portions of the dream-process run a slow and fluctuating course. We have been able to contribute towards the solution of the riddle of dreams which contain a great amount of material compressed into the briefest moment of time; we have suggested that it is a question in such cases of getting hold of ready-made structures already present in the mind.

The fact that dreams are distorted and mutilated by memory [p. 46 f.] is accepted by us but in our opinion constitutes no obstacle; for it is no more than the last and manifest portion of a distorting activity which has been in operation from the very start of the dream's formation.

As regards the embittered and apparently irreconcilable dispute as to whether the mind sleeps at night [p. 54 f.] or is as much in command of all its faculties as it is by day [p. 60 f.], we have found that both parties are right but that neither is wholly right. We have found evidence in the dream-thoughts of a highly complex intellectual function, operating with almost the whole resources of the mental apparatus. Nevertheless it cannot be disputed that these dream-thoughts originated during the day, and it is imperative to assume that there is such a thing as a sleeping state of the mind. Thus even the theory of partial sleep [p. 77] has shown its value, though we have found that what characterizes the state of sleep is not the disintegration of mental bonds but the concentration of the psychical system which is in command during the day upon the wish to sleep. The factor of withdrawal from the external world [p. 7 f.] retains its significance in our scheme; it helps, though not as the sole determinant, to make possible the regressive character of representation in dreams. The renunciation of voluntary direction of the flow of ideas [p. 49 f.] cannot be disputed; but this does not deprive mental life of all purpose, for we have seen how, after voluntary purposive ideas have been abandoned, involuntary ones assume command. We have not merely accepted the fact of the looseness of associative connections in dreams [p. 58], but we have shown that it extends far further than had been suspected; we have found, however, that these loose connections are merely obligatory substitutes for others which are valid and significant. It is quite true that we have described dreams as absurd; but examples have taught us how sensible a dream can be even when it appears to be absurd.

We have no difference of opinion over the functions that are to be assigned to dreams. The view that dreams act as a safety-valve to the mind [p. 79] and that, in the words of Robert [1886, 10 f.], all kinds of harmful things are made harmless by being presented in a dream—not only does this view coincide exactly with our theory of the double wish-fulfilment brought about by dreams, but the way in which it is phrased is more intelligible to us than to Robert himself. The view that the mind has free play in its functioning in dreams [p. 82] is represented in our theory by the fact of the preconscious activity allowing dreams to take their course. Such phrases as 'the return of the mind in dreams to an embryonic point of view' or the words used by Havelock Ellis [1899, 721] to describe dreams—'an archaic world of vast emotions and imperfect thoughts' [p. 60]—strike us as happy anticipations of our own assertions that primitive modes of activity which are suppressed during the day are concerned in the construction of dreams. We have been able to accept entirely as our own what Sully [1893, 362] has written: 'Our dreams are a means of conserving these [earlier] successive personalities. When asleep we go back to the old ways of looking at things and of feeling about them, to impulses and activities which long ago dominated us' [p. 60].[1] For us no less than for Delage [1891] what has been 'suppressed' [p. 82] has become 'the motive force of dreams'.

We have fully appreciated the importance of the part ascribed by Scherner [1861] to 'dream-imagination', as well as Scherner's own interpretations [p. 83 ff.], but we have been obliged to transport them, as it were, to a different position in the problem. The point is not that dreams create the imagination,

---

[1] [This sentence was added in 1914.]

but rather that the unconscious activity of the imagination has a large share in the construction of the dream-thoughts. We remain in Scherner's debt for having indicated the source of the dream-thoughts; but nearly everything that he ascribes to the dream-work is really attributable to the activity of the unconscious during daytime, which is the instigating agent of dreams no less than of neurotic symptoms. We have been obliged to distinguish the 'dream-work' as something quite different and with a much narrower connotation.

Finally, we have by no means abandoned the relation between dreams and mental disorders [p. 89 ff.], but have established it more firmly on fresh ground.

We have thus been able to find a place in our structure for the most various and contradictory findings of earlier writers, thanks to the novelty of our theory of dreams, which combines them, as it were, into a higher unity. Some of those findings we have put to other uses, but we have wholly rejected only a few. Nevertheless our edifice is still uncompleted. Apart from the many perplexing questions in which we have become involved in making our way into the obscurities of psychology, we seem to be troubled by a fresh contradiction. On the one hand we have supposed that the dream-thoughts arise through entirely normal mental activity; but on the other hand we have discovered a number of quite abnormal processes of thought among the dream-thoughts, which extend into the dream-content, and which we then repeat in the course of our dream-interpretation. Everything that we have described as the 'dream-work' seems to depart so widely from what we recognize as rational thought-processes that the most severe strictures passed by earlier writers on the low level of psychical functioning in dreams must appear fully justified.

It may be that we shall only find enlightenment and assistance in this difficulty by carrying our investigation still further. And I will begin by picking out for closer examination one of the conjunctures which may lead to the formation of a dream.

A dream, as we have discovered, takes the place of a number of thoughts which are derived from our daily life and which form a completely logical sequence. We cannot doubt, then, that these thoughts originate from our normal mental life. All the attributes which we value highly in our trains of thought, and which characterize them as complex achievements of a high order, are to be found once more in dream-thoughts. There is no need to assume, however, that this activity of thought is performed during sleep—a possibility which would gravely confuse what has hitherto been our settled picture of the psychical state of sleep. On the contrary, these thoughts may very well have originated from the previous day, they may have proceeded unobserved by our consciousness from their start, and may already have been completed at the onset of sleep. The most that we can conclude from this is that it proves that *the most complicated achievements of thought are possible without the assistance of consciousness*—a fact which we could not fail to learn in any case from every psycho-analysis of a patient suffering from hysteria or from obsessional ideas. These dream-thoughts are certainly not in themselves inadmissible to consciousness; there may have been a number of reasons for their not having become conscious to us during the day. Becoming conscious is connected with the application of a particular psychical function [p. 541], that of attention—a function which, as it seems, is only available in a specific quantity, and this may have been diverted from the train of thought in question on to some other purpose.[1] There is another way, too, in which trains of thought of this kind may be withheld from consciousness. The course of our conscious reflections shows us that we follow a particular path in our application of attention. If, as we follow this path, we come upon an idea which will not bear criticism, we break off: we drop the cathexis of attention. Now it seems that the train of thought which has thus been initiated and dropped can continue to spin itself out without attention being turned to it again, unless at some point or other it reaches a specially high degree of intensity which forces attention to it. Thus, if a train of thought is initially rejected (consciously, perhaps) by a judgement that it is wrong or that it is useless for the immediate intellectual purposes in view, the result may be that this train of thought will proceed, unobserved by consciousness, until the onset of sleep.

To sum up—we describe a train of thought such as this as

[1] [The concept of 'attention' plays a very small part in Freud's later writings. It figures prominently, on the other hand, in his 'Project for a Scientific Psychology' (Freud, 1950a), e.g. in the opening section of Part III. Cf. also pp. 575 and 615.]

'preconscious'; we regard it as completely rational and believe that it may either have been simply neglected or broken off and suppressed. Let us add a frank account of how we picture the occurrence of a train of ideas. We believe that, starting from a purposive idea, a given amount of excitation, which we term 'cathectic energy', is displaced along the associative paths selected by that purposive idea. A train of thought which is 'neglected' is one which has *not received* this cathexis; a train of thought which is 'suppressed' or 'repudiated' is one from which this cathexis has been *withdrawn*. In both cases they are left to their own excitations. Under certain conditions a train of thought with a purposive cathexis is capable of attracting the attention of consciousness to itself and in that event, through the agency of consciousness, receives a 'hypercathexis'. We shall be obliged presently to explain our view of the nature and function of consciousness. [See p. 615 ff.]

A train of thought that has been set going like this in the preconscious may either cease spontaneously or persist. We picture the first of these outcomes as implying that the energy attaching to the train of thought is diffused along all the associative paths that radiate from it; this energy sets the whole network of thoughts in a state of excitation which lasts for a certain time and then dies away as the excitation in search of discharge becomes transformed into a quiescent cathexis. If this first outcome supervenes, the process is of no further significance so far as dream-formation is concerned. Lurking in our preconscious, however, there are other purposive ideas, which are derived from sources in our unconscious and from wishes which are always on the alert. These may take control of the excitation attaching to the group of thoughts which has been left to its own devices, they may establish a connection between it and an unconscious wish, and they may 'transfer' to it the energy belonging to the unconscious wish. Thenceforward the neglected or suppressed train of thought is in a position to persist, though the reinforcement it has received gives it no right of entry into consciousness. We may express this by saying that what has hitherto been a preconscious train of thought has now been 'drawn into the unconscious'.

There are other conjunctures which may lead to the formation of a dream. The preconscious train of thought may have been linked to the unconscious wish from the first and may for that reason have been repudiated by the dominant purposive cathexis; or an unconscious wish may become active for other reasons (from somatic causes, perhaps) and may seek to effect a transference on to the psychical residues that are uncathected by the *Pcs.* without their coming halfway to meet it. But all three cases have the same final outcome: a train of thought comes into being in the preconscious which is without a preconscious cathexis but has received a cathexis from an unconscious wish.

From this point onwards the train of thought undergoes a series of transformations which we can no longer recognize as normal psychical processes and which lead to a result that bewilders us—a psychopathological structure. I will enumerate these processes and classify them.

(1) The intensities of the individual ideas become capable of discharge *en bloc* and pass over from one idea to another, so that certain ideas are formed which are endowed with great intensity. [Cf. p. 330.] And since this process is repeated several times, the intensity of a whole train of thought may eventually be concentrated in a single ideational element. Here we have the fact of 'compression' or 'condensation', which has become familiar in the dream-work. It is this that is mainly responsible for the bewildering impression made on us by dreams, for nothing at all analogous to it is known to us in mental life that is normal and accessible to consciousness. In normal mental life, too, we find ideas which, being the nodal points or end-results of whole chains of thought, possess a high degree of psychical significance; but their significance is not expressed by any feature that is obvious in a *sensory* manner to internal perception; their perceptual presentation is not in any respect more intense on account of their psychical significance. In the process of condensation, on the other hand, every psychical interconnection is transformed into an *intensification* of its ideational content. The case is the same as when, in preparing a book for the press, I have some word which is of special importance for understanding the text printed in spaced or heavy type; or in speech I should pronounce the same word loudly and slowly and with special emphasis. The first of these two analogies reminds us at once of an example provided by the dream-work itself: the word '*trimethylamin*' in the dream of Irma's injection [p. 116]. Art historians have drawn our attention to the fact that the

earliest historical sculptures obey a similar principle: they express the rank of the persons represented by their size. A king is represented twice or three times as large as his attendants or as his defeated enemies. A sculpture of Roman date would make use of subtler means for producing the same result. The figure of the Emperor would be placed in the middle, standing erect, and would be modelled with especial care, while his enemies would be prostrate at his feet; but he would no longer be a giant among dwarfs. The bows with which inferiors greet their superiors among ourselves to-day are an echo of the same ancient principle of representation.

The direction in which condensations in dreams proceed is determined on the one hand by the rational preconscious relations of the dream-thoughts, and on the other by the attraction exercised by visual memories in the unconscious. The outcome of the activity of condensation is the achievement of the intensities required for forcing a way through into the perceptual systems.

(2) Owing, once more, to the freedom with which the intensities can be transferred, 'intermediate ideas', resembling compromises, are constructed under the sway of condensation. (Cf. the numerous instances I have given of this [e.g. p. 293 ff.].) This is again something unheard-of in normal chains of ideas, where the main stress is laid on the selection and retention of the 'right' ideational element. On the other hand, composite structures and compromises occur with remarkable frequency when we try to express preconscious thoughts in speech. They are then regarded as species of 'slips of the tongue'.

(3) The ideas which transfer their intensities to each other stand in the loosest mutual relations. They are linked by associations of a kind that is scorned by our normal thinking and relegated to the use of jokes. In particular, we find associations based on homonyms and verbal similarities treated as equal in value to the rest.

(4) Thoughts which are mutually contradictory make no attempt to do away with each other, but persist side by side. They often combine to form condensations, just as though there were no contradiction between them, or arrive at compromises such as our conscious thoughts would never tolerate but such as are often admitted in our actions.

These are some of the most striking of the abnormal processes to which the dream-thoughts, previously constructed on rational lines, are subjected in the course of the dream-work. It will be seen that the chief characteristic of these processes is that the whole stress is laid upon making the cathecting energy mobile and capable of discharge; the content and the proper meaning of the psychical elements to which the cathexes are attached are treated as of little consequence. It might have been supposed that condensation and the formation of compromises is only carried out for the sake of facilitating regression, that is, when it is a question of transforming thoughts into images. But the analysis—and still more the synthesis—of dreams which include no such regression to images, e.g. the dream of 'Auto-didasker' [p. 298 ff.], exhibits the same processes of displacement and condensation as the rest.

Thus we are driven to conclude that two fundamentally different kinds of psychical process are concerned in the formation of dreams. One of these produces perfectly rational dream-thoughts, of no less validity than normal thinking; while the other treats these thoughts in a manner which is in the highest degree bewildering and irrational. We have already in Chapter VI segregated this second psychical process as being the dream-work proper. What light have we now to throw upon its origin?

It would not be possible for us to answer this question if we had not made some headway in the study of the psychology of the neuroses, and particularly of hysteria. We have found from this that the same irrational psychical processes, and others that we have not specified, dominate the production of hysterical symptoms. In hysteria, too, we come across a series of perfectly rational thoughts, equal in validity to our conscious thoughts; but to begin with we know nothing of their existence in this form and we can only reconstruct them subsequently. If they force themselves upon our notice at any point, we discover by analysing the symptom which has been produced that these normal thoughts have been submitted to abnormal treatment: *they have been transformed into the symptom by means of condensation and the formation of compromises, by way of superficial associations and in disregard of contradictions, and also, it may be, along the path of regression.* In view of the complete identity between the characteristic features of the dream-work and those of the psychical activity which issues in psychoneurotic symptoms, we feel justified in carrying over to dreams the conclusions we have been led to by hysteria.

We accordingly borrow the following thesis from the theory of hysteria: *a normal train of thought is only submitted to abnormal psychical treatment of the sort we have been describing if an unconscious wish, derived from infancy and in a state of repression, has been transferred on to it.* In accordance with this thesis we have constructed our theory of dreams on the assumption that the dream-wish which provides the motive power invariably originates from the unconscious—an assumption which, as I myself am ready to admit, cannot be proved to hold generally, though neither can it be disproved. But in order to explain what is meant by 'repression', a term with which we have already made play so many times, it is necessary to proceed a stage further with our psychological scaffolding.

We have already [p. 565 ff.] explored the fiction of a primitive psychical apparatus whose activities are regulated by an effort to avoid an accumulation of excitation and to maintain itself so far as possible without excitation. For that reason it is built upon the plan of a reflex apparatus. The power of movement, which is in the first instance a means of bringing about internal alterations in its body, is at its disposal as the path to discharge. We went on to discuss the psychical consequences of an 'experience of satisfaction'; and in that connection we were already able to add a second hypothesis, to the effect that the accumulation of excitation (brought about in various ways that need not concern us) is felt as unpleasure and that it sets the apparatus in action with a view to repeating the experience of satisfaction, which involved a diminution of excitation and was felt as pleasure. A current of this kind in the apparatus, starting from unpleasure and aiming at pleasure, we have termed a 'wish'; and we have asserted that only a wish is able to set the apparatus in motion and that the course of the excitation in it is automatically regulated by feelings of pleasure and unpleasure. The first wishing seems to have been a hallucinatory cathecting of the memory of satisfaction. Such hallucinations, however, if they were not to be maintained to the point of exhaustion, proved to be inadequate to bring about the cessation of the need or, accordingly, the pleasure attaching to satisfaction.

A second activity—or, as we put it, the activity of a second system—became necessary, which would not allow the mnemic cathexis to proceed as far as perception and from there to bind the psychical forces; instead, it diverted the excitation arising from the need along a roundabout path which ultimately, by means of voluntary movement, altered the external world in such a way that it became possible to arrive at a real perception of the object of satisfaction. We have already outlined our schematic picture of the psychical apparatus up to this point; the two systems are the germ of what, in the fully developed apparatus, we have described as the *Ucs.* and *Pcs.*

In order to be able to employ the power of movement to make alterations in the external world that shall be effective, it is necessary to accumulate a great number of experiences in the mnemic systems and a multiplicity of permanent records of the associations called up in this mnemic material by different purposive ideas. [Cf. p. 539.] We can now carry our hypotheses a step further. The activity of this second system, constantly feeling its way, and alternately sending out and withdrawing cathexes, needs on the one hand to have the whole of the material of memory freely at its command; but on the other hand it would be an unnecessary expenditure of energy if it sent out large quantities of cathexis along the various paths of thought and thus caused them to drain away to no useful purpose and diminish the quantity available for altering the external world. I therefore postulate that for the sake of efficiency the second system succeeds in retaining the major part of its cathexes of energy in a state of quiescence and in employing only a small part on displacement. The mechanics of these processes are quite unknown to me; anyone who wished to take these ideas seriously would have to look for physical analogies to them and find a means of picturing the movements that accompany excitation of neurones. All that I insist upon is the idea that the activity of the *first* ψ-system is directed towards securing the *free discharge* of the quantities of excitation, while the *second* system, by means of the cathexes emanating from it, succeeds in *inhibiting* this discharge and in transforming the cathexis into a quiescent one, no doubt with a simultaneous raising of its level. I presume, therefore, that under the dominion of the second system the discharge of excitation is governed by quite different mechanical conditions from those in force under the dominion of the first system. When once the second system has concluded its exploratory thought-activity, it releases the inhibition and damming-up of the excitations and allows them to discharge themselves in movement.

Some interesting reflections follow if we consider the relations between this inhibition upon discharge exercised by the second system and the regulation effected by the unpleasure principle.[1] Let us examine the antithesis to the primary experience of satisfaction—namely, the experience of an external fright. Let us suppose that the primitive apparatus is impinged upon by a perceptual stimulus which is a source of painful excitation. Uncoordinated motor manifestations will follow until one of them withdraws the apparatus from the perception and at the same time from the pain. If the perception reappears, the movement will at once be repeated (a movement of flight, it may be) till the perception has disappeared once more. In this case, no inclination will remain to recathect the perception of the source of pain, either hallucinatorily or in any other way. On the contrary, there will be an inclination in the primitive apparatus to drop the distressing mnemic image immediately, if anything happens to revive it, for the very reason that if its excitation were to overflow into perception it would provoke unpleasure (or, more precisely, would *begin* to provoke it). The avoidance of the memory, which is no more than a repetition of the previous flight from the perception, is also facilitated by the fact that the memory, unlike the perception, does not possess enough quality to excite consciousness and thus to attract fresh cathexis to itself. This effortless and regular avoidance by the psychical process of the memory of anything that had once been distressing affords us the prototype and first example of *psychical repression*. It is a familiar fact that much of this avoidance of what is distressing—this ostrich policy—is still to be seen in the normal mental life of adults.

As a result of the unpleasure principle, then, the first ψ-system is totally incapable of bringing anything disagreeable into the context of its thoughts. It is unable to do anything but wish. If things remained at that point, the thought-activity of the second system would be obstructed, since it requires free access to *all* the memories laid down by experience. Two possibilities now present themselves. Either the activity of the second system might set itself entirely free from the unpleasure principle and

---

[1] [In his later works Freud speaks of it as the 'pleasure principle'.]

proceed without troubling about the unpleasure of memories; or it might find a method of cathecting unpleasurable memories which would enable it to avoid releasing the unpleasure. We may dismiss the first of these possibilities, for the unpleasure principle clearly regulates the course of excitation in the second system as much as in the first. We are consequently left with the remaining possibility that the second system cathects memories in such a way that there is an inhibition of their discharge, including, therefore, an inhibition of discharge (comparable to that of a motor innervation) in the direction of the development of unpleasure. We have therefore been led from two directions to the hypothesis that cathexis by the second system implies a simultaneous inhibition of the discharge of excitation: we have been led to it by regard for the unpleasure principle and also [as was shown in the last paragraph but one] by the principle of the least expenditure of innervation. Let us bear this firmly in mind, for it is the key to the whole theory of repression: *the second system can only cathect an idea if it is in a position to inhibit any development of unpleasure that may proceed from it.* Anything that could evade that inhibition would be inaccessible to the second system as well as to the first; for it would promptly be dropped in obedience to the unpleasure principle. The inhibition of unpleasure need not, however, be a complete one: a beginning of it must be allowed, since that is what informs the second system of the nature of the memory concerned and of its possible unsuitability for the purpose which the thought-process has in view.

I propose to describe the psychical process of which the first system alone admits as the 'primary process', and the process which results from the inhibition imposed by the second system as the 'secondary process'.[1]

---

[1] [The distinction between the primary and secondary systems, and the hypothesis that psychical functioning operates differently in them, are among the most fundamental of Freud's concepts. They are associated with the theory (indicated on p. 599 f. and at the opening of the next Section) that psychical energy occurs in two forms: 'free' or 'mobile' (as it occurs in the system *Ucs.*) and 'bound' or 'quiescent' (as it occurs in the system *Pcs.*). Where Freud discusses this subject in his later writings (e.g. in his paper on 'The Unconscious', 1915*e*, end of Section V, and in *Beyond the Pleasure Principle*, 1920*g*, Chapter IV) he attributes this latter distinction to some statement of Breuer's in their joint *Studies on Hysteria* (1895). There is some difficulty in identifying any such state-

There is yet another reason for which, as I can show, the second system is obliged to correct the primary process. The primary process endeavours to bring about a discharge of excitation in order that, with the help of the amount of excitation thus accumulated, it may establish a 'perceptual identity' [with the experience of satisfaction (see pp. 565-6)]. The secondary process, however, has abandoned this intention and taken on another in its place—the establishment of a *'thought' identity* [with that experience]. All thinking is no more than a circuitous path from the memory of a satisfaction (a memory which has been adopted as a purposive idea) to an identical cathexis of the same memory which it is hoped to attain once more through an intermediate stage of motor experiences. Thinking must concern itself with the connecting paths between ideas, without being led astray by the *intensities* of those ideas. But it is obvious that condensations of ideas, as well as intermediate and compromise structures, must obstruct the attainment of the identity aimed at. Since they substitute one idea for another, they cause a deviation from the path which would have led on from the first idea. Processes of this kind are therefore scrupulously avoided in secondary thinking. It is easy to see, too, that the unpleasure principle, which in other respects supplies the thought-process with its most important signposts, puts difficulties in its path towards establishing 'thought identity'. Accordingly, thinking must aim at freeing itself more and more from exclusive regulation by the unpleasure principle and at restricting the development of affect in thought-activity to the minimum required for acting as a signal.[1] The achievement of this greater delicacy in functioning is aimed at by means of a further

ment in Breuer's contribution to that work (Chapter III). The nearest approach to it is a footnote near the beginning of Section 2, in which Breuer distinguishes *three* forms of nervous energy: 'a potential energy which lies quiescent in the chemical substance of the cell', 'a kinetic energy which is discharged when the fibres are in a state of excitation' and 'yet another quiescent state of nervous excitation: tonic excitation or nervous tension'. On the other hand, the question of 'bound' energy is discussed at some length towards the end of the first section of Part III of Freud's 'Project' (1950a), written only a few months after the publication of the *Studies on Hysteria*.]

[1] [This idea of a small amount of unpleasure acting as a 'signal' to prevent the occurrence of a much larger amount was taken up by Freud many years later and applied to the problem of anxiety. See Freud, 1926d, Chapter XI, Section A(b).]

hypercathexis, brought about by consciousness. [See below, p. 615 ff.] As we well know, however, that aim is seldom attained completely, even in normal mental life, and our thinking always remains exposed to falsification by interference from the unpleasure principle.

This, however, is not the gap in the functional efficiency of our mental apparatus which makes it possible for thoughts, which represent themselves as products of the secondary thought-activity, to become subject to the primary psychical process—for such is the formula in which we can now describe the activity which leads to dreams and to hysterical symptoms. Inefficiency arises from the convergence of two factors derived from our developmental history. One of these factors devolves entirely upon the mental apparatus and has had a decisive influence on the relation between the two systems, while the other makes itself felt to a variable degree and introduces instinctual forces of organic origin into mental life. Both of them originate in childhood and are a precipitate of the modifications undergone by our mental and somatic organism since our infancy.

When I described one of the psychical processes occurring in the mental apparatus as the 'primary' one, what I had in mind was not merely considerations of relative importance and efficiency; I intended also to choose a name which would give an indication of its chronological priority. It is true that, so far as we know, no psychical apparatus exists which possesses a primary process only and that such an apparatus is to that extent a theoretical fiction. But this much is a fact: the primary processes are present in the mental apparatus from the first, while it is only during the course of life that the secondary processes unfold, and come to inhibit and overlay the primary ones; it may even be that their complete domination is not attained until the prime of life. In consequence of the belated appearance of the secondary processes, the core of our being, consisting of unconscious wishful impulses, remains inaccessible to the understanding and inhibition of the preconscious; the part played by the latter is restricted once and for all to directing along the most expedient paths the wishful impulses that arise from the unconscious. These unconscious wishes exercise a compelling force upon all later mental trends, a force which those trends are obliged to fall in with or which they may perhaps endeavour to divert and direct to higher aims. A further result of the belated appearance of the secondary process is that a wide sphere of mnemic material is inaccessible to preconscious cathexis.

Among these wishful impulses derived from infancy, which can neither be destroyed nor inhibited, there are some whose fulfilment would be a contradiction of the purposive ideas of secondary thinking. The fulfilment of these wishes would no longer generate an affect of pleasure but of unpleasure; and *it is precisely this transformation of affect which constitutes the essence of what we term 'repression'*. The problem of repression lies in the question of how it is and owing to what motive forces that this transformation occurs; but it is a problem that we need only touch upon here.[1] It is enough for us to be clear that a transformation of this kind does occur in the course of development —we have only to recall the way in which disgust emerges in childhood after having been absent to begin with—and that it is related to the activity of the secondary system. The memories on the basis of which the unconscious wish brings about the release of affect were never accessible to the *Pcs.*, and consequently the release of the affect attaching to those memories cannot be inhibited either. It is for the very reason of this generation of affect that these ideas are now inaccessible even by way of the preconscious thoughts on to which they have transferred their wishful force. On the contrary, the unpleasure principle takes control and causes the *Pcs.* to turn away from the transference thoughts. They are left to themselves—'repressed'—and thus it is that the presence of a store of infantile memories, which has from the first been held back from the *Pcs.*, becomes a *sine qua non* of repression.

In the most favourable cases the generation of unpleasure ceases along with the withdrawal of cathexis from the transference thoughts in the *Pcs.*; and this outcome signifies that the intervention of the unpleasure principle has served a useful purpose. But it is another matter when the repressed unconscious wish receives an organic reinforcement, which it passes on to its transference thoughts; in that way it may place them in a

[1] [The subject was afterwards dealt with by Freud at much greater length in his paper on 'Repression' (1915*d*); his later views on the subject are given in Lecture XXXII of his *New Introductory Lectures* (1933*a*).]

position to make an attempt at forcing their way through with their excitation, even if they have lost their cathexis from the *Pcs.* There then follows a defensive struggle—for the *Pcs.* in turn reinforces its opposition to the repressed thoughts (i.e. produces an 'anticathexis')—and thereafter the transference thoughts, which are the vehicles of the unconscious wish, force their way through in some form of compromise which is reached by the production of a symptom. But from the moment at which the repressed thoughts are strongly cathected by the unconscious wishful impulse and, on the other hand, abandoned by the preconscious cathexis, they become subject to the primary psychical process and their one aim is motor discharge or, if the path is open, hallucinatory revival of the desired perceptual identity. We have already found empirically that the irrational processes we have described are only carried out with thoughts that are under repression. We can now see our way a little further into the whole position. The irrational processes which occur in the psychical apparatus are the *primary* ones. They appear wherever ideas are abandoned by the preconscious cathexis, are left to themselves and can become charged with the uninhibited energy from the unconscious which is striving to find an outlet. Some other observations lend support to the view that these processes which are described as irrational are not in fact falsifications of normal processes—intellectual errors —but are modes of activity of the psychical apparatus that have been freed from an inhibition. Thus we find that the transition from preconscious excitation to movement is governed by the same processes, and that the linking of preconscious ideas to words may easily exhibit the same displacements and confusions, which are then attributed to inattention. Evidence, finally, of the increase in activity which becomes necessary when these primary modes of functioning are inhibited is to be found in the fact that we produce a *comic* effect, that is, a surplus of energy which has to be discharged in *laughter, if we allow these modes of thinking to force their way through into consciousness.*[1]

The theory of the psychoneuroses asserts as an indisputable and invariable fact that only sexual wishful impulses from

[1] [This topic was dealt with by Freud at greater length in Chapter V of his book on jokes (1905*c*). The question of intellectual errors was discussed more fully in the closing pages of the 'Project' (1950*a*).]

infancy, which have undergone repression (i.e. a transformation of their affect) during the developmental period of childhood, are capable of being revived during *later* developmental periods (whether as a result of the subject's sexual constitution, which is derived from an initial bisexuality, or as a result of unfavourable influences acting upon the course of his sexual life) and are thus able to furnish the motive force for the formation of psychoneurotic symptoms of every kind.[1] It is only by reference to these sexual forces that we can close the gaps that are still patent in the theory of repression. I will leave it an open question whether these sexual and infantile factors are equally required in the theory of dreams: I will leave that theory incomplete at this point, since I have already gone a step beyond what can be demonstrated in assuming that dream-wishes are invariably derived from the unconscious.[2] Nor do I propose to enquire

---

[1] [The theme of this sentence was elaborated by Freud in his *Three Essays on the Theory of Sexuality* (1905d).]

[2] Here and elsewhere I have intentionally left gaps in the treatment of my theme because to fill them would on the one hand require too great an effort and on the other would involve my basing myself on material that is alien to the subject of dreams. For instance, I have omitted to state whether I attribute different meanings to the words 'suppressed' and 'repressed'. It should have been clear, however, that the latter lays more stress than the former upon the fact of attachment to the unconscious. Nor have I entered into the obvious problem of why the dream-thoughts are subjected to distortion by the censorship even in cases where they have abandoned the progressive path towards consciousness and have chosen the regressive one. And there are many similar omissions. What I was above all anxious to do was to create an impression of the problems to which a further analysis of the dream-work must lead and to give a hint of the other topics with which that further analysis would come into contact. It has not always been easy for me to decide the point at which to break off my pursuit of this line of exposition.—There are special reasons, which may not be what my readers expect, why I have not given any exhaustive treatment to the part played in dreams by the world of sexual ideas and why I have avoided analysing dreams of obviously sexual content. Nothing could be further from my own views or from the theoretical opinions which I hold in neuropathology than to regard sexual life as something shameful, with which neither a physician nor a scientific research worker has any concern. Moreover, the moral indignation by which the translator of the *Oneirocritica* of Artemidorus of Daldis allowed himself to be led into withholding the chapter on sexual dreams from the knowledge of his readers strikes me as laughable. What governed my decision was simply my seeing that an explanation of sexual dreams would involve

further into the nature of the distinction between the play of psychical forces in the formation of dreams and in that of hysterical symptoms: we are still without a sufficiently accurate knowledge of one of the two objects of the comparison.

There is, however, another point to which I attach importance; and I must confess that it is solely on its account that I have embarked here upon all these discussions of the two psychical systems and their modes of activity and of repression. It is not now a question of whether I have formed an approximately correct opinion of the psychological factors with which we are concerned, or whether, which is quite possible in such difficult matters, my picture of them is distorted and incomplete. However many changes may be made in our reading of the psychical censorship and of the rational and abnormal revisions made of the dream-content, it remains true that processes of this sort are at work in the formation of dreams and that they show the closest analogy in their essentials to the processes observable in the formation of hysterical symptoms. A dream, however, is no pathological phenomenon; it presupposes no disturbance of psychical equilibrium; it leaves behind it no loss of efficiency. The suggestion may be made that no conclusions as to the dreams of normal people can be drawn from my dreams or those of my patients; but this, I think, is an objection which can be safely disregarded. If, then, we may argue back from the phenomena to their motive forces, we must recognize that the psychical mechanism employed by neuroses is not created by the impact of a pathological disturbance upon the mind but is present already in the normal structure of the mental apparatus. The two psychical systems, the censorship upon the passage from one of them to the other, the inhibition and overlaying of one activity by the other, the relations of both of them to consciousness—or whatever more correct interpretations of the observed facts may take their place—all of these form part of the normal structure of our mental instrument, and dreams show us one of the paths leading to an understand-

me deeply in the still unsolved problems of perversion and bisexuality; and I accordingly reserved this material for another occasion. [It should perhaps be added that the translator of *Oneirocritica*, F. S. Krauss, himself subsequently published the omitted chapter in his periodical *Anthropophyteia*, from which Freud has quoted above (p. 356 *n.*) and of which he speaks so highly elsewhere (1910*f* and 1913*k*).]

ing of its structure. If we restrict ourselves to the minimum of new knowledge which has been established with certainty, we can still say this of dreams: they have proved that *what is suppressed continues to exist in normal people as well as abnormal, and remains capable of psychical functioning.* Dreams themselves are among the manifestations of this suppressed material; this is so theoretically in every case, and it can be observed empirically in a great number of cases at least, and precisely in cases which exhibit most clearly the striking peculiarities of dream-life. In waking life the suppressed material in the mind is prevented from finding expression and is cut off from internal perception owing to the fact that the contradictions present in it are eliminated—one side being disposed of in favour of the other; but during the night, under the sway of an impetus towards the construction of compromises, this suppressed material finds methods and means of forcing its way into consciousness.

Flectere si nequeo superos, Acheronta movebo.[1]

The interpretation of dreams is the royal road to a knowledge of the unconscious activities of the mind.

By analysing dreams we can take a step forward in our understanding of the composition of that most marvellous and most mysterious of all instruments. Only a small step, no doubt; but a beginning. And this beginning will enable us to proceed further with its analysis, on the basis of other structures which must be termed pathological. For illnesses—those, at least, which are rightly named 'functional'—do not presuppose the disintegration of the apparatus or the production of fresh splits in its interior. They are to be explained on a *dynamic* basis—by the strengthening and weakening of the various components in the interplay of forces, so many of whose effects are hidden from view while functions are normal. I hope to be able to show elsewhere how the compounding of the apparatus out of two

---

[1] ['If I cannot bend the Higher Powers, I will move the Infernal Regions.' Freud remarks in a note in *Ges. Schr.*, **3** (1925), 169, that 'this line of Virgil [*Aeneid*, VII, 312] is intended to picture the efforts of the repressed instinctual impulses'. He has used the same line as the motto for the whole volume. In a letter to Fliess of December 4, 1896 (Freud, 1950*a*, Letter 51) he proposed using it as a motto for a chapter on 'Symptom Formation' in some projected but unrealized work.—The next sentence was added in 1909. It was included in the same year in the third of his lectures at Clark University (Freud, 1910*a*).]

agencies makes it possible for the normal mind too to function with greater delicacy than would be possible with only one of them.[1]

[1] Dreams are not the only phenomena which allow us to find a basis for psychopathology in psychology. In a short series of papers (1898*b* and 1899*a*) which is not yet completed, I have attempted to interpret a number of phenomena of daily life as evidence in favour of the same conclusions. [*Added* 1909:] These, together with some further papers on forgetting, slips of the tongue, bungled actions, etc., have since been collected under the title of *The Psychopathology of Everyday Life* (Freud, 1901*b*).

THE UNCONSCIOUS AND CONSCIOUSNESS—
REALITY

It will be seen on closer consideration that what the psychological discussion in the preceding sections invites us to assume is not the existence of two *systems* near the motor end of the apparatus but the existence of two kinds of *processes of excitation* or *modes of its discharge*. It is all one to us, for we must always be prepared to drop our conceptual scaffolding if we feel that we are in a position to replace it by something that approximates more closely to the unknown reality. So let us try to correct some conceptions which might be misleading so long as we looked upon the two systems in the most literal and crudest sense as two localities in the mental apparatus—conceptions which have left their traces in the expressions 'to repress' and 'to force a way through'. Thus, we may speak of an unconscious thought seeking to convey itself into the preconscious so as to be able then to force its way through into consciousness. What we have in mind here is not the forming of a second thought situated in a new place, like a transcription which continues to exist alongside the original; and the notion of forcing a way through into consciousness must be kept carefully free from any idea of a change of locality. Again, we may speak of a preconscious thought being repressed or driven out and then taken over by the unconscious. These images, derived from a set of ideas relating to a struggle for a piece of ground, may tempt us to suppose that it is literally true that a mental grouping in one locality has been brought to an end and replaced by a fresh one in another locality. Let us replace these metaphors by something that seems to correspond better to the real state of affairs, and let us say instead that some particular mental grouping has had a cathexis of energy attached to it or withdrawn from it, so that the structure in question has come under the sway of a particular agency or been withdrawn from it. What we are doing here is once again to replace a topographical way of representing things by a dynamic one. What we

610

regard as mobile is not the psychical structure itself but its innervation.[1]

Nevertheless, I consider it expedient and justifiable to continue to make use of the figurative image of the two systems. We can avoid any possible abuse of this method of representation by recollecting that ideas, thoughts and psychical structures in general must never be regarded as localized in organic elements of the nervous system but rather, as one might say, *between* them, where resistances and facilitations [*Bahnungen*] provide the corresponding correlates. Everything that can be an object of our internal perception is *virtual*, like the image produced in a telescope by the passage of light-rays. But we are justified in assuming the existence of the systems (which are not in any way psychical entities themselves and can never be accessible to our psychical perception) like the lenses of the telescope, which cast the image. And, if we pursue this analogy, we may compare the censorship between two systems to the refraction which takes place when a ray of light passes into a new medium.

So far we have been psychologizing on our own account. It is time now to consider the theoretical views which govern present-day psychology and to examine their relation to our hypotheses. The problem of the unconscious in psychology is, in the forcible words of Lipps (1897), less *a* psychological problem than *the* problem of psychology. So long as psychology dealt with this problem by a verbal explanation to the effect that 'psychical' *meant* 'conscious' and that to speak of 'unconscious psychical processes' was palpable nonsense, any psychological evaluation of the observations made by physicians upon abnormal mental states was out of the question. The physician and the philosopher can only come together if they both recognize that the term 'unconscious psychical processes' is 'the appropriate and justified expression of a solidly established

[1] [*Footnote added* 1925:] It became necessary to elaborate and modify this view after it was recognized that the essential feature of a preconscious idea was the fact of its being connected with the residues of verbal presentations. Cf. 'The Unconscious' (1915*e*, [Section VII]). [As is there pointed out, however, this was already indicated in the first edition of the present work. (See pp. 574 and 617.) It is also foreshadowed in the 'Project' (1950*a*), Part III, Sections 1 and 2.]

fact'. The physician can only shrug his shoulders when he is assured that 'consciousness is an indispensable characteristic of what is psychical', and perhaps, if he still feels enough respect for the utterances of philosophers, he may presume that they have not been dealing with the same thing or working at the same science. For even a single understanding observation of a neurotic's mental life or a single analysis of a dream must leave him with an unshakeable conviction that the most complicated and most rational thought-processes, which can surely not be denied the name of psychical processes, can occur without exciting the subject's consciousness.[1] It is true that the physician cannot learn of these unconscious processes until they have produced some effect upon consciousness which can be communicated or observed. But this conscious effect may exhibit a psychical character quite different from that of the unconscious process, so that internal perception cannot possibly regard the one as a substitute for the other. The physician must feel at liberty to proceed by *inference* from the conscious effect to the unconscious psychical process. He thus learns that the conscious effect is only a remote psychical result of the unconscious process and that the latter has not become conscious as such; and moreover that the latter was present and operative even without betraying its existence in any way to consciousness.

It is essential to abandon the overvaluation of the property of being conscious before it becomes possible to form any correct view of the origin of what is mental. In Lipps's words [1897, 146 f.], the unconscious must be assumed to be the general basis of psychical life. The unconscious is the larger sphere, which includes within it the smaller sphere of the conscious. Everything conscious has an unconscious preliminary stage; whereas

---

[1] [*Footnote added* 1914:] I am happy to be able to point to an author who has drawn from the study of dreams the same conclusions as I have on the relation between conscious and unconscious activity. Du Prel (1885, 47) writes: 'The problem of the nature of the mind evidently calls for a preliminary investigation as to whether consciousness and mind are identical. This preliminary question is answered in the negative by dreams, which show that the concept of the mind is a wider one than that of consciousness, in the same kind of way in which the gravitational force of a heavenly body extends beyond its range of luminosity.' And again (ibid., 306 [quoting Maudsley, 1868, 15]): 'It is a truth which cannot be too distinctly borne in mind that consciousness is not co-extensive with mind.'

what is unconscious may remain at that stage and nevertheless claim to be regarded as having the full value of a psychical process. The unconscious is the true psychical reality; *in its innermost nature it is as much unknown to us as the reality of the external world, and it is as incompletely presented by the data of consciousness as is the external world by the communications of our sense organs.*

Now that the old antithesis between conscious life and dream-life has been reduced to its proper proportions by the establishment of unconscious psychical reality, a number of dream-problems with which earlier writers were deeply concerned have lost their significance. Thus some of the activities whose successful performance in dreams excited astonishment are now no longer to be attributed to dreams but to unconscious thinking, which is active during the day no less than at night. If, as Scherner [1861, 114 f.] has said, dreams appear to engage in making symbolic representations of the body [p. 85], we now know that those representations are the product of certain unconscious phantasies (deriving, probably, from sexual impulses) which find expression not only in dreams but also in hysterical phobias and other symptoms. If a dream carries on the activities of the day and completes them and even brings valuable fresh ideas to light, all we need do is to strip it of the dream disguise, which is the product of dream-work and the mark of assistance rendered by obscure forces from the depths of the mind (cf. the Devil in Tartini's sonata dream);[1] the intellectual achievement is due to the same mental forces which produce every similar result during the daytime. We are probably inclined greatly to over-estimate the conscious character of intellectual and artistic production as well. Accounts given us by some of the most highly productive men, such as Goethe and Helmholtz, show rather that what is essential and new in their creations came to them without premeditation and as an almost ready-made whole. There is nothing strange if in other cases, where a concentration of every intellectual faculty was needed, conscious activity also contributed its share. But it is the much-abused

[1] [Tartini, the composer and violinist (1692–1770), is said to have dreamt that he sold his soul to the devil, who thereupon seized a violin and played a sonata of exquisite beauty upon it with consummate skill. When the composer awoke he at once wrote down what he could recollect of it, and the result was his famous 'Trillo del Diavolo'.]

privilege of conscious activity, wherever it plays a part, to conceal every other activity from our eyes.

It would scarcely repay the trouble if we were to treat the historical significance of dreams as a separate topic. A dream may have impelled some chieftain to embark upon a bold enterprise the success of which has changed history. But this only raises a fresh problem so long as a dream is regarded as an alien power in contrast to the other more familiar forces of the mind; no such problem remains if a dream is recognized as a *form of expression* of impulses which are under the pressure of resistance during the day but which have been able to find reinforcement during the night from deep-lying sources of excitation.[1] The respect paid to dreams in antiquity is, however, based upon correct psychological insight and is the homage paid to the uncontrolled and indestructible forces in the human mind, to the 'daemonic' power which produces the dream-wish and which we find at work in our unconscious.

It is not without intention that I speak of 'our' unconscious. For what I thus describe is not the same as the unconscious of the philosophers or even the unconscious of Lipps. By them the term is used merely to indicate a contrast with the conscious: the thesis which they dispute with so much heat and defend with so much energy is the thesis that apart from conscious there are also unconscious psychical processes. Lipps carries things further with his assertion that the whole of what is psychical exists unconsciously and that a part of it also exists consciously. But it is not in order to establish *this* thesis that we have summoned up the phenomena of dreams and of the formation of hysterical symptoms; the observation of normal waking life would by itself suffice to prove it beyond any doubt. The new discovery that we have been taught by the analysis of psychopathological structures and of the first member of that class— the dream—lies in the fact that the unconscious (that is, the psychical) is found as a function of two separate systems and that this is the case in normal as well as in pathological life. Thus there are two kinds of unconscious, which have not yet been distinguished by psychologists. Both of them are unconscious in the sense used by psychology; but in our sense one of them,

[1] [*Footnote added* 1911:] Cf. in this connection Alexander the Great's dream during his siege of Tyre (σά-τυρος). [See p. 99 n.]

which we term the *Ucs.*, is also *inadmissible to consciousness*, while we term the other the *Pcs.* because its excitations—after observing certain rules, it is true, and perhaps only after passing a fresh censorship, though nonetheless without regard to the *Ucs.* —are able to reach consciousness. The fact that excitations in order to reach consciousness must pass through a fixed series or hierarchy of agencies (which is revealed to us by the modifications made in them by censorship) has enabled us to construct a spatial analogy. We have described the relations of the two systems to each other and to consciousness by saying that the system *Pcs.* stands like a screen between the system *Ucs.* and consciousness. The system *Pcs.* not merely bars access to consciousness, it also controls access to the power of voluntary movement and has at its disposal for distribution a mobile cathectic energy, a part of which is familiar to us in the form of attention.[1] [See p. 593.]

We must avoid, too, the distinction between 'supraconscious' and 'subconscious', which has become so popular in the more recent literature of the psychoneuroses, for such a distinction seems precisely calculated to stress the equivalence of what is psychical to what is conscious.

But what part is there left to be played in our scheme by consciousness, which was once so omnipotent and hid all else from view? *Only that of a sense-organ for the perception of psychical qualities.*[2] In accordance with the ideas underlying our attempt at a schematic picture, we can only regard conscious perception as the function proper to a particular system; and for this the abbreviation *Cs.* seems appropriate. In its mechanical properties we regard this system as resembling the perceptual systems *Pcpt.*: as being susceptible to excitation by qualities but incapable of retaining traces of alterations—that is to say, as having no memory. The psychical apparatus, which is turned towards

[1] [*Footnote added* 1914:] Cf. my remarks on the concept of the unconscious in psycho-analysis (Freud, 1912*g*), first published in English in the *Proceedings* of the Society for Psychical Research, 26 [312], in which I have distinguished the descriptive, dynamic and systematic meanings of the highly ambiguous word 'unconscious'. [The whole topic is discussed in the light of Freud's later views in Chapter I of *The Ego and the Id* (1923*b*).]

[2] [Freud's use of the terms 'quantity' and 'quality' is fully explained in Part I of his 'Project' (1950*a*).]

the external world with its sense-organ of the *Pcpt.* systems, is itself the external world in relation to the sense-organ of the *Cs.*, whose teleological justification resides in this circumstance. Here we once more meet the principle of the hierarchy of agencies, which seems to govern the structure of the apparatus. Excitatory material flows in to the *Cs.* sense-organ from two directions: from the *Pcpt.* system, whose excitation, determined by qualities, is probably submitted to a fresh revision before it becomes a conscious sensation, and from the interior of the apparatus itself, whose quantitative processes are felt qualitatively in the pleasure-unpleasure series when, subject to certain modifications, they make their way to consciousness.

Those philosophers who have become aware that rational and highly complex thought-structures are possible without consciousness playing any part in them have found difficulty in assigning any function to consciousness; it has seemed to them that it can be no more than a superfluous reflected picture of the completed psychical process. We, on the other hand, are rescued from this embarrassment by the analogy between our *Cs.* system and the perceptual systems. We know that perception by our sense-organs has the result of directing a cathexis of attention to the paths along which the in-coming sensory excitation is spreading: the qualitative excitation of the *Pcpt.* system acts as a regulator of the discharge of the mobile quantity in the psychical apparatus. We can attribute the same function to the overlying sense-organ of the *Cs.* system. By perceiving new qualities, it makes a new contribution to directing the mobile quantities of cathexis and distributing them in an expedient fashion. By the help of its perception of pleasure and unpleasure it influences the discharge of the cathexes within what is otherwise an unconscious apparatus operating by means of the displacement of quantities. It seems probable that in the first instance the unpleasure principle regulates the displacement of cathexes automatically. But it is quite possible that consciousness of these qualities may introduce in addition a second and more discriminating regulation, which is even able to oppose the former one, and which perfects the efficiency of the apparatus by enabling it, in contradiction to its original plan, to cathect and work over even what is associated with the release of unpleasure. We learn from the psychology of the neuroses that these processes of regulation carried out by the qualitative excitation of the sense organs play a great part in the functional activity of the apparatus. The automatic domination of the primary unpleasure principle and the consequent restriction imposed upon efficiency are interrupted by the processes of sensory regulation, which are themselves in turn automatic in action. We find that repression (which, though it served a useful purpose to begin with, leads ultimately to a damaging loss of inhibition and mental control) affects memories so much more easily than perceptions because the former can receive no extra cathexis from the excitation of the psychical sense·organs. It is true on the one hand that a thought which has to be warded off cannot become conscious, because it has undergone repression; but on the other hand it sometimes happens that a thought of this kind is only repressed because for other reasons it has been withdrawn from conscious perception. Here are some hints of which we take advantage in our therapeutic procedure in order to undo repressions which have already been effected.

The value of the hypercathexis which is set up in the mobile quantities by the regulating influence of the sense organ of the *Cs.* cannot be better illustrated in its teleological aspect than by the fact of its creation of a new series of qualities and consequently of a new process of regulation which constitutes the superiority of men over animals. Thought-processes are in themselves without quality, except for the pleasurable and unpleasurable excitations which accompany them, and which, in view of their possible disturbing effect upon thinking, must be kept within bounds. In order that thought-processes may acquire quality, they are associated in human beings with verbal memories, whose residues of quality are sufficient to draw the attention of consciousness to them and to endow the process of thinking with a new mobile cathexis from consciousness. [Cf. pp. 574 and 611 *n.*]

The whole multiplicity of the problems of consciousness can only be grasped by an analysis of the thought-processes in hysteria. These give one the impression that the transition from a preconscious to a conscious cathexis is marked by a censorship similar to that between the *Ucs.* and the *Pcs.*[1] This censorship, too, only comes into force above a certain quantitative

[1] [The censorship between the *Pcs.* and the *Cs.* appears only rarely in Freud's later writings. It is, however, discussed at length in Section VI of his paper on 'The Unconscious' (1915e).]

limit, so that thought-structures of low intensity escape it. Examples of every possible variety of how a thought can be withheld from consciousness or can force its way into consciousness under certain limitations are to be found included within the framework of psychoneurotic phenomena; and they all point to the intimate and reciprocal relations between censorship and consciousness. I will bring these psychological reflections to an end with a report of two such examples.

I was called in to a consultation last year to examine an intelligent and unembarrassed-looking girl. She was most surprisingly dressed. For though as a rule a woman's clothes are carefully considered down to the last detail, she was wearing one of her stockings hanging down and two of the buttons on her blouse were undone. She complained of having pains in her leg and, without being asked, exposed her calf. But what she principally complained of was, to use her own words, that she had a feeling in her body as though there was something 'stuck into it' which was 'moving backwards and forwards' and was 'shaking' her through and through: sometimes it made her whole body feel 'stiff'. My medical colleague, who was present at the examination, looked at me; he found no difficulty in understanding the meaning of her complaint. But what struck both of us as extraordinary was the fact that it meant nothing to the patient's mother—though she must often have found herself in the situation which her child was describing. The girl herself had no notion of the bearing of her remarks; for if she had, she would never have given voice to them. In this case it had been possible to hoodwink the censorship into allowing a phantasy which would normally have been kept in the preconscious to emerge into consciousness under the innocent disguise of making a complaint.

Here is another example. A fourteen-year-old boy came to me for psycho-analytic treatment suffering from *tic convulsif*, hysterical vomiting, headaches, etc. I began the treatment by assuring him that if he shut his eyes he would see pictures or have ideas, which he was then to communicate to me. He replied in pictures. His last impression before coming to me was revived visually in his memory. He had been playing at draughts with his uncle and saw the board in front of him. He thought of various positions, favourable or unfavourable, and of moves that one must not make. He then saw a dagger lying on the board—an object that belonged to his father but which his imagination placed on the board. Then there was a sickle lying on the board and next a scythe. And there now appeared a picture of an old peasant mowing the grass in front of the patient's distant home with a scythe. After a few days I discovered the meaning of this series of pictures. The boy had been upset by an unhappy family situation. He had a father who was a hard man, liable to fits of rage, who had been unhappily married to the patient's mother, and whose educational methods had consisted of threats. His father had been divorced from his mother, a tender and affectionate woman, had married again and had one day brought a young woman home with him who was to be the boy's new mother. It was during the first few days after this that the fourteen-year-old boy's illness had come on. His suppressed rage against his father was what had constructed this series of pictures with their understandable allusions. The material for them was provided by a recollection from mythology. The sickle was the one with which Zeus castrated his father; the scythe and the picture of the old peasant represented Kronos, the violent old man who devoured his children and on whom Zeus took such unfilial vengeance. [See p. 256.] His father's marriage gave the boy an opportunity of repaying the reproaches and threats which he had heard from his father long before because he had played with his genitals. (Cf. the playing at draughts; the forbidden moves; the dagger which could be used to kill.) In this case long-repressed memories and derivatives from them which had remained unconscious slipped into consciousness by a roundabout path in the form of apparently meaningless pictures.

Thus I would look for the *theoretical* value of the study of dreams in the contributions it makes to psychological knowledge and in the preliminary light it throws on the problems of the psychoneuroses. Who can guess the importance of the results which might be obtained from a thorough understanding of the structure and functions of the mental apparatus, since even the present state of our knowledge allows us to exert a favourable therapeutic influence on the curable forms of psychoneurosis? But what of the *practical* value of this study—I hear the question raised—as a means towards an understanding of the mind, towards a revelation of the hidden characteristics of individual men? Have not the unconscious impulses brought out by dreams the importance of real forces in mental life? Is the ethical significance of suppressed wishes to be made light of—wishes which, just as they lead to dreams, may some day lead to other things?

I do not feel justified in answering these questions. I have not considered this side of the problem of dreams further. I think, however, that the Roman emperor was in the wrong when he had one of his subjects executed because he had dreamt of murdering the emperor. [See above, p. 67.] He should have begun by trying to find out what the dream meant; most probably its meaning was not what it appeared to be. And even if a dream with another content had had this act of *lèse majesté* as its meaning, would it not be right to bear in mind Plato's dictum that the virtuous man is content to *dream* what a wicked man really *does* [p. 67]? I think it is best, therefore, to acquit dreams. Whether we are to attribute *reality* to unconscious wishes, I cannot say. It must be denied, of course, to any transitional or intermediate thoughts. If we look at unconscious wishes reduced to their most fundamental and truest shape, we shall have to conclude, no doubt, that *psychical* reality is a particular form of existence not to be confused with *material* reality.[1] Thus there seems to be no justification for people's reluctance in accepting responsibility for the immorality of their dreams. When the mode of functioning of the mental apparatus is rightly appreciated and the relation between the conscious and the unconscious understood, the greater part of what is ethically objectionable in our dream and phantasy lives will be found to disappear. In the words of Hanns Sachs [1912, 569]: 'If we look in our consciousness at something that has been told us by a dream about a contemporary (real) situation, we ought not

---

[1] [This sentence does not appear in the first edition. In 1909 it appeared in the following form: 'If we look at unconscious wishes reduced to their most fundamental and truest shape, we shall have to remember, no doubt, that psychical reality too has more than one form of existence.' In 1914 the sentence first appeared as printed in the text, except that the last word but one was 'factual' and not 'material'. 'Material' was substituted in 1919.—The remainder of this paragraph was added in 1914.—Freud had already drawn a distinction between 'thought reality' and 'external reality' in the second section of Part III of his 'Project' (1950a).]

to be surprised to find that the monster which we saw under the magnifying glass of analysis turns out to be a tiny infusorian.'

Actions and consciously expressed opinions are as a rule enough for practical purposes in judging men's characters. Actions deserve to be considered first and foremost; for many impulses which force their way through to consciousness are even then brought to nothing by the real forces of mental life before they can mature into deeds. In fact, such impulses often meet with no psychical obstacles to their progress, for the very reason that the unconscious is certain that they will be stopped at some other stage. It is in any case instructive to get to know the much trampled soil from which our virtues proudly spring. Very rarely does the complexity of a human character, driven hither and thither by dynamic forces, submit to a choice between simple alternatives, as our antiquated morality would have us believe.[1]

And the value of dreams for giving us knowledge of the future? There is of course no question of that.[2] [Cf. p. 5 _n._] It would be truer to say instead that they give us knowledge of the past. For dreams are derived from the past in every sense. Nevertheless the ancient belief that dreams foretell the future is not wholly devoid of truth. By picturing our wishes as fulfilled, dreams are after all leading us into the future. But this future, which the dreamer pictures as the present, has been moulded by his indestructible wish into a perfect likeness of the past.

[1] [This subject is further discussed in Freud, 1925_i_ (Section B).]

[2] [In the 1911 edition only, the following footnote appeared at this point: 'Professor Ernst Oppenheim of Vienna has shown me, from the evidence of folklore, that there is a class of dreams in which the prophetic meaning has been dropped even in popular belief and which are perfectly correctly traced back to wishes and needs emerging during sleep. He will shortly be giving a detailed account of these dreams, which are as a rule narrated in the form of comic stories.'—Cf. the paper on dreams in folklore written jointly by Freud and Oppenheim (1957_a_ [1911]) in _Standard Ed._, **12**, 177.]

APPENDIX A

A PREMONITORY DREAM FULFILLED [1]

FRAU B., an estimable woman who moreover possesses a critical sense, told me in another connection and without the slightest *arrière pensée* that once some years ago she dreamt she had met Dr. K., a friend and former family doctor of hers, in the Kärntnerstrasse [2] in front of Hiess's shop. The next morning, while she was walking along the same street, she in fact met the person in question at the very spot she had dreamt of. So much for my theme. I will only add that no subsequent event proved the importance of this miraculous coincidence, which cannot therefore be accounted for by what lay in the future.

Analysis of the dream was helped by questioning, which established the fact that there was no evidence of her having had any recollection at all of the dream on the morning after she dreamt it, until after her walk—evidence such as her having written the dream down or told it to someone before it was fulfilled. On the contrary, she was obliged to accept the following account of what happened, which seems to me more plausible, without raising any objection to it. She was walking along the Kärntnerstrasse one morning and met her old family doctor in front of Hiess's shop. On seeing him she felt convinced that she had dreamt the night before of having this very meeting at that precise spot. According to the rules that apply to the interpretation of neurotic symptoms, her conviction must have been justified; its content may, however, require to be re-interpreted.

---

[1] [The manuscript of this paper is dated November 10, 1899—six days after the publication of *The Interpretation of Dreams*. In the same letter to Fliess in which Freud announced that event (Freud, 1950a, Letter 123, of November 5, 1899) he remarked that he had just discovered the origin and meaning of premonitory dreams. The paper was first published posthumously in *Ges. Werke*, 17 (1941), 21. The present English translation (by James Strachey) first appeared in *Coll. Papers*, 5 (1950), 70.—The same incident was reported by Freud very much more briefly in his *Psychopathology of Everyday Life* (1901b), Chapter XII, Section D.—The topic of premonitory dreams is touched upon in *The Interpretation of Dreams* on pp. 65 and 621.]

[2] [The principal shopping-street in the centre of Vienna.]

The following is an episode with which Dr. K. is connected from Frau B.'s earlier life. When she was young she was married, without her wholehearted consent, to an elderly but wealthy man. A few years later he lost his money, fell ill of tuberculosis and died. For many years the young woman supported herself and her sick husband by giving music lessons. Among her friends in misfortune was her family doctor, Dr. K., who devoted himself to looking after her husband and helped her in finding her first pupils. Another friend was a barrister, also a Dr. K., who put the chaotic affairs of the ruined merchant in order, while at the same time he made love to the young woman and—for the first and last time—set her passion aflame. This love affair brought her no real happiness, for the scruples created by her upbringing and her cast of mind interfered with her complete surrender while she was married and later when she was a widow. In the same connection in which she told me the dream, she also told me of a real occurrence dating from this unhappy period of her life, an occurrence which in her opinion was a remarkable coincidence. She was in her room, kneeling on the floor with her head buried in a chair and sobbing in passionate longing for her friend and helper the barrister, when at that very moment the door opened and in he came to visit her. We shall find nothing at all remarkable in this coincidence when we consider how often she thought of him and how often he probably visited her. Moreover, accidents which seem preconcerted like this are to be found in every love story. Nevertheless this coincidence was probably the true content of her dream and the sole basis of her conviction that it had come true.

Between the scene in which her wish had been fulfilled and the time of the dream more than twenty-five years elapsed. In the meantime Frau B. had become the widow of a second husband who left her with a child and a fortune. The old lady's affection was still centred on Dr. K., who was now her adviser and the administrator of her estate and whom she saw frequently. Let us suppose that during the few days before the dream she had been expecting a visit from him, but that this had not taken place—he was no longer so pressing as he used to be. She may then have quite well had a nostalgic dream one night which took her back to the old days. Her dream was probably of a *rendez-vous* at the time of her love affair, and the chain of her dream-thoughts carried her back to the occasion when, without any pre-arrangement, he had come in at the very moment at which she had been longing for him. She probably had dreams of this kind quite often now; they were a part of the belated punishment with which a woman pays for her youthful cruelty. But such dreams—derivatives of a suppressed current of thought, filled with memories of *rendez-vous* of which, since her second marriage, she no longer liked to think—such dreams were put aside on waking. And that was what happened to our ostensibly prophetic dream. She then went out, and in the Kärntnerstrasse, at a spot which was in itself indifferent, she met her old family doctor, Dr. K. It was a very long time since she had seen him. He was intimately associated with the excitements of that happy-unhappy time. He too had been a helper, and we may suppose that he had been used in her thoughts, and perhaps in her dreams as well, as a screen figure behind which she concealed the better-loved figure of the other Dr. K. This meeting now revived her recollection of the dream. She must have thought: 'Yes, I had a dream last night of my *rendez-vous* with Dr. K.' But this recollection had to undergo the distortion which the dream escaped only because it had been completely forgotten. She inserted the indifferent K. (who had reminded her of the dream) in place of the beloved K. The content of the dream—the *rendez-vous*—was transferred to a belief that she had dreamt of that particular spot, for a *rendez-vous* consists in two people coming to the same spot at the same time. And if she then had an impression that a dream had been fulfilled, she was only giving effect in that way to her memory of the scene in which she had longed in her misery for him to come and her longing had at once been fulfilled.

Thus the creation of a dream after the event, which alone makes prophetic dreams possible, is nothing other than a form of censoring, thanks to which the dream is able to make its way through into consciousness.

10 *Nov.* 99

APPENDIX B

LIST OF WRITINGS BY FREUD DEALING PREDOMINANTLY OR LARGELY WITH DREAMS

[*It would scarcely be an exaggeration to say that dreams are alluded to in the majority of Freud's writings. The following list of works (of greatly varying importance) may however be of some practical use. The date at the beginning of each entry is that of the year during which the work in question was written. The date at the end is that of publication; and under that date fuller particulars of the work will be found in the General Bibliography. The items in square brackets were published posthumously.*]

[1895 'Project for a Scientific Psychology' (Sections 19, 20 and 21 of Part I). (1950*a*.))]

1899 *The Interpretation of Dreams*. (1900*a*.)

[1899 'A Premonitory Dream Fulfilled.' (1941*c*.))]

1901 *On Dreams*. (1901*a*.)

1901 'Fragment of an Analysis of a Case of Hysteria.' [Original title: 'Dreams and Hysteria.'] (1905*e*.)

1905 *Jokes and their Relation to the Unconscious* (Chapter VI). (1905*c*.)

1907 *Delusions and Dreams in Jensen's 'Gradiva'*. (1907*a*.)

1910 'A Typical Example of a Disguised Oedipus Dream.' (1910*l*.)

1911 'Additions to the Interpretation of Dreams.' (1911*a*.)

1911 'The Handling of Dream-Interpretation in Psycho-Analysis.' (1911*e*.)

1911 'Dreams in Folklore' (with Ernst Oppenheim). (1957*a*.)

1913 'An Evidential Dream.' (1913*a*.)

1913 'The Occurrence in Dreams of Material from Fairy Tales.' (1913*d*.)

1913 'Observations and Examples from Analytic Practice.' (1913*h*.)

1914   'The Representation in a Dream of a "Great Achievement".' (1914*e*.)

1914   'From the History of an Infantile Neurosis' (Section IV). (1918*b*.)

1916   *Introductory Lectures on Psycho-Analysis* (Part II). (1916–1917.)

1917   'A Metapsychological Supplement to the Theory of Dreams.' (1917*d*.)

1920   'Supplements to the Theory of Dreams.' (1920*f*.)

1922   'Dreams and Telepathy.' (1922*a*.)

1923   'Remarks upon the Theory and Practice of Dream-Interpretation.' (1923*c*.)

1923   'Josef Popper-Lynkeus and the Theory of Dreams.' (1923*f*.)

1925   'Some Additional Notes on Dream-Interpretation as a Whole.' (1925*i*.)

1929   'A Letter to Maxime Leroy on a Dream of Descartes.' (1929*b*.)

1932   'My Contact with Josef Popper-Lynkeus.' (1932*c*.)

1932   *New Introductory Lectures on Psycho-Analysis* (Lectures XXIX and XXX). (1933*a*.)

[1938   *An Outline of Psycho-Analysis* (Chapter V). (1940*a*.)]

N.B.—An unauthorized concoction of portions of *The Interpretation of Dreams* and *On Dreams* has appeared in two editions in America under the title of *Dream Psychology: Psychoanalysis for Beginners* (with an introduction by André Tridon). New York: McCann, 1920 and 1921. Pp. xi + 237.

ON DREAMS
(1901)

EDITOR'S NOTE

(*a*) GERMAN EDITIONS:

1901 *Über den Traum.* First published as part (pp. 307–344) of a serial publication, *Grenzfragen des Nerven- und Seelenlebens*, edited by L. Löwenfeld and H. Kurella. Wiesbaden: Bergmann.

1911 2nd ed. (Issued as a separate brochure, enlarged.) Same publishers. Pp. 44.

1921 3rd ed. Munich and Wiesbaden: Bergmann. Pp. 44.

1925 In Freud's *Gesammelte Schriften*, **3**, 189–256. Leipzig, Vienna and Zurich: Internationaler Psychoanalytischer Verlag.

1931 In Freud's collective volume *Sexualtheorie und Traumlehre*, 246–307. Same publishers.

1942 In Freud's *Gesammelte Werke*, **2** and **3**, 643–700. London: Imago Publishing Co.

(*b*) ENGLISH TRANSLATIONS:

1914 By M. D. Eder (with introduction by W. L. Mackenzie). London: Heinemann. New York: Rebman. Pp. xxxii + 110.

1952 By James Strachey. London: Hogarth Press and Institute of Psycho-Analysis. Pp. viii + 80. New York: Norton. Pp. 120.

The present translation is a revised reprint of the one published in 1952.

Only three or four months after the publication of *The Interpretation of Dreams* the notion of writing a shortened version of his book was already in Freud's mind. Fliess had evidently written to suggest something of the sort, for in a letter of April 4, 1900 (Freud, 1950*a*, Letter 132), Freud rejected the proposal on the ground, among others, that he had 'already promised to let Löwenfeld have an essay of the same kind'. He also commented on his distaste for embarking on such a job so soon after finishing the large book. Evidently this reluctance persisted, for on May 20 (ibid., Letter 136) he mentions that he has not even *started* the 'brochure', and on July 10 (ibid., Letter 138) announces that he has put it off till October. His last reference to it in the Fliess correspondence is on October 14, 1900 (ibid., Letter 139), where he remarks that he is writing the essay 'without any real enjoyment', since his mind is full of material for the *Psychopathology of Everyday Life* (which was to be his next production). In this latter work, incidentally, there is a reference (near the end of Chapter VII) to the essay *On Dreams* and to the question of whether the issue of a *résumé* might interfere with the sales of the big book.

As will be seen, the only addition of importance made by Freud in the later issues of the essay was the section on symbolism introduced into the second edition.

ON DREAMS

I

During the epoch which may be described as pre-scientific, men had no difficulty in finding an explanation of dreams. When they remembered a dream after waking up, they regarded it as either a favourable or a hostile manifestation by higher powers, daemonic and divine. When modes of thought belonging to natural science began to flourish, all this ingenious mythology was transformed into psychology, and to-day only a small minority of educated people doubt that dreams are a product of the dreamer's own mind.

Since the rejection of the mythological hypothesis, however, dreams have stood in need of explanation. The conditions of their origin, their relation to waking mental life, their dependence upon stimuli which force their way upon perception during the state of sleep, the many peculiarities of their content which are repugnant to waking thought, the inconsistency between their ideational images and the affects attaching to them, and lastly their transitory character, the manner in which waking thought pushes them on one side as something alien to it, and mutilates or extinguishes them in memory—all of these and other problems besides have been awaiting clarification for many hundreds of years, and till now no satisfactory solution of them has been advanced. But what stands in the foreground of our interest is the question of the *significance* of dreams, a question which bears a double sense. It enquires in the first place as to the psychical significance of dreaming, as to the relation of dreams to other mental processes, and as to any biological function that they may have; in the second place it seeks to discover whether dreams can be interpreted, whether the content of individual dreams has a 'meaning', such as we are accustomed to find in other psychical structures.

In the assessment of the significance of dreams three lines of thought can be distinguished. One of these, which echoes, as it were, the ancient overvaluation of dreams, is expressed in the writings of certain philosophers. They consider that the basis of dream-life is a peculiar state of mental activity, and even go so far as to acclaim that state as an elevation to a higher level. For instance, Schubert [1814] declares that dreams are a liberation of the spirit from the power of external nature, and a freeing of the soul from the bonds of the senses. Other thinkers, without going so far as this, insist nevertheless that dreams arise essentially from mental impulses and represent manifestations of mental forces which have been prevented from expanding freely during the daytime. (Cf. the 'dream imagination' of Scherner [1861, 97 f.] and Volkelt [1875, 28 f.].) A large number of observers agree in attributing to dream-life a capacity for superior functioning in certain departments at least (e.g. in memory).

In sharp contrast to this, the majority of medical writers adopt a view according to which dreams scarcely reach the level of being psychical phenomena at all. On their theory, the sole instigators of dreams are the sensory and somatic stimuli which either impinge upon the sleeper from outside or become active accidentally in his internal organs. What is dreamt, they contend, has no more claim to sense and meaning than, for instance, the sounds which would be produced if 'the ten fingers of a man who knows nothing of music were wandering over the keys of a piano'. [Strümpell, 1877, 84.] Dreams are described by Binz [1878, 35] as being no more than 'somatic processes which are in every case useless and in many cases positively pathological'. All the characteristics of dream-life would thus be explained as being due to the disconnected activity of separate organs or groups of cells in an otherwise sleeping brain, an activity forced upon them by physiological stimuli.

Popular opinion is but little affected by this scientific judgement, and is not concerned as to the sources of dreams; it seems to persist in the belief that nevertheless dreams have a meaning, which relates to the prediction of the future and which can be discovered by some process of interpretation of a content which is often confused and puzzling. The methods of interpretation employed consist in transforming the content of the dream as it is remembered, either by replacing it piecemeal in accordance with a fixed key, or by replacing the dream as a whole by another whole to which it stands in a symbolic relation. Serious-minded people smile at these efforts: '*Träume sind Schäume*'— 'dreams are froth'.

One day I discovered to my great astonishment that the view of dreams which came nearest to the truth was not the medical but the popular one, half involved though it still was in superstition. For I had been led to fresh conclusions on the subject of dreams by applying to them a new method of psychological investigation which had done excellent service in the solution of phobias, obsessions and delusions, etc. Since then, under the name of 'psycho-analysis', it has found acceptance by a whole school of research workers. The numerous analogies that exist between dream-life and a great variety of conditions of psychical illness in waking life have indeed been correctly observed by many medical investigators. There seemed, therefore, good ground for hoping that a method of investigation which had given satisfactory results in the case of psychopathic structures would also be of use in throwing light upon dreams. Phobias and obsessions are as alien to normal consciousness as dreams are to waking consciousness; their origin is as unknown to consciousness as that of dreams. In the case of these psychopathic structures practical considerations led to an investigation of their origin and mode of development; for experience had shown that the discovery of the trains of thought which, concealed from consciousness, connect the pathological ideas with the remaining contents of the mind is equivalent to a resolution of the symptoms and has as its consequence the mastering of ideas which till then could not be inhibited. Thus psychotherapy was the starting-point of the procedure of which I made use for the explanation of dreams.

This procedure is easily described, although instruction and practice would be necessary before it could be put into effect.

If we make use of it on someone else, let us say on a patient with a phobia, we require him to direct his attention on to the idea in question, not, however, to reflect upon it as he has done so often already, but to take notice of *whatever occurs to his mind without any exception* and report it to the physician. If he should then assert that his attention is unable to grasp anything at all, we dismiss this with an energetic assurance that a complete absence of any ideational subject-matter is quite impossible.

And in fact very soon numerous ideas will occur to him and will lead on to others; but they will invariably be prefaced by a judgement on the part of the self-observer to the effect that they are senseless or unimportant, that they are irrelevant, and that they occurred to him by chance and without any connection with the topic under consideration. We perceive at once that it was this critical attitude which prevented the subject from reporting any of these ideas, and which indeed had previously prevented them from becoming conscious. If we can induce him to abandon his criticism of the ideas that occur to him, and to continue pursuing the trains of thought which will emerge so long as he keeps his attention turned upon them, we find ourselves in possession of a quantity of psychical material, which we soon find is clearly connected with the pathological idea which was our starting-point; this material will soon reveal connections between the pathological idea and other ideas, and will eventually enable us to replace the pathological idea by a new one which fits into the nexus of thought in an intelligible fashion.

This is not the place in which to give a detailed account of the premises upon which this experiment was based, or the consequences which follow from its invariable success. It will therefore be enough to say that we obtain material that enables us to resolve any pathological idea if we turn our attention precisely to those associations which are 'involuntary', which 'interfere with our reflection', and which are normally dismissed by our critical faculty as worthless rubbish.

If we make use of this procedure upon *ourselves*, we can best assist the investigation by at once writing down what are at first unintelligible associations.

I will now show what results follow if I apply this method of investigation to dreams. Any example of a dream should in fact be equally appropriate for the purpose; but for particular reasons I will choose some dream of my own, one which seems obscure and meaningless as I remember it, and one which has the advantage of brevity. A dream which I actually had last night will perhaps meet these requirements. Its content, as I noted it down immediately after waking up, was as follows:

'*Company at table or table d'hôte . . . spinach was being eaten . . . Frau E. L. was sitting beside me; she was turning her whole attention to me and laid her hand on my knee in an intimate manner. I removed*

*her hand unresponsively. She then said: "But you've always had such
beautiful eyes." . . . I then had an indistinct picture of two eyes, as
though it were a drawing or like the outline of a pair of spectacles. . . .'*

This was the whole of the dream, or at least all that I could
remember of it. It seemed to me obscure and meaningless, but
above all surprising. Frau E. L. is a person with whom I have
hardly at any time been on friendly terms, nor, so far as I know,
have I ever wished to have any closer relations with her. I have
not seen her for a long time, and her name has not, I believe,
been mentioned during the last few days. The dream-process
was not accompanied by affects of any kind.

Reflecting over this dream brought me no nearer to understanding it. I determined, however, to set down without any
premeditation or criticism the associations which presented
themselves to my self-observation. As I have found, it is advisable for this purpose to divide a dream into its elements and
to find the associations attaching to each of these fragments
separately.

Company at table or table d'hôte. This at once reminded me of an
episode which occurred late yesterday evening. I came away
from a small party in the company of a friend who offered to
take a cab and drive me home in it. 'I prefer taking a cab with
a taximeter,' he said, 'it occupies one's mind so agreeably; one
always has something to look at.' When we had taken our
places in the cab and the driver had set the dial, so that the
first charge of sixty hellers[1] became visible, I carried the joke
further. 'We've only just got in,' I said, 'and already we owe
him sixty hellers. A cab with a taximeter always reminds me of
a table d'hôte. It makes me avaricious and selfish, because it
keeps on reminding me of what I owe. My debt seems to be
growing too fast, and I'm afraid of getting the worst of the
bargain; and in just the same way at a table d'hôte I can't avoid
feeling in a comic way that I'm getting too little, and must keep
an eye on my own interests.' I went on to quote, somewhat
discursively:

> Ihr führt ins Leben uns hinein,
> Ihr lasst den Armen schuldig werden.[2]

---

[1] [Equivalent at the time to 6*d*. or 12½ cents.]

[2] [These lines are from one of the Harp-player's songs in Goethe's
Wilhelm Meister. In the original the words are addressed to the Heavenly
Powers and may be translated literally: 'You lead us into life, you make

And now a second association to 'table d'hôte'. A few weeks ago, while we were at table in a hotel at a mountain resort in the Tyrol, I was very much annoyed because I thought my wife was not being sufficiently reserved towards some people sitting near us whose acquaintance I had no desire at all to make.[1] I asked her to concern herself more with me than with these strangers. This was again *as though I were getting the worst of the bargain at the table d'hôte*. I was struck too by the contrast between my wife's behaviour at table and that of Frau E. L. in the dream, who 'turned her whole attention to me'.

To proceed. I now saw that the events in the dream were a reproduction of a small episode of a precisely similar kind which occurred between my wife and me at the time at which I was secretly courting her. The caress which she gave me under the table-cloth was her reply to a pressing love letter. In the dream, however, my wife was replaced by a comparative stranger —E. L.

Frau E. L. is the daughter of a man to whom I was once *in debt*. I could not help noticing that this revealed an unsuspected connection between parts of the content of the dream and my associations. If one follows the train of association starting out from one element of a dream's content, one is soon brought back to another of its elements. My associations to the dream were bringing to light connections which were not visible in the dream itself.

If a person expects one to keep an eye on his interests without any advantage to oneself, his artlessness is apt to provoke the scornful question: 'Do you suppose I'm going to do this or that for the sake of your *beaux yeux* [*beautiful eyes*]?' That being so, Frau E. L.'s speech in the dream, 'You've always had such beautiful eyes', can only have meant: 'People have always done everything for you for love; you have always had everything *without paying for it*.' The truth is, of course, just the contrary: I have always paid dearly for whatever advantage I have had

the poor creature guilty.' But the words '*Armen*' and '*schuldig*' are both capable of bearing another meaning. '*Armen*' might mean 'poor' in the financial sense and '*schuldig*' might mean 'in debt'. So in the present context the last line could be rendered: 'You make the poor man fall into debt.'—The lines were quoted again by Freud at the end of Chapter VII of *Civilization and its Discontents* (1930a).]

[1] [The episode is also referred to in *The Psychopathology of Everyday Life* (1901b), Chapter VII (A).]

from other people. The fact that my friend took me home yesterday in a cab *without my paying for it* must, after all, have made an impression on me.

Incidentally, the friend whose guests we were yesterday has often put me in his debt. Only recently I allowed an opportunity of repaying him to slip by. He has had only one present from me—an antique bowl, round which there are *eyes* painted: what is known as an '*occhiale*', to avert the *evil eye*. Moreover he is an *eye surgeon*. The same evening I asked him after a woman patient, whom I had sent on to him for a consultation to fit her with *spectacles*.

As I now perceived, almost all the elements of the dream's content had been brought into the new context. For the sake of consistency, however, the further question might be asked of why *spinach*, of all things, was being served in the dream. The answer was that *spinach* reminded me of an episode which occurred not long ago at our family table, when one of the children—and precisely the one who really deserves to be admired for his *beautiful eyes*—refused to eat any spinach. I myself behaved in just the same way when I was a child; for a long time I detested spinach, till eventually my taste changed and promoted that vegetable into one of my favourite foods. My own early life and my child's were thus brought together by the mention of this dish. 'You ought to be glad to have spinach,' the little *gourmet's* mother exclaimed; 'there are children who would be only too pleased to have spinach.' Thus I was reminded of the duties of parents to their children. Goethe's words

> Ihr führt ins Leben uns hinein,
> Ihr lasst den Armen schuldig werden.

gained a fresh meaning in this connection.[1]

I will pause here to survey the results I had so far reached in my dream-analysis. By following the associations which arose from the separate elements of the dream divorced from their context, I arrived at a number of thoughts and recollections, which I could not fail to recognize as important products of my mental life. This material revealed by the analysis of the dream was intimately connected with the dream's content, yet the connection was of such a kind that I could never have inferred the

[1] [See footnote 2 on p. 637. The first line of the couplet might now be taken to mean that the verses are addressed to parents.]

fresh material from that content. The dream was unemotional, disconnected and unintelligible; but while I was producing the thoughts behind the dream, I was aware of intense and well-founded affective impulses; the thoughts themselves fell at once into logical chains, in which certain central ideas made their appearance more than once. Thus, the contrast between 'selfish' and 'unselfish', and the elements 'being in debt' and 'without paying for it' were central ideas of this kind, not represented in the dream itself. I might draw closer together the threads in the material revealed by the analysis, and I might then show that they converge upon a single nodal point, but considerations of a personal and not of a scientific nature prevent my doing so in public. I should be obliged to betray many things which had better remain my secret, for on my way to discovering the solution of the dream all kinds of things were revealed which I was unwilling to admit even to myself. Why then, it will be asked, have I not chosen some other dream, whose analysis is better suited for reporting, so that I could produce more convincing evidence of the meaning and connectedness of the material uncovered by analysis? The answer is that *every* dream with which I might try to deal would lead to things equally hard to report and would impose an equal discretion upon me. Nor should I avoid this difficulty by bringing up someone else's dream for analysis, unless circumstances enabled me to drop all disguise without damage to the person who had confided in me.

At the point which I have now reached, I am led to regard the dream as a sort of *substitute* for the thought-processes, full of meaning and emotion, at which I arrived after the completion of the analysis. We do not yet know the nature of the process which has caused the dream to be generated from these thoughts, but we can see that it is wrong to regard it as purely physical and without psychical meaning, as a process which has arisen from the isolated activity of separate groups of brain cells aroused from sleep.

Two other things are already clear. The content of the dream is very much shorter than the thoughts for which I regard it as a substitute; and analysis has revealed that the instigator of the dream was an unimportant event of the evening before I dreamt it.

I should, of course, not draw such far-reaching conclusions if only a single dream-analysis was at my disposal. If experience shows me, however, that by uncritically pursuing the associations arising from *any* dream I can arrive at a similar train of thoughts, among the elements of which the constituents of the dream re-appear and which are interconnected in a rational and intelligible manner, then it will be safe to disregard the slight possibility that the connections observed in a first experiment might be due to chance. I think I am justified, therefore, in adopting a terminology which will crystallize our new discovery. In order to contrast the dream as it is retained in my memory with the relevant material discovered by analysing it, I shall speak of the former as the '*manifest* content of the dream' and the latter—without, in the first instance, making any further distinction—as the '*latent* content of the dream'. I am now faced by two new problems which have not hitherto been formulated. (1) What is the psychical process which has transformed the latent content of the dream into the manifest one which is known to me from my memory? (2) What are the motive or motives which have necessitated this transformation? I shall describe the process which transforms the latent into the manifest content of dreams as the 'dream-work'. The counterpart to this activity—one which brings about a transformation in the opposite direction—is already known to us as the work of analysis. The remaining problems arising out of dreams—questions as to the instigators of dreams, as to the origin of their material, as to their possible meaning, as to the possible function of dreaming, and as to the reasons for dreams being forgotten—all these problems will be discussed by me on the basis, not of the manifest, but of the newly discovered latent dream-content. Since I attribute all the contradictory and incorrect views upon dream-life which appear in the literature of the subject to ignorance of the latent content of dreams as revealed by analysis, I shall be at the greatest pains henceforward to avoid confusing the *manifest dream* with the *latent dream-thoughts*.

III

The transformation of the latent dream-thoughts into the manifest dream-content deserves all our attention, since it is the first instance known to us of psychical material being changed over from one mode of expression to another, from a mode of expression which is immediately intelligible to us to another which we can only come to understand with the help of guidance and effort, though it too must be recognized as a function of our mental activity.

Dreams can be divided into three categories in respect of the relation between their latent and manifest content. In the first place, we may distinguish those dreams which *make sense* and are at the same time *intelligible*, which, that is to say, can be inserted without further difficulty into the context of our mental life. We have numbers of such dreams. They are for the most part short and appear to us in general to deserve little attention, since there is nothing astonishing or strange about them. Incidentally, their occurrence constitutes a powerful argument against the theory according to which dreams originate from the isolated activity of separate groups of brain cells. They give no indication of reduced or fragmentary psychical activity, but nevertheless we never question the fact of their being dreams, and do not confuse them with the products of waking life. A second group is formed by those dreams which, though they are connected in themselves and have a clear sense, nevertheless have a *bewildering* effect, because we cannot see how to fit that sense into our mental life. Such would be the case if we were to dream, for instance, that a relative of whom we were fond had died of the plague, when we had no reason for expecting, fearing or assuming any such thing; we should ask in astonishment: 'How did I get hold of such an idea?' The third group, finally, contains those dreams which are without either sense or intelligibility, which seem *disconnected, confused* and *meaningless*. The preponderant majority of the products of our dreaming exhibit these characteristics, which are the basis of the low opinion in which dreams are held and of the medical theory that they are the outcome of a restricted mental activity. The most evident signs of incoherence are seldom absent, especially in dream-compositions of any considerable length and complexity.

The contrast between the manifest and latent content of dreams is clearly of significance only for dreams of the second and more particularly of the third category. It is there that we are faced by riddles which only disappear after we have replaced the manifest dream by the latent thoughts behind it; and it was on a specimen of the last category—a confused and unintelligible dream—that the analysis which I have just recorded was carried out. Contrary to our expectation, however, we came up against motives which prevented us from becoming fully acquainted with the latent dream-thoughts. A repetition of similar experiences may lead us to suspect that *there is an intimate and regular relation between the unintelligible and confused nature of dreams and the difficulty of reporting the thoughts behind them*. Before enquiring into the nature of this relation, we may with advantage turn our attention to the more easily intelligible dreams of the first category, in which the manifest and latent content coincide, and there appears to be a consequent saving in dream-work.

Moreover, an examination of these dreams offers advantages from another standpoint. For *children's* dreams are of that kind —significant and not puzzling. Here, incidentally, we have a further argument against tracing the origin of dreams to dissociated cerebral activity during sleep. For why should a reduction in psychical functioning of this kind be a characteristic of the state of sleep in the case of adults but not in that of children? On the other hand, we shall be fully justified in expecting that an explanation of psychical processes in children, in whom they may well be greatly simplified, may turn out to be an indispensable prelude to the investigation of the psychology of adults.

I will therefore record a few instances of dreams which I have collected from children. A little girl nineteen months old had been kept without food all day because she had had an attack of vomiting in the morning; her nurse declared that she had been upset by eating strawberries. During the night after this day of starvation she was heard saying her own name in her sleep and adding: '*Stwawbewwies, wild stwawbewwies, omblet, pudden!*' She was thus dreaming of eating a meal, and she laid special stress in her menu on the particular delicacy of which, as she had reason to expect, she would only be allowed scanty quantities in the near future.—A little boy of twenty-two months had a similar dream of a feast which he had been denied. The day before, he had been obliged to present his uncle with a gift of a basket of fresh cherries, of which he himself, of course, had only been allowed to taste a single sample. He awoke with this cheerful news: '*Hermann eaten all the chewwies!*'—One day a girl of three and a quarter made a trip across a lake. The voyage was evidently not long enough for her, for she cried when she had to get off the boat. Next morning she reported that during the night she had been for a trip on the lake: she had been continuing her interrupted voyage.—A boy of five and a quarter showed signs of dissatisfaction in the course of a walk in the neighbourhood of the Dachstein.[1] Each time a new mountain came into view he asked if it was the Dachstein and finally refused to visit a waterfall with the rest of the company. His behaviour was attributed to fatigue; but it found a better explanation when next morning he reported that he had dreamt that *he had climbed up the Dachstein*. He had evidently had the idea that the expedition would end in a climb up the Dachstein, and had become depressed when the promised mountain never came in view. He made up in his dream for what the previous day had failed to give him.—A six-year-old girl[2] had an exactly similar dream. In the course of a walk her father had stopped short of their intended goal as the hour was getting late. On their way back she had noticed a signpost bearing the name of another landmark; and her father had promised to take her there as well another time. Next morning she met her father with the news that she had dreamt that *he had been with her to both places*.

The common element in all these children's dreams is obvious. All of them fulfilled wishes which were active during the day but had remained unfulfilled. The dreams were simple and undisguised *wish-fulfilments*.

Here is another child's dream, which, though at first sight it is not quite easy to understand, is also nothing more than a wish-fulfilment. A little girl not quite four years old had been brought to town from the country because she was suffering

[1] [A mountain in the Austrian Alps.]

[2] [In *The Interpretation of Dreams*, where the same dream is reported (*Standard Ed.*, **4**, 129), the girl's age is twice given as 'eight'.]

from an attack of poliomyelitis. She spent the night with an aunt who had no children, and was put to sleep in a large bed —much too large for her, of course. Next morning she said she had had a dream that *the bed had been far too small for her, and that there had been no room for her in it.* It is easy to recognize this dream as a wishful dream if we remember that children very often express a wish '*to be big*'. The size of the bed was a disagreeable reminder of her smallness to the would-be big child; she therefore corrected the unwelcome relation in her dream, and grew so big that even the large bed was too small for her.

Even when the content of children's dreams becomes complicated and subtle, there is never any difficulty in recognizing them as wish-fulfilments. An eight-year-old boy had a dream that he was driving in a chariot with Achilles and that Diomede was the charioteer. It was shown that the day before he had been deep in a book of legends about the Greek heroes; and it was easy to see that he had taken the heroes as his models and was sorry not to be living in their days.[1]

This small collection throws a direct light on a further characteristic of children's dreams: their connection with daytime life. The wishes which are fulfilled in them are carried over from daytime and as a rule from the day before, and in waking life they have been accompanied by intense emotion. Nothing unimportant or indifferent, or nothing which would strike a child as such, finds its way into the content of their dreams.

Numerous examples of dreams of this infantile type can be found occurring in adults as well, though, as I have said, they are usually brief in content. Thus a number of people regularly respond to a stimulus of thirst during the night with dreams of drinking, which thus endeavour to get rid of the stimulus and enable sleep to continue. In some people 'dreams of convenience' of this kind often occur before waking, when the necessity for getting up presents itself. They dream that they are already up and at the washing-stand, or that they are already at the school or office where they are due at some particular time. During the night before a journey we not infrequently dream of having arrived at our destination; so too, before a visit to the theatre or a party, a dream will often anticipate the pleasure

[1] [Most of these children's dreams will be found reported in greater detail in *The Interpretation of Dreams* (1900a), Chapter III, and in the eighth of Freud's *Introductory Lectures* (1916–17).]

that lies ahead—out of impatience, as it were. In other dreams the wish-fulfilment is expressed a stage more indirectly: some connection or implication must be established—that is, the work of interpretation must be begun—before the wish-fulfilment can be recognized. A man told me, for instance, that his young wife had had a dream that her period had started. I reflected that if this young woman had missed her period she must have known that she was faced with a pregnancy. Thus when she reported her dream she was announcing her pregnancy, and the meaning of the dream was to represent as fulfilled her wish that the pregnancy might be postponed for a while. Under unusual or extreme conditions dreams of this infantile character are particularly common. Thus the leader of a polar expedition has recorded that the members of his expedition, while they were wintering in the ice-field and living on a monotonous diet and short rations, regularly dreamt like children of large meals, of mountains of tobacco, and of being back at home.[1]

It by no means rarely happens that in the course of a comparatively long, complicated and on the whole confused dream one particularly clear portion stands out, which contains an unmistakable wish-fulfilment, but which is bound up with some other, unintelligible material. But in the case of adults, anyone with some experience in analysing their dreams will find to his surprise that even those dreams which have an appearance of being transparently clear[2] are seldom as simple as those of children, and that behind the obvious wish-fulfilment some other meaning may lie concealed.

It would indeed be a simple and satisfactory solution of the riddle of dreams if the work of analysis were to enable us to trace even the meaningless and confused dreams of adults back to the infantile type of fulfilment of an intensely felt wish of the previous day. There can be no doubt, however, that appearances do not speak in favour of such an expectation. Dreams are usually full of the most indifferent and strangest material, and there is no sign in their content of the fulfilment of any wish.

---

[1] [Quoted in full from 1911 onwards in *The Interpretation of Dreams* (*Standard Ed.*, 4, 131 *n*).—The last two sentences of this paragraph were added in 1911.]

[2] [*'Durchsichtigen.'* So in the first edition. In the second and subsequent editions misprinted *'undurchsichtigen'.*]

But before taking leave of infantile dreams with their undisguised wish-fulfilments, I must not omit to mention one principal feature of dreams, which has long been evident and which emerges particularly clearly precisely in this group. Every one of these dreams can be replaced by an optative clause: 'Oh, if only the trip on the lake had lasted longer!'—'If only I were already washed and dressed!'—'If only I could have kept the cherries instead of giving them to Uncle!' But dreams give us more than such optative clauses. They show us the wish as already fulfilled; they represent its fulfilment as real and present; and the material employed in dream-representation consists principally, though not exclusively, of situations and of sensory images, mostly of a visual character. Thus, even in this infantile group, a species of transformation, which deserves to be described as dream-work, is not completely absent: *a thought expressed in the optative has been replaced by a representation in the present tense.*

IV

We shall be inclined to suppose that a transformation of some such kind has occurred even in confused dreams, though we cannot tell whether what has been transformed was an optative in their case too. There are, however, two passages in the specimen dream which I have reported, and with whose analysis we have made some headway, that give us reason to suspect something of the kind. The analysis showed that my wife had concerned herself with some other people at table, and that I had found this disagreeable; the dream contained precisely the opposite of this—the person who took the place of my wife was turning her whole attention to me. But a disagreeable experience can give rise to no more suitable wish than that its opposite might have occurred—which was what the dream represented as fulfilled. There was an exactly similar relation between the bitter thought revealed in the analysis that I had never had anything free of cost and the remark made by the woman in the dream—'You've always had such beautiful eyes'. Some part of the opposition between the manifest and latent content of dreams is thus attributable to wish-fulfilment.

But another achievement of the dream-work, tending as it does to produce incoherent dreams, is even more striking. If in any particular instance we compare the number of ideational elements or the space taken up in writing them down in the case of the dream and of the dream-thoughts to which the analysis leads us and of which traces are to be found in the dream itself, we shall be left in no doubt that the dream-work has carried out a work of compression or *condensation* on a large scale. It is impossible at first to form any judgement of the degree of this condensation; but the deeper we plunge into a dream-analysis the more impressive it seems. From every element in a dream's content associative threads branch out in two or more directions; every situation in a dream seems to be put together out of two or more impressions or experiences. For instance, I once had a dream of a sort of swimming-pool, in which the bathers were scattering in all directions; at one point on the edge of the pool someone was standing and bending towards one of the people bathing, as though to help her out of the water. The situation was put together from a memory of an experience I had had at puberty and from two paintings, one of which I had seen shortly before the dream. One was a picture from Schwind's series illustrating the legend of Mélusine, which showed the water-nymphs surprised in their pool (cf. the scattering bathers in the dream); the other was a picture of the Deluge by an Italian Master; while the little experience remembered from my puberty was of having seen the instructor at a swimming-school helping a lady out of the water who had stopped in until after the time set aside for men bathers.—In the case of the example which I chose for interpretation, an analysis of the situation led me to a small series of recollections each of which contributed something to the content of the dream. In the first place, there was the episode from the time of my engagement of which I have already spoken. The pressure upon my hand under the table, which was a part of that episode, provided the dream with the detail 'under the table'—a detail which I had to add as an afterthought to my memory of the dream. In the episode itself there was of course no question of 'turning to me'; the analysis showed that this element was the fulfilment of a wish by presenting the opposite of an actual event, and that it related to my wife's behaviour at the table d'hôte. But behind this recent recollection there lay concealed an exactly similar and far more important scene from the time of our engagement, which estranged us for a whole day. The intimate laying of a hand on my knee belonged to a quite different context and was concerned with quite other people. This element in the dream was in turn the starting-point of two separate sets of memories —and so on.

The material in the dream-thoughts which is packed together for the purpose of constructing a dream-situation must of course in itself be adaptable for that purpose. There must be one or more *common elements* in all the components. The dream-work then proceeds just as Francis Galton did in constructing his family photographs. It superimposes, as it were, the different components upon one another. The common element in them then stands out clearly in the composite picture, while contradictory details more or less wipe one another out. This method of production also explains to some extent the varying degrees of characteristic vagueness shown by so many elements in the content of dreams. Basing itself on this discovery, dream-interpretation has laid down the following rule: in analysing a dream, if an uncertainty can be resolved into an 'either—or', we must replace it for purposes of interpretation by an 'and', and take each of the apparent alternatives as an independent starting-point for a series of associations.

If a common element of this kind between the dream-thoughts is not present, the dream-work sets about *creating* one, so that it may be possible for the thoughts to be given a common representation in the dream. The most convenient way of bringing together two dream-thoughts which, to start with, have nothing in common, is to alter the verbal form of one of them, and thus bring it half-way to meet the other, which may be similarly clothed in a new form of words. A parallel process is involved in hammering out a rhyme, where a similar sound has to be sought for in the same way as a common element is in our present case. A large part of the dream-work consists in the creation of intermediate thoughts of this kind which are often highly ingenious, though they frequently appear far-fetched; these then form a link between the composite picture in the manifest content of the dream and the dream-thoughts, which are themselves diverse both in form and essence and have been determined by the exciting factors of the dream. The analysis of our sample dream affords us an instance of this kind in which a thought has been given a new form in order to bring it into contact with another which is essentially foreign to it. In carrying out the analysis I came upon the following thought: '*I should like to get something sometimes without paying for it.*' But in that form the thought could not be employed in the dream-content. It was therefore given a fresh form: '*I should like to get some enjoyment without cost* ["*Kosten*"].'[1] Now the word '*Kosten*' in its second sense fits into the 'table d'hôte' circle of ideas, and could thus be represented in the '*spinach*' which was served in the dream. When a dish appears at our table and the children refuse it, their mother begins by trying persuasion, and urges them '*just to taste* ["*kosten*"] *a bit of it*'. It may seem strange that the dream-work should make such free use of verbal ambiguity, but further experience will teach us that the occurrence is quite a common one.

The process of condensation further explains certain con-

---

[1] [The German word '*Kosten*' means both 'cost' and 'to taste'.]

stituents of the content of dreams which are peculiar to them and are not found in waking ideation. What I have in mind are 'collective' and 'composite figures' and the strange 'composite structures', which are creations not unlike the composite animals invented by the folk-imagination of the Orient. The latter, however, have already assumed stereotyped shapes in our thought, whereas in dreams fresh composite forms are being perpetually constructed in an inexhaustible variety. We are all of us familiar with such structures from our own dreams.

There are many sorts of ways in which figures of this kind can be put together. I may build up a figure by giving it the features of two people; or I may give it the *form* of one person but think of it in the dream as having the *name* of another person; or I may have a visual picture of one person, but put it in a situation which is appropriate to another. In all these cases the combination of different persons into a single representative in the content of the dream has a meaning; it is intended to indicate an 'and' or 'just as', or to compare the original persons with each other in some particular respect, which may even be specified in the dream itself. As a rule, however, this common element between the combined persons can only be discovered by analysis, and is only indicated in the contents of the dream by the formation of the collective figure.

The composite structures which occur in dreams in such immense numbers are put together in an equal variety of ways, and the same rules apply to their resolution. There is no need for me to quote any instances. Their strangeness disappears completely when once we have made up our minds not to class them with the objects of our waking perception, but to remember that they are products of dream-condensation and are emphasizing in an effectively abbreviated form some common characteristic of the objects which they are thus combining. Here again the common element has as a rule to be discovered by analysis. The content of the dream merely says as it were: 'All these things have an element *x* in common.' The dissection of these composite structures by means of analysis is often the shortest way to finding the meaning of a dream.—Thus, I dreamt on one occasion that I was sitting on a bench with one of my former University teachers, and that the bench, which was surrounded by other benches, was moving forward at a rapid pace. This was a combination of a lecture theatre and a

trottoir roulant.[1] I will not pursue this train of ideas further.
—Another time I was sitting in a railway carriage and holding
on my lap an object in the shape of a top-hat ['*Zylinderhut*',
literally 'cylinder-hat'], which however was made of transparent
glass. The situation made me think at once of the proverb:
'*Mit dem Hute in der Hand kommt man durchs ganze Land.*'[2] The
glass cylinder led me by a short *détour* to think of an incan-
descent gas-mantle; and I soon saw that I should like to make
a discovery which would make me as rich and independent
as my fellow-countryman Dr. Auer von Welsbach was made
by his, and that I should like to travel instead of stopping in
Vienna. In the dream I was travelling with my discovery, the
hat in the shape of a glass cylinder—a discovery which, it is
true, was not as yet of any great practical use.—The dream-
work is particularly fond of representing two *contrary* ideas by
the same composite structure. Thus, for instance, a woman had
a dream in which she saw herself carrying a tall spray of flowers,
such as the angel is represented as holding in pictures of the
Annunciation. (This stood for innocence; incidentally, her own
name was Maria.) On the other hand, the spray was covered
with large white[3] flowers like camellias. (This stood for the
opposite of innocence; it was associated with *La dame aux
camélias.*)

A good proportion of what we have learnt about condensation in dreams may be summarized in this formula: each
element in the content of a dream is 'overdetermined' by
material in the dream-thoughts; it is not derived from a *single*
element in the dream-thoughts, but may be traced back to a
whole number. These elements need not necessarily be closely
related to each other in the dream-thoughts themselves; they
may belong to the most widely separated regions of the fabric
of those thoughts. A dream-element is, in the strictest sense of
the word, the 'representative' of all this disparate material in
the content of the dream. But analysis reveals yet another side
of the complicated relation between the content of the dream

---

[1] [The '*trottoir roulant*' was a moving roadway installed at the Paris
Exhibition of 1900.]

[2] ['If you go hat in hand, you can cross the whole land.']

[3] [This should probably be 'red'. The flowers are so described in the
much fuller account of the dream given in *The Interpretation of Dreams*
(*Standard Ed.*, 5, 347).]

and the dream-thoughts. Just as connections lead from each element of the dream to several dream-thoughts, so as a rule a single dream-thought is represented by more than one dream-element; the threads of association do not simply converge from the dream-thoughts to the dream-content, they cross and interweave with each other many times over in the course of their journey.

Condensation, together with the transformation of thoughts into situations ('dramatization'), is the most important and peculiar characteristic of the dream-work. So far, however, nothing has transpired as to any *motive* necessitating this compression of the material.

V

In the case of the complicated and confused dreams with which we are now concerned, condensation and dramatization alone are not enough to account for the whole of the impression that we gain of the dissimilarity between the content of the dream and the dream-thoughts. We have evidence of the operation of a third factor, and this evidence deserves careful sifting.

First and foremost, when by means of analysis we have arrived at a knowledge of the dream-thoughts, we observe that the manifest dream-content deals with quite different material from the latent thoughts. This, to be sure, is no more than an appearance, which evaporates under closer examination, for we find ultimately that the whole of the dream-content is derived from the dream-thoughts, and that almost all the dream-thoughts are represented in the dream-content. Nevertheless, something of the distinction still remains. What stands out boldly and clearly in the dream as its essential content must, after analysis, be satisfied with playing an extremely subordinate role among the dream-thoughts; and what, on the evidence of our feelings, can claim to be the most prominent among the dream-thoughts is either not present at all as ideational material in the content of the dream or is only remotely alluded to in some obscure region of it. We may put it in this way: *in the course of the dream-work the psychical intensity passes over from the thoughts and ideas to which it properly belongs on to others which in our judgement have no claim to any such emphasis*. No other process contributes so much to concealing the meaning of a dream and to making the connection between the dream-content and the dream-thoughts unrecognizable. In the course of this process, which I shall describe as 'dream-displacement', the psychical intensity, significance or affective potentiality of the thoughts is, as we further find, transformed into sensory vividness. We assume as a matter of course that the most distinct element in the manifest content of a dream is the most important one; but in fact [owing to the displacement that has occurred] it is often an *indistinct* element which turns out to be the most direct derivative of the essential dream-thought.

What I have called dream-displacement might equally be

described [in Nietzsche's phrase] as 'a transvaluation of psychical values'. I shall not have given an exhaustive estimate of
this phenomenon, however, unless I add that this work of displacement or transvaluation is performed to a very varying
degree in different dreams. There are dreams which come about
almost without any displacement. These are the ones which
make sense and are intelligible, such, for instance, as those
which we have recognized as undisguised wishful dreams. On
the other hand, there are dreams in which not a single piece
of the dream-thoughts has retained its own psychical value, or
in which everything that is essential in the dream-thoughts has
been replaced by something trivial. And we can find a complete
series of transitional cases between these two extremes. The
more obscure and confused a dream appears to be, the greater
the share in its construction which may be attributed to the
factor of displacement.

Our specimen dream exhibits displacement to this extent at
least, that its content seems to have a different *centre* from its
dream-thoughts. In the foreground of the dream-content a
prominent place is taken by a situation in which a woman seems
to be making advances to me; while in the dream-thoughts
the chief emphasis is laid on a wish for once to enjoy unselfish
love, love which 'costs nothing'—an idea concealed behind the
phrase about 'beautiful eyes' and the far-fetched allusion to
'spinach'.

If we undo dream-displacement by means of analysis, we
obtain what seems to be completely trustworthy information
on two much-disputed problems concerning dreams: as to their
instigators and as to their connection with waking life. There
are dreams which immediately reveal their derivation from
events of the day; there are others in which no trace of any
such derivation is to be discovered. If we seek the help of
analysis, we find that every dream without any possible exception goes back to an impression of the past few days, or, it is
probably more correct to say, of the day immediately preceding
the dream, of the 'dream-day'. The impression which plays the
part of dream-instigator may be such an important one that we
feel no surprise at being concerned with it in the daytime, and
in that case we rightly speak of the dream as carrying on with
the significant interests of our waking life. As a rule, however,
if a connection is to be found in the content of the dream with

any impression of the previous day, that impression is so trivial, insignificant and unmemorable, that it is only with difficulty that we ourselves can recall it. And in such cases the content of the dream itself, even if it is connected and intelligible, seems to be concerned with the most indifferent trivialities, which would be unworthy of our interest if we were awake. A good deal of the contempt in which dreams are held is due to the preference thus shown in their content for what is indifferent and trivial.

Analysis does away with the misleading appearance upon which this derogatory judgement is founded. If the content of a dream puts forward some indifferent impression as being its instigator, analysis invariably brings to light a significant experience, and one by which the dreamer has good reason to be stirred. This experience has been replaced by the indifferent one, with which it is connected by copious associative links. Where the content of the dream treats of insignificant and uninteresting ideational material, analysis uncovers the numerous associative paths connecting these trivialities with things that are of the highest psychical importance in the dreamer's estimation. *If what make their way into the content of dreams are impressions and material which are indifferent and trivial rather than justifiably stirring and interesting, that is only the effect of the process of displacement.* If we answer our questions about dream-instigators and the connection between dreaming and daily affairs on the basis of the new insight we have gained from replacing the manifest by the latent content of dreams, we arrive at these conclusions: *dreams are never concerned with things which we should not think it worth while to be concerned with during the day, and trivialities which do not affect us during the day are unable to pursue us in our sleep.*

What was the dream-instigator in the specimen that we have chosen for analysis? It was the definitely insignificant event of my friend giving me *a drive in a cab free of cost.* The situation in the dream at the table d'hôte contained an allusion to this insignificant precipitating cause, for in my conversation I had compared the taximeter cab with a table d'hôte. But I can also point to the important experience which was represented by this trivial one. A few days earlier I had paid out a considerable sum of money on behalf of a member of my family of whom I am fond. No wonder, said the dream-thoughts, if this person were to feel grateful to me: love of that sort would not be 'free of cost'. Love that is free of cost, however, stood in the forefront of the dream-thoughts. The fact that not long before I had had several *cab-drives* with the relative in question, made it possible for the cab-drive with my friend to remind me of my connections with this other person.

The indifferent impression which becomes a dream-instigator owing to associations of this kind is subject to a further condition which does not apply to the true source of the dream: it must always be a *recent* impression, derived from the dream-day.

I cannot leave the subject of dream-displacement without drawing attention to a remarkable process which occurs in the formation of dreams and in which condensation and displacement *combine* to produce the result. In considering condensation we have already seen the way in which two ideas in the dream-thoughts which have something in common, some point of contact, are replaced in the dream-content by a composite idea, in which a relatively distinct nucleus represents what they have in common, while indistinct subordinate details correspond to the respects in which they differ from each other. If displacement takes place in addition to condensation, what is constructed is not a composite idea but an 'intermediate common entity', which stands in a relation to the two different elements similar to that in which the resultant in a parallelogram of forces stands to its components. For instance, in the content of one of my dreams there was a question of an injection with *propyl*. To begin with, the analysis only led me to an indifferent experience which had acted as dream-instigator, and in which a part was played by *amyl*. I was not yet able to justify the confusion between amyl and propyl. In the group of ideas behind this same dream, however, there was also a recollection of my first visit to Munich, where I had been struck by the *Propylaea*.[1] The details of the analysis made it plausible to suppose that it was the influence of this second group of ideas upon the first one that was responsible for the displacement from amyl to propyl. *Propyl* is as it were an intermediate idea between *amyl* and *Propylaea*, and found its way into the content of the dream as a kind of *compromise*, by means of simultaneous condensation and displacement.[2]

---

[1] [A ceremonial portico on the Athenian model.]

[2] [The dream from which this detail is taken was the first one to be exhaustively analysed by Freud. It is reported at length in *The Interpretation of Dreams*. (Cf. *Standard Ed.*, **4**, 106 ff., and, for this particular detail, **4**, 294.)]

There is a still more urgent necessity in the case of the process of displacement than in that of condensation to discover the motive for these puzzling efforts on the part of the dream-work.

It is the process of displacement which is chiefly responsible for our being unable to discover or recognize the dream-thoughts in the dream-content, unless we understand the reason for their distortion. Nevertheless, the dream-thoughts are also submitted to another and milder sort of transformation, which leads to our discovering a new achievement on the part of the dream-work —one, however, which is easily intelligible. The dream-thoughts which we first come across as we proceed with our analysis often strike us by the unusual form in which they are expressed; they are not clothed in the prosaic language usually employed by our thoughts, but are on the contrary represented symbolically by means of similes and metaphors, in images resembling those of poetic speech. There is no difficulty in accounting for the constraint imposed upon the form in which the dream-thoughts are expressed. The manifest content of dreams consists for the most part in pictorial situations; and the dream-thoughts must accordingly be submitted in the first place to a treatment which will make them suitable for a representation of this kind. If we imagine ourselves faced by the problem of representing the arguments in a political leading article or the speeches of counsel before a court of law in a series of pictures, we shall easily understand the modifications which must necessarily be carried out by the dream-work owing to *considerations of representability in the content of the dream.*

The psychical material of the dream-thoughts habitually includes recollections of impressive experiences—not infrequently dating back to early childhood—which are thus themselves perceived as a rule as situations having a visual subject-matter. Wherever the possibility arises, this portion of the dream-thoughts exercises a determining influence upon the form taken by the content of the dream; it constitutes, as it were, a nucleus of crystallization, attracting the material of the dream-thoughts to itself and thus affecting their distribution. The situation in a dream is often nothing other than a modified repetition, complicated by interpolations, of an impressive experience of this kind; on the other hand, faithful and straightforward reproductions of real scenes only rarely appear in dreams.

The content of dreams, however, does not consist entirely of situations, but also includes disconnected fragments of visual images, speeches and even bits of unmodified thoughts. It may therefore perhaps be of interest to enumerate very briefly the modes of representation available to the dream-work for reproducing the dream-thoughts in the peculiar form of expression necessary in dreams.

The dream-thoughts which we arrive at by means of analysis reveal themselves as a psychical complex of the most intricate possible structure. Its portions stand in the most manifold logical relations to one another: they represent foreground and background, conditions, digressions and illustrations, chains of evidence and counter-arguments. Each train of thought is almost invariably accompanied by its contradictory counterpart. This material lacks none of the characteristics that are familiar to us from our waking thinking. If now all of this is to be turned into a dream, the psychical material will be submitted to a pressure which will condense it greatly, to an internal fragmentation and displacement which will, as it were, create new surfaces, and to a selective operation in favour of those portions of it which are the most appropriate for the construction of situations. If we take into account the genesis of the material, a process of this sort deserves to be described as a 'regression'. In the course of this transformation, however, the logical links which have hitherto held the psychical material together are lost. It is only, as it were, the substantive content of the dream-thoughts that the dream-work takes over and manipulates. The restoration of the connections which the dream-work has destroyed is a task which has to be performed by the work of analysis.

The modes of expression open to a dream may therefore be qualified as meagre by comparison with those of our intellectual speech; nevertheless a dream need not wholly abandon the possibility of reproducing the logical relations present in the dream-thoughts. On the contrary, it succeeds often enough in replacing them by formal characteristics in its own texture.

In the first place, dreams take into account the connection which undeniably exists between all the portions of the dream-thoughts by combining the whole material into a single situation. They reproduce *logical connection* by *approximation in time and space*, just as a painter will represent all the poets in a single group in a picture of Parnassus. It is true that they were never in fact assembled on a single mountain-top; but they certainly form a conceptual group. Dreams carry this method of reproduction down to details; and often when they show us two elements in the dream-content close together, this indicates that there is some specially intimate connection between what correspond to them among the dream-thoughts. Incidentally, it is to be observed that all dreams produced during a single night will be found on analysis to be derived from the same circle of thoughts.

A *causal relation* between two thoughts is either left unrepresented or is replaced by a *sequence* of two pieces of dream of different lengths. Here the representation is often reversed, the beginning of the dream standing for the consequence and its conclusion for the premise. An immediate *transformation* of one thing into another in a dream seems to represent the relation of *cause and effect*.

The alternative '*either—or*' is never expressed in dreams, both of the alternatives being inserted in the text of the dream as though they were equally valid. I have already mentioned that an 'either—or' used in *recording* a dream is to be translated by 'and'. [See p. 650.]

Ideas which are contraries are by preference expressed in dreams by one and the same element.[1] 'No' seems not to exist so far as dreams are concerned. Opposition between two thoughts, the relation of *reversal*, may be represented in dreams in a most remarkable way. It may be represented by some *other* piece of the dream-content being turned into its opposite—as it were by an afterthought. We shall hear presently of a further method of expressing contradiction. The sensation of *inhibition of movement* which is so common in dreams also serves to express a contradiction between two impulses, a *conflict of will*.

One and one only of these logical relations—that of *similarity, consonance, the possession of common attributes*—is very highly

---

[1] [*Footnote added* 1911:] It deserves to be remarked that well-known philologists have asserted that the most ancient human languages tended in general to express contradictory opposites by the same word. (E.g. 'strong-weak', 'inside-outside'. This has been described as 'the antithetical meaning of primal words'.) [Cf. Freud, 1910*e*.]

favoured by the mechanism of dream-formation. The dream-work makes use of such cases as a foundation for dream-condensation, by bringing together everything that shows an agreement of this kind into a new unity.

This short series of rough comments is of course inadequate to deal with the full extent of the formal means employed by dreams for the expression of logical relations in the dream-thoughts. Different dreams are more or less carefully constructed in this respect; they keep more or less closely to the text presented to them; they make more or less use of the expedients that are open to the dream-work. In the second case they appear obscure, confused and disconnected. If, however, a dream strikes one as *obviously* absurd, if its content includes a piece of palpable nonsense, this is intentionally so; its apparent disregard of all the requirements of logic is expressing a piece of the intellectual content of the dream-thoughts. Absurdity in a dream signifies the presence in the dream-thoughts of *contradiction, ridicule and derision*. Since this statement is in the most marked opposition to the view that dreams are the product of a dissociated and uncritical mental activity, I will emphasize it by means of an example.

One of my acquaintances, Herr M., had been attacked in an essay with an unjustifiable degree of violence, as we all thought—by no less a person than Goethe. Herr M. was naturally crushed by the attack. He complained of it bitterly to some company at table; his veneration for Goethe had not been affected, however, by this personal experience. I now tried to throw a little light on the chronological data, which seemed to me improbable. Goethe died in 1832. Since his attack on Herr M. must naturally have been made earlier than that, Herr M. must have been quite a young man at the time. It seemed to be a plausible notion that he was eighteen. I was not quite sure, however, what year we were actually in, so that my whole calculation melted into obscurity. Incidentally, the attack was contained in Goethe's well-known essay on 'Nature'.

The nonsensical character of this dream will be even more glaringly obvious, if I explain that Herr M. is a youngish business man, who is far removed from any poetical and literary interests. I have no doubt, however, that when I have entered into the analysis of the dream I shall succeed in showing how much 'method' there is in its nonsense.

The material of the dream was derived from three sources:

(1) Herr M., whom I had got to know among some *company*

at table, asked me one day to examine his elder brother, who was showing signs of [general paralysis]. In the course of my conversation with the patient an awkward episode occurred, for he gave his brother away for no accountable reason by talking of his *youthful follies*. I had asked the patient the *year of his birth* (cf. the *year of* Goethe's *death* in the dream) and had made him carry out a number of calculations in order to test the weakness of his memory.

(2) A medical journal, which bore my name among others on its title-page, had published a positively '*crushing*' criticism by a *youthful* reviewer of a book by my friend F. in Berlin. I took the editor to task over this; but, though he expressed his regret, he would not undertake to offer any redress. I therefore severed my connection with the journal, but in my letter of resignation expressed a hope that *our personal relations would not be affected by the event.* This was the true source of the dream. The unfavourable reception of my friend's work had made a profound impression on me. It contained, in my opinion, a fundamental biological discovery, which is only now—many years later—beginning to find favour with the experts.

(3) A woman patient of mine had given me an account a short time before of her brother's illness, and how he had broken out in a frenzy with cries of '*Nature! Nature!*' The doctors believed that his exclamation came from his having read *Goethe's* striking essay on that subject and that it showed he had been overworking at his studies. I had remarked that *it seemed to me more plausible* that his exclamation of the word 'Nature' should be taken in the sexual sense in which it is used by the less educated people here. This idea of mine was at least not disproved by the fact that the unfortunate young man subsequently mutilated his own genitals. He was *eighteen* at the time of his outbreak.

Behind my own ego in the dream-content there lay concealed, in the first instance, my friend who had been so badly treated by the critic. '*I tried to throw a little light on the chronological data.*' My friend's book dealt with the *chronological data* of life and among other things showed that the length of *Goethe's* life was a multiple of a number of days that has a significance in biology. But this ego was compared with a paralytic: '*I was not quite sure what year we were in.*' Thus the dream made out that my friend was behaving like a paralytic, and in this respect it was a mass

of absurdities. The dream-thoughts, however, were saying
ironically: 'Naturally, it's *he* [my friend F.] who is the crazy
fool and it's *you* [the critics] who are the men of genius and
know better. Surely it couldn't be the *reverse?*' There were
plenty of examples of this *reversal* in the dream. For instance,
Goethe attacked the young man, which is absurd, whereas it is
still easy for quite a young man to attack the great Goethe.

I should like to lay it down that no dream is prompted by
motives other than egoistic ones.[1] In fact, the ego in the present
dream does not stand only for my friend but for myself as well.
I was identifying myself with him, because the fate of his discovery seemed to foreshadow the reception of my own findings.
If I were to bring forward my theory emphasizing the part
played by sexuality in the aetiology of psychoneurotic disorders
(cf. the allusion to the eighteen-year-old patient's cry of
'Nature! Nature!'), I should come across the same criticisms;
and I was already preparing to meet them with the same
derision.

If we pursue the dream-thoughts further, we shall keep on
finding ridicule and derision as correlates of the absurdities of
the manifest dream. It is well known that it was the discovery
of the split skull of a sheep on the Lido of Venice that gave
Goethe the idea of the so-called 'vertebral' theory of the skull.
My friend boasts that, when he was a student, he released a
storm which led to the resignation of an old Professor who,
though he had once been distinguished (among other things in
connection precisely with the same branch of comparative
anatomy), had become incapable of teaching owing to *senile
dementia.* Thus the agitation which my friend promoted served
to combat the mischievous system according to which there is
no *age limit* for academic workers in German universities—for
age is proverbially no defence against folly.—In the hospital here I
had the honour of serving for years under a chief who had long
been a *fossil* and had for decades been notoriously *feeble-minded,*
but who was allowed to continue carrying on his responsible
duties. At this point I thought of a descriptive term based upon
the discovery on the Lido.[2] Some of my young contemporaries

---

[1] [Freud has, however, qualified this statement in an additional footnote written in 1925, which will be found near the end of Chapter V of
The Interpretation of Dreams (Standard Ed., **4,** 270).]

[2] ['*Schafkopf*', literally 'sheep's head', = 'silly ass'.]

at the hospital concocted, in connection with this man, a version of what was then a popular song: '*Das hat kein Goethe g'schrieben, das hat kein Schiller g'dicht . . .*'[1]

[1] ['This was written by no Goethe, this was composed by no Schiller.' —This dream is also discussed at length in *The Interpretation of Dreams* (*Standard Ed.*, 5, 439, etc.).]

VII

We have not yet come to the end of our consideration of the dream-work. In addition to condensation, displacement and pictorial arrangement of the psychical material, we are obliged to assign it yet another activity, though this is not to be found in operation in *every* dream. I shall not deal exhaustively with this part of the dream-work, and will therefore merely remark that the easiest way of forming an idea of its nature is to suppose —though the supposition probably does not meet the facts— that *it only comes into operation* AFTER *the dream-content has already been constructed*. Its function would then consist in arranging the constituents of the dream in such a way that they form an approximately connected whole, a dream-composition. In this way the dream is given a kind of façade (though this does not, it is true, hide its content at every point), and thus receives a first, preliminary interpretation, which is supported by interpolations and slight modifications. Incidentally, this revision of the dream-content is only possible if it is not too punctiliously carried out; nor does it present us with anything more than a glaring misunderstanding of the dream-thoughts. Before we start upon the analysis of a dream we have to clear the ground of this attempt at an interpretation.

The motive for this part of the dream-work is particularly obvious. *Considerations of intelligibility* are what lead to this final revision of a dream; and this reveals the origin of the activity. It behaves towards the dream-content lying before it just as our normal psychical activity behaves in general towards any perceptual content that may be presented to it. It understands that content on the basis of certain anticipatory ideas, and arranges it, even at the moment of perceiving it, on the presupposition of its being intelligible; in so doing it runs a risk of falsifying it, and in fact, if it cannot bring it into line with anything familiar, is a prey to the strangest misunderstandings. As is well known, we are incapable of seeing a series of unfamiliar signs or of hearing a succession of unknown words, without at once falsifying the perception from considerations of intelligibility, on the basis of something already known to us.

Dreams which have undergone a revision of this kind at the

hands of a psychical activity completely analogous to waking thought may be described as 'well-constructed'. In the case of other dreams this activity has completely broken down; no attempt even has been made to arrange or interpret the material, and, since after we have woken up we feel ourselves identical with this last part of the dream-work, we make a judgement that the dream was 'hopelessly confused'. From the point of view of analysis, however, a dream that resembles a disordered heap of disconnected fragments is just as valuable as one that has been beautifully polished and provided with a surface. In the former case, indeed, we are saved the trouble of demolishing what has been superimposed upon the dream-content.

It would be a mistake, however, to suppose[1] that these dream-façades are nothing other than mistaken and somewhat arbitrary revisions of the dream-content by the conscious agency of our mental life. In the erection of a dream-façade use is not infrequently made of wishful phantasies which are present in the dream-thoughts in a pre-constructed form, and are of the same character as the appropriately named 'day-dreams' familiar to us in waking life. The wishful phantasies revealed by analysis in night-dreams often turn out to be repetitions or modified versions of scenes from infancy; thus in some cases the façade of the dream directly reveals the dream's actual nucleus, distorted by an admixture of other material.

The dream-work exhibits no activities other than the four that have already been mentioned. If we keep to the definition of 'dream-work' as the process of transforming the dream-thoughts into the dream-content, it follows that the dream-work is not creative, that it develops no phantasies of its own, that it makes no judgements and draws no conclusions; it has no functions whatever other than condensation and displacement of the material and its modification into pictorial form, to which must be added as a variable factor the final bit of interpretative revision. It is true that we find various things in the dream-content which we should be inclined to regard as a product of some other and higher intellectual function; but in every case analysis shows convincingly that *these intellectual operations have already been performed in the dream-thoughts and have only been* TAKEN OVER *by the dream-content.* A conclusion

[1] [This paragraph was added in 1911.]

drawn in a dream is nothing other than the repetition of a conclusion in the dream-thoughts; if the conclusion is taken over into the dream unmodified, it will appear impeccable; if the dream-work has displaced it on to some other material, it will appear nonsensical. A calculation in the dream-content signifies nothing more than that there is a calculation in the dream-thoughts; but while the latter is always rational, a dream-calculation may produce the wildest results if its factors are condensed or if its mathematical operations are displaced on to other material. Not even the speeches that occur in the dream-content are original compositions; they turn out to be a hotchpotch of speeches made, heard or read, which have been revived in the dream-thoughts and whose wording is exactly reproduced, while their origin is entirely disregarded and their meaning is violently changed.

It will perhaps be as well to support these last assertions by a few examples.

(I) Here is an innocent-sounding, well-constructed dream dreamt by a woman patient:

She dreamt she was going to the market with her cook, who was carrying the basket. After she had asked for something, the butcher said to her: 'That's not obtainable any longer,' and offered her something else, adding: 'This is good too.' She rejected it and went on to the woman who sells vegetables, who tried to get her to buy a peculiar vegetable that was tied up in bundles but was of a black colour. She said: 'I don't recognize that: I won't take it.'

The remark '*That's not obtainable any longer*' originated from the treatment itself. A few days earlier I had explained to the patient in those very words that the earliest memories of childhood were '*not obtainable any longer* as such', but were replaced in analysis by 'transferences' and dreams. So *I* was the butcher.

The second speech—'*I don't recognize that*'—occurred in an entirely different connection. On the previous day she had reproved her cook, who incidentally also appeared in the dream, with the words: '*Behave yourself properly! I don't recognize that!*' meaning, no doubt, that she did not understand such behaviour and would not put up with it. As the result of a displacement, it was the more innocent part of this speech which made its way into the content of the dream; but in the dream-thoughts it was only the other part of the speech that played a part. For the dream-work had reduced to complete unintelligibility and extreme innocence an imaginary situation in which *I* was *behaving improperly* to the lady in a particular way. But this situation which the patient was expecting in her imagination was itself only a new edition of something she had once actually experienced.[1]

(II) Here is an apparently quite meaningless dream containing figures. *She was going to pay for something. Her daughter took 3 florins and 65 kreuzers from her (the mother's) purse. The dreamer said to her: 'What are you doing? It only costs 21 kreuzers.'*

The dreamer came from abroad and her daughter was at school here. She was in a position to carry on her treatment with me as long as her daughter remained in Vienna. The day before the dream the head-mistress had suggested to her that she should leave her daughter at school for another year. In that case she could also have continued her treatment for a year. The figures in the dream become significant if we remember that 'time is money'. One year is equal to 365 days, or, expressed in money, 365 kreuzers or 3 florins 65 kreuzers. The 21 kreuzers corresponded to the 3 weeks which had still to run between the dream-day and the end of the school term and also to the end of the patient's treatment. It was clearly financial considerations which had induced the lady to refuse the head-mistress's proposal, and which were responsible for the smallness of the sums mentioned in the dream.[2]

(III) A lady who, though she was still young, had been married for a number of years, received news that an acquaintance of hers, Fräulein Elise L., who was almost exactly her contemporary, had become engaged. This was the precipitating cause of the following dream:

She was at the theatre with her husband. One side of the stalls was completely empty. Her husband told her that Elise L. and her fiancé had wanted to go too, but had only been able to get bad seats—three for 1 florin 50 kreuzers—and of course they could not take those. She thought it would not really have done any harm if they had.

What interests us here is the source of the figures in the material of the dream-thoughts and the transformations which

[1] [This dream is reported in greater detail in *The Interpretation of Dreams (Standard Ed.*, 4, 183).]

[2] [For this dream see *The Interpretation of Dreams (Standard Ed.*, 5, 414).—An Austrian florin was worth approximately 1s. 10d. or 40 cents at the end of the nineteenth century.]

they underwent. What was the origin of the 1 florin 50 kreuzers? It came from what was in fact an indifferent event of the previous day. Her sister-in-law had been given a present of 150 florins by her husband and had *been in a hurry* to get rid of them by buying a piece of jewellery. It is to be noticed that 150 florins is a *hundred* times as much as 1 florin 50 kreuzers. The only connection with the 'three', which was the number of the theatre tickets, was that her newly engaged friend was that number of months—three—her junior. The situation in the dream was a repetition of a small incident which her husband often teased her about. On one occasion she had been in a great hurry to buy tickets for a play in advance, and when she got to the theatre she had found that one side of the stalls was almost completely empty. There had been *no need for her to be in such a hurry*. Finally, we must not overlook the *absurdity* in the dream of two people taking three tickets for a play.

Now for the dream-thoughts: 'It was *absurd* to marry so early. There was *no need for me to be in such a hurry*. I see from Elise L.'s example that I should have got a husband in the end. Indeed, I should have got one *a hundred times* better' (a treasure) 'if I had only waited. My money' (or dowry) 'could have bought *three* men just as good.'[1]

---

[1] [This dream, which is mentioned again below, on p. 673, is discussed in *The Interpretation of Dreams* (*Standard Ed.*, 5, 415) and at greater length in Freud's *Introductory Lectures* (1916–17), especially in Lectures VII and XIV.]

VIII

Having been made acquainted with the dream-work by the foregoing discussion, we shall no doubt be inclined to pronounce it a quite peculiar psychical process, the like of which, so far as we are aware, does not exist elsewhere. It is as though we were carrying over on to the dream-work all the astonishment which used formerly to be aroused in us by its product, the dream. In fact, however, the dream-work is only the first to be discovered of a whole series of psychical processes, responsible for the generation of hysterical symptoms, of phobias, obsessions and delusions. Condensation and, above all, displacement are invariable characteristics of these other processes as well. Modification into a pictorial form, on the other hand, remains a peculiarity of the dream-work. If this explanation places dreams in a single series alongside the structures produced by psychical illness, this makes it all the more important for us to discover the essential determining conditions of such processes as those of dream-formation. We shall probably be surprised to hear that neither the state of sleep nor illness is among these indispensable conditions. A whole number of the phenomena of the everyday life of healthy people—such as forgetting, slips of the tongue, bungled actions and a particular class of errors—owe their origin to a psychical mechanism analogous to that of dreams and of the other members of the series.[1]

The heart of the problem lies in displacement, which is by far the most striking of the special achievements of the dream-work. If we enter deeply into the subject, we come to realize that the essential determining condition of displacement is a purely psychological one: something in the nature of a *motive*. One comes upon its track if one takes into consideration certain experiences which one cannot escape in analysing dreams. In analysing my specimen dream I was obliged to break off my report of the dream-thoughts on page 640, because, as I confessed, there were some among them which I should prefer to conceal from strangers and which I could not communicate to other people without doing serious mischief in important directions. I added that nothing would be gained if I were to

[1] [See Freud's *Psychopathology of Everyday Life* (1901*b*).]

choose another dream instead of that particular one with a view to reporting its analysis: I should come upon dream-thoughts which required to be kept secret in the case of *every* dream with an obscure or confused content. If, however, I were to continue the analysis on my own account, without any reference to other people (whom, indeed, an experience so personal as my dream cannot possibly have been intended to reach), I should eventually arrive at thoughts which would surprise me, whose presence in me I was unaware of, which were not only *alien* but also *disagreeable* to me, and which I should therefore feel inclined to dispute energetically, although the chain of thoughts running through the analysis insisted upon them remorselessly. There is only one way of accounting for this state of affairs, which is of quite universal occurrence; and that is to suppose that these thoughts really were present in my mind, and in possession of a certain amount of psychical intensity or energy, but that they were in a peculiar psychological situation, as a consequence of which they *could not become conscious* to me. (I describe this particular condition as one of 'repression'.) We cannot help concluding, then, that there is a causal connection between the obscurity of the dream-content and the state of repression (inadmissibility to consciousness) of certain of the dream-thoughts, and that the dream had to be obscure so as not to betray the proscribed dream-thoughts. Thus we are led to the concept of a 'dream-distortion', which is the product of the dream-work and serves the purpose of dissimulation, that is, of disguise.

I will test this on the specimen dream which I chose for analysis, and enquire what the thought was which made its way into that dream in a distorted form, and which I should be inclined to repudiate if it were undistorted. I recall that my free cab-drive reminded me of my recent expensive drive with a member of my family, that the interpretation of the dream was 'I wish I might for once experience love that cost me nothing', and that a short time before the dream I had been obliged to spend a considerable sum of money on this same person's account. Bearing this context in mind, I cannot escape the conclusion that *I regret having made that expenditure*. Not until I have recognized this impulse does my wish in the dream for the love which would call for *no* expenditure acquire a meaning. Yet I can honestly say that when I decided to spend this sum of money I did not hesitate for a moment. My regret at having to do so—the contrary current of feeling—did not become conscious to me. *Why* it did not, is another and a far-reaching question, the answer to which is known to me but belongs in another connection.

If the dream that I analyse is not my own, but someone else's, the conclusion will be the same, though the grounds for believing it will be different. If the dreamer is a healthy person, there is no other means open to me of obliging him to recognize the repressed ideas that have been discovered than by pointing out the context of the dream-thoughts; and I cannot help it if he refuses to recognize them. If, however, I am dealing with a neurotic patient, with a hysteric for instance, he will find the acceptance of the repressed thought forced upon him, owing to its connection with the symptoms of his illness, and owing to the improvement he experiences when he exchanges those symptoms for the repressed ideas. In the case, for instance, of the woman patient who had the dream I have just quoted about the three theatre tickets which cost 1 florin 50 kreuzers, the analysis led to the inevitable conclusion that she had a low estimate of her husband (cf. her idea that she could have got one 'a hundred times better'), that she regretted having married him, and that she would have liked to exchange him for another one. It is true that she asserted that she loved her husband, and that her emotional life knew nothing of any such low estimate of him, but all her symptoms led to the same conclusion as the dream. And after her repressed memories had been revived of a particular period during which she had consciously not loved her husband, her symptoms cleared up and her resistance against the interpretation of the dream disappeared.

IX

Now that we have established the concept of repression and have brought dream-distortion into relation with repressed psychical material, we can express in general terms the principal finding to which we have been led by the analysis of dreams. In the case of dreams which are intelligible and have a meaning, we have found that they are undisguised wish-fulfilments; that is, that in their case the dream-situation represents as fulfilled a wish which is known to consciousness, which is left over from daytime life, and which is deservedly of interest. Analysis has taught us something entirely analogous in the case of obscure and confused dreams: once again the dream-situation represents a wish as fulfilled—a wish which invariably arises from the dream-thoughts, but one which is represented in an unrecognizable form and can only be explained when it has been traced back in analysis. The wish in such cases is either itself a repressed one and alien to consciousness, or it is intimately connected with repressed thoughts and is based upon them. Thus the formula for such dreams is as follows: *they are disguised fulfilments of repressed wishes*. It is interesting in this connection to observe that the popular belief that dreams always foretell the future is confirmed. Actually the future which the dream shows us is not the one which *will* occur but the one which we should *like* to occur. The popular mind is behaving here as it usually does: what it wishes, it believes.

Dreams fall into three classes according to their attitude to wish-fulfilment. The first class consists of those which represent an unrepressed wish undisguisedly; these are the dreams of an infantile type which become ever rarer in adults. Secondly there are the dreams which express a repressed wish disguisedly; these no doubt form the overwhelming majority of all our dreams, and require analysis before they can be understood. In the third place there are the dreams which represent a repressed wish, but do so with insufficient or no disguise. These last dreams are invariably accompanied by anxiety, which interrupts them. In their case anxiety takes the place of dream-distortion; and in dreams of the second class anxiety is only avoided owing to the dream-work. There is no great difficulty in proving that the ideational content which produces anxiety in us in dreams was once a wish but has since undergone repression.

There are also clear dreams with a distressing content, which, however, is not felt as distressing in the dream itself. For this reason they cannot be counted as anxiety-dreams; but they have always been taken as evidence of the fact that dreams are without meaning and have no psychical value. An analysis of a dream of this kind will show that we are dealing with well-disguised fulfilments of repressed wishes, that is to say with a dream of the second class; it will also show how admirably the process of displacement is adapted for disguising wishes.

A girl had a dream of seeing her sister's only surviving child lying dead in the same surroundings in which a few years earlier she had in fact seen the dead body of her sister's *first* child. She felt no pain over this; but she naturally rejected the idea that this situation represented any wish of hers. Nor was there any need to suppose this. It had been beside the first child's coffin, however, that, years before, she had seen and spoken to the man she was in love with; if the second child died, she would no doubt meet the man again in her sister's house. She longed for such a meeting, but fought against the feeling. On the dream-day she had bought a ticket for a lecture which was to be given by this same man, to whom she was still devoted. Her dream was a simple dream of impatience of the kind that often occurs before journeys, visits to the theatre, and similar enjoyments that lie ahead. But in order to disguise this longing from her, the situation was displaced on to an event of a kind most unsuitable for producing a feeling of enjoyment, though it had in fact done so in the past. It is to be observed that the emotional behaviour in the dream was appropriate to the real content which lay in the background and not to what was pushed into the foreground. The dream-situation anticipated the meeting she had so long desired; it offered no basis for any painful feelings.[1]

---

[1] [This dream is reported in greater detail in *The Interpretation of Dreams* (*Standard Ed.*, 4, 152 ff.).]

X

Hitherto philosophers have had no occasion to concern themselves with a psychology of repression. We may therefore be permitted to make a first approach to this hitherto unknown topic by constructing a pictorial image of the course of events in dream-formation. It is true that the schematic picture we have arrived at—not only from the study of dreams—is a fairly complicated one; but we cannot manage with anything simpler. Our hypothesis is that in our mental apparatus there are two thought-constructing agencies, of which the second enjoys the privilege of having free access to consciousness for its products, whereas the activity of the first is in itself unconscious and can only reach consciousness by way of the second. On the frontier between the two agencies, where the first passes over to the second, there is a censorship, which only allows what is agreeable to it to pass through and holds back everything else. According to our definition, then, what is rejected by the censorship is in a state of repression. Under certain conditions, of which the state of sleep is one, the relation between the strength of the two agencies is modified in such a way that what is repressed can no longer be held back. In the state of sleep this probably occurs owing to a relaxation of the censorship; when this happens it becomes possible for what has hitherto been repressed to make a path for itself to consciousness. Since, however, the censorship is never completely eliminated but merely reduced, the repressed material must submit to certain alterations which mitigate its offensive features. What becomes conscious in such cases is a compromise between the intentions of one agency and the demands of the other. *Repression—relaxation of the censorship—the formation of a compromise*, this is the fundamental pattern for the generation not only of dreams but of many other psychopathological structures; and in the latter cases too we may observe that the formation of compromises is accompanied by processes of condensation and displacement and by the employment of superficial associations, which we have become familiar with in the dream-work.

We have no reason to disguise the fact that in the hypothesis which we have set up in order to explain the dream-work a part is played by what might be described as a 'daemonic' element. We have gathered an impression that the formation of obscure dreams occurs *as though* one person who was dependent upon a second person had to make a remark which was bound to be disagreeable in the ears of this second one; and it is on the basis of this simile that we have arrived at the concepts of dream-distortion and censorship, and have endeavoured to translate our impression into a psychological theory which is no doubt crude but is at least lucid. Whatever it may be with which a further investigation of the subject may enable us to identify our first and second agencies, we may safely expect to find a confirmation of some correlate of our hypothesis that the second agency controls access to consciousness and can bar the first agency from such access.

When the state of sleep is over, the censorship quickly recovers its full strength; and it can now wipe out all that was won from it during the period of its weakness. This must be one part at least of the explanation of the forgetting of dreams, as is shown by an observation which has been confirmed on countless occasions. It not infrequently happens that during the narration of a dream or during its analysis a fragment of the dream-content which had seemed to be forgotten re-emerges. This fragment which has been rescued from oblivion invariably affords us the best and most direct access to the meaning of the dream. And that, in all probability, must have been the only reason for its having been forgotten, that is, for its having been once more suppressed.

XI

When once we have recognized that the content of a dream is the representation of a fulfilled wish and that its obscurity is due to alterations in repressed material made by the censorship, we shall no longer have any difficulty in discovering the *function* of dreams. It is commonly said that sleep is disturbed by dreams; strangely enough, we are led to a contrary view and must regard dreams as *the guardians of sleep*.

In the case of children's dreams there should be no difficulty in accepting this statement. The state of sleep or the psychical modification involved in sleep, whatever that may be, is brought about by a resolve to sleep which is either imposed upon the child or is reached on the basis of sensations of fatigue; and it is only made possible by the withholding of stimuli which might suggest to the psychical apparatus aims other than that of sleeping. The means by which *external* stimuli can be kept off are familiar to us; but what are the means available for controlling *internal* mental stimuli which set themselves against falling asleep? Let us observe a mother putting her child to sleep. The child gives vent to an unceasing stream of desires: he wants one more kiss, he wants to go on playing. His mother satisfies some of these desires, but uses her authority to postpone others of them to the next day. It is clear that any wishes or needs that may arise have an inhibiting effect upon falling asleep. We all know the amusing story told by Balduin Groller [a popular nineteenth-century Austrian novelist] of the bad little boy who woke up in the middle of the night and shouted across the night-nursery: 'I want the rhino!' A better behaved child, instead of shouting, would have *dreamt* that he was playing with the rhino. Since a dream that shows a wish as fulfilled is *believed* during sleep, it does away with the wish and makes sleep possible. It cannot be disputed that dream-images are believed in in this way, for they are clothed in the psychical appearance of perceptions, and children have not yet acquired the later faculty of distinguishing hallucinations or phantasies from reality.

Adults have learnt to make this distinction; they have also grasped the uselessness of wishing, and after lengthy practice know how to postpone their desires until they can find satisfaction by the long and roundabout path of altering the external world. In their case, accordingly, wish-fulfilments along the short psychical path are rare in sleep too; it is even possible, indeed, that they never occur at all, and that anything that may seem to us to be constructed on the pattern of a child's dream in fact requires a far more complicated solution. On the other hand, in the case of adults—and this no doubt applies without exception to everyone in full possession of his senses—a differentiation has occurred in the psychical material, which was not present in children. A psychical agency has come into being, which, taught by experience of life, exercises a dominating and inhibiting influence upon mental impulses and maintains that influence with jealous severity, and which, owing to its relation to consciousness and to voluntary movement, is armed with the strongest instruments of psychical power. A portion of the impulses of childhood has been suppressed by this agency as being useless to life, and any thought-material derived from those impulses is in a state of repression.

Now while this agency, in which we recognize our normal ego, is concentrated on the wish to sleep, it appears to be compelled by the psycho-physiological conditions of sleep to relax the energy with which it is accustomed to hold down the repressed material during the day. In itself, no doubt, this relaxation does no harm; however much the suppressed impulses of the childish mind may prance around, their access to consciousness is still difficult and their access to movement is barred, as the result of this same state of sleep. The danger of sleep being disturbed by them must, however, be guarded against. We must in any case suppose that even during deep sleep a certain amount of free attention is on duty as a guard against sensory stimuli, and that this guard may sometimes consider waking more advisable than a continuation of sleep. Otherwise there would be no explanation of how it is that we can be woken up at any moment by sensory stimuli of some particular *quality*. As the physiologist Burdach [1838, 486] insisted long ago, a mother, for instance, will be roused by the whimpering of her baby, or a miller if his mill comes to a stop, or most people if they are called softly by their own name. Now the attention which is thus on guard is also directed towards internal wishful stimuli arising from the repressed material, and combines with them to form the dream which, as a compromise, simultaneously satisfies both of the two agencies. The dream provides a kind of psychical consummation for the wish that has been suppressed (or formed with the help of repressed material) by representing it as fulfilled; but it also satisfies the other agency by allowing sleep to continue. In this respect our ego is ready to behave like a child; it gives credence to the dream-images, as though what it wanted to say was: 'Yes, yes! you're quite right, but let me go on sleeping!' The low estimate which we form of dreams when we are awake, and which we relate to their confused and apparently illogical character, is probably nothing other than the judgement passed by our sleeping ego upon the repressed impulses, a judgement based, with better right, upon the motor impotence of these disturbers of sleep. We are sometimes aware in our sleep of this contemptuous judgement. If the content of a dream goes too far in overstepping the censorship, we think: 'After all, it's only a dream!'—and go on sleeping.

This view is not traversed by the fact that there are marginal cases in which the dream—as happens with anxiety-dreams—can no longer perform its function of preventing an interruption of sleep, but assumes instead the other function of promptly bringing sleep to an end. In doing so it is merely behaving like a conscientious night-watchman, who first carries out his duty by suppressing disturbances so that the townsmen may not be woken up, but afterwards continues to do his duty by himself waking the townsmen up, if the causes of the disturbance seem to him serious and of a kind that he cannot cope with alone.

The function of the dream as a guardian of sleep becomes particularly evident when an external stimulus impinges upon the senses of a sleeper. It is generally recognized that sensory stimuli arising during sleep influence the content of dreams; this can be proved experimentally and is among the few certain (but, incidentally, greatly overvalued) findings of medical investigation into dreams. But this finding involves a puzzle which has hitherto proved insoluble. For the sensory stimulus which the experimenter causes to impinge upon the sleeper is not correctly recognized in the dream; it is subjected to one of an indefinite number of possible interpretations, the choice being apparently left to an arbitrary psychical determination. But there is, of course, no such thing as arbitrary determination in the mind. There are several ways in which a sleeper may react to an external sensory stimulus. He may wake up or he may succeed in continuing his sleep in spite of it. In the latter case he may make use of a dream in order to get rid of the external stimulus, and here again there is more than one method open to him. For instance, he may get rid of the stimulus by dreaming that he is in a situation which is absolutely incompatible with the stimulus. Such was the line taken by a sleeper who was subject to disturbance by a painful abscess on the perineum. He dreamt that he was riding on a horse, making use of the poultice that was intended to mitigate his pain as a saddle, and in this way he avoided being disturbed.[1] Or, as happens more frequently, the external stimulus is given an interpretation which brings it into the context of a repressed wish which is at the moment awaiting fulfilment; in this way the external stimulus is robbed of its reality and is treated as though it were a portion of the psychical material. Thus someone dreamt that he had written a comedy with a particular plot; it was produced in a theatre, the first act was over, and there were thunders of applause; the clapping was terrific. . . . The dreamer must have succeeded in prolonging his sleep till after the interference had ceased; for when he woke up he no longer heard the noise, but rightly concluded that someone must have been beating a carpet or mattress. Every dream which occurs immediately before the sleeper is woken by a loud noise has made an attempt at explaining away the arousing stimulus by providing another explanation of it and has thus sought to prolong sleep, even if only for a moment.

[1] [This dream is reported in full in *The Interpretation of Dreams* (1900a) *Standard Ed.*, 4, 229).]

XII [1]

No one who accepts the view that the censorship is the chief reason for dream-distortion will be surprised to learn from the results of dream-interpretation that most of the dreams of adults are traced back by analysis to *erotic wishes*. This assertion is not aimed at dreams with an *undisguised* sexual content, which are no doubt familiar to all dreamers from their own experience and are as a rule the only ones to be described as 'sexual dreams'. Even dreams of this latter kind offer enough surprises in their choice of the people whom they make into sexual objects, in their disregard of all the limitations which the dreamer imposes in his waking life upon his sexual desires, and by their many strange details, hinting at what are commonly known as 'perversions'. A great many other dreams, however, which show no sign of being erotic in their manifest content, are revealed by the work of interpretation in analysis as sexual wish-fulfilments; and, on the other hand, analysis proves that a great many of the thoughts left over from the activity of waking life as 'residues of the previous day' only find their way to representation in dreams through the assistance of repressed erotic wishes.

There is no theoretical necessity why this should be so; but to explain the fact it may be pointed out that no other group of instincts has been submitted to such far-reaching suppression by the demands of cultural education, while at the same time the sexual instincts are also the ones which, in most people, find it easiest to escape from the control of the highest mental agencies. Since we have become acquainted with infantile sexuality, which is often so unobtrusive in its manifestations and is always overlooked and misunderstood, we are justified in saying that almost every civilized man retains the infantile forms of sexual life in some respect or other. We can thus understand how it is that repressed infantile sexual wishes provide the most frequent and strongest motive-forces for the construction of dreams.[2]

There is only one method by which a dream which expresses erotic wishes can succeed in appearing innocently non-sexual in

[1] [The whole of this section was added in 1911.]
[2] See my *Three Essays on the Theory of Sexuality* (1905*d*).

its manifest content. The material of the sexual ideas must not be represented as such, but must be replaced in the content of the dream by hints, allusions and similar forms of indirect representation. But, unlike other forms of indirect representation, that which is employed in dreams must not be immediately intelligible. The modes of representation which fulfil these conditions are usually described as 'symbols' of the things which they represent. Particular interest has been directed to them since it has been noticed that dreamers speaking the same language make use of the same symbols, and that in some cases, indeed, the use of the same symbols extends beyond the use of the same language. Since dreamers themselves are unaware of the meaning of the symbols they use, it is difficult at first sight to discover the source of the connection between the symbols and what they replace and represent. The fact itself, however, is beyond doubt, and it is important for the technique of dream-interpretation. For, with the help of a knowledge of dream-symbolism, it is possible to understand the meaning of separate elements of the content of a dream or separate pieces of a dream or in some cases even whole dreams, without having to ask the dreamer for his associations.[1] Here we are approaching the popular ideal of translating dreams and on the other hand are returning to the technique of interpretation used by the ancients, to whom dream-interpretation was identical with interpretation by means of symbols.

Although the study of dream-symbols is far from being complete, we are in a position to lay down with certainty a number of general statements and a quantity of special information on the subject. There are some symbols which bear a single meaning almost universally: thus the Emperor and Empress (or the King and Queen) stand for the parents, rooms represent women[2] and their entrances and exits the openings of the body. The majority of dream-symbols serve to represent persons, parts of the body and activities invested with erotic interest; in particular, the genitals are represented by a number of often very surprising symbols, and the greatest variety of objects are employed to denote them symbolically. Sharp weapons, long and stiff objects, such as tree-trunks and sticks, stand for the

---

[1] [See, however, the qualification three paragraphs lower down.]

[2] Cf. '*Frauenzimmer*' [literally 'women's apartment,' commonly used in German as a slightly derogatory word for 'woman'].

male genital; while cupboards, boxes, carriages or ovens may represent the uterus. In such cases as these the *tertium comparationis*, the common element in these substitutions, is immediately intelligible; but there are other symbols in which it is not so easy to grasp the connection. Symbols such as a staircase or going upstairs to represent sexual intercourse, a tie or cravat for the male organ, or wood for the female one, provoke our unbelief until we can arrive at an understanding of the symbolic relation underlying them by some other means. Moreover a whole number of dream-symbols are bisexual and can relate to the male or female genitals according to the context.

Some symbols are universally disseminated and can be met with in all dreamers belonging to a single linguistic or cultural group; there are others which occur only within the most restricted and individual limits, symbols constructed by an individual out of his own ideational material. Of the former class we can distinguish some whose claim to represent sexual ideas is immediately justified by linguistic usage (such, for instance, as those derived from agriculture, e.g. 'fertilization' or 'seed') and others whose relation to sexual ideas appears to reach back into the very earliest ages and to the most obscure depths of our conceptual functioning. The power of constructing symbols has not been exhausted in our own days in the case of either of the two sorts of symbols which I have distinguished at the beginning of this paragraph. Newly discovered objects (such as airships) are, as we may observe, at once adopted as universally available sexual symbols.

It would, incidentally, be a mistake to expect that if we had a still profounder knowledge of dream-symbolism (of the 'language of dreams') we could do without asking the dreamer for his associations to the dream and go back entirely to the technique of dream-interpretation of antiquity. Quite apart from individual symbols and oscillations in the use of universal ones, one can never tell whether any particular element in the content of a dream is to be interpreted symbolically or in its proper sense, and one can be certain that the *whole* content of a dream is not to be interpreted symbolically. A knowledge of dream-symbolism will never do more than enable us to translate certain constituents of the dream-content, and will not relieve us of the necessity for applying the technical rules which I gave earlier. It will, however, afford the most valuable assistance to interpretation precisely at points at which the dreamer's associations are insufficient or fail altogether.

Dream-symbolism is also indispensable to an understanding of what are known as 'typical' dreams, which are common to everyone, and of 'recurrent' dreams in individuals.

If the account I have given in this short discussion of the symbolic mode of expression in dreams appears incomplete, I can justify my neglect by drawing attention to one of the most important pieces of knowledge that we possess on this subject. Dream-symbolism extends far beyond dreams: it is not peculiar to dreams, but exercises a similar dominating influence on representation in fairy-tales, myths and legends, in jokes and in folk-lore. It enables us to trace the intimate connections between dreams and these latter productions. We must not suppose that dream-symbolism is a creation of the dream-work; it is in all probability a characteristic of the unconscious thinking which provides the dream-work with the material for condensation, displacement and dramatization.[1]

[1] Further information on dream-symbolism may be found in the works of early writers on dream-interpretation, e.g. Artemidorus of Daldis and Scherner (1861), and also in my own *Interpretation of Dreams* (1900a) [Chapter VI, Section E], in the mythological studies of the psycho-analytic school, as well as in some of W. Stekel's writings (e.g. 1911). [See further Lecture X (on 'Symbolism in Dreams') in Freud's *Introductory Lectures* (1916–17).]

XIII

I lay no claim to having thrown light in these pages upon *all* the problems of dreams, nor to having dealt in a convincing way with those that I *have* discussed. Anyone who is interested in the whole extent of the literature of dreams may be referred to a work by Sante de Sanctis (*I sogni*, 1899); and anyone who wishes to hear more detailed arguments in favour of the view of dreams which I myself have put forward should turn to my volume *The Interpretation of Dreams*, 1900.[1] It only remains for me now to indicate the direction in which my exposition of the subject of the dream-work calls for pursuit.

I have laid it down as the task of dream-interpretation to replace the dream by the latent dream-thoughts, that is, to unravel what the dream-work has woven. In so doing I have raised a number of new psychological problems dealing with the mechanism of this dream-work itself, as well as with the nature and conditions of what is described as repression; on the other hand I have asserted the existence of the dream-thoughts —a copious store of psychical structures of the highest order, which is characterized by all the signs of normal intellectual functioning, but is nevertheless withdrawn from consciousness till it emerges in distorted form in the dream-content. I cannot but assume that thoughts of this kind are present in everyone, since almost everyone, including the most normal people, is capable of dreaming. The unconscious material of the dream-thoughts and its relation to consciousness and to repression raise further questions of significance to psychology, the answers to which must no doubt be postponed until analysis has clarified the origin of other psychopathological structures, such as hysterical symptoms and obsessional ideas.

[1] [Cf. also the eleven lectures on dreams which constitute Part II of Freud's *Introductory Lectures* (1916–17).]

BIBLIOGRAPHIES

[Titles of books and periodicals are in italics; titles of papers are in inverted commas. Abbreviations are in accordance with the *World List of Scientific Periodicals* (London, 1952). Numerals in thick type refer to volumes; ordinary numerals refer to pages. *G.S.* = Freud, *Gesammelte Schriften* (12 vols.), Vienna, 1924–34. *G.W.* = Freud, *Gesammelte Werke* (18 vols.), London, from 1940. *C.P.* = Freud, *Collected Papers* (5 vols.), London, 1924–50. *Standard Ed.* = Freud, *Standard Edition* (24 vols.), London, from 1953. Entries marked with an asterisk have not been verified for the present edition. See Editor's Introduction, p. xxi. For non-technical authors, and for technical authors where no specific work is mentioned, see the *General Index*.]

A

AUTHOR INDEX AND LIST OF WORKS REFERRED TO IN THE TEXT

[The figures in round brackets at the end of each entry indicate the page or pages of this volume on which the work in question is mentioned. In the case of the Freud entries, the letters attached to the dates of publication are in accordance with the corresponding entries in the complete bibliography of Freud's writings to be included in the last volume of the *Standard Edition*.]

ABEL, K. (1884) *Der Gegensinn der Urworte*, Leipzig. (318, *n.* 3)

ABRAHAM, K. (1909) *Traum und Mythus*, Vienna. (351, *n.* 2, 401)

ADLER, A. (1910) 'Der psychische Hermaphroditismus im Leben und in der Neurose', *Fortschr. Med.*, **28**, 486. (396–7)

(1911) 'Beitrag zur Lehre vom Widerstand', *Zbl. Psychoanal.*, **1**, 214. (579 *n.*)

ALLISON, A. (1868) 'Nocturnal Insanity', *Med. Times & Gaz.*, **947**, 210. (89)

ALMOLI, S. See SALOMON ALMOLI.

AMRAM, N. (1901) Sepher pithrôn chalômôth, Jerusalem. (4, *n.* 2)

ARISTOTLE *De somniis* and *De divinatione per somnum*. (2–3, 33, 97, *n.* 2, 320 *n.*, 550)
[*Trans.* by W. S. Hett (in volume 'On the Soul', Loeb Classical Library), London & New York, 1935.]

ARTEMIDORUS OF DALDIS *Oneirocritica*. (3, 4, 98, 99 *n.*, 354 *n.*, 606, *n.* 2, 685 *n.*) [*German trans.*: *Symbolik der Träume* by F. S. Krauss,

Vienna, 1881, and 'Erotische Träume und ihre Symbolik', *Anthropophyteia*, **9**, 316, by Hans Licht. *Engl. trans.* (abridged): *The Interpretation of Dreams*, by R. Wood, London, 1644.]

ARTIGUES, R. (1884) *Essai sur la valeur séméiologique du rêve*, (Thesis) Paris. (34)

BENINI, V. (1898) 'La memoria e la durata dei sogni', *Riv. ital. Filos.*, **13a**, 149. (45, 71)

BERNARD-LEROY and TOBOWOLSKA, J. (1901) 'Mécanisme intellectuel du rêve', *Rev. phil.*, **51**, 570. (502)

BERNFELD, S. (1944) 'Freud's Earliest Theories and the School of Helmholtz', *Psychoanal. Quart.*, **13**, 341. (xvi n., 482 n.)

BERNSTEIN, I., and SEGEL, B. W. (1908) *Jüdische Sprichwörter und Redensarten*, Warsaw. (132, n. 1)

BETLHEIM, S., and HARTMANN, H. (1924) 'Über Fehlreaktionen des Gedächtnisses bei Korsakoffschen Psychose', *Arch. Psychiat. Nervenkr.*, **72**, 278. (384)

BIANCHIERI, F. (1912) 'I sogni dei bambini di cinque anni', *Riv. Psicol.*, **8**, 325. (131 n.)
See also DOGLIA and BIANCHIERI.

BINZ, C. (1878) *Über den Traum*, Bonn. (19, 56, 77, 87, 634)

BLEULER, E. (1910) 'Die Psychoanalyse Freuds', *Jb. psychoanal. psychopath. Forsch.*, **2**, 623. (351, n. 2)

BONATELLI, F. (1880) 'Del sogno', *La filosofia delle scuole italiane*, Feb., 16. (45)

BÖRNER, J. (1855) *Das Alpdrücken, seine Begründung und Verhütung*, Würzburg. (34)

BÖTTINGER (1795) In C. P. J. SPRENGEL: *Beiträge zur Geschichte der Medizin*, **2**. (34 n.)

BOUCHÉ-LECLERCQ, A. (1879–82) *Histoire de la divination dans l'antiquité*, Paris. (34 n.)

BREUER, J., and FREUD, S. (1895) see FREUD, S. (1895d)
(1940 [1892]) see FREUD, S. (1940d)

BÜCHSENSCHÜTZ, B. (1868) *Traum und Traumdeutung im Altertum*, Berlin. (2, n. 1, 97, n. 2, 132, n. 2)

BURDACH, K. F. (1838) *Die Physiologie als Erfahrungswissenschaft*, Vol. 3 of 2nd ed., 1832–40. (1st ed. 1826–32.) (7, 50, 52–3, 78, 83, 223–4, 679)

BUSEMANN, A. (1909) 'Traumleben der Schulkinder', *Z. päd. Psychol.*, **10**, 294. (131 n.)
(1910) 'Psychologie der kindlichen Traumerlebnisse', *Z. päd. Psychol.*, **11**, 320. (131 n.)

CABANIS, P. J. G. (1802) *Rapports du physique et du moral de l'homme*, Paris. (90)

CALKINS, M. W. (1893) 'Statistics of Dreams', *Amer. J. Psychol.*, **5**, 311. (19, 21, 43, 221)

CAREÑA, CAESAR (1641) *Tractatus de Officio Sanctissimae Inquisitionis*, Cremona. (70, *n*. 1)

CHABANEIX, P. (1897) *Physiologie cérébrale: le subconscient chez les artistes, les savants, et les écrivains*, Paris. (44 *n*., 64)

CICERO: *De divinatione*. (9, 55)
[*Trans.* by W. A. Falconer (Loeb Classical Library), London & New York, 1922.]

CLAPARÈDE, E. (1905) 'Esquisse d'une théorie biologique du sommeil', *Arch. psychol.*, **4**, 245. (53 *n*.)

CLERK-MAXWELL, J. (1876) *Matter and Motion*, London. (456, 520)

CORIAT, I. H. (1913) 'Zwei sexual-symbolische Beispiele von Zahnarzt-Träumen', *Zbl. Psychoanal. Psychother.*, **3**, 440. (387, *n*. 1)

DATTNER, B. (1913) 'Gold und Kot', *Int. Z. Psychoanal.*, **1**, 495. (403)

DAVIDSON, WOLF (1799) *Versuch über den Schlaf*, Berlin. 2nd ed. (1st ed., 1795.) (62)

DEBACKER, F. (1881) *Des hallucinations et terreurs nocturnes chez les enfants*, (Thesis) Paris. (135, *n*. 1, 585–7)

DELACROIX, H. (1904) 'Sur la structure logique du rêve', *Rev. Métaphys.*, **12**, 921. (501)

DELAGE, Y. (1891) 'Essai sur la théorie du rêve', *Rev. industr.*, **2**, 40. (18, 80–82, 179 *n*., 591)

DELBŒUF, I. (1885) *Le sommeil et les rêves*, Paris. (11–12, 20–21, 51, 52 *n*., 58, 60, 105, 179 *n*., 184, *n*. 1)

DIEPGEN, P. (1912) *Traum und Traumdeutung als mediz. naturwissenschaftl. Problem im Mittelalter*, Berlin. (4, *n*. 2, 542 *n*.)

DOGLIA, S., and BIANCHIERI, F. (1910–11) 'I sogni dei bambini di tre anni', *Contrib. psicol.*, **1**, 9. (131 *n*.)

DÖLLINGER, J. (1857) *Heidenthum und Judenthum*, Regensburg. (34 *n*.)

DREXL, F. X. (1909) *Achmets Traumbuch: Einleitung und Probe eines kritischen Textes*, (Thesis) Munich. (4, *n*. 2)

DUGAS, L. (1897a) 'Le sommeil et la cérébration inconsciente durant le sommeil', *Rev. phil.*, **43**, 410. (55, 59)
(1897b) 'Le souvenir du rêve', *Rev. phil.*, **44**, 220. (575)

DU PREL, C. (1885) *Die Philosophie der Mystik*, Leipzig. (63, *n*. 2, 131 *n*., 134 *n*., 280, *n*. 1, 528 *n*., 612 *n*.)

EDER, M. D. (1913) 'Augenträume', *Int. Z. Psychoanal.*, **1**, 157. (398 *n*.)

EGGER, V. (1895) 'La durée apparente des rêves', *Rev. phil.*, **40**, 41. (27, 64, 496)
(1898) 'Le souvenir dans le rêve', *Rev. phil.*, **46**, 154. (46)

ELLIS, HAVELOCK (1899) 'The Stuff that Dreams are made of', *Popular Science Monthly*, **54**, 721. (19, 60, 591)

(1911) *The World of Dreams*, London. (65, *n.* 1, 169, 182 *n.*, 353, 373, 402, 501, 542)

ERDMANN, J. E. (1852) *Psychologische Briefe* (Brief VI), Leipzig. (71)

FECHNER, G. T. (1860) *Elemente der Psychophysik*, Leipzig. (48, 55, 536)

FEDERN, P. (1914) 'Über zwei typische Traumsensationen', *Jb. Psychoanal.*, **6**, 89. (394)

FÉRÉ, C. (1886) 'Note sur un cas de paralysie hystérique consécutive à un rêve', *Soc. biolog.*, **41** (Nov. 20). (89)

(1887) 'A Contribution to the Pathology of Dreams and of Hysterical Paralysis', *Brain*, **9**, 488. (88, *n.* 1)

FERENCZI, S. (1910) 'Die Psychoanalyse der Träume', *Psychiat.-neurol. Wschr.*, **12**, Nos. 11–13. (99 *n.*, 132, *n.* 1, 245 *n.*, 325)
[*Trans.:* 'The Psychological Analysis of Dreams', Chap. III of *Contributions to Psychoanalysis*, Boston, 1916.]

(1911) 'Über lenkbare Träume', *Zbl. Psychoanal.*, **2**, 31. (572)

(1912) 'Symbolische Darstellung des Lust- und Realitätsprinzips im Ödipus-Mythos', *Imago*, **1**, 276. (263, *n.* 2)
[*Trans.:* 'The Symbolic Representation of the Pleasure and Reality Principles in the Oedipus Myth', Chap. X, Part I of *Contributions to Psycho-Analysis*, Boston, 1916.]

(1913) 'Zur Augensymbolik', *Int. Z. Psychoanal.*, **1**, 161. (398 *n.*)
[*Trans.:* 'On Eye Symbolism', Chap. X, Pt. II of *Contributions to Psycho-Analysis*, Boston, 1916.]

(1916) 'Affektvertauschung im Traume', *Int. Z. Psychoanal.*, **4**, 112. (472–3)
[*Trans.:* 'Interchange of Affect in Dreams', No. LV in *Further Contributions*, London, 1926.]

(1917) 'Träume der Ahnungslosen', *Int. Z. Psychoanal.*, **4**, 208. (377)
[*Trans.:* 'Dreams of the Unsuspecting', No. LVI of *Further Contributions*, London, 1926.]

FICHTE, I. H. (1864) *Psychologie: die Lehre vom bewussten Geiste des Menschen*, (2 vols.), Leipzig. (7, 63, 71)

FISCHER, K. P. (1850) *Grundzüge des Systems der Anthropologie*, Erlangen. (Pt. I, Vol. 2, in *Grundzüge des Systems der Philosophie*.) (66)

FLIESS, W. (1906) *Der Ablauf des Lebens*, Vienna. (94, 166, *n.* 2)

FÖRSTER, M. (1910) 'Das lateinisch-altenglische pseudo-Danielsche Traumbuch in Tiberius A. III', *Archiv Stud. neueren Sprachen und Literaturen*, **125**, 39. (4, *n.* 2)

(1911) 'Ein mittelenglisches Vers-Traumbuch des 13 Jahrhunderts', *Archiv Stud. neueren Sprachen und Literaturen*, **127**, 31. (4, *n.* 2)

FOUCAULT, M. (1906) *Le rêve: études et observations*, Paris. (502, 512 *n.*)

FREUD, S. (1877a) 'Über den Ursprung der hinteren Nervenwurzeln im Rückenmarke von Ammocoetes (Petromyzon Planeri)', *Sitzungsber. k. Akad. Wiss.*, III Abt., Bd. 75, January. (413)

(1884e) 'Über Coca', *Centralbl. ges. Therap.*, **2**, 289. (170)

FREUD, S. (*cont.*)

[*Trans.*: (abbreviated) 'Coca', *Saint Louis Med. Surg. J.*, 47 (1884), 502.]

(1893c) 'Quelques considérations pour une étude comparative des paralysies motrices organiques et hystériques', *G.S.*, 1, 273; *G.W.*, 1, 37. (563 *n.*)
[*Trans.*: 'Some Points for a Comparative Study of Organic and Hysterical Motor Paralyses', *C.P.*, 1, 42; *Standard Ed.*, 1.]

(1894a) 'Die Abwehr-Neuropsychosen', *G.S.*, 1, 290; *G.W.*, 1, 57. (xvi, 230 *n.*)
[*Trans.*: 'The Neuro-Psychoses of Defence', *C.P.*, 1, 59; *Standard Ed.*, 3.]

(1895b) 'Über die Berechtigung, von der Neurasthenie einen bestimmten Symptomenkomplex als "Angstneurose" abzutrennen', *G.S.*, 1, 306; *G.W.*, 1, 313. (156, 161)
[*Trans.*: 'On the Grounds for Detaching a Particular Syndrome from Neurasthenia under the Description "Anxiety Neurosis"', *C.P.*, 1, 76; *Standard Ed.*, 3.]

(1895d) With BREUER, J., *Studien über Hysterie*, Vienna. (*G.S.*, 1; *G.W.*, 1, 75. Omitting Breuer's contributions.) (xiv–xvii, 80 *n.*, 100, 106 *n.*, 142, *n.* 2, 179 *n.*, 482 *n.*, 522, 538, 542 *n.*, 546, 569, *n.* 3, 601 *n.*)
[*Trans.*: *Studies on Hysteria*, *Standard Ed.*, 2. (Including Breuer's contributions.)]

(1896b) 'Weitere Bemerkungen über die Abwehr-Neuropsychosen', *G.S.*, 1, 363; *G.W.*, 1, 377. (142, *n.* 2, 230 *n.*, 545)
[*Trans.*: 'Further Remarks on the Neuro-Psychoses of Defence', *C.P.*, 1, 155; *Standard Ed.*, 3.]

(1898b) 'Zum psychischen Mechanismus der Vergesslichkeit', *G.W.*, 1, 517. (170, *n.* 1, 518 *n.*, 609 *n.*)
[*Trans.*: 'The Psychical Mechanism of Forgetting', *Standard Ed.*, 3.]

(1899a) 'Über Deckerinnerungen', *G.S.*, 1, 465; *G.W.*, 1, 531. (17 *n.*, 173 *n.*, 246 *n.*, 288, *n.* 2, 348, *n.* 2, 425 *n.*, 609 *n.*)
[*Trans.*: 'Screen Memories', *C.P.*, 5, 47; *Standard Ed.*, 3.]

(1900a) *Die Traumdeutung*, Vienna. (*G.S.*, 2–3; *G.W.*, 2–3.) (263, *n.* 2, 390, 392, 397, 410, 644, *n.* 2, 645 *n.*, 646, *n.* 1, 652, *n.* 3, 657, *n.* 2, 664, *n.* 1, 665 *n.*, 669, *n.* 2, 670 *n.*, 675 *n.*, 681 *n.*, 685 *n.*, 686)
[*Trans.*: *The Interpretation of Dreams*, London and New York, 1955; *Standard Ed.*, 4–5.]

(1901a) *Über den Traum*, Wiesbaden. (*G.S.*, 3, 189; *G.W.*, 2–3, 643.) (133 *n.*, 154, *n.* 1, 184, *n.* 1, 416 *n.*, 441 *n.*)
[*Trans.*: *On Dreams*, London, 1951; *Standard Ed.*, 5, 629.]

(1901b) *Zur Psychopathologie des Alltagslebens*, Berlin, 1904. (*G.S.*, 4; *G.W.*, 4.) (118, *n.* 1, 170, *n.* 1, 197, *n.* 1, 211, *n.* 1, 248 *n.*, 256, *n.* 2, 296, *n.* 2, 399, *n.* 1, 456, *n.* 2, 501, *n.* 1, 515, *n.* 1, 518 *n.*, 532 *n.*, 535 *n.*, 609 *n.*, 632, 671, *n.*)
[*Trans.*: *The Psychopathology of Everyday Life*, *Standard Ed.*, 6.]

FREUD, S. (*cont.*)

(1904*a*) 'Die Freud'sche psychoanalytische Methode', *G.S.*, **6**, 3; *G.W.*, **5**, 3. (101, *n.* 1)

[*Trans.:* 'Freud's Psycho-Analytic Procedure', *C.P.*, **1**, 264; *Standard Ed.*, **7**, 249.]

(1905*c*) *Der Witz und seine Beziehung zum Unbewussten*, Vienna. (*G.S.*, **9**; *G.W.*, **6**.) (120 *n.*, 195, *n.* 1, 268 *n.*, 297 *n.*, 303, *n.* 1, 341, *n.* 1, 356, *n.* 2, 445, *n.* 1, 480 *n.*, 505 *n.*)

[*Trans.: Jokes and their Relation to the Unconscious, Standard Ed.*, **8**.]

(1905*d*) *Drei Abhandlungen zur Sexualtheorie*, Vienna. (*G.S.*, **5**, 3; *G.W.*, **5**, 29.) (xii, 130, *n.* 2, 244, *n.* 2, 272, *n.* 2, 355, *n.* 1, 396, 492 *n.*, 606, *n.* 1, 682, *n.* 2.)

[*Trans.: Three Essays on the Theory of Sexuality*, London, 1949; *Standard Ed.*, **7**, 125.]

(1905*e*) 'Bruchstück einer Hysterie-Analyse', *G.S.*, **8**, 3; *G.W.*, **5**, 163. (xiv, 190, *n.* 1, 310 *n.*, 341, *n.* 1, 354, 387, *n.* 2, 395, 494 *n.*, 516 *n.*, 519, *n.* 1, 531 *n.*, 561, *n.* 1, 562, *n.* 2, 579 *n.*)

[*Trans.:* 'Fragment of an Analysis of a Case of Hysteria', *C.P.*, **3**, 13; *Standard Ed.*, **7**, 3.]

(1906*a*) 'Meine Ansichten über die Rolle der Sexualität in der Ätiologie der Neurosen', *G.S.*, **5**, 123; *G.W.*, **5**, 149 (288, *n.* 1)

[*Trans.:* 'My Views on the Part played by Sexuality in the Aetiology of the Neuroses', *C.P.*, **1**, 272; *Standard Ed.*, **7**, 271.]

(1907*a*) *Der Wahn und die Träume in W. Jensens 'Gradiva'*, Vienna. (*G.S.*, **9**, 273; *G.W.*, **7**, 31.) (97, *n.* 1, 372 *n.*)

[*Trans.: Delusions and Dreams in Jensen's 'Gradiva', Standard Ed.*, **9**.]

(1908*a*) 'Hysterische Phantasien und ihre Beziehung zur Bisexualität', *G.S.*, **5**, 246; *G.W.*, **7**, 191. (491, *n.* 3, 569)

[*Trans.:* 'Hysterical Phantasies and their Relation to Bisexuality', *C.P.*, **2**, 51; *Standard Ed.*, **9**.]

(1908*b*) 'Charakter und Analerotik', *G.S.*, **5**, 261; *G.W.*, **7**, 203. (216, *n.* 1, 403)

[*Trans.:* 'Character and Anal Erotism', *C.P.*, **2**, 45; *Standard Ed.*, **9**.]

(1908*c*) 'Über infantile Sexualtheorien', *G.S.*, **5**, 168; *G.W.*, **7**, 171. (250 *n.*)

[*Trans.:* 'On the Sexual Theories of Children', *C.P.*, **2**, 59; *Standard Ed.*, **9**.]

(1908*e*) 'Der Dichter und das Phantasieren', *G.S.*, **10**, 229; *G.W.*, **7**, 213. (491, *n.* 3)

[*Trans.:* 'Creative Writers and Day-Dreaming', *C.P.*, **4**, 173; *Standard Ed.*, **9**.]

(1909*b*) 'Analyse der Phobie eines fünfjährigen Knaben', *G.S.*, **8**, 129; *G.W.*, **7**, 243. (131 *n.*, 250 *n.*, 251 *n.*, 253 *n.*)

[*Trans.:* 'Analysis of a Phobia in a Five-Year-Old Boy', *C.P.*, **3**, 149; *Standard Ed.*, **10**, 30.]

(1909*d*) 'Bemerkungen über einen Fall von Zwangsneurose', *G.S.*, **8**, 269; *G.W.*, **7**, 381. (304 *n.*, 341, *n.* 1, 445, *n.* 1)

FREUD, S. (cont.)

[Trans.: 'Notes upon a Case of Obsessional Neurosis', C.P., 3, 293; Standard Ed., 10, 155.]

(1910a) Über Psychoanalyse, Vienna. (G.S., 4, 349; G.W., 8, 3.) (608n.)
[Trans.: Five Lectures on Psycho-Analysis, Standard Ed., 11, 3.]

(1910d) 'Die zukünftigen Chancen der psychoanalytischen Therapie', G.S., 6, 25; G.W., 8, 104. (355, n. 2, 365, 370, 403, n. 2)
[Trans.: 'The Future Prospects of Psycho-Analytic Therapy', C.P., 2, 285; Standard Ed., 11, 141.]

(1910e) ' "Über den Gegensinn der Urworte" ', G.S., 10, 221; G.W., 8, 214. (318, n. 3, 661 n.)
[Trans.: ' "The Antithetical Meaning of Primal Words" ', C.P., 4, 184; Standard Ed., 11, 155.]

(1910f) 'Brief an Dr. Friedrich S. Krauss über die Anthropophyteia', G.S., 11, 242; G.W., 8, 224. (606, n. 2)
[Trans.: 'Letter to Dr. Friedrich S. Krauss on Anthropophyteia', Standard Ed., 11, 233.]

(1910h) 'Über einen besonderen Typus der Objektwahl beim Manne' ('Beiträge zur Psychologie des Liebeslebens' I), G.S., 5, 186; G.W., 8, 66. (263, n. 2, 403, n. 2)
[Trans.: 'A Special Type of Choice of Object made by Men' ('Contributions to the Psychology of Love' I), C.P., 4, 192; Standard Ed., 11, 165.]

(1910l) 'Typisches Beispiel eines verkappten Ödipustraumes', Zentralbl. Psychoanal., 1, 45; reprinted in Die Traumdeutung, G.S., 3, 118 n.; G.W., 2–3, 404 n. (145 n., 398 n.)
[Trans.: 'A Typical Example of a Disguised Oedipus Dream'; included in The Interpretation of Dreams, Standard Ed., 5, 398 n.]

(1911a) 'Nachträge zur Traumdeutung', Zentralbl. Psychoanal., 1, 187. (Partly reprinted G.S., 3, 77 ff. and 126 f.; G.W., 2–3, 365 ff. and 412 f.) (360 n., 366, n. 1, 408 n.)
[Trans.: 'Additions to the Interpretation of Dreams' (wholly incorporated in The Interpretation of Dreams, Standard Ed., 5, 360 ff. and 408 f.)]

(1911b) 'Formulierungen über die zwei Prinzipien des psychischen Geschehens', G.S., 5, 409; G.W., 8, 230. (431, n. 1, 567, n. 2)
[Trans.: 'Formulations on the Two Principles of Mental Functioning', C.P., 4, 13; Standard Ed., 12, 215.]

(1911e) 'Die Handhabung der Traumdeutung in der Psychoanalyse', G.S., 6, 45; G.W., 8, 350. (104, n. 1, 514 n.)
[Trans.: 'The Handling of Dream-Interpretation in Psycho-Analysis', C.P., 2, 305; Standard Ed., 12, 91.]

(1912g) 'A Note on the Unconscious in Psycho-Analysis' [in English], C.P., 4, 22; Standard Ed., 12, 257. (615, n. 1)
[German Trans. (by Hanns Sachs): 'Einige Bemerkungen über den Begriff des Unbewussten in der Psychoanalyse, G.S., 5, 433; G.W., 8, 430.]

FREUD, S. (*cont.*)

(1912–13) *Totem und Tabu*, Vienna. (*G.S.*, **10**; *G.W.*, **9**.) (255, *n.* 2, 256, *n.* 2, 263, *n.* 2, 410 *n.*, 501, *n.* 1)
[*Trans.*: *Totem and Taboo*, London, 1950; *Standard Ed.*, **13**, 1.]

(1913*a*) 'Ein Traum als Beweismittel', *G.S.*, **3**, 267; *G.W.*, **10**, 12. (351, *n.* 1, 490, *n.* 1, 562, *n.* 1)
[*Trans.*: 'An Evidential Dream', *C.P.*, **2**, 133; *Standard Ed.*, **12**, 269.]

(1913*d*) 'Märchenstoffe in Träumen', *G.S.*, **3**, 259; *G.W.*, **10**, 2. (Appendix B, 626)
[*Trans.*: 'The Occurrence in Dreams of Material from Fairy Tales', *C.P.*, **4**, 236; *Standard Ed.*, **12**, 281.]

(1913*f*) 'Das Motiv der Kästchenwahl', *G.S.*, **10**, 243; *G.W.*, **10**, 244. (255, *n.* 2)
[*Trans.*: 'The Theme of the Three Caskets', *C.P.*, **4**, 244; *Standard Ed.*, **12**, 291.]

(1913*h*) 'Erfahrungen und Beispiele aus der analytischen Praxis', *Int. Z. Psychoanal.*, **1**, 377. (Partly reprinted *G.S.*, **11**, 301; *G.W.*, **10**, 40. Partly included in *Traumdeutung*, *G.S.*, **3**, 41, 71 f., 127 and 135; *G.W.*, **2–3**, 238, 359 ff., 413 f. and 433.) (232 *n.*, 409, *n.* 2, 431, *n.* 2)
[*Trans.*: 'Observations and Examples from Analytic Practice', *Standard Ed.*, **13**, 193 (in full). Also partly incorporated in *The Interpretation of Dreams*, *Standard Ed.*, **4**, 232, and **5**, 409 f.]

(1913*k*) 'Geleitwort zu Bourke's *Der Unrat in Sitte, Brauch, Glauben und Gewohnheitsrecht der Völker*', *G.S.*, **11**, 249; *G.W.*, **10**, 453. (606, *n.* 2)
[*Trans.*: 'Preface to Bourke, *Scatalogic Rites of All Nations*', *C.P.*, **5**, 88; *Standard Ed.*, **12**, 335.]

(1914*a*) 'Über fausse reconnaissance ("déjà raconté") während der psychoanalytischen Arbeit', *G.S.*, **6**, 76; *G.W.*, **10**, 116. (399, *n.* 1)
[*Trans.*: 'Fausse reconnaissance ("déjà raconté") in Psycho-Analytic Treatment', *C.P.*, **2**, 334; *Standard Ed.*, **13**, 201.]

(1914*c*) 'Zur Einführung des Narzissmus', *G.S.*, **6**, 155; *G.W.*, **10**, 138. (505, *n.* 2)
[*Trans.*: 'On Narcissism: an Introduction', *C.P.*, **4**, 30; *Standard Ed.*, **14**, 69.]

(1914*d*) 'Zur Geschichte der psychoanalytischen Bewegung', *G.S.*, **4**, 411; *G.W.*, **10**, 44. (xii, xiv, 348, *n.* 5)
[*Trans.*: 'On the History of the Psycho-Analytic Movement', *C.P.*, **1**, 287; *Standard Ed.*, **14**, 3.]

(1914*e*) 'Darstellungen der "grossen Leistung" im Traume', *Int. Z. Psychoanal.*, **2**, 384; reprinted in *Die Traumdeutung*, *G.S.*, **3**, 130; *G.W.*, **2–3**, 416. (412 *n.*)
[*Trans.*: 'The Representation in a Dream of a "Great Achievement" '; included in *The Interpretation of Dreams*, *Standard Ed.*, **5**, 412.]

(1915*a*) 'Weitere Ratschläge zur Technik der Psychoanalyse III: Bemerkungen über die Übertragungsliebe', *G.S.*, **6**, 120; *G.W.*, **10**, 306. (562, *n.* 2)
[*Trans.*: 'Observations on Transference-Love (Further Recom-

FREUD, S. (*cont.*)

mendations on the Technique of Psycho-Analysis, III)', *C.P.*, **2**, 377; *Standard Ed.*, **12**, 159.]

(1915*b*) 'Zeitgemässes über Krieg und Tod', *G.S.*, **10**, 315; *G.W.*, **10**, 324. (255, *n.* 2, 714)
[*Trans.:* 'Thoughts for the Times on War and Death', *C.P.*, **4**, 288; *Standard Ed.*, **14**, 275.]

(1915*d*) 'Die Verdrängung', *G.S.*, **5**, 466; *G.W.*, **10**, 248. (547, *n.* 2, 604 *n.*)
[*Trans.:* 'Repression', *C.P.*, **4**, 84; *Standard Ed.*, **14**, 143.]

(1915*e*) 'Das Unbewusste', *G.S.*, **5**, 480; *G.W.*, **10**, 264. (601 *n.*, 611 *n.*, 617 *n.*)
[*Trans.:* 'The Unconscious', *C.P.*, **4**, 98; *Standard Ed.*, **14**, 161.]

(1916*c*) 'Eine Beziehung zwischen einem Symbol und einem Symptom', *G.S.*, **5**, 310; *G.W.*, **10**, 394. (362 *n.*)
[*Trans.:* 'A Connection between a Symbol and a Symptom', *C.P.*, **2**, 162; *Standard Ed.*, **14**, 339.]

(1916*d*) 'Einige Charaktertypen aus der psychoanalytischen Arbeit', *G.S.*, **10**, 287; *G.W.*, **10**, 364. (266 *n.*)
[*Trans.:* 'Some Character-Types Met with in Psycho-Analytic Work', *C.P.*, **4**, 318; *Standard Ed.*, **14**, 311.]

(1916–17) *Vorlesungen zur Einführung in die Psychoanalyse*, Vienna. (*G.S.*, **7**; *G.W.*, **11**.) (xxix, 17 *n.*, 133 *n.*, 142, *n.* 3, 155, *n.* 1, 232 *n.*, 277 *n.*, 297 *n.*, 359, 364, *n.* 1, 405 *n.*, 409, *n.* 1, 414, *n.* 1, 416 *n.*, 431, *n.* 1, 517, *n.* 2, 580 *n.*, 645 *n.*, 670 *n.*)
[*Trans.: Introductory Lectures on Psycho-Analysis*, revised ed. London, 1929; *A General Introduction to Psychoanalysis*, New York, 1935; *Standard Ed.*, **15** and **16**.]

(1917*d*) 'Metapsychologische Ergänzung zur Traumlehre', *G.S.*, **5**, 520; *G.W.*, **10**, 412. (34 *n.*, 524, *n.* 1, 541 *n.*, 548, 555 *n.*)
[*Trans.:* 'A Metapsychological Supplement to the Theory of Dreams', *C.P.*, **4**, 137; *Standard Ed.*, **14**, 219.]

(1918*b*) 'Aus der Geschichte einer infantilen Neurose', *G.S.*, **8**, 439; *G.W.*, **12**, 29. (184, *n.* 2, 310 *n.*, 372 *n.*, 522 *n.*)
[*Trans.:* 'From the History of an Infantile Neurosis', *C.P.*, **3**, 473; *Standard Ed.*, **17**, 3.]

(1919*h*) 'Das Unheimliche', *G.S.*, **10**, 369; *G.W.*, **12**, 229. (357 *n.*, 414, *n.* 3)
[*Trans.:* ' "The Uncanny" ', *C.P.*, **4**, 368; *Standard Ed.*, **17**, 219.]

(1920*a*) 'Über die Psychogenese eines Falles von weiblicher Homosexualität', *G.S.*, **5**, 312; *G.W.*, **12**, 271. (476, *n.* 3)
[*Trans.:* 'The Psychogenesis of a Case of Female Homosexuality', *C.P.*, **2**, 202; *Standard Ed.*, **18**, 147.]

(1920*f*) 'Ergänzungen zur Traumlehre' (Author's Abstract of Congress Address), *Int. Z. Psychoanal.*, **6**, 397. (Appendix B, 627)
[*Trans.:* 'Supplements to the Theory of Dreams', *Int. J. Psycho-Anal.*, **1**, 354; *Standard Ed.*, **18**, 4.]

(1920*g*) *Jenseits des Lustprinzips*, Vienna. (*G.S.*, **6**, 191; *G.W.*, **13**, 3.) (245 *n.*, 268 *n.*, 461 *n.*, 540 *n.*, 558, *n.* 1, 565 *n.*, 601 *n.*)

FREUD, S. (cont.)

[Trans.: Beyond the Pleasure Principle, London, 1950; Standard Ed., 18, 3.]

(1921b) Introduction [in English] to Varendonck, The Psychology of Day-Dreams, London. (Standard Ed., 18, 271.) (491, n. 3) [German Text (part only): G.S., 11, 264; G.W., 13, 439.]

(1921c) Massenpsychologie und Ich-Analyse, Vienna. (G.S., 6, 261; G.W., 13, 73.) (151 n., 476, n. 2)

[Trans.: Group Psychology and the Analysis of the Ego, London, 1922; Standard Ed., 18, 67.]

(1922a) 'Traum und Telepathie', G.S., 3, 278; G.W., 13, 165. (5 n., 161, n. 1, 331 n., 403, n. 2, 524, n. 1, 560, n. 2, 579 n.)

[Trans.: 'Dreams and Telepathy', C.P., 4, 408; Standard Ed., 18, 197.]

(1922b) 'Über einige neurotische Mechanismen bei Eifersucht, Paranoia und Homosexualität', G.S., 5, 387; G.W., 13, 195. (89n.)

[Trans.: 'Some Neurotic Mechanisms in Jealousy, Paranoia and Homosexuality', C.P., 2, 232; Standard Ed., 18, 223.]

(1922c) 'Nachschrift zur Analyse des kleinen Hans', G.S., 8, 264; G.W., 13, 431. (521 n.)

[Trans.: 'Postscript to the "Analysis of a Phobia in a Five-Year-Old Boy"', C.P., 3, 288; Standard Ed., 10, 148.]

(1923a) [1922]) '"Psychoanalyse" und "Libido Theorie"', G.S., 11, 201; G.W., 13, 211. (490, n. 1)

[Trans.: 'Two Encyclopædia Articles', C.P., 5, 107; Standard Ed., 18, 235.]

(1923b) Das Ich und das Es, Vienna. (G.S., 6, 353; G.W., 13, 237.) (160 n., 476, n. 2, 541 n., 564 n., 615, n. 1)

[Trans.: The Ego and the Id, London, 1927; Standard Ed., 19.]

(1923c) 'Bemerkungen zur Theorie und Praxis der Traumdeutung,' G.S., 3, 305; G.W., 13, 301. (104, n. 1, 165 n., 323, n. 2, 476, n. 2)

[Trans.: 'Remarks on the Theory and Practice of Dream-Interpretation', C.P., 5, 136; Standard Ed., 19.]

(1923d) 'Eine Teufelsneurose im siebzehnten Jahrhundert', G.S., 10, 409; G.W., 13, 317. (358, n. 3)

[Trans.: 'A Seventeenth Century Demonological Neurosis', C.P., 4, 436; Standard Ed., 19.]

(1923f) 'Josef Popper-Lynkeus und die Theorie des Traumes', G.S., 11, 295; G.W., 13, 357. (95 n., 308, n. 2)

[Trans.: 'Josef Popper-Lynkeus and the Theory of Dreams', Standard Ed., 19.]

(1924-34) Gesammelte Schriften, Vienna. (xii, xxxi, 2, n. 2, 21, n. 1, 127, n. 1, 190, n. 2, 311, n. 1, 508 n.)

(1924c) 'Das ökonomische Problem des Masochismus', G.S., 5, 374; G.W., 13, 371. (159, n. 2)

[Trans.: 'The Economic Problem of Masochism', C.P., 2, 255; Standard Ed., 19.]

(1925a) 'Notiz über den Wunderblock', G.S., 6, 415; G.W., 14, 3. (540 n.)

FREUD, S. (cont.)

[Trans.: 'A Note upon the "Mystic Writing-Pad" ', C.P., 5, 175; Standard Ed., 19.]

(1925d) 'Selbstdarstellung', G.S., 11, 119; G.W., 14, 33. (438 n., 714)
[Trans.: An Autobiographical Study, London, 1935; Standard Ed., 20.]

(1925i) 'Einige Nachträge zum Ganzen der Traumdeutung', G.S., 3, 172; G.W., 1, 559. (5 n., 74 n., 524, n. 2, 621, n. 1)
[Trans.: 'Some Additional Notes upon Dream-Interpretation as a Whole', C.P., 5, 150; Standard Ed., 20.]

(1925j) 'Einige psychische Folgen des anatomischen Geschlechtsunterschieds', G.S., 11, 8; G.W., 14, 19. (257 n.)
[Trans.: 'Some Psychological Consequences of the Anatomical Distinction between the Sexes', C.P., 5, 186; Standard Ed., 19.]

(1926d) Hemmung, Symptom und Angst, Vienna. (G.S., 11, 23; G.W., 14, 113.) (161, n. 2, 338, n. 1, 400, n. 3, 602 n.)
[Trans.: Inhibitions, Symptoms and Anxiety, London, 1936; The Problem of Anxiety, New York, 1936; Standard Ed., 20.]

(1927c) Die Zukunft einer Illusion, Vienna. (G.S., 11, 411; G.W., 14, 325.) (455, n. 1)
[Trans.: The Future of an Illusion, London, 1928; Standard Ed., 21.]

(1929b) 'Brief an Maxim Leroy über einen Traum des Cartesius', G.S., 12, 403; G.W., 14, 558. (Appendix B, 627)
[Trans.: 'A Letter to Maxime Leroy on a Dream of Descartes', Standard Ed., 21.]

(1930a) Das Unbehagen in der Kultur, Vienna. (G.S., 12, 29; G.W., 14, 421.) (78 n.)
[Trans.: Civilization and its Discontents, London and New York, 1930; Standard Ed., 21.]

(1930e) 'Goethe-Preis 1930', G.S., 12, 408; G.W., 14, 547. (142, n. 1, 266 n.)
[Trans.: 'Address delivered in the Goethe House at Frankfort', Standard Ed., 21.]

(1931b) 'Über die weibliche Sexualität', G.S., 12, 120; G.W., 14, 517. (257 n.)
[Trans.: 'Female Sexuality', C.P., 5, 252; Standard Ed., 21.]

(1932c) 'Meine Berührung mit Josef Popper-Lynkeus', G.S., 12, 415; G.W., 16, 261. (xii, 95 n., 308, n. 2)
[Trans.: 'My Contact with Josef Popper-Lynkeus', C.P., 5, 295; Standard Ed., 22.]

(1933a) Neue Folge der Vorlesungen zur Einführung in die Psychoanalyse, Vienna. (G.S., 12, 151; G.W., 15.) (5 n., 92 n., 334 n., 490, n. 2, 505, n. 1, 530, n. 2, 541 n., 558, n. 1, 604 n.)
[Trans.: New Introductory Lectures on Psycho-Analysis, London and New York, 1933; Standard Ed., 22.]

(1940a [1938]) Abriss der Psychoanalyse, (G.W., 17, 67.) (Appendix B, 627)
[Trans.: An Outline of Psycho-Analysis, London and New York, 1949; Standard Ed., 23.]

FREUD, S. (cont.)

(1940c [1922]) 'Das Medusenhaupt', G.W., 17, 47. (357 n.)
[Trans.: 'Medusa's Head', C.P., 5, 105; Standard Ed., 18, 273.]

(1940d [1892]) With BREUER, J., 'Zur Theorie des hysterischen Anfalls', G.W., 17, 9. (xvi)
[Trans.: 'On the Theory of Hysterical Attacks', C.P., 5, 27; Standard Ed., 1.]

(1941a [1892]) 'Brief an Josef Breuer', G.W., 17, 5. (565 n.)
[Trans.: 'A Letter to Josef Breuer', C.P., 5, 25; Standard Ed., 1.]

(1941c [1899]) 'Eine erfüllte Traumahnung', G.W., 17, 21. (5 n., 65, n. 2, 623–5)
[Trans.: 'A Premonitory Dream Fulfilled', C.P., 5, 70; Standard Ed., 5, 623.]

(1950a [1887–1902]) Aus den Anfängen der Psychoanalyse, London. Includes 'Entwurf einer Psychologie' (1895). (xii, xiv–xx, xxxvi, 17 n., 94, n. 2, 112, n. 1, 116, n. 2, 117 n., 118, n. 1, 121 n., 122 n., 125 n., 130, n. 1, 136 n., 142, n. 1, 145 n., 151 n., 157, n. 1, 161, n. 1, 172 n., 193, n. 2, 194, n. 1, 195, nn. 1 and 3, 200 n., 205, nn. 1 and 2, 214, n. 1, 231 n., 240 n., 243, n. 2, 248 n., 263, n. 2, 268 n., 297 n., 317 n., 318, n. 1, 387, n. 2, 425 n., 436 n., 439 n., 454 n., 464 n., 468 n., 491, n. 4, 499 n., 509 n., 515, n. 1, 536 n., 540 n., 565 n., 593 n., 601 n., 605 n., 608 n., 615, n. 2, 620 n., 623, n. 1, 631–2, 714.)
[Trans.: The Origins of Psycho-Analysis, London and New York, 1954. (Partly, including 'A Project for a Scientific Psychology', in Standard Ed., 1.)]

(1957a [1911]) With OPPENHEIM, E., 'Dreams in Folklore', Standard Ed., 12, 177. (621)

FUCHS, E. (1909–12) Illustrierte Sittengeschichte (Ergänzungsbände), Munich. (346 n.)

GALTON, F. (1907) Inquiries into Human Faculty and its Development, 2nd ed., London. (1st ed., 1883.) (139, 293, 494, 649)

GARNIER, A. (1872) Traité des facultés de l'âme, contenant l'histoire des principales théories psychologiques, (3 vols.), Paris. (1st ed., 1852.) (26, 233)

GIESSLER, C. M. (1888) Beiträge zur Phänomenologie des Traumlebens, Halle. (88, n. 1)

(1890) Aus den Tiefen des Traumlebens, Halle. (88, n. 1)

(1896) Die physiologischen Beziehungen der Traumvorgänge, Halle. (88, n. 1)

GIROU DE BOUZAREINGES, C., and GIROU DE BOUZAREINGES, L. (1848) Physiologie: essai sur le mécanisme des sensations, des idées et des sentiments, Paris. (25)

GOBLOT, E. (1896) 'Sur le souvenir des rêves', Rev. phil., 42, 288. (502, 575)

GOMPERZ, T. (1866) Traumdeutung und Zauberei, Vienna. (98 n.)

GOTTHARDT, O. (1912) Die Traumbücher des Mittelalters, Eisleben. (4, n. 2)

GRIESINGER, W. (1845) *Pathologie und Therapie der psychischen Krankheiten*, Stuttgart. (134)
(1861) do., 2nd ed. (quoted by Radestock). (91, 230 n.)

GRUPPE, O. (1906) *Griechische Mythologie und Religionsgeschichte*, Munich. (In Müller, *Handbuch der klassischen Altertums-Wissenschaft*, 5, 2.) (3)

GUISLAIN, J. (1833) *Leçons orales sur les phrénopathies* (3 vols.), Brussels. (89) [Quotation in text is from German trans.: *Abhandlungen über die Phrenopathien*, Nuremberg, 1838.]

HAFFNER, P. (1887) 'Schlafen und Träumen', *Sammlung zeitgemässer Broschüren*, 226, Frankfurt. (5, 52 n., 63, n. 1, 67–9)

HAGEN, F. W. (1846) 'Psychologie und Psychiatrie', *Wagner's Handwörterbuch der Physiologie*, 2, 692, Brunswick. (90)

HALLAM, F., and WEED, S. (1896) 'A Study of Dream Consciousness', *Amer. J. Psychol.*, 7, 405. (18, 134, 163)

HARTMANN, E. VON (1890) *Philosophie des Unbewussten*, 10th ed., Leipzig. (1st ed., 1869.) (134, 528 n.)
[*Trans.: Philosophy of the Unconscious*, by W. C. Coupland, London, 1884.]

HARTMANN, H. See BETLHEIM and HARTMANN.

HENNINGS, J. C. (1784) *Von den Träumen und Nachtwandlern*, Weimar. (13, 24)

HENZEN, W. (1890) *Über die Träume in der altnordischen Sagaliteratur*, (Thesis) Leipzig. (407)

HERBART, J. F. (1892) *Psychologie als Wissenschaft neu gegründet auf Erfahrung, Metaphysik und Mathematik. (Zweiter, analytischer Teil)*; Vol. 6 in *Herbart's Sämtliche Werke* (ed. K. Kehrbach), Langensalza. (1st ed., Königsberg, 1825.) (76)

HERMANN, K. F. (1858) *Lehrbuch der gottesdienstlichen Alterthümer der Griechen*, 2nd ed., Heidelberg. (Pt. II of *Lehrbuch der griechischen Antiquitäten*.) (34 n.)
(1882) *Lehrbuch der griechischen Privatalterthümer*, 3rd ed., Freiburg. (Pt. IV of *Lehrbuch der griechischen Antiquitäten*). (34 n.)

HERODOTUS *History*. (398 n.)
[*Trans.* by A. D. Godley, Vol. III (Loeb Classical Library), London and New York, 1922.]

HERVEY DE SAINT-DENYS, Marquis d', (1867) *Les rêves et les moyens de les diriger*, Paris. (Published anonymously.) (13–14, 26, 60–1, 572)

HILDEBRANDT, F. W. (1875) *Der Traum und seine Verwerthung für's Leben*, Leipzig. (9–10, 15, 18–20, 26–28, 56, 62–4, 67–72, 163)

HIPPOCRATES *Ancient Medicine* and *Regimen*. (3, n. 2, 34 n., 402)
[*Trans.* by W. H. S. Jones, Vols. I and IV (Loeb Classical Library), London and New York, 1923 and 1931.]

HITSCHMANN, E. (1913) 'Goethe als Vatersymbol', *Int. Z. Psychoanal.*, 1, 569. (354)

700   BIBLIOGRAPHY A

HOBBES, T. (1651) *Leviathan*, London. (542 *n*.)

HOFFBAUER, J. C. (1796) *Naturlehre der Seele*, Halle. (24)

HOHNBAUM (1830) In C. F. NASSE: *Jb. Anthrop.*, **1**. (88)

HUG-HELLMUTH, H. VON (1911) 'Analyse eines Traumes eines 5½
     jährigen Knaben', *Zbl. Psychoanal.*, **2**, 122. (131 *n*.)
     (1913) 'Kinderträume', *Int. Z. Psychoanal.*, **1**, 470. (131 *n*.)
     (1915) 'Ein Traum der sich selbst deutet', *Int. Z. Psychoanal.*, **3**,
     33. (142, *n*. 3)

*IDELER, K. W. (1862) 'Die Enstehung des Wahnsinns aus den Träu-
     men', *Charité Annalen*, **3**, Berlin. (88, *n*. 1)

*IWAYA, S. (1902) 'Traumdeutung in Japan', *Ostasien*, 302. (4, *n*. 2)

JEKELS, L. (1917) 'Shakespeare's Macbeth', *Imago*, **5**, 170. (266 *n*.)

JESSEN, P. (1855) *Versuch einer wissenschaftlichen Begründung der Psychologie*,
     Berlin. (8, 13, 23–4, 46, 66, 72)

JODL, F. (1896) *Lehrbuch der Psychologie*, Stuttgart. (57)

JONES, E. (1910a) 'The Oedipus Complex as an Explanation of Hamlet's
     Mystery', *Amer. J. Psychol.*, **21**, 72. (266 *n*.)
     (1910b) 'Freud's Theory of Dreams', *Amer. J. Psychol.*, **21**, 283.
     (401)
     (1911) 'The Relationship between Dreams and Psychoneurotic
     Symptoms', *Am. J. Insanity*, **68**, 57. (569, *n*. 2)
     (1912a) 'Unbewusste Zahlenbehandlung', *Zbl. Psychoanal.*, **2**, 241.
     (418, *n*. 1)
     (1912b) 'A Forgotten Dream', *J. abnorm. Psychol.*, **7**, 5. (520, *n*. 2)
     (1914a) 'Frau und Zimmer', *Int. Z. Psychoanal.*, **2**, 380. (354 *n*.)
     (1914b) 'Zahnziehen und Geburt', *Int. Z. Psychoanal.*, **2**, 380.
     (387, *n*. 3)
     (1916) 'The Theory of Symbolism', *Brit. J. Psychol.*, **9**, 181.
     (351, *n*. 2)
     (1949) *Hamlet and Oedipus*, London. (266 *n*.)
     (1953) *Sigmund Freud: Life and Work*, **1**, London. (xxii, 111, *n*. 2,
     170, *n*. 2, 714)

JOSEPHUS, FLAVIUS *Antiquitates Judaicae*. (334)
     [*Trans.*: *Ancient History of the Jews* by W. Whiston, London,
     1874.]

JUNG, C. G. (ed.) (1906) *Diagnostische Assoziationsstudien* (2 vols.),
     Leipzig. (532 *n*.)
     [*Trans.*: *Studies in Word-Association*, London.]
     (1907) *Über die Psychologie der Dementia præcox*, Halle. (530, *n*. 1)
     [*Trans.*: *The Psychology of Dementia Præcox*, New York, 1909.]
     (1910a) 'Über Konflikte der kindlichen Seele', *Jb. psychoanal.
     psychopath. Forsch.*, **2**, 33. (131 *n*.)
     (1910b) 'Ein Beitrag zur Psychologie des Gerüchtes', *Zbl. Psy-
     choanal.*, **1**, 81. (334)
     (1911) 'Ein Beitrag zur Kenntnis des Zahlentraumes', *Zbl.
     Psychoanal.*, **1**, 567. (418, *n*. 1)

KANT, I. (1764) *Versuch über die Krankheiten des Kopfes*. (90)
(1798) *Anthropologie in pragmatischer Hinsicht*. (70–1)

KARPINSKA, L. VON (1914) 'Ein Beitrag zur Analyse "sinnloser" Worte in Traume', *Int. Z̧. Psychoanal.*, 2, 164. (303)

KAZOWSKY, A. D. (1901) 'Zur Frage nach dem Zusammenhange von Träumen und Wahnvorstellungen', *Neurol. Z̧bl.*, 440 and 508. (88, *n.* 1)

KIRCHGRABER, F. (1912) 'Der Hut als Symbol des Genitales', *Z̧bl. Psychoanal. Psychother.*, 3, 95. (362 *n.*)

KLEINPAUL, R. (1898) *Die Lebendigen und die Toten in Volksglauben, Religion und Sage*, Leipzig. (351, *n.* 2)

KRAUSS, A. (1858–59) 'Der Sinn im Wahnsinn', *Allg. Z̧. Psychol.*, 15, 617 and 16, 222. (36–7, 88–90, 92)

KRAUSS, F. S. See ARTEMIDORUS. (356, *n.* 1)

LADD, G. T. (1892) 'Contribution to the Psychology of Visual Dreams', *Mind*, (New Series) 1, 299. (32–3, 589)

LANDAUER, K. (1918) 'Handlungen des Schlafenden', *Z̧. ges. Neur. Psychiat.*, 39, 329. (224, *n.* 1)

*LASÈGUE, C. (1881) 'Le délire alcoolique n'est pas un délire, mais un rêve', *Arch. gén. Méd.* (88, *n.* 1)

LAUER, C. (1913) 'Das Wesen des Traumes in der Beurteilung der talmudischen und rabbinischen Literatur', *Int. Z̧. Psychoanal.*, 1, 459. (4, *n.* 2)

LEHMANN, A. (1908) *Aberglaube und Z̧auberei von den ältesten Z̧eiten bis in die Gegenwart* (German trans. by Petersen), Stuttgart. (34 *n.*)

LE LORRAIN, J. (1894) 'La durée du temps dans les rêves', *Rev. phil.*, 38, 275. (27, 64, 496)
(1895) 'Le rêve', *Rev. phil.*, 40, 59. (496, 567, *n.* 1)

LÉLUT. (1852) 'Mémoire sur les sommeil, les songes et le sonnambulisme', *Ann. méd.-psychol.*, 4, 331. (90)

LEMOINE, A. (1855) *Du sommeil au point de vue physiologique et psychologique*. Paris. (55)

LEROY. See BERNARD-LEROY.

LEURET, F. (1834) *Fragments psychologiques sur la folie*, Paris. (529)

LIÉBEAULT, A. A. (1889) *Le sommeil provoqué et les états analogues*, Paris. (570 *n.*)

LIPPS, T. (1883) *Grundtatsachen des Seelenlebens*, Bonn. (223–4)
(1897) 'Der Begriff des Unbewussten in der Psychologie', *Records of the Third Internat. Congr. Psychol.*, Munich. (611–12, 614)

*LLOYD, W. (1877) *Magnetism and Mesmerism in Antiquity*, London. (34 *n.*)

LÖWINGER. (1908) 'Der Traum in der jüdischen Literatur', *Mitt. jüd. Volksk.*, 10. (4, *n.* 2)

LUCRETIUS *De rerum natura*. (8)
[*Trans.* by W. H. D. Rouse (Loeb Classical Library), London and New York, 1924.]

'LYNKEUS' (J. POPPER) (1899) *Phantasien eines Realisten*, Dresden. (95, 308, *n.* 2)

MAASS, J. G. E. (1805) *Versuch über die Leidenschaften*, Halle. (8)

MACARIO, M. M. A. (1847) 'Des rêves, considérés sous le rapport physiologique et pathologique', Pt. II, *Ann. méd-psychol.*, 9, 27. (89)

(1857) *Du sommeil, des rêves et du sonnambulisme dans l'état de santé et de maladie*, Paris-Lyons. (498)

MACNISH, R. (1830) *Philosophy of Sleep*, Glasgow. (24–5)
[*German trans.*: *Der Schlaf in allen seinen Gestalten*, Leipzig, 1835.]

MAEDER, A. (1908) 'Die Symbolik in den Legenden, Märchen, Gebräuchen, und Träumen', *Psychiat.-neurol. Wschr.*, 10, 55. (351, *n.* 2)

(1912) 'Über die Funktion des Traumes', *Jb. psychoanal. psychopath. Forsch.*, 4, 692. (579 *n.*)

MAINE DE BIRAN, M. F. P. (1834) *Nouvelles considérations sur les rapports du physique et du moral de l'homme*, (ed. by V. Cousin), Paris. (90)

MARCINOWSKI, J. (1911) 'Eine kleine Mitteilung', *Zbl. Psychoanal.*, 1, 575. (302–3)

(1912a) 'Gezeichnete Träume', *Zbl. Psychoanal.*, 2, 490 (356)

(1912b) 'Drei Romane in Zahlen', *Zbl. Psychoanal.*, 2, 619. (418, *n.* 1)

MAUDSLEY, H. (1868) *Psychology and Pathology of the Mind*, London. (1st ed., 1867.) (612 *n.*)

MAURY, L. F. A. (1853) 'Nouvelles observations sur les analogies des phénomènes du rêve et de l'aliénation mentale', Pt. II, *Ann. méd-psychol.*, 5, 404. (27, 90, 495–7)

(1878) *Le sommeil et les rêves*, Paris. (1st ed., 1861.) (8, 13, 16–17, 25–7, 31–2, 34–5, 55–7, 59–61, 64, 72–4, 77, 88, 90, 92, 189, 523, *n.* 2, 531 *n.*, 575)

*MEIER, G. F. (1758) *Versuch einer Erklärung des Nachtwandelns*, Halle. (24)

MEYNERT, T. (1892) *Sammlung von populärwissenschaftlichen Vorträgen über den Bau und die Leistungen des Gehirns*, Vienna. (223, 250)

MIURA K. (1906) 'Über japanische Traumdeuterei', *Mitt. dtsch. Ges. Naturk. Ostasiens*, 10, 291. (4, *n.* 2)

MOREAU, J. (1855) 'De l'identité de l'état de rêve et de folie', *Ann. méd.-psychol.*, 1, 361. (90)

MÜLLER, J. (1826) *Über die phantastischen Gesichtserscheinungen*, Coblenz. (31–2)

MYERS, F. W. H. (1892) 'Hypermnesic Dreams', *Proc. Soc. Psych. Res.*, 8, 362. (14)

*NÄCKE, P. (1903) 'Über sexuelle Träume', *Arch. Kriminalanthropol.*, 307. (396)

    (1905) 'Der Traum als feinstes Reagens f. d. Art d. sexuellen Empfindens', *Monatschr. f. Krim.-Psychol.*, **2**, 500. (396)

    (1907) 'Kontrastträume und spez. sexuelle Kontrastträume', *Arch. Kriminalanthropol.*, **24**, 1. (396)

    (1908) 'Beiträge zu den sexuellen Träumen', *Arch. Kriminalanthropol.*, **29**, 363. (396)

    (1911) 'Die diagnostische und prognostische Brauchbarkeit der sex. Träume', *Ärztl. Sachv.-Ztg.*, **2**. (396)

NEGELEIN, J. VON (1912) 'Der Traumschlüssel des Jaggadeva', *Relig. Gesch. Vers.*, **11**, 4. (4, *n.* 2)

NELSON, J. (1888) 'A Study of Dreams', *Amer. J. Psychol.*, **1**, 367. (18)

NORDENSKJÖLD, O. *et al.* (1904) *Antarctic. Zwei Jahre in Schnee und Eis am Südpol*, (2 vols.), Berlin. (131 *n.*)
    [*English trans.* (abr.): *Antarctica*, London, 1905.]

PACHANTONI, D. (1909) 'Der Traum als Urschprung von Wahnideen bei Alkoholdelirianten', *Zbl. Nervenheilk.*, **32**, 796. (88, *n.* 1)

PAULHAN, F. (1894) 'À propos de l'activité de l'esprit dans le rêve'; under 'Correspondence' in *Rev. phil*, **38**, 546. (502)

PEISSE, L. (1857) *La médecine et les médecins*, Paris. (92)

PFAFF, E. R. (1868) *Das Traumleben und seine Deutung nach den Prinzipien der Araber, Perser, Griechen, Inder und Ägypter*, Leipzig. (67)

*PFISTER, O. (1909) 'Ein Fall von psychoanalytischer Seelsorge und Seelenheilung', *Evangelische Freiheit*, Tübingen. (403, *n.* 2)

    (1911–12) 'Die psychologische Enträtselung der religiösen Glossolalie und der automatischen Kryptographie', *Jb. psychoanal. psychopath. Forsch.*, **3**, 427 and 730. (356)

    (1913) 'Kryptolalie, Kryptographie und unbewusstes Vexierbild bei Normalen', *Jb. psychoanal. und psychopath. Forsch.*, **5**, 115. (356)

PICHON, A. E. (1896) *Contribution à l'étude des délires oniriques ou délires de rêve*, Bordeaux. (88, *n.* 1)

PILCZ, A. (1899) 'Über eine gewisse Gesetzmässigkeit in den Träumen', Author's Abstract, *Mschr. Psychiat. Neurol.*, **5**, 231, Berlin. (20)

PLATO *Republic*. (67 and *n.*, 620)
    [*Trans.* by B. Jowett (Dialogues, Vol. II), Oxford, 1871.]

POHORILLES, N. E. (1913) 'Eduard von Hartmanns Gesetz der von unbewussten Zielvorstellungen geleiteten Assoziationen', *Int. Z. Psychoanal.*, **1**, 605. (528 *n.*)

PÖTZL, O. (1917) 'Experimentell erregte Traumbilder in ihren Beziehungen zum indirekten Sehen', *Z. ges. Neurol. Psychiat.*, **37**, 278. (181, *n.* 2)

PRINCE, MORTON (1910) 'The Mechanism and Interpretation of Dreams', *J. abnorm. Psychol.*, **5**, 139. (521)

Purkinje, J. E. (1846) 'Wachen, Schlaf, Traum und verwandte Zustände', R. *Wagner's Handwörterbuch der Physiologie*, 3, 412, Brunswick. (83, 134)

Putnam, J. J. (1912) 'Ein charakteristischer Kindertraum', *Zbl. Psychoanal.*, 2, 328. (131 *n*.)

*Raalte, F. van (1912) 'Kinderdroomen', *Het Kind*, Jan. (131 *n*.)

Radestock, P. (1879) *Schlaf und Traum*, Leipzig. (8, 34, 44–5, 56–7, 66, 71, 88–92, 134)

Rank, O. (1909) *Der Mythus von der Geburt des Helden*, Leipzig and Vienna. (256, *n*. 2, 400, *n*. 2)
   [*Trans.: Myth of the Birth of the Hero*, New York, 1913]
   (1910) 'Ein Traum der sich selbst deutet', *Jb. Psychoanal. psychopath. Forsch.*, 2, 465. (160 *n*., 238 *n*., 310 *n*., 335, 348 *n*., 398 *n*., 406)
   (1911a) 'Beispiel eines verkappten Ödipustraumes', *Zbl. Psychoanal.*, 1, 167. (398 *n*.)
   (1911b) 'Belege zur Rettungsphantasie', *Zbl. Psychoanal.*, 1, 331. (403, *n*. 2)
   (1911c) 'Zum Thema der Zahnreizträume', *Zbl. Psychoanal.*, 1, 408. (388–92)
   (1912a) 'Die Symbolschichtung im Wecktraum und ihre Wiederkehr im mythischen Denken', *Jb. psychoanal. psychopath. Forsch.*, 4, 51. (219 *n*., 238 *n*., 352, *n*. 2, 367, 402–3)
   (1912b) 'Aktuelle Sexualregungen als Traumanlässe', *Zbl. Psychoanal.*, 2, 596. (238 *n*.)
   (1912c) *Das Inzest-Motiv in Dichtung und Sage*, Leipzig and Vienna. (256, *n*. 2)
   (1913) 'Eine noch nicht beschriebene Form des Ödipus-Traumes', *Int. Z. Psychoanal.*, 1, 151. (398 *n*.)
   (1914) 'Die "Geburts-Rettungsphantasie" in Traum und Dichtung', *Int. Z. Psychoanal.*, 2, 43. (403, *n*. 2)

Rank, O., and Sachs, H. (1913) *Die Bedeutung der Psychoanalyse für die Geisteswissenschaften*, Wiesbaden. (351, *n*. 2)
   [*Trans.: The Significance of Psychoanalysis for the Mental Sciences*, New York, 1915.]

Régis, E. (1894) 'Les hallucinations oniriques ou du sommeil des dégénérés mystiques', *Compte rendu Congrès Méd. Alién.*, 260, Paris, 1895. (88, *n*. 1)

Reik, T. (1911) 'Zur Rettungssymbolik', *Zbl. Psychoanal.*, 1, 499. (403, *n*. 2)
   (1915) 'Gold und Kot', *Int. Z. Psychoanal.*, 3, 183. (403)

Reitler, R. (1913a) 'Zur Augensymbolik', *Int. Z. Psychoanal.*, 1, 159. (398 *n*.)
   (1913b) 'Zur Genital- und Sekret-Symbolik', *Int. Z. Psychoanal.*, 1, 492. (359)

Robert, W. (1886) *Der Traum als Naturnotwendigkeit erklärt*, Hamburg. (17–18, 79–81, 163, 164 *n*., 177–8, 189, 579, 591)

RODITSEK, A. (1912) 'Zur Frage der Symbolik in dem Träumen Gesunder', *Zbl. Psychoanal.*, **2**, 340. (373–7)

ROFFENSTEIN, G. (1923) 'Experimentelle Symbolträume', *Z. ges. Neurol. Psychiat.*, **87**, 362. (384)

R[ORSCHACH], H. (1912) 'Zur Symbolik der Schlange und der Kravatte', *Zbl. Psychoanal.*, **2**, 675. (356, *n*. 1)

SACHS, H. (1911) 'Zur Darstellungs-Technik des Traumes', *Zbl. Psychoanal.*, **1**, 413. (410–11)

— (1912) 'Traumdeutung und Menschenkenntnis', *Jb. Psychoanal. psychopath. Forsch.*, **3**, 568. (620–1)

— (1913) 'Ein Traum Bismarcks', *Int. Z Psychoanal.*, **1**, 80. (378–81)

— (1914) 'Das Zimmer als Traumdarstellung des Weibes', *Int. Z. Psychoanal.*, **2**, 35. (354)

See also RANK and SACHS.

SALOMON ALMOLI BEN JACOB (1637) *Pithrôn Chalômôth*, Amsterdam. (4, *n*. 2)

SANCTIS, SANTE DE (1896) *I sogni e il sonno nell' isterismo e nella epilepsia*, Rome. (88)

— (1897a) 'Les maladies mentales et les rêves', extrait des *Ann. Soc. Méd. de Gand*, **76**, 177. (88)

*— (1897b) 'Sui rapporti d'identità, di somiglianza, di analogia e di equivalenza fra sogno e pazzia', *Riv. quindicinale Psicol. Psichiat. Neuropatol.*, Nov. 15. (88)

— (1898a) 'Psychoses et rêves', *Rapport au Congrès de neurol. et d'hypnologie de Bruxelles 1897; Comptes rendus*, **1**, 137. (88)

— (1898b) 'I sogni dei neuropatici e dei pazzi', *Arch. psichiat. antrop. crim.*, **19**, 342. (88)

— (1899) *I sogni*, Turin. (89, 94)

[*German transl.* by O. Schmidt, Halle, 1901.]

SCHERNER, K. A. (1861) *Das Leben des Traumes*, Berlin. (36–7, 83–7, 132 *n*. 2, 224–7, 334–5, 346, 353, 359 *n*., 402, 546, 591–2, 613, 634, 685 *n*.)

SCHLEIERMACHER, F. (1862) *Psychologie*, (Vol. 6, Sec. 3 in *Collected Works*, ed. L. George), Berlin. (49, 71, 102)

SCHOLZ, F. (1887) *Schlaf und Traum*, Leipzig. (20, 57–8, 67, 134)

[*Trans.: Sleep and Dreams* by H. M. Jewett, New York, 1893.]

SCHOPENHAUER, A. (1862) 'Versuch über das Geistersehen und was damit zusammenhängt', *Parerga und Paralipomena* (Essay V), **1**, 213, 2nd ed., Berlin. (1st ed. 1851.) (36, 66, 90)

SCHRÖTTER, K. (1912) 'Experimentelle Träume', *Zbl. Psychoanal.*, **2**, 638. (384)

SCHUBERT, G. H. VON (1814) *Die Symbolik des Traumes*, Bamberg. (63, 352)

SCHWARZ, F. (1913) 'Traum und Traumdeutung nach "Abdalgan an-Nabulusi" ', *Z. deutsch. morgenl. Ges.*, **67**, 473. (4, *n*. 2)

*Secker, F. (1909–10) 'Chinesische Ansichten über den Traum', *Neue metaph. Rndschr.*, **17**, 101. (4, *n.* 2)

Siebeck, H. (1877) 'Das Traumleben der Seele', *Sammlung gemeinverständlicher Vorträge*, Berlin. (58)

Silberer, H. (1909) 'Bericht über eine Methode, gewisse symbolische Halluzinations-Erscheinungen hervorzurufen und zu beobachten', *Jb. psychoanal. psychopath. Forsch.*, **1**, 513. (49, *n.* 2, 102, *n.*1, 344–5, 378, 412 *n.*, 503–5)

— (1910) 'Phantasie und Mythos', *Jb. psychoanal. psychopath. Forsch.*, **2**, 541. (102, *n.* 1, 214, *n.* 4)

— (1912) 'Symbolik des Erwachens und Schwellensymbolik überhaupt', *Jb. psychoanal. psychopath. Forsch.*, **3**, 621. (102, *n.* 1, 503–5, 559)

— (1914) *Probleme der Mystik und ihrer Symbolik*, Vienna and Leipzig. (524)

Simon, P. M. (1888) *Le monde des rêves*, Paris. (30, 34, 38, 134)

*Sperber, H. (1912) 'Über den Einfluss sexueller Momente auf Entstehung und Entwicklung der Sprache', *Imago*, **1**, 405. (352, *n.* 1)

Spielrein, S. (1913) 'Traum von "Pater Freudenreich" ', *Int. Z. Psychoanal.*, **1**, 484. (131 *n.*)

Spitta, H. (1882) *Die Schlaf- und Traumzustände der menschlichen Seele*, Tübingen. (1st ed., 1878.) (34, 47, 50, 55, 57–9, 63, *n.* 1, 66–7, 70, 72, 88, 90, 221, 512)

Spitteler, C. (1914) *Meine frühesten Erlebnisse*, Jena. (160, *n.* 1, 252, *n.* 2)

Stannius, H. (1849) *Das peripherische Nervensystem der Fische, anatomisch und physiologisch untersucht*, Rostock. (413, 452, *n.* 1)

Stärcke, A. (1911) 'Ein Traum der das Gegenteil einer Wunscherfüllung zu verwirklichen schien', *Zbl. Psychoanal.*, **2**, 86. (158)

Stärcke, J. (1913) 'Neue Traumexperimente in Zusammenhang mit älteren und neueren Traumtheorien', *Jb. psychoanal. psychopath. Forsch.*, **5**, 233. (62, 132, *n.* 2)

Stekel, W. (1909) 'Beiträge zur Traumdeutung', *Jb. psychoanal. psychopath. Forsch.*, **1**, 458. (276, 338, 348, *n.* 5, 357–8, 362 *n.*, 363 *n.*, 380)

— (1911) *Die Sprache des Traumes*, Wiesbaden. (350, 357–9, 385, *n.* 1, 396–7, 411, 685 *n.*)

Stricker, S. (1879) *Studien über das Bewusstsein*, Vienna. (57, 74, 460)

Strümpell, A. von (1883–84) *Lehrbuch der speciellen Pathologie und Therapie der inneren Krankheiten*, Leipzig. (23)
[*Trans.*: *Text-book of Medicine*, (2 vols.), 4th Amer. Ed., New York, 1912.]

Strümpell, L. (1877) *Die Natur und Enstehung der Träume*, Leipzig (7, 15–16, 19, 20–1, 28–9, 33, 37–8, 43–6, 51, 53–4, 57–8, 78 127, 182, 222–3, 226, 234, 460)

Stumpf, E. J. G. (1899) *Der Traum und seine Deutung*, Leipzig. (100, *n.* 1)

SULLY, J. (1893) 'The Dream as a Revelation', *Fortnightly Rev.*, **53**, 354. (60, 135, n. 2, 501–2, 591)

SWOBODA, H. (1904) *Die Perioden des Menschlichen Organismus*, Vienna. (94, 166 and n. 2, 384)

TANNERY, M. P. (1898) 'Sur la mémoire dans le rêve', *Rev. phil.*, **45**, 637. (512 n.)

TAUSK, V. (1913) 'Zur Psychologie der Kindersexualität', *Int. Z. Psychoanal.*, **1**, 444. (131 n., 304)
(1914) 'Kleider und Farben im Dienste der Traumdarstellung', *Int. Z. Psychoanal.*, **2**, 464. (411)

TFINKDJI, J. (1913) 'Essai sur les songes et l'art de les interpréter (onirocritie) en Mésopotomie', *Anthropos*, **8**, 505. (4, n. 2, 98 n.)

THOMAYER, S., and SIMERKA (1897) 'Sur la signification de quelques rêves', *Rev. neurol.*, **5**, 98. (89)

TISSIÉ, P. (1898) *Les rêves, physiologie et pathologie*, Paris. (1st ed., 1870.) (34, 36, 41, 45, 88–9, 134)

TOBOWOLSKA, J. (1900) *Etude sur les illusions de temps dans les rêves du sommeil normal*, (Thesis) Paris. (64 n., 498, 502)
See also BERNARD-LEROY and TOBOWOLSKA.

VARENDONCK, J. (1912) *The Psychology of Day-Dreams*, London. (491, n. 3)

VASCHIDE, N. (1911) *Le sommeil et les rêves*, Paris. (11 n., 13–14, 61, 572)

VESPA, B. (1897) 'Il sonno e i sogni nei neuro- e psicopatici', *Boll. Soc. Lancisiana Osp.*, **17**, 193. (88, n. 1)

VOLD, J. MOURLY (1896) 'Expériences sur les rêves et en particulier sur ceux d'origine musculaire et optique' (review), *Rev. phil.*, **42**, 542. (38)
(1910–12) *Über den Traum* (2 vols.) (*German transl.* by O. Klemm), Leipzig. (39 n., 223, n. 2, 394)

VOLKELT, J. (1875) *Die Traum-Phantasie*, Stuttgart. (16, 27, 36, 40, 55, 58–9, 66, 71, 83–7, 134, 224–7, 346, 634)

WEED, S. See HALLAM and WEED.

WEYGANDT, W. (1893) *Entstehung der Träume*, Leipzig. (7–8, 26, 35, 41, 58, 124 n.)

WHITON CALKINS. See CALKINS, WHITON.

WIGGAM, A. (1909) 'A Contribution to the Data of Dream Psychology', *Ped. Sem. J. Genet. Psychol.*, **16**, 250. (131 n.)

WINTERSTEIN, A. VON (1912) 'Zwei Belege für die Wunscherfüllung im Traume', *Zbl. Psychoanal.*, **2**, 292. (8)

WITTELS, F. (1924) *Sigmund Freud: der Mann, die Lehre, die Schule*, Vienna. (214, n. 1, 423, n. 1)
[*Trans.: Sigmund Freud: his Personality, his Teaching and his School*, by Eden and Cedar Paul, London, 1924.]
(1931) *Freud and his Time* (trans. by Louise Brink), New York. (441 n.)

WUNDT, W. (1874) *Grundzüge der physiologischen Psychologie*, Leipzig. (28, 30–1, 40–1, 57–8, 90, 222–3, 234)

ZELLER, A. (1818) 'Irre', *Ersch and Gruber: Allgemeine Encyclopedie der Wissenschaften*, **24**, 120. (70)

B

LIST OF OTHER WORKS ON DREAMS PUBLISHED BEFORE THE YEAR 1900

[*These are works included in Freud's Bibliographies but not referred to in the text.*]

AHMAD IBN SĪRĪN, *Achmetis f. Seirim Oneirocriticae*, ed. N. Rigaltius, Paris, 1603.

*ALBERTI, MICHAEL (1744) *Diss. de insomniorum influxi in sanitatem et morbos*. Resp. Titius Halae M.

ALIX (1883) 'Les rêves', *Rev. Sci. Industr.* 3rd series, **6**, 554.

*ANON (1890) 'Rêves et l'hypnotisme', *Le Monde*, Aug. 25.
   *(1890) 'Science of Dreams', *The Lyceum*, p. 28, Dublin.
   (1893) 'The Utility of Dreams', *J. Comp. Neurol.*, **3**, 17, Granville.

BACCI, DOMENICO (1857) *Sui sogni e sul sonnambulismo, pensiero fisiologico-metafisici*, Venice.

BALL, B. (1885) *La morphinomanie, les rêves prolongés*, Paris.

BENEZÉ, EMIL (1897) 'Das Traummotiv in der mittelhochdeutschen Dichtung bis 1250 und in alten deutschen Volksliedern', Benezé: *Sageng. und lit.-hist. Unters*, 1, *Das Traummotiv*, Halle.

*BENINI, V. (1898) 'Nel moneto dei sogni', *Il Pensiero nuovo*, Apr.

*BIRKMAIER, HIERON (1715) *Licht im Finsterniss der nächtlichen Gesichte und Träume*, Nuremberg.

BISLAND, E. (1896) 'Dreams and their Mysteries', *N. Am. Rev.*, **162**, 716.

BRADLEY, F. H. (1894) 'On the Failure of Movement in Dream', *Mind*, (new series), **3**, 373, London.

BRANDER, R. (1884) *Der Schlaf und das Traumleben*, Leipzig.

BREMER, L. (1893) 'Traum und Krankheit', *New York med. Monatschr.*, **5**, 281.

*BUSSOLA, SERAFINO (1834) *De somniis*, (Thesis) Ticini Reg.

*CAETANI-LOVATELLI (1889) 'I sogni e l'ipnotismo nel mondo antico', *Nuova Antol.*, Dec. 1.

CANE, FRANCIS E. (1889) 'The Physiology of Dreams', *The Lancet*, **67**, II, 1330 (Dec. 28)

CARDANO, GIROLAMO (1562) *Somiorum synesiorum, omnis generis insomnia explicantes libri IV*, Bâle.
   (2nd ed. in *Opera omnia Cardani*, **5**, 593, Lyons, 1663.)

CARIERO, ALESSANDRO (1575) *De somniis deque divinatione per somnia*, Padua.

CARPENTER (1849–52) 'Dreaming' (under 'Sleep'), *Cyclop. of Anat. and Physiol.*, **4**, 687, London.

CLAVIÈRE (1897) La rapidité de la pensée dans le rêve, *Rev. phil.*, **43**, 507.

COUTTS, G. A. (1896) 'Night-terrors', *Amer. J. med. Sc.*

D. L. (1895) 'A propos de l'appréciation du temps dans le rêve', *Rev. phil.*, **40**, 69.

DAGONET, H. (1889) 'Du rêve et du délire alcoolique', *Ann. méd.-psychol.*, Series 7, **10**, 193.

DANDOLO, G. (1889) *La conscienza nel sogno*, Padua.

DECHAMBRE, A. (1880) 'Cauchemar', *Dict. encycl. sc. méd.*, **2**, 48.

*DIETRICH, J. D. (1726) *An ea, quae hominibus in somno et somnio accidunt, iisdem possint imputari?* resp. Gava, Wittemberg.

*DOCHMASA, A. M. (1890) *Dreams and their Significance as Forebodings of Disease*, Kazan.

DREHER, E. (1890) 'Sinneswahrnehmung und Traumbild', *Reichs-med. Anzeiger*, **15**, Nos. 20, 21, 22, 23, 24; **16**, Nos. 3, 8, Leipzig.

DUCOSTÉ, M. (1899) 'Les songes d'attaques des épileptiques', *Journ. Méd. Bordeaux*, Nov. 26 and Dec. 3.

*DU PREL, C. (1869) 'Oneirokritikon: der Traum vom Standpunkte des transcend. Idealismus', *Deutsche Vierteljahrschrift*, **2**, Stuttgart.
(1880) *Psychologie der Lyrik*, Leipzig.
*(1889) 'Künstliche Träume' *Sphinx*, July.

EGGER, V. (1888) 'Le sommeil et la certitude, le sommeil et la mémoire', *Critique philos.*, **1**, 341, Paris.

ELLIS, HAVELOCK (1895) 'On Dreaming of the Dead', *Psychol. Rev.*, **2**, 458.
(1897) 'A Note on hypnagogic Paramnesia', *Mind*, **6**, 283.

ERDMANN, J. E. (1855) 'Das Träumen', *Ernste Spiele*, Chap. 12, Berlin.

ERK, VINZ. VON (1874) *Über den Unterschied von Traum und Wachen*, Prague.

*ESCANDE DE MESSIÈRES (1895) 'Les rêves chez les hystériques', (Thesis) Bordeaux.

FAURE (1876) 'Études sur les rêves morbides. Rêves persistants', *Arch. génér. Méd.*, 6th ser., **27**, 550.

*FENIZIA (1896) 'L'azione suggestiva delle cause esterne nei sogni', *Arch. per l'Antrop.*, 26.

*FÉRÉ, C. (1897) 'Les rêves d'accès chez les épileptiques', *Méd. mod.* Dec. 8.

*FISCHER, JOH. (1899) *Ad artis veterum onirocriticae historiam symbola*, (Thesis) Jena.

*FLORENTIN, V. (1899) 'Das Traumleben: Plauderei', *Die alte und die neue Welt*, 33, 725.

FORNASCHON, H. (1897) 'Die Geschichte eines Traumes als Beitrag der Transcendentalpsychologie', *Psychische Studien*, 24, 274.

FRENSBERG. (1885) 'Schlaf und Traum', *Sammlung gemeinverst. wiss. Vortr.*, Virchow-Holtzendorf, Ser. 20, 466.

FRERICHS, J. H. (1866) *Der Mensch: Traum, Herz, Verstand*, Norden.

GALEN. *De praecognitione, ad Epigenem*, Lyons, 1540.

*GIRGENSOHN, L. (1845) *Der Traum: psychol.-physiol. Versuch.*

*GLEICHEN-RUSSWURM, A. VON (1899) 'Traum in der Dichtung', *Nat. Z.*, Nos. 553–559.

*GLEY, E. (1898) 'Appréciation du temps pendant le sommeil', *L'intermédiaire des Biologistes*, 10, 228.

GORTON, D. A. (1896) 'Psychology of the Unconscious', *Amer. med. Times*, 24, 33, 37.

GOULD, G. M. (1889) 'Dreams, Sleep, and Consciousness', *The Open Court* (Chicago), 2, 1433–6 and 1444–7.

*GRABENER, G. C. (1710) *Ex antiquitate judaica de menûdim bachalôm sive excommunicatis per insomnia exerc. resp. Klebius*, Wittemberg.

GRAFFUNDER, P. C. (1894) 'Traum und Traumdeutung', *Samml. gemeinw. wiss. Vorträge*, 197.

GREENWOOD, F. (1894) *Imaginations in Dreams and their Study*, London.

*GROT, N. (1878) *Dreams, a Subject of Scientific Analysis* (in Russian), Kiev.

GUARDIA, J. M. (1892) 'La personnalité dans les rêves', *Rev. phil.* 34, 225.

GUTFELDT, I. (1899) 'Ein Traum', *Psychol. Studien*, 26, 491.

*HAMPE, T. (1896) 'Über Hans Sachsens Traumgedichte', *Z. deutsch. Unterricht*, 10, 616.

HEERWAGEN (1889) 'Statist. Untersuch. über Träume u. Schlaf', *Philos. Stud.*, 5, 301.

HILLER, G. (1899) 'Traum, Ein Kapitel zu den zwölf Nächten', *Leipz. Tagbl. und Anz.*, No. 657, Suppl. 1.

HITSCHMANN, F. (1894) 'Über das Traumleben der Blinden', *Z. Psychol.*, 7, 387.

JASTROW, J. (1888) 'The Dreams of the Blind', *New Princeton Rev.*, 5, 18.

JENSEN, J. (1871) 'Träumen und Denken', *Samml. gemeinw. wiss. Vortr.*, Virchow-Holtzendorff Ser. 6, 134.

KINGSFORD, A. (1888) *Dreams and Dream-Stories*, (ed. E. Maitland), London. (2nd ed.)

KLOEPFEL, F. (1899) 'Träumerei und Traum: Allerlei aus unserem Traumleben', *Universum*, 15, 2469 and 2607.

*KRAMAR, OLDRICH (1882) *O spànku a snu*, Prager Akad. Gymn.

KRASNICKI, E. VON (1897) 'Karls IV Wahrtraum', *Psych. Stud.*, **24**, 697.

KUCERA, E. (1895) 'Aus dem Traumleben', *Mähr-Weisskirchen, Gymn.*

LAISTNER, L. (1889) *Das Rätsel der Sphinx*, (2 vols.), Berlin.

*LANDAU, M. (1892) 'Aus dem Traumleben', *Münchner Neueste Nachrichten*, Jan. 9.

LAUPTS. (1895) 'Le fonctionnement cérébral pendant le rêve et pendant le sommeil hypnotique', *Ann. méd.-psychol.*, Ser. 8, **2**, 354.

*LEIDESDORF, M. (1880) 'Das Traumleben', *Sammlung der 'Alma Mater'*, Vienna.

*LERCH, M. F. (1883–84) 'Das Traumleben und sein Bedeutung', *Gymn. Progr.*, Komotau.

*LIBERALI, FRANCESCO (1834) *Dei sogni*, (Thesis) Padua.

LIÉBEAULT, A. (1893) 'A travers les états passifs, le sommeil et les rêves', *Rev. hypnot.*, **8**, 41, 65, 106.

LUKSCH, L. (1894) *Wunderbare Traumerfüllung als Inhalt des wirklichen Lebens*, Leipzig.

MACARIO, M. M. A. (1846) 'Des rêves, considérés sous le rapport physiologique et pathologique', Pt. I, *Ann. méd-psychol.*, **8**, 170. (1889). 'Des rêves morbides', *Gaz. méd. de Paris*, **8**, 1, 85, 97, 109, 121.

MACFARLANE, A. W. (1890) 'Dreaming', *Edinb. med. J.*, **36**, 499.

MAINE DE BIRAN, M. F. P. (1792) 'Nouvelles Considérations sur le sommeil, les songes, et le sonnambulisme', *Œuvres Philosophiques*, 209, (Ed. V. Cousin), Paris, 1841.

MAURY, L. F. A. (1857) 'De certains faits observés dans les rêves', *Ann. méd.-psychol.*, Ser. 3, **3**, 157.

*MEISEL (pseud.) (1783) *Natürlich-göttliche und teuflische Träume*, Seighartstein.

MELINAND, M. C. (1898) 'Dream and Reality', *Pop. Sc. Mo.*, **54**, 96.

MELZENTIN, C. (1899) 'Über wissenschaftliche Traumdeutung', *Gegenwart*, 50, Leipzig.

MENTZ, R. (1888) *Die Träume in den altfranzösischen Karls- und Artusepen*, Marburg.

MONROE, W. S. (1899) 'A study of taste-dreams', *Am. J. Psychol.*, **10**, 326.

MOREAU DE LA SARTHE, J. L. (1820) 'Rêve', *Dict. sc. méd.*, **48**, 245.

MOTET (1829–36) 'Cauchemar', *Dict. méd. chir. pratiques*, Paris.

MURRAY, J. C. (1894) 'Do we ever dream of tasting?' *Proc. Am. psychol. Ass.*, 20.

*NAGELE, A. (1889) 'Der Traum in der epischen Dichtung', *Programm der Realschule*, Marburg.

NEWBOLD, W. R. (1896) 'Sub-conscious Reasoning', *Proc. Soc. psychic. Res.*, **12**, 11, London.

PASSAVANTI, J. (1891) *Libro die sogni*, Rome.

PAULHAN, F. (1894) 'A propos de l'activité de l'esprit dans le rêve',
    Rev. phil., **38**, 546.

PICK, A. (1896) 'Über pathologische Träumerie und ihre Beziehungen
    zur Hysterie', *Jb. Psychiat.*, **14**, 280.

*RAMM, K. (1889) *Diss. pertractans somnia*, Vienna.

*RÉGIS, E. (1890) 'Les rêves Bordeaux', *La Gironde* (Variétés), May 31.

RICHARD, JEROME (1766) *La théorie des songes*, Paris.

RICHARDSON, B. W. (1892) 'The Physiology of Dreams', *Asclep.*, **9**,
    129.

RICHTER, E. (1816) *Onéirologie ou dissertation sur les songes, considérés dans
    l'état de maladie*, (Thesis) Paris.

*RICHTER, J. P. (Jean Paul) (1813) 'Blicke in die Traumwelt', *Museum*,
    2, (also in *Werke*, ed. Hempel, **44**, 128.)
    *'Über Wahl- und Halbträume', *Werke*, **44**, 142.
    (1826–33) *Wahrheit aus Jean Pauls Leben.*

ROBINSON, L. (1893) 'What Dreams are made of', *N. Am. Rev.*, **157**, 687.

ROUSSET, C. (1876) *Contribution à l'étude du cauchemar*, (Thesis) Paris.

ROUX, J. (1898) 'Le rêve et les délires onitiques', *Province méd. Lyons*, **12**,
    212.

*RYFF, W. H. (1554) *Traumbüchlein*, Strassburg.

*SANTEL, A. (1874) 'Poskus raz kladbe nekterih pomentjivih prokazni
    spanja in sanj', *Progr. Gymn.*, Görz.

SARLO, F. DE (1887) *I sogni. Saggio psicologico*, Naples.

SCH. FR. (1897) 'Etwas über Träume', *Psych. Studien*, **24**, 686.

SCHLEICH, K. L. (1899) 'Schlaf und Traum', *Zukunft*, **29**, 14; 54.

SCHWARTZKOPFF, P. (1887) *Das Leben im Traum: eine Studie*, Leipzig.

STEVENSON, R. L. (1892) 'A Chapter on Dreams', *Across the Plain.*

STRYK, M. VON (1899) 'Der Traum und die Wirklichkeit', (after C.
    Mélinand), *Baltische Mschr.*, 189, Riga.

SULLY, J. (1881) *Illusions, a Psychological Study*, London.
    (1882) 'Études sur les rêves', *Rev. scientif.*, Ser. 3, **3**, 385.
    (1892) *The Human Mind*, (2 vols.), London.
    (1875–89) 'Dreams', *Enc. Brit.*, 9th ed.

SUMMERS, T. O. (1895) 'The Physiology of Dreaming', *St. Louis Clin.*,
    8, 401.

SURBLED, G. (1895) 'Origine des rêves', *Rev. quest. scient.*
    (1898) *Le rêve*, Paris.

SYNESIUS OF SYRENE *Liber de insomniis.*
    [*German trans.: Oneiromantik* by Krauss, Vienna, 1888.]

TANNERY, M. P. (1894) 'Sur l'activité de l'esprit dans le rêve', *Rev.
    phil.*, **38**, 630.
    (1898) 'Sur la paramnésie dans les rêves', *Rev. phil.*, **46**, 420.

THIÉRY, A. (1896) 'Aristote et la psychologie physiologique du rêve', *Rev. neo-scol.*, **3**, 260.

*THOMAYER, S. (1897) 'Contributions to the Pathology of Dreams' (in Czech), *Policlinic of the Czech University*, Prague.

TISSIÉ, P. (1896) 'Les rêves; rêves pathogènes et thérapeutiques; rêves photographiés', *Journ. méd. Bordeaux*, **36**, 293, 308, 320.

TITCHENER, E. B. (1895) 'Taste Dreams', *Am. J. Psychol.*, **6**, 505.

TONNINI, S. (1887) 'Suggestione e sogni', *Arch. psichiatr. antrop. crim.*, **8**, 264.

*TONSOR, J. H. (1627) *Disp. de vigilia, somno et somniis, prop. Lucas*, Marburg.

TUKE, D. H. (1892) 'Dreaming', *Dict. of Psychol. Med.* (ed. Tuke), London.

ULLRICH, M. W. (1896) *Der Schlaf und das Traumleben, Geisteskraft und Geistesschwäche*, (3rd ed.), Berlin.

UNGER, F. (1898) *'Die Magie des Traumes als Unsterblichkeitsbeweis. Nebst e. Vorwort: Okkultismus und Sozialismus von C. du Prel*, (2nd ed.), Münster.

VIGNOLI, T. (1879) *Mito e scienza: Saggio*, Milan.
[*Trans.: Myth and Science: An Essay*, London, 1882 (Chap. VIII).]

*VISCHER, F. T. (1876) 'Studien über den Traum', *Beilage allg. Z.*, 105.

VOLD, J. MOURLY (1897) 'Einige Experimente über Gesichtsbilder im Traume', *Report of 3rd. Psych. Congr.*, Munich, and *Z. Psychol. Physiol. Sinnesorgane*, **13**, 66.

*VYKOUKAL, F. V. (1898) *On Dreams and Dream-interpretations*, (in Czech) Prague.

WEDEL, R. (1899) 'Untersuchungen ausländischer Gelehrter über gew. Traumphänomene', *Beitr. zur Grenzwissenschaft*, p. 24.

*WEHR, H. (1887) 'Das Unbewusste im menschlichen Denken', *Programm der Oberrealschule*, Klagenfurt.

WEILL, A. (1872) *Qu'est-ce que le rêve?* Paris.

*WENDT, K. (1858) *Kriemhilds Traum*, (Thesis) Rostock.

WILKS, S. (1893–94) 'On the Nature of Dreams', *Med. Mag.*, **2**, 597, London.

WILLIAMS, H. S. (1891–92) 'The Dream State and its Psychic Correlatives, *Amer. J. Insanity*, **48**, 445.

WOODWORTH, R. S. (1897) 'Note on the Rapidity of Dreams', *Psychol. Rev.*, **4**, 524.
 *(1886) 'Ce qu'on peut rêver en cinq secondes', *Rev. sc.*, 3rd. ser., **11**, 572.

ZUCCARELLI (1894–95) 'Polluzioni notturne ed epilepsia', *L'anomalo*, **1, 2, 3**.

ADDITIONAL NOTES

P. xiii, bottom. A letter from Freud to André Breton, dated December 14, 1932 (1933e), states explicitly that in the fourth edition and afterwards the bibliographies were entirely in the hands of Rank.

P. 171, l. 11. '*Festschrift*'. This *Festschrift* was in honour of Professor Stricker, Director of the Institute of Pathological Anatomy, at which Dr. Gärtner was Assistant, and where Freud had worked in his student days.

P. 398 footnote, l. 7 from bottom. The case of Goethe is mentioned by Freud as an instance of the success in life of a mother's favourite, in his paper on 'A Childhood Recollection from *Dichtung und Wahrheit*' (1917b), *Standard Ed.*, **17**, 156.

P. 419, footnote. '*Nächtlich am Busento*' are the opening words of a well-known poem by Von Platen.

P. 439, l. 3 from bottom. The journal in question was the *Wiener klinische Rundschau*.

P. 485. The anecdote about moving to Paris was quoted by Freud again in the second section of his paper 'Thoughts for the Times on War and Death' (1915b).

P. 519, l. 14. 'Nineteen'. In the first edition only (but not in the 1925 reprint of it) this read 'seventeen'. See Jones (1953), 35–6.

P. 599, l. 4 from bottom. 'Level'. Some light is thrown on Freud's use of the concept of 'level' of cathexis in the 3rd Part of his 'Project' of 1895 (Freud, 1950a).

P. 441, footnote. R. Pestalozzi, writing in the *Neue Zürcher Zeitung*, July 1, 1956 (p. 5), has shown that the essay was not in fact by Goethe but by a Swiss writer, G. C. Tobler. See also Section I of Freud's *Autobiographical Study* (1925d).

INDEX OF DREAMS

A

B

DREAMT BY OTHERS

(The names or descriptions in brackets are the dreamer's followed by the reporter's.)

GENERAL INDEX

The names of non-technical authors are included in this index. The names of technical authors are also included, where the reference in the text is not to any particular work. For references to particular works, *Bibliography A* should be consulted.

Above and below as dream-symbols, 285–9, 305, 326, 410
Abraham, K. (see also Bibliography A), 93 *n.*
Abrantès, the Duchess of, 25
Abstract thought represented in dreams, 341, 524
Absurd dreams, 343 *n.*, 416, 426–45, 448–51, 513, 662–5, 670
Absurdity of dreams, 20, 55–7, 60, 76, 96, 339, 591, 662
Accelerated flow of ideas in dreams, 498
Achilles, 129, 645
Acrobatic performances
  and dreams of flying or falling, 272, 393
  and hysterical attacks, 272
  and unconscious memories of sexual intercourse, 272 *n.*
Adam Bede, 290
Addenda to dreams, 155 *n.*, 376, 456, 489, 518–19, 677
Adler, V., 213 *n.,* 214
Admissibility to Consciousness (*see also* Censorship; Repression), 144–5, 177, 236, 540–2, 547, 593, 615, 672, 676–7, 679
Adonis, 401
Adriatic, 465–6
Aeneid, the, 608
Aesculapius, 34 *n.*
Affect in anxiety-dreams, 236, 267, 385, 401 *n.,* 557
Affect in dreams, 66–7, 74, 377, 459–87, 633, 640
  absence of, 462–4, 477, 637
  displacement of, 177, 267, 463–7, 478, 485–6, 654
  nature of the generation of, 582
  of death of loved person, 248–9, 463, 583–4, 675
  overdetermination of, 480

Affect in dreams—*cont.*
  release of, a centrifugal process, 467–8
  reversal of, 141, 237, 455, 463, 471–7
  suppression of, 461, 467–8, 471, 507, 556–7, 582
  the combined product of several sources, 480, 507
  transformation of, 604, 606
  transposed to the moment after waking, 478
Affect in neurotic characters, 479
Affect in waking life, 177, 460, 471, 478–9, 602, 645
Agathe (in *Der Freischütz*), 419 *n.*
Age, representation of, in dreams, 409–10, 416, 438–9, 513, 669–70
Agencies, the two psychical (*see also* Primary process; Secondary process), xv, xviii, 144–6, 177, 235–6, 260, 308, 479, 598–611, 676–80
Aggressiveness, 159
Agoraphobia, 360, 362, 581
Ahnfrau, Die (Grillparzer), 262
Alarm-clock dreams (*see also* Arousal dreams), 26–8, 221
'*Albert*', 586
Albertus Magnus, 542 *n.*
Alcoholism, 89
Alexander the Great, 99 *n.,* 614 *n.*
'Allegorical' dream-interpretation, 524
Alliteration (*see also* Play upon words), 59, 206, 531 *n.*
Almaviva, Count (in *Nozze di Figaro*), 209
Alpelhofer, 474
Alps, the, 198, 378–9
Alternatives in dreams, 312, 316–18, 650, 661
Ambition, and bed-wetting, 216
Ambivalence, emotional, 431

723

Death-wishes—*cont.*
  of loved person, 249–67, 328, 430
  repression of, 145 *n.*, 154–5
'Decoding' method of dream-interpretation, 97–100, 104–5, 225, 351, 388, 471
Defaecate, need to, as dream-instigator, 161 *n.*, 213, 402–3, 411
Defaecation, referred to in dreams (*see also* Faeces), 200, 213–14, 332, 403, 429, 448, 468–9, 520
Defensive mechanisms, 260
'Deferred action', theory of, 205
Déjà vu in dreams, 399, 447, 478
Deliria, 36, 72, 90–1, 529
Deluge, the, 649
Delusions, xxiii, 36–7, 59, 88–9, 91, 185 *n.*, 249, 470, 573, 635, 671
Dementia praecox, 351, 530 *n.*
Dental stimuli as dream-instigators (*see also* Teeth as dream-symbols; Teeth, dreams of loss of), 37, 86, 225–7, 385–392
Departure as dream-symbol, 385
Depression, 89, 332 *n.*
Derision in the dream-thoughts expressed by absurdity in dream-content, 430, 434–5, 444–5, 451, 662, 664
Destructiveness, 161 *n.*
Devil, the, 585, 613
'Devil's trill', the, 613 *n.*
Diable, Ile du, 166
Diagnostic value of dreams, 3, 33–4, 72
Digestive processes as dream-instigators, 22, 35, 37, 85–6, 168, 220–1, 226, 403
Diomede, 129, 645
Disease, organic, and dreams, 3, 33–5, 72, 236
Disgust, emergence of, in childhood, 604
Displacement (*see also* Psychical intensity; Transvaluation of psychical values)
  an essential part of the dream-work, 307–8, 507, 516, 543, 561–4, 589, 595–7, 654–5, 666–668, 671, 685
  by change of verbal expression of the dream-thoughts, 339–41
  combines with condensation to

Displacement—*cont.*
  make composite structures, 294, 322, 482, 657–8
  in psychoneuroses, 182, 461, 671, 676
  of affect in dreams, 177, 267, 463–7, 485–6, 654
  of affect in waking life, 177
  of important by superficial associations, 176–82, 531, 656
  of psychical intensity, xv–xvi, 117 *n.*, 176–82, 305–9, 339, 410, 460, 561–4, 654–60, 675
Dissociation, 521
Distortion
  a function of the Censorship, 144, 160, 175–7, 267, 308, 525–6, 573, 576, 606 *n.*
  and affect, 461
  and secondary revision, 514, 590
  disguises the dream-wish, 134–45, 182, 218, 308, 381, 552, 559, 570, 589
  in children's dreams, 127 *n.*, 268
  in dreams of the death of loved persons, 248–9
  in exhibitionist dreams, 243
  in 'innocent' dreams, 182–9
  in neurosis, 374, 419 *n.*
  in waking life, 141–2
  involves withdrawal of psychical value, 516
  reversal a tool of, 327–8
  verbal ambiguity a tool of, 341
Distressing dreams (*see also* Anxiety-dreams), 134–6, 145–6, 152–60, 556–8, 675
Doll's House, A (*Ibsen*), 296
Don Giovanni (*Mozart*), 497
Door as dream-symbol, 346, 397, 683
'*Dora*', 190 *n.*, 341 *n.*, 354, 387 *n.*, 395, 516 *n.*, 519 *n.*, 531 *n.*, 561 *n.*
Dordogne, 13
Dornbach, 129, 432
'*Doubles entendres*' compared to dreams (*see also* Verbal ambiguity), 186
Doubt, 335, 448–9, 515–17
Dover, 518 *n.*
Draconian code, 255 *n.*
Dramatization in dreams, 50, 653–4, 685
'Dream within a dream', 338, 575
'Dream-book' method of dream-interpretation, 97–100, 104–5, 225, 351, 388, 471

Dream-thoughts (latent)—*cont.*

psychical intensity of, 329–30, 561–2, 595–6, 654–6

regression and, 543, 546, 548

relation to manifest content of, 118, 122–3, 277, 295, 305–8, 311, 329, 356, 506, 640–3, 654

repressed wish in, 244, 266, 470–1, 598, 606 *n.*

representation of, by the dream-work, 288, 311–23, 326–9, 335–7, 352, 394, 410, 660–2

secondary revision and, 488–93, 495, 499, 666–8

sexual material in, 396–9

somatic stimuli and, 237

uncovered by analysis of dream, 144, 174, 517, 522–7, 530–2, 641, 686

Dream-work

affect and, 461 *n.*, 465, 467–8, 471–2, 480, 487, 507, 556–8

and absurd dreams, 426–45

and calculations in dreams, 414–418

and intellectual activity in dreams, 445–59

and speeches in dreams, 418–25

censorship and, 320–2, 507

combines dream-sources in a single unity, 178–9, 228

condensation a function of, 179, 279–304, 445, 507, 519, 595, 648–53

considerations of representability and, 329–49, 445, 507

day-time functioning of, under control of pre-conscious, 575–7

differs qualitatively from waking thought, 507

displacement a function of, 178, 304–9, 445, 507, 543, 561–2, 654–7, 671

experimentally produced dreams and, 181 *n.*

irrational character of, 592–8, 671

means of representation and, 311–38, 360–414, 660–2

preconscious and, 575–7

regressive character of, 547–8

secondary revision and, 488–503, 507–8, 666–8

sensory stimuli and, 225–6, 236

symbolic representation and, 350–360, 659, 685

Dream-work—*cont.*

transforms dream-thoughts into dream-content, 277–8, 445, 506–7, 641–3

unravelling of, in dream-interpretation, 522–5, 686

Dreyfus, 166

Droit du Seigneur, 209

Duino, 464

Dumas, A. (*fils*), 319, 347 *n.*

Dupuy, 500

Duration of dreams (*see also* Time, sense of, in dreams), 26–7, 64, 495–8, 575, 590

Dyspnoea, 285

Eberstein, Count, Ballad of, 354

Echerntal, the, 127

Egg as dream-symbol, 346

Ego, 52, 55, 84, 234, 267, 322–3, 327, 410, 484 *n.*

and repressed wishes, 557–8, 679–80

and the libido, 410

and the super-ego, 476 *n.*

Egoism of children, 250, 267

Egoistic character of dreams, 267–271, 322–3, 440–1, 485, 664

Ehniger, Dr., 70 *n.*

'Either-or' in dreams, 312, 316–18, 650, 661

Ekdal (in *The Wild Duck*), 296

Eliot, George, 290

Embarrassment dreams, 37, 238–40, 242–7, 264, 285, 336

'*Emil*', 128

Emission (*see also* Erection; Orgasm; Sexual content, dreams with)

consciously withheld in dream, 572

dreams ending in, 238 *n.*, 316, 335, 369–71, 388, 391–2, 394, 402

symbolized in dream, 403 *n.*

Emmersdorf, 211

Emperor's New Clothes, the, 243–4

Energy, psychical, bound and free, 599–601, 610–11

Enuresis, 216, 371, 395, 403 *n.*, 404

Epilepsy, 89, 202, 545

Erection symbolized in dreams (*see also* Impotence; Emission), 354, 377, 380, 394

Ereutophobia, 298

Logical relations represented in dreams, 312-20, 449-50, 507, 543, 660-2

Lopez, General, 59, 531 *n.*

'Louise', 452-4

Löwenfeld, L., 631

Lubbock, Sir John, 2

Lübeck, 194

Ludwig, King of Bavaria, 435 *n.*

Luggage as a dream-symbol, 358

Lyons, Miss, 462

Lys Rouge, Le (Anatole France), 82 *n.*

Macbeth, 266

Macrobius, 3

Madeira, 355

Magdeburg, 132 *n.*

Magic Flute, The, 291

Malade Imaginaire, Le (Molière), 520

Mania, 89, 356 *n.*

Manifest content (*see* Dream-content, manifest)

Map as dream-symbol, 356

Marat, J. P., 26

Marathon, 398 *n.*

Marbach, 456 *n.*

Marburg, 456

Marcuse, 490 *n.*

Maria Theresa, Empress of Austria, 428

Marriage represented in dream-symbols, 354, 358

Marxow, Fleischl von (see Fleischl von Marxow)

Masochism, 159, 375, 476

'mental', 159

Masséna, 197-8

Masturbation, 186-7, 348, 357, 363, 365, 371-2, 380-3, 385-92, 544, 586, 619

dreams with dental stimuli and, 385-92

prohibition of, in childhood, referred to in dreams, 363, 380-1, 544, 586, 619

symbolized in dreams, 186-7, 348 *n.*, 357, 365, 371-2, 378-83

'Mathilde', 111-12, 117-18, 120

Matter and Motion (by Clerk-Maxwell), 456, 520

Maupassant, Guy de, 290

Meaux, 16

Mecca, 59

'Medical' theory of dreams, 76-8, 82, 87, 92, 180, 590, 634-5, 680

Meeres und der Liebe Wellen, Des (by *Grillparzer*), 214

Megalomania, 215-16, 218, 470, 556

of fathers, 448

Melancholia, 89, 332 *n.*

Mélusine, legend of, 649

Memory (*see also* Forgetting of dreams; Mnemic system)

as source of dreams, 180-1

function of, 538-40, 543, 565-6, 573-4, 578, 599-604, 617

in dreams, xviii, 11-21, 29, 57, 64, 68, 90, 163-4, 218-19, 589

in waking life, 11, 57, 163, 529 *n.*

of dreams, 43-7, 512, 517-21, 522 *n.*

Memory-traces, xvi-xviii, 228, 507, 538-9, 540 *n.*, 565, 578

Menelaus (in *Offenbach's La Belle Hélène*), 488 *n.*

Menstruation, 319, 347 *n.*

Mental deficiency, 76

Mental disease (*see also* Dementia praecox; Mania; Melancholia)

aetiology of, 36

regressive functioning in, 567-8

relation of dreams to, 88-92, 569 *n.*, 592

'Mental masochists', 159

Mephistopheles (in *Goethe's Faust*), 78, 142 *n.*

Meredith, George, 300 *n.*

Meyer, Conrad F., 470

Meyer, Karl, 125-6

Meynert, Theodor (*see also* Bibliography A), 437-8

Micturition (*see also* Bed-wetting; Urinary stimuli as dream-instigators)

represented in dreams, 201, 210-219, 227, 352 *n.*, 367, 373, 402-3, 469

verbally referred to in dreams, 304

Middle Ages, dream-interpretation in, 4 *n.*

Midsummer Night's Dream, A, 462

Milton, 135 *n.*

Miramare, 464

Missing a train, dreams of, 385

Mnem. (*see* Mnemic)

Mnemic elements, 539

Mnemic systems (*Mnem.*) (*see also* Memory; Memory-traces), xviii, 538-43, 565-6, 573-4, 578, 599-604, 617

Mödling, 298
'*Moi splanchnique*', 36
Molière, 520
Money
 avariciousness for, equated with
  uncleanliness, 200
 equated with faeces, 403
Montbrison, 16–17
Mood during sleep, and affect in
 dreams, 487
Moor, Karl (in *Schiller's Die Räuber*),
 424 *n.*
Mora, Duc de (in *Daudet's Le Nabab*),
 291
Moral responsibility for dreams,
 68–70
Moral sense
 and dreams, 54, 58, 66–74, 90,
  244
 and the Oedipus complex, 263
 in children, 250
Moravia, 196
Moscheles, 371
Moses, 380–1, 401
Motor activity and the psychical
 apparatus, 537, 541, 544, 555,
 565–8, 578, 598–602, 605
Motor paralysis in sleep, xv, 336–7,
 468, 555, 568
Mozart, 208–9, 291, 434, 497
Müller, Herr, 494
Müllerin Verrat, der (Goethe), 319
Multiple determination of the
 dream-content, 149, 219 *n.*,
 283–4, 306–8, 309 *n.*, 330, 489,
 505, 652–3
  examples of, 292–3, 295, 417,
   452 *n.*, 510
Munich, 294–5, 657
Music
 in psychoneurotic hallucination,
  418 *n.*
 phrase of, carried over into
  dream, 50
 recollections aroused by, 497
Mussidan, 13
Muthmann, 93 *n.*
Myths, xxvii, 256, 266 *n.*, 345, 351,
 357, 398, 400–1, 619, 633, 685

Nabab, Le (by *Daudet*), 291, 491,
 535 *n.*
'*Nächtlich am Busento lispeln*', 419 *n.*
Nail-file as dream-symbol, 354

Nakedness or undress, dreams of,
 24, 37, 238–40, 242–7, 264, 285,
 336
Nansen, F., 191
Naples, 196
Napoleon I, 9–10, 26, 197–8, 233–4,
 497–8, 554
Narcissism of children, 255 *n.*
Narrow space as dream-symbol, 86,
 397, 399 *n.*, 401
Nature, Philosophy of, 5 *n.*, 41
Nausicaä, 246–7
Neck-tie as dream-symbol, 356,
 684
Negative
 does not exist in dreams, 318,
  326, 337, 661
 expression of, in dreams, 246, 326,
  337
Neologisms, 296–300, 302–4, 356,
 441–3
'Nervous stimulation', dreams due
 to, 40, 221–2
Neue Ghetto, Das, 442
Neurones, xvii–xviii, 540, 599
Neuroses
 affect in, qualitatively justified
  but quantitatively excessive,
  461, 479
 death of loved person and,
  251 *n.*, 257–8
 hallucinations in, 418 *n.*, 535
 incestuous wishes of children and,
  257–63
 of defence, 230 *n.*
 regressive character of, 544–5,
  548–9
 relation of dreams to, xxiii, xv,
  xix, 151 *n.*, 303, 418 *n.*, 522,
  549, 597–8, 606–7, 619, 635
 repression and, 235–6, 530, 618
 sexual basis of, 185 *n.*, 236, 257,
  260–1, 300–1, 346–7, 349 *n.*,
  441, 605–6, 664
 theory of, xxv–xxvii, xxxii, 104,
  128, 441, 451, 469–70, 483, 588,
  605–6
 unconscious psychical processes
  in, 611–12, 614, 616–18
Neurotic fears (*see also* Anxiety,
 neurotic; Phobias), 346–7
Neurotic symptoms
 as fulfilment of unconscious wish,
  553, 558, 562–4, 569, 577–8,
  605–6

Neurotic symptoms—*cont.*
  capable of over-interpretation, 266
  constructed to avoid anxiety-attack, 581
  in the case of '*Irma*', 108–10
  patient's attitude to, 410
  product of conflict between *Ucs.* and *Pcs.*, 581, 592
Neurotics
  bed-wetting in, 216
  compared to children, 251, 268 *n.*
  compulsion towards free association in, xiv
  dreams of, xxiii, 14, 104, 146, 162, 185, 203, 244, 273, 346, 371–4, 623
  preoccupation of, with their own body, 346
  psycho-analysis of, xxv, xxvii, 14, 104, 146, 162, 182, 216, 244, 257–8, 273, 310, 522, 531, 553, 593, 612, 673
Newly-married couples, dreams of, 81
Nibelungenlied, 515 *n.*
Nietzsche, 330, 549, 655
Night fears, 135 *n.*, 585
Nightmare, 3, 34–5
Nonsense words in dreams, 296–300, 302–4, 356, 441–3
Nora in *A Doll's House*, 296
Normal persons
  only quantitatively distinguished from neurotics, 373
  symbolism in the dreams of, 373–7
Norse sagas, 407
Notre-Dame, Cathedral of, 469
Novalis, F., 83
Nozze di Figaro, 208, 434, 497
Numbers
  as dream-symbols, 358
  in dreams, 39, 414–18, 438–9, 513, 668–70
  selected by chance, 514–15, 532 *n.*
Nursing mother and child, 204, 207, 223, 233, 287–9, 326, 372–3, 572, 577, 679

Obscurity of dreams (*see also* Incoherence of dreams; Sensory intensity)
  relation of, to repression, 518 *n.*, 672, 674, 677–8

Obscurity of dreams—*cont.*
  secondary revision and, 500
  significance of, 1, 329–35, 365, 445–6, 512, 516, 518 *n.*, 649, 654–5
Obsessional neuroses, xxiii, 89, 245, 251, 304 *n.*, 351 *n.*, 445 *n.*, 573, 593, 671, 686
  dreams in, 91, 328, 367, 399
  fear of murderous impulses in, 260, 457–8
  psycho-analytic treatment of, 100, 635
Obsessions
  affect and, 461
  compared to clock-face, 223
  formation of, and secondary revision, 244, 501 *n.*
  verbal forms of, 303–4, 340–1
Odhin's Trost (by *Dahn*), 216 *n.*
Odin, 216 *n.*
Odysseus, 246
Odyssey, The, 246, 249, 553 *n.*
Oedipus complex (*see also* Incestuous wishes), xviii–xix, 261–3, 452
Oedipus dreams, 145 *n.*, 397–9
Oedipus Rex, 261–4, 501 *n.*
l'Oeuvre (*Zola*), 300
Offenbach, 488
Olfactory stimuli as dream-instigators, 23, 25
Olmütz, 296–7
One night, dreams of (*see also* Series of dreams), 13, 315–16, 333–5, 347, 403, 441–4, 520 *n.*, 525, 661
Ophelia, 265
Oppenheim, Prof. Ernst, 621 *n.*
Opposites
  dream-interpretation by, 99 *n.*, 471
  representation by (*see* Reversal)
Optative in dream-thoughts expressed by present indicative in dream-content, 534–5, 647–8
Organic disease and dreams, 3, 33–5, 72, 236
Organic stimuli as dream-instigators, 33–42, 58, 80, 85–6, 220–221, 226, 235, 237–8, 402, 565, 590
Orgasm, dreams ending in (*see also* Emission; Sexual content, dreams with), 238 *n.*, 316, 335
Oriental dream-books, 99 *n.*

THE POWER OF READING

Visit the Random House website and get connected with information on all our books and authors

EXTRACTS from our recently published books and selected backlist titles

COMPETITIONS AND PRIZE DRAWS Win signed books, audiobooks and more

AUTHOR EVENTS Find out which of our authors are on tour and where you can meet them

LATEST NEWS on bestsellers, awards and new publications

MINISITES with exclusive special features dedicated to our authors and their titles

READING GROUPS Reading guides, special features and all the information you need for your reading group

LISTEN to extracts from the latest audiobook publications

WATCH video clips of interviews and readings with our authors

RANDOM HOUSE INFORMATION including advice for writers, job vacancies and all your general queries answered

Come home to Random House

www.randomhouse.co.uk

THE COMPLETE PSYCHOLOGICAL WORKS OF SIGMUND FREUD
ALSO AVAILABLE FROM VINTAGE

☐	Volume I	0099426528	£11.99
☐	Volume II	0099426536	£10.99
☐	Volume III	0099426544	£10.99
☐	Volume IV	0099426552	£11.99
☐	Volume VI	0099426579	£12.99
☐	Volume VII	0099426587	£10.99
☐	Volume VIII	0099426595	£10.99
☐	Volume IX	0099426625	£9.99
☐	Volume X	0099426633	£10.99
☐	Volume XI	0099426641	£10.99
☐	Volume XII	009942665X	£11.99
☐	Volume XIII	0099426668	£10.99
☐	Volume XIV	0099426676	£10.99
☐	Volume XV	0099426684	£11.99
☐	Volume XVI	0099426692	£10.99
☐	Volume XVII	0099426722	£10.99
☐	Volume XVIII	0099426730	£10.99
☐	Volume XIX	0099426749	£10.99
☐	Volume XX	0099426757	£11.99
☐	Volume XXI	0099426765	£10.99
☐	Volume XXII	0099426773	£10.99
☐	Volume XXIII	0099426781	£10.99
☐	Volume XXIV	009942679X	£9.99

FREE POST AND PACKING
Overseas customers allow £2.00 per paperback

BY PHONE: 01624 677237

BY POST: Random House Books
C/o Bookpost, PO Box 29, Douglas
Isle of Man, IM99 1BQ

BY FAX: 01624 670923

BY EMAIL: bookshop@enterprise.net

Cheques (payable to Bookpost) and credit cards accepted

Prices and availability subject to change without notice.
Allow 28 days for delivery.
When placing your order, please mention if you do not wish to receive
any additional information.

www.randomhouse.co.uk/vintage